17A

R111525

FREEDOM NEXT TIME

ALSO BY JOHN PILGER

The Last Day

Aftermath: The Struggle of Cambodia and Vietnam
(with Anthony Barnett)

The Outsiders
(with Michael Coren)

Heroes

A Secret Country

Distant Voices

Hidden Agendas

The New Rulers of the World

*Tell Me No Lies: Investigative Journalism
and Its Triumphs*
(editor)

FREEDOM NEXT TIME

JOHN PILGER

BANTAM PRESS

LONDON • TORONTO • SYDNEY • AUCKLAND • JOHANNESBURG

TRANSWORLD PUBLISHERS
61–63 Uxbridge Road, London W5 5SA
a division of The Random House Group Ltd

RANDOM HOUSE AUSTRALIA (PTY) LTD
20 Alfred Street, Milsons Point, Sydney,
New South Wales 2061, Australia

RANDOM HOUSE NEW ZEALAND LTD
18 Poland Road, Glenfield, Auckland 10, New Zealand

RANDOM HOUSE SOUTH AFRICA (PTY) LTD
Isle of Houghton, Corner of Boundary and Carse O'Gowrie Roads,
Houghton 2198, South Africa

Published 2006 by Bantam Press
a division of Transworld Publishers

A catalogue record for this book is available from the British Library.
ISBN (tpb) 0593055535
9780593055533 (from Jan 07)
ISBN (cased) 0593055527
9780593055526 (from Jan 07)

Typeset in 11/14pt Sabon by
Falcon Oast Graphic Art Ltd.

Printed in Great Britain by
Clays Ltd, Bungay, Suffolk.

1 3 5 7 9 10 8 6 4 2

Papers used by Transworld Publishers are natural, recyclable products made from
wood grown in sustainable forests. The manufacturing processes conform to the
environmental regulations of the country of origin.

For Louis,
born as this was being written

Contents

Acknowledgements

This book could not have been completed without the help and support of the following people, to whom I give my warmest appreciation: Anthony Arnove, Terry Bell, Patrick Bond, Jill Chisholm, John Cooley, Ania Corless, Ann Cunningham, Cosmas Desmond, Roger Diski, Helen Edwards, Mona El-Farra, Sally Gaminara, Richard Gifford, Amira Hass, Jane Hill, Mike Holderness, Jacqueline Korn, Sheila Lee, Nur Masalha, Ray McGovern, Chris Martin, Gavin Morris, Ilan Pappe, Sam Pilger, Zoë Pilger, Nida Rafa, Jaine Roberts, Vicki Robinson, Stephen Rudoff, Laura Sherlock, Gil Sochat, Gillian Somerscales, Margie Struthers.

Rise like lions after slumber
In unvanquishable number.
Shake your chains to earth like dew.
Which in sleep has fallen on you.
Ye are many – they are few.

Percy Bysshe Shelley
The Mask of Anarchy

Introduction

This book is about empire, its façades and the enduring struggle of people for their freedom. It offers an antidote to authorised versions of contemporary history that censor by omission and impose double standards. It is, I hope, a contribution to what Vandana Shiva calls 'an insurrection of subjugated knowledge'.[1]

When I began as a journalist, there was something called 'slow news'. We would refer to 'slow news days' (usually Sunday) when 'nothing happened' – apart, that is, from triumphs and tragedies in faraway places where most of humanity lived. The triumphs, the painstaking gains of people yearning to be free, were rarely acknowledged. The tragedies were dismissed as acts of nature, regardless of evidence to the contrary. Our terms of reference were those of great power, such as 'our' governments and 'our' institutions. The 'view from the ground' had value only if it reinforced that from on high. Whole societies were described and measured by their relationship with 'us': their usefulness to 'our interests' and their degree of compliance with (or hostility to) our authority. Above all, they were not 'us'.

These colonial assumptions have not changed. To sustain them, millions of people remain invisible, and expendable. On September 11, 2001, while the world lamented the deaths of innocent people in the United States, the UN Food and Agricultural Organisation reported that the daily mortality rate continued: 36,615 children had died from the effects of extreme poverty. This was normal in the age of 'economic growth'.[2]

The expendable people of impoverished Nicaragua fed this statistic. In the early 1980s, the historian Mark Curtis surveyed five hundred articles in the British press that dealt with Nicaragua. He found an almost universal suppression of the triumphs of the Sandinista government in favour of the falsehood of 'the threat of a communist takeover', which was then Anglo-American propaganda. 'It would take considerable intellectual acrobatics,' he wrote, 'to designate Sandinista success in alleviating poverty – remarkable by any standard – as unworthy of much comment by objective indicators ... One might reasonably conclude that the reporting was conditioned by a different set of priorities, one that conformed to the stream of disinformation from Washington and London.'[3]

Meanwhile, the atrocious misadventure known as the 'Iran–Contra affair' was represented in Washington as a domestic embarrassment for the Reagan administration rather than a conspiracy to bleed to death the Nicaraguan government, whose only threat was that of a good example. That countless innocent people were killed or denied the opportunity to free themselves from poverty, disease and illiteracy was never an 'issue'. A subsequent ruling by the International Court of Justice distinguished the Reagan administration as the only government the court has ever condemned for 'terrorism', calling on it to pay the Nicaraguan government $17 billion in reparations. This was ignored and the matter long forgotten, for it was the slowest news.[4]

The following year, 1987, the UN General Assembly passed a resolution that all member states should combat 'terrorism wherever and by whomever it is committed'. Only two states voted against it: the United States and Israel. At the time, this was unreported. When Ronald Reagan died, he was lauded as a 'great communicator', a leader of magnetic personal charm. His terrorism and lawlessness were unmentionable.[5]

The current occupation of Iraq is seen from the same parallel world. When the BBC's Director of News, Helen Boaden, was asked in January 2006 to explain how one of her 'embedded' reporters in Iraq could possibly describe the aim of the Anglo-American invasion as 'bring[ing] democracy and human rights' to Iraq, she replied with sheaves of quotations from Tony Blair that this was indeed his aim, as if his now notorious mendacity and the truth were compatible. No other evidence was required.[6] Such matter-of-fact servility to the state used to bemuse Soviet journalists visiting the West during the Cold War. 'How do you achieve that?' one of them once joked. 'In our country, to get that result, we tear out fingernails!'[7]

On March 28, 2003, during the attack on Iraq, sixty-two people were killed by an American missile that exploded in the al-Shula district of Baghdad. That evening, *Newsnight*, the BBC's only regular televised current affairs programme, devoted forty-five seconds to the massacre – less than one second per death. Contrast that with July 7, 2005, when the terrorist bombing of London killed almost the same number of people and received such coverage that overnight we became intimate with the lives of the victims, and could mourn their loss or salute their courage.

In other words, for the men, women and children blown to pieces in Baghdad, the solidarity we extended naturally to the London victims was denied; we were not allowed to know them. Why? Certainly, they were not 'us', but they *were* 'our' victims – that is, they had died at the hands of forces in collusion with our government, and in our name.

As I write this, early in 2006, three families in three different towns in Iraq have been wiped out by American missiles and bombs. One family had seventeen members and the others fourteen and seven; the victims were mostly women, the elderly and children. Their violent extinction caused not a ripple in that man-made phenomenon known as the 'mainstream', the main source of what we call news. Browsing the internet, I happened to read all seventeen names of the dead of the first family. Their names and ages had been meticulously collected and posted by an independent American reporter, Dahr Jamail, whose outstanding eye-witness and in-vestigative work never appears in the 'mainstream'.[8]

The innocent people killed in London were worthy victims. The innocent people killed in Iraq were unworthy victims. Put another way, the London massacre was worthy of our compassion; the Iraqi outrages were not.

This logic does not always follow a true course. When Saddam Hussein was in power and being courted and armed to the teeth by 'us', notably with the technology to build weapons of mass destruction, Iraqi Kurds massacred by him were slow news. When, in 1988, Saddam attacked the Kurdish village of Halabja with nerve gas, killing five thousand people, the British and American governments did their best to discourage coverage of the atrocity; the Americans went as far as blaming it on Iran. When I enquired at the time, I was told by the Foreign Office in London that it was 'far too easy' to blame Saddam.

However, in 1991, when Saddam displeased his sponsors in Washington and London by attacking another of their clients, Kuwait, and was now an official enemy, the plight of Iraqi Kurds suddenly became a great charitable cause in the West. Headlines and TV footage were lavished on them. They were made worthy victims *par excellence*. Alas, this change of status did not apply to the Kurds across the border in Turkey, even though they were part of the same dispossessed nation and were being slaughtered in far greater numbers by the Turkish military. The Ankara regime is a member of NATO and beneficiary of Anglo-American, World Bank and IMF 'aid'. Indeed, at the height of the Turkish Kurds' agony, the Turkish military received $8 billion worth of American gifts of tanks, planes, helicopters and ships.[9] In 2006, Turkey's Kurds remain unworthy victims.

By the same rule of thumb, a crime is only a crime if the perpetrators are 'them', not 'us'. In his epic acceptance of the 2005 Nobel Prize in Literature, Harold Pinter referred to 'a vast tapestry of lies, upon which we feed'. He asked why 'the systematic brutality, the widespread atrocities, the ruthless suppression of independent thought' of Stalinist Russia were well known in the West while American imperial crimes were merely 'superficially recorded, let alone documented, let alone acknowledged'.

He was referring to a great silence, unbroken by the incessant din of the media age. Across the world, the extinction and suffering of countless human beings could be attributed to rampant America. 'But you wouldn't know it,' said Pinter. 'It never happened. Nothing ever happened. Even while it was happening it never happened. It didn't matter. It was of no interest.'[10]

To its shame, though unsurprisingly, the BBC ignored Pinter's warning. All that drawing-room flatulence about the arts, all that preening for the cameras at Booker prizegivings, yet the national broadcaster could not make room for Britain's greatest living dramatist, so honoured, to tell the truth. For the BBC, it never happened.

Soon afterwards, bereft of irony, the newsreader Fiona Bruce introduced, as news, a Christmas propaganda film about George W. Bush's dogs. The film showed how kind the President and his family were. That happened. Now imagine Bruce reading this: 'Here is delayed news, just in. From 1945 to 2005, the United States attempted to overthrow fifty governments, many of them democracies, and to crush thirty popular movements fighting tyrannical regimes. In the process, twenty-five countries were bombed, causing the loss of several million lives and the despair of millions more.'[11]

One of the striking features of the post-Cold War era has been the public rehabilitation of the concept of empire. Like Prime Minister Harold Macmillan secretly in the 1950s, a new crop of imperialists now openly laments the 'loss of white prestige' that was the old imperialism and the denigration of 'our' culture.[12] 'Culture' has become the code for race and class; revisionism is all the rage. The *Wall Street Journal* has lauded Britain's and France's disastrous imperial adventure in Suez in 1956, describing American opposition as 'perhaps the biggest strategic mistake in the post-war era'.[13] The Cambridge academic John Casey has rejoiced that the Western powers now 'can do what they like [in the developing world]'.[14]

'It is easy to forget,' wrote Frank Furedi in *The New Ideology of Imperialism*, 'that until the 1930s the moral claims of imperialism were seldom questioned in the West. Imperialism and the global expansion of the Western powers were represented in unambiguously positive terms as a major contributor to human civilisation . . . To be an imperialist was considered a respectable, political badge.'[15] As the United States emerged from the Second World War and shed what 'Atlanticists' like to call its 'age of innocence' (forgetting the slaughter of the Native Americans, slavery, the theft of Texas from Mexico, the bloody subjugation of Central America, Cuba and the Philippines, and other innocent pursuits), 'imperialism' was dropped from American textbooks and declared a European affair. One of the difficulties for proud imperialists in the immediate post-war period was that Hitler and fascism, and all their ideas of racial and cultural superiority, had left a legacy of guilt by association. The Nazis had been proud imperialists, too.

A serious, if farcical, campaign to expunge the word from the language followed 'on the grounds that it falsely attributed immoral motives to Western foreign policy'. The term was deemed to no longer have 'relevance'. Those who persisted in using it as a pejorative term were 'disreputable' and 'sinister'. They were, wrote one American historian, 'inspired by the Communist doctrine', or they were 'Negro intellectuals who had grievances of their own against white capitalism'.[16]

In the best Stalinist tradition, imperialism was airbrushed out. 'The Cold War intelligentsia,' wrote Furedi, 'by denying the centrality of the imperial identity to Western society, were denying their own past. They did not deny that imperialism was something to be ashamed of, they merely denied all association with it.'[17]

That changed in the 1990s. With the collapse of the Soviet Union, the imperialists took heart. The economic and political crises in the 'developing' world, caused by the collapse in commodity prices and the ravages of debt, would now serve as retrospective justification for imperialism. Once again, the 'third world' needed to be saved from itself. Imperialism's return journey to establishment respectability had begun.

Written up by Bush's ideological sponsors shortly before he came to power in 2000, a messianic conspiracy theory called the 'Project for the New American Century' foresaw his administration as an imperial dictatorship behind a democratic façade: 'the cavalry on the new American frontier' that could 'fight and win multiple, simultaneous major theatre wars'.[18] The attacks on the United States on September 11, 2001 ensured the theory became practice; a fraudulent 'war on terror' became a war of terror.

A Pentagon plan entitled 'Vision 2020' had already identified the goal as 'full spectrum dominance'. This would allow 'the medium of space, the fourth medium of warfare – along with land, sea and air – to close the ever-widening gap between diminishing resources and increasing military commitments'.[19] General John Jumper of the US Air Force predicted that the planet could be easily mastered because American forces enjoyed 'God's eye' from satellites and commanded 'the global information grid'.[20] He had a point. More than 725 American bases are now placed strategically in compliant countries, notably at gateways to sources of fossil fuels and encircling the Middle East and Central Asia.[21]

No longer whispered, 'empire' is a word to be embraced again. The British treasurer Gordon Brown has told the *Daily Mail*, 'The days of Britain having to apologise for the British empire are over. We should celebrate.'[22] The historian Andrew Roberts insisted in the *Daily Express* that for 'the vast majority of its half-millennium-long history, the British empire was an exemplary force for good'.[23] In the *Daily Telegraph*, the military historian John Keegan declared the empire 'highly benevolent and moralistic'.[24] Applauding Blair's moral gunboats and Gladstonian convictions of superiority, Niall Ferguson, professor of politics at Oxford, said, 'Imperialism may be a dirty word, but when Tony Blair is essentially calling for the imposition of Western values – democracy and so on – it is really the language of liberal imperialism . . . imposing your views and practices on others.'[25]

Ferguson's honesty is provocative to the 'liberal realists' who dominate the study of international relations in Britain and teach that the new imperialists are the world's crisis managers, rather than the cause of a crisis. With honourable exceptions, these scholars of 'geopolitics' have taken the humanity out of the study of nations and congealed it with a jargon that serves great power. Laying out whole societies for autopsy, they identify 'failed states' and 'rogue states', inviting 'humanitarian intervention' – a term used by imperial Japan to describe its bloody invasion of Manchuria. (Mussolini also used it to justify seizing Ethiopia, as did Hitler when the Nazis drove into the Sudetenland.)[26]

There are minor variations. Michael Ignatieff, former professor of human rights at Harvard and an enthusiastic backer of the West's invasions, prefers 'liberal intervention'.[27] From the same lexicon of modern imperial euphemisms have come 'good international citizen' (a Western vassal) and 'good governance' (a neo-liberal economy run by the World Bank/IMF). Once noble concepts have been appropriated: 'democracy' (pro-Washington regime) and 'reform' (dismantling genuine social reforms) and 'peacemaking' (war). Remarkably, academics and commentators still describe Tony Blair and Bill Clinton as 'centre-left', a denial of the historical record.

The 'centre', of course, is liberal and reasonable, because liberalism is non-ideological. That is the mythical touchstone of the world's most powerful ideology. Tony Blair, wrote the *Guardian* columnist Hugo Young in 1997, 'wants to create a world none of us have known, where the laws of political gravity are overturned [and] ideology has surrendered entirely to "values"'.[28] That Blair would commit, in pursuit of these 'values', the crime of invading, unprovoked, a defenceless country, which the Nuremberg judges described as 'the paramount war crime', was unthinkable. 'It's a nice and convenient myth that liberals are the peacemakers and conservatives the warmongers,' wrote Hywel Williams, 'but the imperialism of the liberal may be more dangerous because of its open-ended nature – its conviction that it represents a superior form of life.'[29]

It is not surprising that the 'liberal' Blair has taken Britain to war more often than any Prime Minister in the modern era, or that his closest ally, or mentor, is George W. Bush, considered by a large section of humanity the most dangerous man on earth. What unites them is not their extremism, but a time-honoured orthodoxy, celebrated relentlessly in the 'mainstream'. This, wrote Richard Falk, professor of international relations at Princeton and a distinguished dissenter, 'regards law and morality as irrelevant to the identification of rational policy'. Thus, Western policies and actions have long been formulated 'through a self-righteous, one-way, legal/moral screen [with] positive images of Western values and innocence portrayed as threatened, validating a campaign of unrestricted political violence . . .' This 'is so widely accepted . . . as to be virtually unchallengeable'.[30]

Freedom Next Time pushes back this one-way moral screen to demonstrate that imperialism, in whatever guise, is the antithesis of the 'benevolent and moralistic'. Each chapter is set in a country with which I have had long association as a reporter and film-maker. Along with a sense of history, I have tried to convey something of what I have seen and what has moved me – the everyday pain, dark humour and generosity of lives lived a long way away and conveniently dehumanised in a surreal assembly line of 'sound-bites', from the children playing among cluster bombs in Kabul to the ritual humiliations forced upon Palestinians, to the determination of impoverished South African women in erecting their own modern homes. The stories are those both of eye-witnesses and of the powerful, including voices that speak from the bunkers of British imperialism where they wrote their true intentions, not intended for our eyes.

These phantom truth-tellers appear in chapter 1, 'Stealing a Nation'. Knowing this story as I do, I still find its criminal audacity almost incredible. In high secrecy, during the late 1960s and early 1970s, British governments tricked, coerced and finally expelled the entire population of the Chagos Islands in the Indian Ocean in order to give the principal island, Diego Garcia, a paradise, to the Americans for a military base. From here, Iraq and Afghanistan have been attacked. That the islanders were British citizens and had roots in the islands that went back to the eighteenth century, that they spoke their own language and practised their own culture, made no difference. Methodically, they were kidnapped by their own government and sent into exile to the slums of Mauritius, where untold numbers have wasted away, including children who died 'simply of sadness', as their mothers told me.

The ruthlessness was explicit – 'the object is to get some rocks which will remain *ours*'. The United Nations was lied to, as if none of this was happening. While Margaret Thatcher and the British media cheered on the Royal Navy as it sped to the rescue of two thousand white Falkland islanders in 1982, not a word was uttered about the brutal dispossession of two thousand Chagos islanders, who are black. When, eighteen years later, the islanders glimpsed their freedom in a High Court judgement that ruled they had been wronged and could go home, they were tricked again by the Blair government; a decree passed by 'royal prerogative', an archaic, secretive mechanism, was used to circumvent the law and justice.

At the time of writing, the High Court is conducting a 'judicial review' and its latest ruling is anxiously awaited by the islanders. The injustice already done is a metaphor for the great piracy begun more than five hundred years ago when European buccaneers were granted the privileges of 'discovery and conquest' in a world the Pope and kings considered their property, to be disposed of according to their divine right. This assumption of divinity has not changed.

The title of chapter 2, 'The Last Taboo', is taken from an essay by the Palestinian-born writer and scholar Edward Said, published shortly before his death in 2002. He wrote, 'The extermination of the Native Americans can be admitted, the morality of Hiroshima attacked, the national flag [of the United States] publicly committed to the flames. But the systematic continuity of Israel's 52-year oppression and maltreatment of the Palestinians is virtually unmentionable, a narrative that has no permission to appear.'[31]

The narrative begins almost forty years ago when I arrived in Palestine as a young correspondent and listened to Palestinians and Israelis, and saw the barren refugee camps. In describing the 'destructive role' of foreign journalists who ignored the history and context of Palestinian frustration and violence, Edward Said understood the taboo many of us saw and privately deplored while nourishing and prolonging lethal myths.

In 2002, a Glasgow University study found that barely 9 per cent of young British viewers of television news knew that the Israelis were the occupying force and that the illegal settlers were Jewish: many believed them to be Palestinian. The term 'Occupied Territories' was rarely explained, and people were not told that the Palestinians were the victims of an illegal military occupation. Language was used selectively, terms such as 'murder' and 'atrocity' applied exclusively to the deaths of Israelis. Only they were worthy victims. The deaths of Palestinians were not so much slow news as non-existent news.[32]

At the end of 2005, when Israeli Prime Minister Ariel Sharon fell seriously ill and was hailed as a 'man of peace' whose 'hope for a Palestinian state' might be 'lost' should he die, it seemed the ghost of Lewis Carroll had finally made off with the forbidden narrative. And when, soon afterwards, Hamas was elected to office in the Occupied Territories and Gaza, the news was received in the West through the same looking-glass. The wrong kind of democracy had spoken and a Brechtian solution was surely called for: 'To dissolve the people / And elect another'. That the ascent of Hamas was due in no small part to the secret, machiavellian support of Israel and to an Anglo-American campaign to destroy secular Arabism and its 'moderate' dreams of freedom was unmentionable.[33]

In his 2001 history, *Late Victorian Holocausts*, Mike Davis writes that as many as twenty-nine million Indians died unnecessarily in famines wilfully imposed by British policies. He relates how in 1876 the Viceroy, Lord Lytton, insisted that nothing should prevent the export of surplus wheat and rice to England and that officials were ordered to 'discourage relief works in every way'. As millions starved, the imperial government launched 'a militarised campaign to collect the tax arrears accumulated during the drought'. In the north-west provinces alone, which had brought in record harvests in the preceding three years, at least one and a quarter million people died.[34]

Stalin in the Ukraine would subsequently match this, infamously; and this was Harold Pinter's point: we know of Stalin's crimes; we know next to nothing of our own. It is a tribute to the elite promotion of that 'exemplary force for good' that the India of the Raj remains mainly a source of nostalgia. While young Britons are taught modern history largely conditioned by the evils of Hitler and the 'good war' – that 'ethical bath where the sins of centuries of conquest, slavery and exploitation were expiated', as Richard Drayton wrote – the story of how the British Raj brought its own dimension of imperial suffering to India is, at most, a footnote.[35]

In my chapter 3, 'Shining India', the legacy of the Raj is present in independent India: in the elite denial of enduring poverty. I first went to India in the 1960s, at the height of a famine in Rajasthan. As in the time of the Raj, the term 'famine' was officially frowned upon; 'emergency' was preferred. Those who enquired too deeply into the criminal absurdity of Indian mass impoverishment were unwelcome; several foreign film-makers were banned. In 2004, after a long absence, I returned to India's greatest city, Bombay, where the mighty freedom movements had rallied and Gandhi had lived and, today, a new empire has arrived: that of Bushite 'free trade', bourgeois consumerism, call centres, a ferocious meritocracy and a new struggle for freedom.

In 1967, I was banned from apartheid South Africa. Thirty years later, I flew back. Nelson Mandela was President, the 'rainbow nation' had been declared and apartheid was dead. Great men and great events had convinced the outside world that freedom had arrived, and black South Africans felt the thrill of freedom as they queued patiently to vote for the first time in their lives.

The betrayal of their struggle, goodwill and optimism is described in chapter 4, 'Apartheid Did Not Die'. This was the title of a documentary film I made on my return, which stirred spirited debate in South Africa. Apartheid took its name and mysticism from the first Boer regime, but its lifeblood flowed from the British imperial legacy of Cecil Rhodes and other 'men of commerce and industry', who at the turn of the twentieth century stole the land, resources and economic birthright of the majority. The poverty they created has not been turned back in 'free' South Africa, as the African National Congress solemnly pledged. In the 'townships', conditions are described as 'desperate', with more than five million hungry children and a health system unable to cope with epidemic disease, such as AIDS and tuberculosis.[36]

A new elite has emerged, the product of 'black empowerment' and the beneficiary of nefarious deals with the white power that still runs South Africa. 'We seek to establish', said Trevor Manuel, the Finance Minister, 'an environment in which winners flourish.'[37] However, members of the tribe known sardonically as the 'waBenzi' (the Mercedes Benz is their preferred means of transport) are beginning to look over their shoulders at the great struggles of the past, for their compatriots are stirring again and demanding more than symbols. Community uprisings are common again as townships and squatter camps are torched, along with the buildings of authority. In the global apartheid created by modern economic imperialism, today's South Africa provides both a spectre and a warning.

As the first American bombs fell on Afghanistan in October 2001, retribution for the attacks on America five weeks earlier, President Bush broadcast the following message to his far-off victims: 'The oppressed people of Afghanistan will know the generosity of America. As we strike military targets, we will also drop food, medicine and supplies to the starving and suffering men and women and children of Afghanistan. The United States is a friend of the Afghan people.'[38]

The previous week, Tony Blair had said memorably: 'To the Afghan people, we make this commitment. We will not walk away . . . If the Taliban regime changes, we will work with you to make sure its successor is one that is broad-based, that unites all ethnic groups and offers some way out of the poverty that is your miserable existence.'[39]

In the final chapter, 'Liberating Afghanistan', their words are set against the consequences of their actions. The attack on Afghanistan, said to be the first 'victory' in the 'war on terror', caused the deaths of almost seven times the number that died in the Twin Towers. As the Taliban melted away, the country was taken over by some of the world's most brutal men, the same warlords America had nurtured during the Soviet occupation, who had reduced Kabul, the capital, to rubble. The 'liberal intervention' in Afghanistan is today a surreal concoction. The American-arranged 'democracy' includes, for example, Mulavi Qalamuddin, the Taliban's head of the Department for the Prevention of Vice and the Promotion of Virtue, who enforced Sharia law through unusual forms of punishment and physical abuse. The liberation of women is a mirage. While al-Qaida is nowhere to be found, American patrols flying outsized Stars and Stripes and playing rock music at full volume attack isolated villages and 'render' their 'suspects' to a CIA gulag.

When I heard Donald Rumsfeld describe Afghanistan today as a 'model' of democracy, I thought how my favourite chronicler of the absurdities of war, Joseph Heller, would appreciate this assessment. In chapter 5, I relate a conversation I had with a colonel on an American base, who resembled uncannily 'Major Major' in Heller's *Catch-22*. Tony Blair's Defence Secretary, John Reid, also seemed to step from the pages of *Catch-22* when he announced that the 'war on terror' in Afghanistan was 'absolutely interlinked to countering narcotics'.[40] The main export of the 'model' democracy is heroin, which the Taliban had successfully banned and from which the current, democratic warlords are making their fortunes. The drug ends up on the streets of cities like Glasgow. Such is the 'great game of nations' which pith-helmeted Englishmen evolved and their successors do proud.

After leaving Afghanistan, I flew to the United States, where a rebellion within the 'old' establishment is under way. I met Ray McGovern, a former CIA analyst who had once prepared the daily briefing for the White House. When I said to him that Norman Mailer believed that America had entered a 'pre-fascist' state, he was silent, then said, 'I hope he's right, because there are others saying that we are already in a fascist mode. When you see who is controlling the means of production here, when you see who is controlling the newspapers and periodicals, and the TV stations, from which most Americans take their news, and when you see how the so-called war on terror is being conducted, you begin to understand where we are headed . . . so yes, we all ought to be worried about fascism.'[41]

Another establishment voice, Paul Craig Roberts, a former associate editor of the *Wall Street Journal* and Assistant Secretary of the Treasury under Reagan, wrote,

The United States is starting to acquire the image of Nazi Germany. Knowledgeable people should have no trouble drawing up their own list of elements common to both the Bush and Hitler regimes: the use of extraordinary lies to justify military aggression; reliance on coercion and threats in place of diplomacy; total belief in the virtue and righteousness of one's cause; the equating of factual objections or 'reality-based' analysis to treason; the re-direction of patriotism from country to leader; the belief that defeat resides in debate and a weakening of will.[42]

'Fascism' is too easily used as abuse or as a neat label for all the world's evils, but what is striking about the debate in America today is the recurring warning of conservatives who believe in the separation of powers under the constitution. 'In effect,' wrote Roberts, 'Bush is asserting the powers that accrued to Hitler in 1933 . . . Thus has the US arrived at the verge of dictatorship.'[43]

In 2005, the US Senate, in effect, voted to abolish habeas corpus when it passed an amendment that overturned a Supreme Court ruling allowing Guantanamo Bay prisoners access to a federal court. Without habeas corpus and the 'due process' provisions of the Bill of Rights, a government can lock away its opponents and implement a dictatorship. A not untypical case is that of an American doctor who was punished with twenty-two years in prison for founding a charity, Help the Needy, which helped children in Iraq stricken by the economic blockade enforced by America and Britain in the 1990s. In raising money for infants dying from diarrhoea, Dr Rafil Dhafir broke this siege which, according to UNICEF, had caused the deaths of half a million infants under the age of five.[44] The then Attorney-General, John Ashcroft, called Dr Dhafir a 'terrorist', a description derided by even the judge in what was a transparently political trial.[45]

Secretly, Bush has assumed the power of a variety of 'signing statements'. These are little-known decrees that circumvent laws passed by Congress and allow him to ignore legislation, not to mention the Geneva Convention, forbidding torture of prisoners. After all, blurted out the President, the US Constitution 'is just a goddamned piece of paper'.[46]

Along with the intelligence agencies, the Pentagon has expanded its domestic surveillance to 'investigate crimes within the United

States'.[47] In the CIA gulag, torture and murder are admitted. In Iraq, the true extent of the slaughter and the punishment of the civilian population, notably the massacres and use of white phosphorus weapons in the city of Fallujah, is masked by a successful, 'embedded' system of reporting. In 2004, a peer-reviewed study by the Johns Hopkins School of Public Health, published in the British medical journal *The Lancet*, suggested a 'conservative' figure of a hundred thousand killed by mostly American firepower.[48] Four other studies estimate a higher figure.[49]

A once bountiful land is being poisoned by an invisible weapon of mass destruction: radiation from uranium-tipped weapons (known as 'depleted' uranium) and equivalent to many times that released by the Hiroshima and Nagasaki bombs. Children are especially vulnerable because they play in heavily polluted areas, where cancers have increased thirty-fold. More than half of Iraq's cancer sufferers are under the age of five. I have seen the hospital wards filled with these little, mutated ghosts.[50]

Once I believed that if only those with power and responsibility had seen what I had seen, the horror and degradation of war, they would act otherwise. That was naïve, for only the power of popular dissent changes their course, or rids us of them. They understand that. That is why, as the legal powers of the state are criminalised, so is dissent.

In Britain, from January 1, 2006, you can be arrested for the most minor offences. This is clearly directed at peaceful protest. Maya Evans, a vegan chef aged twenty-five, will have a criminal record for the rest of her life. She was arrested under the new Serious Organised Crime and Police Act for reading aloud at the Cenotaph in London the names of ninety-seven British soldiers killed in Iraq. So serious was her crime that it took fourteen policemen in two vans to arrest her.[51]

Eighty-year-old John Catt, who served in the Royal Air Force during the Second World War, was stopped by police in Brighton for wearing an 'offensive' T-shirt which suggested that Bush and Blair be tried for war crimes. He was arrested under the Terrorism Act and handcuffed, with his arms wrenched behind his back. The office record of his arrest says the 'purpose' of searching him was 'terrorism' and the 'grounds for intervention' were 'carrying a plackard and T-shirt with anti-Blair info' (*sic*). At the time of writing, he is awaiting trial for refusing to accept a police caution.[52]

This capture of the law for political ends is no different from the subversion of the High Court's judgement in favour of the Chagos islanders. Is this the beginning of a kind of fascism in which great goose-stepping rallies are quite unnecessary? George Orwell warned that totalitarianism did not require a totalitarian state. The consequences of decisions taken by respectable, 'democratic' politicians are now evocative of decisions taken by fascists.

The difference is distance. The entire population of the British archipelago of Chagos was rounded up and expelled, the women and children forced into the hold of a ship without fresh water in a fashion reminiscent of slavery. While that was going on, Britons at home remained free, protected by laws. Now that is changing. The distance is diminishing.

I have written *Freedom Next Time* to warn against these dangers and to celebrate those who challenge them. It takes up the theme of my previous books, such as *Heroes*, *Distant Voices* and *Hidden Agendas*, the last having been recently distinguished with a 'denied' stamp by the censors of Guantanamo Bay.[53] This is not a pessimistic book. In my experience, most people do not indulge the absurdity of rapacious power's 'rules'. They do not contort their morality and intellect to comply with double standards and the notion of approved evil, of worthy and unworthy victims. They would agree wholeheartedly with Robert Jackson, Chief Counsel of the United States at the Nuremberg trials of the Nazi leaders. 'If certain acts of violation of treaties are crimes,' he said, 'they are crimes whether the United States does them or whether Germany does them, and we are not prepared to lay down a rule of criminal conduct against others which we would not be willing to have invoked against us.'[54]

In Britain, opinion polls show that the majority oppose the invasion and occupation of Iraq and believe the Prime Minister has lied to them. In the 2005 British general election, barely a fifth of the adult population voted for the Blair government in the second lowest turnout since the franchise. This was not apathy; it was an undeclared strike that reflects a rising awareness, consciousness even, offering more than hope.

Since the crusaders in Washington squandered the sympathy of most of humanity for the victims of September 11, 2001, in order to accelerate their own dominance, a critical public intelligence has stirred. Witness the spectacular response of people in the West to the tsunami of December 26, 2004. While Bush offered less than the cost of his inauguration party and Blair one-twentieth of a loan given to the Indonesian regime so that it could buy British military aircraft, ordinary people gave millions. More than charity, this was a reclaiming of the politics of community, morality and internationalism.

The celebrated American commentator Walter Lippmann once described the public as 'a bewildered herd'.[55] This contempt is shared by those who fear the unmasking of their apparent invincibility when the 'herd' suddenly changes direction. During the 1960s, in the United States, the civil rights campaign ended the vestiges of slavery. It was allied to a movement that stopped an all-out military mobilisation which would have set alight Asia and beyond. Like the Chartists and the other crusaders who fought for the freedoms many of us enjoy, they knew that if power was truly invincible it would not fear the people so much as to expend vast resources trying to distract and deceive them.

I offer none of this as rhetoric; human renewal is not a phenomenon. The continuation of a struggle may appear at times frozen, but is a seed beneath the snow. Look at Latin America, long declared invisible, almost expendable in the West. 'Latin Americans have been trained in impotence,' wrote Eduardo Galeano. 'A pedagogy passed down from colonial times, taught by violent soldiers, timorous teachers and frail fatalists, has rooted in our souls the belief that reality is untouchable and that all we can do is swallow in silence the woes every day brings.'[56] Galeano, dissident and poet, was celebrating the rebirth of democracy in his homeland, Uruguay, where people had voted 'against fear'. In Venezuela, Hugo Chavez heads the only government on earth sharing the nation's oil wealth with its poorest. In Bolivia, poorest of them all, the indigenous people, having forced out foreign corporations that 'owned' their water, have elected the continent's first indigenous leader.

These forces are part of a worldwide movement against poverty and war and misinformation that has arisen in less than a decade, and is more diverse, enterprising, internationalist and tolerant of difference than anything in my lifetime. It is also unburdened by Western narcissism, which has no part in freedom, as the wisest know. The wisest also know that just as the conquest of Iraq is unravelling, so a whole system of domination and impoverishment can unravel, too.

1
Stealing a Nation

The object of the exercise is to get some rocks
which will remain *ours*.
                    Foreign Office, London, 1966

The struggle of people against power is the struggle
of memory against forgetting.
                    Milan Kundera

In long-forgotten archives in London and Mauritius is rare film of a
community of contented people. The grainy, flickering images, full
of movement of children playing on sandy beaches, and proud
young women presenting their newborn for christening, and men
setting out to fish, their dogs swimming alongside, are glimpses of
a true paradise. There are thriving villages, a school, a hospital, a
church, a light railway, set in a phenomenon of natural beauty:
strings of coral atolls, floating in turquoise, that were once the peaks
of a Gondwanaland mountain range known as Limuria, long
covered by 21,000 square miles of the Indian Ocean.

Sixty-five of these limestone specks, arranged in groups, make
up the Chagos archipelago: the Salomon Islands and the Peros
Banhos atoll to the north, the Egmont Islands to the west and,
200 miles to the south, an atoll the shape of a tiny Italy, 14 miles
long and 6 miles wide. This is Diego Garcia. Free of serious tropical
storms and with a large protected natural harbour, Diego Garcia lies
almost exactly midway between Africa and Asia.

Some two thousand people lived on the Chagos archipelago,
the majority on Diego Garcia. A gentle, Creole nation, their ancestry
went back to the eighteenth century when the French brought slaves
from Mozambique and Madagascar to work a coconut plantation.
After Napoleon's defeat in 1815 the islands passed from French to
British rule; just under twenty years later, slavery was abolished.

Chagossian society continued to grow with the arrival of
indentured labourers from India in the 1840s and 1850s. Many

stayed and converted to Catholicism, together with the settled population, and by the twentieth century they had developed a distinct language that was a lilting variation of French Creole.

There were now three copra factories, supplying the coconut oil that lit street lamps in London, and a coaling station for ships en route to and from Australia; by the 1960s, there were plans for tourism. The workers received a small wage or payment in kind with commodities such as rice, oil and milk. They supplemented this by fishing in the abundantly stocked coastal waters, growing tomatoes, chilli, pumpkins and aubergines, and rearing chicken and ducks.[1] In one film, shot by missionaries, a boy plays with a pet duck and a dog dives for fish. As if celebrating a perfect vision of empire in such a place, a Colonial Office film from the 1950s describes the population as 'born and brought up . . . in conditions most tranquil and benign'. The camera pans across a laughing woman hanging out clothes to dry in a coconut grove while her children play around her. This is Charlesia Alexis.[2]

I met Charlesia the other day, fifty years after she was filmed. She was sitting in the shade of her small, sparsely furnished house on the edge of Port Louis, the capital of Mauritius, over a thousand miles from her home. I asked her for her fondest memories of Diego Garcia. 'Oh, everything!' she replied. 'The sense of well-being is my fondest souvenir. My family could eat and drink what they liked; we never lacked for anything; we never bought anything, except clothes. Can you imagine that?'

'Why did you leave?'

'I left in 1967. My husband was very ill and I decided to take him to Port Louis to get the special treatment he needed. When we were ready to return, we went to Rogers and Company – they ran the boats – and asked for our tickets. They said they had instructions not to let us go back. They said Diego had been sold.'

'Sold?'

'Yes, that's what they said. We were tricked. Looking back, the day before we left, the administrator told us to take a lot of fruit with us. They tricked us in so many ways, and when this game had run its course, they deported everyone, just like that. I was the fourth generation. Diego was my bird in the sky that was taken from me. I was sent to live in a slum, in rooms previously inhabited by goats and pigs. That's how they saw us.'

Something similar happened to Rita Bancoult. In 1968, one of her six children fell seriously ill, and Rita and her husband had to take her and the rest of their family to Mauritius. When the sick child died, they, like Charlesia, went to the shipping agent in Port Louis harbour to collect their tickets home and were also told they could never return. 'I'm very sorry for you, Rita,' said the agent, 'but your island has been sold.' At that, her husband, who was sitting beside her, suffered a stroke; his arms and mouth were paralysed, and he died a few days later.

Like all the Chagossian women I met in exile in Mauritius, Charlesia Alexis and Rita Bancoult are remarkable simply for having endured; for what happened in the Chagos Islands was so searing, it may seem barely credible. Indeed *La Lutte*, as the Chagossians call their struggle for justice and freedom, arose from a crime that allows us to glimpse how great power works behind its respectable, democratic façade and helps us to understand how much of the world is run for the benefit of the powerful, and how governments justify their actions with lies.

During the 1960s and 1970s British governments, both Labour and Tory, tricked and expelled the entire population of the Chagos, a British colonial dependency, so that their homeland could be given to a foreign power, the United States, as the site for a military base. This 'act of mass kidnapping'[3] was carried out in high secrecy, along with the conspiracy that preceded it. For almost a decade, neither Parliament nor the US Congress knew anything about it, and no journalist revealed it. When the base had been established, a group of 'defence' correspondents were flown out by the Ministry of Defence and reported as expected, as if no-one had ever lived there; BBC newsreaders still refer to US aircraft flying out to bomb Afghanistan and Iraq from the 'uninhabited' island of Diego Garcia.

The Chagossians were treated like Australia's Aborigines in the nineteenth century: they were deemed not to exist. Not only was their homeland stolen from them, they were taken out of history. Until recently, the Foreign Office website denied their very existence. Only a handful of MPs have referred to them in parliamentary debates on Britain's remaining 'overseas territories'. Not a single politician whose policy-making had brutal consequences for the islanders has ever referred to them in his or her memoirs. I know of no work of scholarship on British foreign policy that describes what happened to them, with one admirable exception: the books of Mark Curtis, who has called them 'unpeople'.[4]

Having abandoned them, seven British governments watched their vulnerable, faraway citizens live a nightmare in shanties in the Seychelles and, mainly, Mauritius, where they had been discarded, while ministers and their officials in London mounted a campaign of deception that went all the way up to the Prime Minister. This scandal continues today – even after the High Court in London ruled in 2000 that the islanders' 'wholesale removal' was an 'abject legal failure'.

The year was 1961. Two men strode up the jetty on Diego Garcia, filmed by missionaries unaware of the significance of their visitors. One of them was Rear Admiral Grantham of the US Navy, the leader of an American advance survey team whose objective was to find an island suitable for a military base that would allow Washington to dominate the Indian Ocean and beyond. For the next three years, British and American planners and engineers inspected the Chagos group. Finally they selected the nearby island of Aldabra. Their secret decision leaked out to the scientists of the Royal Society in London, who were horrified. Aldabra has a unique population of Giant Land Tortoises, nesting seabirds and the last surviving flight-less bird in the Indian Ocean; it is a treasure-store of wildlife.

Together with the Smithsonian Institution in Washington, this formidable establishment body mounted a campaign that saw off the Ministry of Defence and Admiral Grantham. The Giant Land Tortoise and the last flightless bird were safe. The second choice, however, was not. This was Diego Garcia which, although rich in terrestrial and marine life, was not unique enough to excite the indignation of naturalists.

As for the presence of a flourishing human population, this was 'not an insurmountable problem', advised the Foreign Office, for people could be 'removed' and 'the outside world [presented] with a scenario in which there were no permanent inhabitants on the archipelago'. This was essential, 'because to recognise that there are permanent inhabitants will imply that there is a population whose democratic rights will have to be safeguarded'.[5] Winston Smith in George Orwell's *1984* could not have put it better.

In February 1964, a secret Anglo-American conference was held in London, at which the final decision was taken. Again, Parliament was not informed. The following April, Anthony Greenwood, the Colonial Secretary in Harold Wilson's Labour government, flew to Mauritius, then a British colony that included the Chagos Islands. Greenwood spelled out the terms for granting independence to Mauritius. Despite United Nations Resolution 1514, which held that all colonial peoples had an inalienable right to independence without conditions, Greenwood offered it with strings. Mauritius could be free as long as Britain could keep the Chagos archipelago. The bribe was a mere £3 million, together with a promise to support Mauritian sugar preferences.

Thus Charlesia's and Rita's homeland was 'sold'. On November 8, 1965, in the twilight of its colonial era, Britain created a new colony, the British Indian Ocean Territory (BIOT), whose principal territory was the Chagos Islands. It was a ruse of which perhaps only Britain's *ancien régime* was capable; for the new colony was a fake, an entity created for the sole purpose of handing it over for the use of the American military. This was made possible by using the archaic powers of the royal prerogative, a throwback to the divine right of kings.

The British Indian Ocean Territory was brought into being by an order-in-council, a decision approved not by Parliament but by the monarch, acting on the advice – in effect, the instructions – of a secretive, unaccountable group known as the Privy Council. The members of this body, the Privy Councillors, include present and former government ministers. They appear before the Queen in Buckingham Palace, standing in a semi-circle around her, heads slightly bowed, like Druids; they never sit down. Items for the Queen's rubber-stamping – the 'orders-in-council' – are read out by title only. There is no discussion; the Queen simply says, 'Agreed.' This is government by fiat: the use of a royal decree by politicians who want to get away with something undemocratically. Most British people have never heard of it. British prime ministers use it to take the nation into unpopular wars, such as the invasions of Egypt in 1956 and Iraq in 2003. Dictators do the same, but without the quaint ritual. The Wilson government used it to deport an entire population so as to hand their country to the Americans. Almost forty years later, the Blair government used it to thwart the High Court's attempt to allow them back.

Although barely reported in the press, word of this manoeuvre reached the United Nations in New York, spurring the General Assembly to pass Resolution 2066, which called on the British government 'to take no action which would dismember the territory of Mauritius and violate its territorial integrity'. This was ignored.

In December 1966, Lord Chalfont, a Foreign Office minister, signed a contract in Washington giving the Pentagon a fifty-year 'lease' on Diego Garcia with an automatic extension of twenty years. Declassified State Department documents obtained under the US Freedom of Information Act in 2005 reveal that Washington wanted the entire population expelled; as one official put it, the islands were to be 'swept' and 'sanitised'. This was described in a secret file as 'a neat, sensible package'.[6]

Robin Cook, who in 1966 had not yet begun his parliamentary career, told me in 2004 that the scandal was not raised in the House of Commons for almost a decade because MPs 'knew nothing about it; the keeping of that secret was amazing'. It was indeed. In December 1974 – the year Cook was first elected as an MP – a joint UK–US question-and-answer primer for officials and embassies around the world asked: 'Is there any native population on the islands?' The reply was: 'No.' A Ministry of Defence spokesman denied this was a lie, in the process uttering perhaps the most amazing lie of all. 'There is nothing in our files,' he said, 'about inhabitants or about an evacuation.'[7]

It was not until 1975, following an exposé in the *Washington Post*, that the US Senate revealed that the British government had been secretly 'compensated' for the Chagos with a discount of $14 million off the price of a Polaris nuclear submarine. This itself was illegal, as it was never submitted to Congress for approval; and the document Chalfont signed stated falsely that the US would pay no rent for acquiring 'base rights'. There was no mention of a population.[8]

Lizette Talate is also in the Colonial Office film. She was fourteen years old at the time and remembers the producer saying to her and her friends, 'Keep smiling, girls!' Sitting in her kitchen in Port Louis, she said, 'We didn't need to be told. I was a happy child, because my roots were deep in Diego. My great-grandmother was born on Diego, and my grandmother was born there, and my mother was born there, and I was born there. I made six children there. Maybe only the English can make a film that showed we were an established community, then deny their own evidence and invent the lie that we were transient workers. That's why they couldn't legally throw us out of our own homes; they had to terrify us into leaving or force us out.'

'How did they terrify you?'

'They tried to starve us. The food ships stopped arriving, and everything was scarce. There was no milk, no dairy products, no oil, no sugar, no salt. When they couldn't starve us out of our homes, they spread rumours that we would be bombed, then they turned on our dogs.'

The Chagossians love their dogs; they are inseparable. A Chagossian home is a profusion of steps-and-stairs children and fawn-coloured, tail-wagging mongrels and pups. The plan to kill all the dogs on the island – with its unsubtle implication that humans might be next – came from Sir Bruce Greatbatch, KCVO, CMG, MBE, then Her Majesty's Governor of the Seychelles, who was responsible for the 'new' colony of the BIOT.

'At first they tried poisoned fish balls,' said Lizette. 'That killed a few and left many in terrible agony. Then they paid a man to walk around with a big stick, beating them to death, or trying to.'

'What year was this?'

'Spring 1971. It was very hot. American soldiers had already begun to arrive to build the base. They backed several of their big vehicles against the brick shed where the coconuts were prepared; hundreds of dogs had been rounded up and imprisoned there. Then they gassed them through a tube from the truck's exhaust. You could hear them crying.'

The bodies of the dogs, many still alive, were thrown on to a shelf that usually held the flesh of coconuts as it was cooked above husks burning below. This was their pyre. Children listened to the howls of their pets being burned to death and watched a few trying to escape on to the beach, and being driven back into the flames by whippers-in. It took more than a ton of husks to complete the slaughter.

'The children cherished their dogs,' said Lizette. 'Nothing was the same after that. We were covered in sadness.'

Robin Mardemootoo, the islanders' Mauritian lawyer, told me: 'The relationship with your pets ought to be the same whether you are Chagossian or British. They were absolutely destroyed by the fate reserved for the dogs, and many of them told me that it was clear to them that if they offered any objection to the depopulation they would suffer the same fate. And if this was not enough, American military helicopters and planes flew very low over the island and people were told the whole place would be bombed very soon. I've listened to women crying, remembering how they ran from the noise when all of a sudden they would see a helicopter, and they would take their children in their arms, terrified.'

Those who refused to leave were summoned to the Administrator's office and told they had no choice because their 'removal' was 'legal' under the rules of the new colony. This was a big lie. A senior judge, Lord Justice Sedley, noted thirty years later that 'legal powers designed for the governance of the islands [were misused] for the illicit purpose of de-populating them'.[9]

The assembled people were told they would be loaded on to ships and deported. There is a photograph of this meeting. A white man wearing shorts and long socks is standing on the steps, addressing the crowd; children are looking up at the adults, who look stunned. Several appear to have dropped down with shock; others seem stricken with grief.

'Magistrate Todd delivered the news,' said Lizette. 'There was a sort of hint that what they did to our dogs they were going to do to us. They were without pity.'

Along with 180 others, Lizette and her family were forced on to the vessel *Nordvaer*, which had plied between the Chagos and Mauritius and the Seychelles, transporting copra and taking supplies back to the islands. The uneventful coming and going of this ship had helped give the Chagossians their best-known name, Ilois, meaning 'islanders'. As a means of transporting this number of passengers across 2,500 miles, it was hopelessly inadequate. They were allowed to take with them only minimal personal possessions; they had to leave behind their furniture, which they had bought with savings from their work in the plantations, and their precious chickens and ducks, donkeys and goats. The descendants of goats and donkeys that were not shot now run wild in the vegetable gardens and graveyards long claimed by bush.

Sir Bruce Greatbatch's military-style commands were sent by satellite from the Seychelles. 'Destroy the dogs and save the horses,' he had ordered Marcel Moulinie, the plantation manager. He now insisted that the horses took pride of place on deck of the *Nordvaer*.[10] For five days, the horses were fed and the people were not. The men were herded onto the bridge and had to stand or crouch in very rough weather; the women and children were made to sleep in the hold on a cargo of fertiliser – bird shit. People vomited and suffered diarrhoea; two women miscarried.

'Even water was scarce,' said Lizette. 'What I can't forget is the fear and uncertainty for myself and my family. When we got to the Seychelles, the police were waiting for us. They marched us up the hill to a prison, where we were kept in cells until the boat was ready to take us on to Mauritius.

'I suppose we took some hope in the promise that in Mauritius we would be granted a house, a piece of land, animals and a sum of money. We got nothing. When the ship got to Mauritius, the only kind person was the captain who let us stay on his ship until he had to go.'

The former President of Mauritius, Cassam Uteem, who has championed the Chagossians' rights, told me: 'You can't imagine how bewildered and terrified they were. Some of them camped on the docks, waiting for the next ship to take them back home. No British official was there to ease their way, even though the British had done this to them and they were British citizens. They needed help to integrate themselves into Mauritian society, which is very different from the society they were used to. For them, life had been simple: they had a house of their own, they grew their own food, they fished from the sea and they worked on a plantation. They were very close to nature, whereas in Mauritius, it's a sophisticated life by comparison. You go out and look for a job; and there is unemployment. What happens to someone who doesn't have any skills besides those of fishermen?

'Many had never seen traffic; at home, they wouldn't think of using even a bicycle to go from one place to the other. These were a people who would sing their way through life; and here they were, weeping their way through life, and they are still weeping. I know of one lady who lost two children within two or three months, and she wasn't able even to perform their funerals because she didn't have any money. The children were taken from the hospital straight to the cemetery. That lady is still weeping.'

Lizette is that lady. She lost Jollice, aged eight, and Regis, aged ten months. Her husband died soon afterwards. She is a wiry, fiercely intelligent woman who wears a mask of grief and determination. 'When the ship docked, Mauritian officials didn't know what to do with us,' she said. 'They eventually took us to an abandoned housing estate called Beau Marchand. Mauritians we met told us this place was not habitable, and we could see why. Goats from Rodriguez Island had been put in the houses, which had no electricity and water, and rubbish and filth were everywhere. It is accurate to say we were treated like animals.

'That was November – I've forgotten the year; I hope I have! – I was so sick I was in hospital and both my children were, too. They died in the January, within eight days of each other.'

'What did they die of?' I asked.

'They died of sadness. When I received the news, I knew the youngest had my milk, which was the milk of sadness. The eight-year-old had heard all the talk, and he'd seen the horror of what had happened to the dogs. He knew he was leaving his home.'

'What did the doctor say about him?'

'The doctor said he could not treat sadness.'

'Do you have photos of them?'

'When I came to Mauritius, I didn't have the opportunity to have their photos taken. I just sat and cried and had no time to take photos . . . But, listen to me, I am going home; we all are going home. We are not here to be pitied, we are here to *fight*.'

Waving away her pups, Rita Bancoult welcomed me into her

home in the Cassis district of Port Louis, where most exiled Chagossians live. Born on the island of Peros Banhos in 1925, she says her 'will never to forget' her previous life has sustained her since her family was tipped on to the dock with 'a bunch of clothes tied in a pillowcase and a straw mattress'. Among family snaps she showed me was a picture of the royal family, from around the 1970s. I asked her why she kept this.

'That's the what?' she said.

'That's the Queen and the Duke. Didn't you know?'

'I didn't think about it. It's one of the pictures my husband's mother kept . . .'

'What are you doing with it, Rita?'

'I'm putting it in the toilet! They have caused us too much suffering. I'm tearing it into pieces and putting it down the toilet.'

And so she did.

'When we arrived in Mauritius,' she said, 'we were not even recognised as human beings. My children had nothing to eat, so I went from house to house in a good-looking street. I got a domestic's job, but when the lady found out I was from the Chagos, she sacked me. All I could do was search bins in the street for plastic bags containing stale bread. In Mauritius, the well-off throw out most of their bread. It would take me all day to collect a meal of this for the children; it's how we lived.'

Four of Rita's children died in Mauritius: first, the baby they had brought over with a gangrenous wound to be treated; then, in the years of exile, Reno, Alec and Eddie.

'What did they die from?' I asked.

'Sorrow.'

I had brought an official British document to show Rita. It was written in 1968 by one Anthony Ivall Aust (pronounced oarst), then a high-flying legal adviser to the Foreign and Commonwealth Office, aged twenty-six. Headed 'Maintaining the fiction', it advised the Wilson government to 'argue' the 'fiction' that the Chagossians were 'only a floating population' because 'this would bolster our arguments that the territory has no indigenous or settled population'. When it was translated into Creole for Rita, she dropped her head in her hands.

'But that's not true!' she cried out. 'All our generations are buried on Diego. How could he write that?'

I did not read her Aust's *pièce de résistance*. 'We are able to make up the rules as we go along,' he wrote, 'and treat the inhabitants of BIOT as not "belonging" to it in any sense.' Aust was subsequently awarded the CMG in the Queen's Birthday Honours.[11]

By 1975, the Chagossians in exile began to die from their imposed poverty. Most were unemployed and penniless and either sharing a slum or sleeping rough. A survey by the Comité Ilois Organisation Fraternelle in Port Louis told of twenty-six families that had 'died together in poverty', nine suicides, and young girls forced into prostitution merely to pay for food. The following is an extract from the report:

> Eliane and Michele Mouza: mother and child, committed suicide.
> Leone Rangasamy: drowned herself because she was prevented from going home.
> Terenne Chiatoux: committed suicide, no job, no roof.
> Daisy Volfrin: obtained no food for three days. Died through poverty.
> Josue and Maude Baptiste: no roof, no food, committed suicide.[12]

This was merely a snapshot of the suffering inflicted by the British government, whose callousness *en passant* was expressed in a letter to a Member of Parliament from a Foreign Office official. 'Although we have no information about deaths,' he wrote, 'some deaths are bound to have occurred in the normal course of events.'[13]

That was a lie. The Foreign Office had sent a senior official, A. R. G. Prosser, to investigate; he had sent back a graphically detailed report on the islanders' living conditions and advised that 'something needs to be done'.[14] The government's response was to offer a minuscule £650,000 in compensation to the entire population. Even this did not arrive until 1978, five years after the last islander had been deported; and even this was dispatched grudgingly. A note from the British High Commission in Port Louis had emphasised,

'We must be satisfied that we could not discharge our obligation . . . more cheaply.'[15]

In 1975, a group of desperate people presented the following petition to the High Commission:

> We, the inhabitants of the Chagos islands . . . have been uprooted from these islands because the Mauritius government sold the islands to the British government to build a base. Our ancestors were slaves on those islands but we know we are the heirs of those islands. Although we were poor we were not dying of hunger. We were living free . . . Here in Mauritius . . . we, being mini-slaves, don't get anybody to help us. We are at a loss not knowing what to do.[16]

The response of the High Commission was that this had nothing to do with the British and the islanders should address their 'concerns' to the Mauritian government, which had assumed responsibility for their resettlement.[17] This was another lie; most of the Chagossians were citizens of the United Kingdom and Colonies. However, as the files disclose, it was all part of the official British strategy towards the islanders, which was to 'grant as few rights with as little formality as possible'.[18]

On March 16, 1981, several hundred Chagossian women converged on the British High Commission in Port Louis, sat down and sang, and demanded proper compensation. Having tried in vain to speak to the High Commissioner, they occupied the entrance hall, and eight women began a hunger strike in the gardens opposite. One of them was seventy-seven years old. Charlesia Alexis was arrested and beaten; a newspaper photograph of her being dragged into the back of a police van sent an embarrassing ripple to London. When the hunger strike was in its eighteenth day, the British agreed to 'talks' – not with the Chagossians, but with the Mauritian government.

In the first few months of 1982, it appeared that progress was being made on compensation. On March 27, a group of the most impoverished islanders accepted a 'full and final' settlement of £4 million – less than half the estimated minimum they could survive on. Rita Bancoult showed me a strange, pseudo-official document that bore her name and her thumbprint. In exchange for a 'settlement' amounting to around £1,000, and unaware of what she was agreeing to, Rita unwittingly 'signed' an agreement to renounce her rights to return to the Chagos.

'I can't read or write,' she said. 'I was told that if I signed this I would get some welfare assistance in Mauritius. I later realised it allowed the British government to say they had compensated us. They didn't; they tricked us. The money we got didn't begin to pay our debts.'

Robin Mardemootoo, their lawyer, said, 'It was entirely improper, unethical and dictatorial to have the Chagossians put their thumbprint on an English legal document, where the Chagossian, who doesn't read or speak any English, is basically made to renounce his rights as a human being.'

Compounding deception with confusion, a Foreign Office delegation to Mauritius, led by Sir Leonard Allison, announced, 'We shall not insist upon renunciations,' while leaving unchanged both the terms of the settlement, which required renunciation, and the documents, which could not be read by those desperate for some compensation.[19]

Such a crude expedient may well have been a product of the Falklands War. In 1982, Britain's treatment of the Chagossians was being contrasted in the United Nations with its expenditure that year of £2 billion defending the rights of the Falkland islanders.[20] The Falklands and the Chagos each had a population of 2,000 British citizens. One population was white, the other black. While the Argentine invasion of the Falklands was furiously resisted by British forces sent 8,000 miles for the purpose, the American invasion of Diego Garcia was accommodated in every detail by the British government, which even arranged for the inhabitants' expulsion.

In 1982, the *Financial Times* called the Falklands invasion an 'illegal and immoral means to make good territorial claims', as well as an 'outrage' that should not be allowed to 'pass over the wishes of the Falkland islanders'.[21] Echoing Margaret Thatcher, the *Daily Telegraph* said that 'the wishes of the [Falkland] islanders were paramount', that 'these islanders' must not be 'betrayed', and 'principle dictates' that the British and American governments could not possibly 'be indifferent to the imposition of foreign rule on people who have no desire for it'.[22] Such fine indignation applied precisely to the people of the Chagos, but was never expressed.

I asked Marcel Moulinie about this. A ruddy, Buddha-shaped man, at ease with a pink gin, a billowing shirt and a tropical sunset, he was the last manager of the plantation on Diego Garcia which his family had owned. He had moved in the pith-helmeted milieu of Sir Bruce Greatbatch, and now he was a troubled man.

'First, let's set the record straight,' he said, 'Operation Stampede – getting those people off the islands – was a *faux pas* of Sir Bruce.'

'A *faux pas*?'

'I don't think he meant it. He had some wonderful ideas for developing the islands for tourism. That's why he wanted to get the horses off and try it somewhere else.'

'Yes,' I said, 'he put them on deck and the women and children in the hold.'

'Oh, he did that without really thinking. But it wasn't good; it was terrible actually. In giving the horses priority, we had to put wooden stables on board and, God, as the ship rolled, you had horse dung everywhere; it was disgusting actually.'

'What else disgusted you?'

'The invention in London that the Chagossians were mere contract workers who could be sent back to places they had never come from. The man who looked after my cattle on Diego was fifth generation.'

'Why did they do it?'

'Let's face it: do any of these boys in the Colonial Office, do they really care about this? Come on . . . You had your standard of living and you kept to it . . . your pink gin at lunchtime . . .'

'So the people were just "the natives"?'

'The natives, yes. That was the truth of colonial life, whether you were in Kenya, Uganda, the Seychelles; and who cared about the Chagos? Oh, just bung them on a ship, you know. That was the situation. It was hell. One young fellow jumped overboard to his death. I've read about the slave ships from Africa to America. This was the same. The only difference was the absence of chains. I couldn't get the people out of my mind; I still can't. In their first few years in Mauritius, I went to see them. They had no water and no sanitation, and the children had no clothes; they looked as though they had been rolled in ash and earth.'

'You sound full of regret.'

'I am.'

'What do you regret most?'

'Where does one start? Getting rid of the dogs; I did that for Sir Bruce. It was not fun. We had about eight hundred dogs on Diego. I'm sorry to say I tried to poison them. I used strychnine, which the Americans used to poison coyotes back home. The moment I saw the poison having an effect I would shoot them in the head. The Americans helped, but a platoon of us couldn't shoot all the dogs. So I talked to the American medical boys, who suggested carbon monoxide. That did it. Then we burnt them, eight or nine hundred. We didn't do the cats . . . couldn't catch them.'

'While all this was going on, did anyone express any regrets?'

'Well, my uncle, who owned the plantation, was very annoyed about the whole thing.'

'Annoyed?'

'He wasn't happy with the price he got for the plantation.'

'What do you think of the compensation the people got?'

'You call that compensation? Now come on, these things should be done properly, not brushed under the carpet.'

'Do you remember the Royal Navy going to the rescue of the Falkland islanders?'

'Ha! How many times I've thought of that.'

'What was the difference?'

'Can't you hear her, the Queen, in her Christmas broadcast and birthday broadcasts? "My people," she would say. So you go to the rescue of two thousand of her people in the Falklands, and you kick out two thousand of her people in the Chagos.'

'What's the difference?'

'I wouldn't like to answer that.'

'Why not?'

'I love the British.'

'Go on, answer it.'

'I think we both know the answer.'

*

Olivier Bancoult is Rita's surviving son. At dawn every morning he puts on his green overalls and cycles down a stony dirt path past corrugated shacks, from which people greet him warmly. During the day he is an electrician with Port Louis city council. In the evening, from a small lock-up beneath a hand-painted sign, 'CHAGOS REFUGEE GROUP', he takes *La Lutte* to the world. Of the four thousand Chagossians on Mauritius, only Olivier speaks fluent English. A paragon of patience and grace, he leads a community dominated by matriarchs who intend to go home before they die.

As you enter the lock-up, there is a 'picture of paradise', as Olivier calls it. It is an incandescent, wall-sized mural, green and lush and dream-like. (It is not unlike the mural tapestries that hang in Palestinian refugee homes.) Above it are photographs of Olivier with Nelson Mandela and Olivier with the late Pope. 'We compare our struggle to Mandela's,' he said. 'It is almost forty years since they stole our country and imprisoned us here. We are all like Mandela.'

The lock-up contains a computer: 'My messenger to the world,' says Olivier. 'We send our press releases out from here.'

'Does anyone publish them?'

'Sometimes, but I keep sending them anyway; I keep explaining who we are, and what was done to us. I remember the words of Martin Luther King: "With this faith, we will be able to hew out of the mountain despair, a stone of hope."'

'Do you get angry?'

'Yes, I get very angry when I think of the Americans on Diego, with their bombers coming down a two-mile runway, and their swimming pools and bars and barbecues, and their Miss Diego Garcia contests.'

'What upsets you the most?'

'The lie that we didn't exist.'

The 1975 Ministry of Defence lie that 'there is nothing in our files about inhabitants [of the Chagos] or about an evacuation' has special notoriety. For the truth was, there was everything in their files.[23]

In the 1990s the islanders' struggle took a dramatic turn when a treasure trove of declassified official documents was discovered in the National Archives at Kew in south-west London. This provided the narrative of a conspiracy between two governments to carry out, in the words of Article 7 of the Statute of the International Criminal Court, the 'deportation or forcible transfer of a population . . . a crime against humanity'.[24]

For the conspirators, secrecy and deception were vital. In May 1964, a Foreign Office 'memorandum of guidance' warned that 'these steps [the depopulation of the Chagos] should be timed to attract the least attention and should have some logical cover where possible worked out in advance [otherwise] they will arouse suspicions as to their purpose'.[25] The 'logical cover' was the invention of the BIOT, which would be presented to the world as 'temporarily' populated by 'contract workers' who could be 'returned' to Mauritius and the Seychelles. A senior Foreign Office official, T. C. D. Jerrom, called this a 'solution to the population problem'.

On July 28, 1965, Jerrom wrote to the British Representative at the United Nations, F. D. W. Brown, instructing him to lie to the General Assembly that the Chagos Islands were 'uninhabited when the United Kingdom government first acquired them'. This Brown did on November 16, 1965. He also misrepresented the population as 'labourers from Mauritius and the Seychelles' for whom Britain's obligations under the United Nations Charter 'did not apply', and he lied that the 'new administrative arrangements' had been 'freely worked out with the . . . elected representatives of the people concerned'.[26]

In a secret memorandum, a Colonial Office official, K. W. S. MacKenzie, spelt out the truth. 'One of the things we would like to do in the new Territory', he wrote, 'is to convert all the existing residents into short-term, temporary residents by giving them temporary immigration permits, describing them as inhabitants of Mauritius or the Seychelles.'[27]

Reading the files, it is clear that the British government did as it was told by Washington. Mass deportation, wrote a Foreign Office official, 'was made virtually a condition of the agreement [with the Americans] when we negotiated it in 1965'. Another official, I. McCluney, wrote, 'I smell trouble here . . . I don't see why the Americans shouldn't allow some to stay. Could they not be useful?'[28]

At the British Mission to the United Nations in New York, C. E. King fretted about the 'risks of damaging publicity'. He wrote to

London: 'It would be desirable, in any necessary publicity about the proposed installations, to avoid as far as possible the use of the word "base".' At the Foreign Office, J. H. Lambert warned that 'if interest in [the Chagossians] became strong enough, the press may well discover that they exist in significant numbers'.[29]

Secretly, among themselves, the officials recognised they were open to 'charges of dishonesty' because they were planning to 'cook the books'. One expressed 'old fashioned' concerns about telling 'whopping fibs'. But even 'fib', however whopping, hardly describes the lie of the message from Sir Bruce Greatbatch to the Foreign Office in which he described those he had been unable to trick into leaving as 'all contract expired [who] have exercised their right to leave Chagos.'[30]

From 1965, instructions issued by the Foreign Office and Commonwealth Relations Office, as it was then called, to British embassies around the world emphasised the need to avoid all reference to 'permanent inhabitants'. Anthony Aust, the young Foreign Office legal adviser who had written that 'we are able to make up the rules as we go along', advised that the official line should be 'to maintain the fiction that the inhabitants of Chagos are not a permanent or semi-permanent population'.[31]

A debate was conducted between these appointed officials, clearly aware of their power. One commented, '[On Diego Garcia] there is a civilian population. In practice, however, I would advise a policy of "quiet disregard" – in other words, let's forget about this one until the United Nations challenge us on it.'[32] The gravity of this apparently cavalier remark is evident when it is set against Article 73 of the United Nations Charter, which obliges colonial powers like Britain not only to protect the human rights of their dependent peoples but 'to develop self government'. This is called 'a sacred trust'.[33] H. G. Darwin wrote, 'This is all fairly unsatisfactory . . . we propose to certify [the] islanders, more or less fraudulently, as belonging somewhere else. This all seems difficult to reconcile with the "sacred trust" of Article 73.'[34]

Perhaps with this problem in mind, Eleanor Emery, head of the Pacific Dependent Territories Department at the Foreign Office, wrote the following 'secret and personal' letter to Sir Bruce Greatbatch: 'We shall continue to try and say as little as possible to avoid embarrassing the United States Administration . . . We would not wish it to become general knowledge that some of the inhabitants have lived on Diego Garcia for at least two generations and could, therefore, be regarded as "belongers".' The Foreign Office, she wrote, would therefore advise government ministers to say 'there is only a small number of contract labourers from Mauritius and the Seychelles engaged to work on the copra plantations' and that 'should a Member [of Parliament] ask about what would happen to these contract labourers in the event of a base being set up on the island, we hope that, for the present, this can be brushed aside as a hypothetical question.'[35]

What these files reveal is a trail of lies, yes, but also an imperious attitude of brutality and contempt. On August 24, 1966, Sir Paul Gore-Booth, Permanent Under-Secretary at the Foreign Office, wrote: 'We must surely be very tough about this. The object of the exercise is to get some rocks which will remain *ours*. There will be no indigenous population except seagulls who have not yet got a Committee (the Status of Women Committee does *not* cover the rights of birds)' (original emphasis).

At the bottom of the page is a postscript handwritten by D. A. Greenhill, another senior official, who became Baron Greenhill of Harrow. 'Unfortunately,' he wrote, 'along with the Birds go some few Tarzans or Men Fridays whose origins are obscure, and who are being hopefully wished on to Mauritius etc. When this has been done, I agree we must be very tough.'[36]

In the early 1970s, Andrew Stuart was head of the Hong Kong and Indian Ocean Department at the Foreign Office, a very senior position. In 1973, he proposed that he go to Diego Garcia to see for himself if the population had been 'temporary or permanent'. More than thirty years later, in August 2004, we met in London and I asked him what he had found.

'I found what had been a regular community,' he said, '. . . a church and shops and all that, and I reported back that there had been a permanent community.'

'What happened then?'

'I assumed they were properly compensated . . .'

'When you look at official documents now, here you have some of your former colleagues talking about needing some rocks and getting rid of a bunch of Tarzans and Man Fridays . . .'

'Actually, I knew the person you're referring to, and I have the greatest respect for him; he's dead now. I'm sure that if he had any clue that his throwaway remarks would become public he would never have written that . . . You know, people put things in minutes on official papers they don't really mean.'

'Really? . . . Did any of your colleagues ever say that what was being done to the Chagos was wrong?'

'No, I don't think so . . . There was a need in the West for a base in the Indian Ocean in the post-Vietnam situation. I didn't feel that it was wrong, provided that the inhabitants were properly compensated. Do you find that shocking?'

'Having spoken to many people from the Chagos who are suffering terribly, I would like to say I find it shocking, but I am not surprised. It's how undemocratic power works, isn't it?'

'Supposing,' he said, '. . . sorry, I'm quizzing you . . . supposing they had been offered a tropical paradise to live in, and money to live on, and that the whole thing had been carried out sensitively and generously, would you regard that as shocking?'

'Well, it would be up to the Chagossians, but in fact they were prepared to live on the outer islands, Peros Banhos and Salomon, and they were prevented from going there, and they are still prevented from going there, even though these islands are two hundred miles from Diego Garcia. They offered that as a solution and it was denied them.'

'The Americans would have regarded that as unacceptable.'

'But this was British territory, and these people were British subjects. Why should their basic rights be suspended because the Americans found something unacceptable?'

'There were overriding defence needs . . . and a lot of Cold War paranoia.'

'These days there is no Cold War, no Soviet Union, and this is an American base far from America, yet the British government is still putting American interests above the rights of its people. You were one of a group of retired British ambassadors who recently signed a letter opposing the invasion of Iraq. If attacking Iraq was wrong, why wasn't the Chagos episode wrong?'

'Attacking Iraq was stupid. I'm not against the United States as the policeman of the world, but they've got to be more sensible about it. On Iraq, I was not making a moral judgement. It was a pragmatic judgement of the unwisdom of their action.'

'Do you think morality plays a part in foreign policy?'

'Oh yes, sure. I mean, if there is no moral basis to what you are doing, then you are no different from the dictators.'

'The Chagos must have slipped by that principle.'

'Why do you keep on bringing me back to a moral judgement?'

'The United Nations Charter says that Britain held what it calls a "sacred trust" towards looking after the people of the Chagos . . .'

'I'm sorry; you keep on bringing me back to the same point. I don't personally use words like sacred trust.'

'The United Nations Charter does, and Britain is a signatory.'

'I know that, but when people start talking about sacred trust, I turn off. I spent my whole colonial life working for the independence first of Uganda, then the Seychelles and the New Hebrides, and that was my sacred trust . . . of course, I realise you have an agenda and that you are unlikely to give a huge amount of strength to my point of view.'

'The only agenda here is the agenda of a number of British governments whose behaviour has caused such suffering to people. Otherwise, I wouldn't be asking you these questions. We wouldn't like it done to us, would we?'

'No, of course not.'

The cover-up went to the top of government. On November 5 and 8, 1965, the Colonial Secretary, Anthony Greenwood, wrote two secret minutes to Prime Minister Harold Wilson, in which he described the problem of a 'population of one thousand inhabitants' living in the Chagos. He urged that the Queen quickly approve the 'order-in-council detaching the islands' so that the new colony could be declared and 'we should be able to present the UN with a *fait accompli*'.[37]

So when Prime Minister Wilson gave the green light to the order-in-council, he was aware he was overriding the legal and human rights of British citizens. He was stealing their country and ignoring the risks of 'dumping unemployables in heavily over-populated Mauritius', as one honest Foreign Office official warned, not to mention the incalculable suffering this ensured.[38]

The Foreign Secretary, Michael Stewart, a quiet, grey-haired, grandfatherly-looking man, took charge of the cover-up. Writing secretly to Wilson on July 25, 1968, he proposed that the government lie to the world that there was 'no indigenous population' even though he had signed a memorandum circulating in the Cabinet which said, 'By any stretch of the English language, there was an indigenous population and the Foreign Office knew it.'[39]

Not only did the Foreign Office know, it was busily working out how ministers should lie about it. 'We would not wish it to become general knowledge', said one memorandum, 'that some of the inhabitants [were] "belongers". We shall therefore advise ministers in handling supplementary questions about whether Diego Garcia is inhabited to say there is only a small number of contract workers from the Seychelles and Mauritius engaged in work on the copra plantations on the island. That is being economical with the truth.'[40]

In his letter to Wilson, Stewart wrote: 'Officials have examined closely the possibility of giving them [the Chagossians] some element of choice, but have advised that this would seem wholly impracticable.'[41]

Compare his words with those of Britain's Representative to the United Nations, F. D. W. Brown, who told the General Assembly that 'the new administrative arrangements' for the Chagos had been 'freely worked out with the . . . elected representatives of the people concerned'. Stewart also wrote that 'it would be helpful if we can present any move as a change of employment for contract workers . . . rather than as a population resettlement'.[42]

On April 26, 1969, Wilson's private secretary wrote to Stewart that the Prime Minister approved the 'plan'.[43] Seven successive British governments have – to recall the memorable expression of the Foreign Office legal adviser in 1969 – maintained the fiction.[44]

Richard Gifford has read all these documents since he first visited Mauritius on holiday in 1997 and became aware of the Chagossians' plight. Since then, he has been their indefatigable and brave lawyer. 'It was quite shocking to find there was a policy being formulated in flagrant breach of international law,' he told me. 'The documents show that it was decided at the highest level, by the Prime Minister, most particularly Harold Wilson. He knew very well there was a population and they were going to be removed. This is policy made almost on the back of an envelope. There is no democratic input, nobody was asking questions, nobody was knocking on the door, nobody was there to represent the interests of the islanders. They just didn't exist as a political factor to take into account.'

In his two autobiographies, totalling more than a thousand pages, Denis Healey, who was Defence Secretary in the Wilson government and responsible for turning Diego Garcia over to the Pentagon, makes not a single mention of the expulsion of the population. In 2004 I asked Healey for an interview. He replied, 'I fear I have no memories of the Chagos archipelago. Sorry.'

On May 6, 1969, Healey's private secretary wrote to 10 Downing Street, confirming that the Defence Secretary had read Stewart's plan and 'agrees with its recommendations'. Healey even queried the cost of expelling the population and sought an assurance that any 'excess' above £10 million would not be borne by his department.[45]

Wilson sought the approval of all his senior Cabinet ministers, including the Attorney-General, his principal adviser on international law, and they all gave it in writing. From the mid-1960s to 1974, three prime ministers and thirteen Cabinet ministers had personal knowledge of the expulsion of the population of the Chagos Islands. None of them raised an objection.

'It's very difficult to accept that British cabinets would do this,' said Gifford. 'I couldn't begin to justify it, for it was known to be illegal under international law, and it's now accepted as an international crime against humanity. We have since then had the problems of ethnic cleansing in the Balkans, and although the degree of force may not have been the same, it is nonetheless the same objective, to clear a group of people by reason of their ethnic origin from a territory because they are not wanted. I don't see how anybody in their right mind could have conceived or executed that policy.'

I asked him why he thought they did it.

'One can only say they were looking at another prize, and that this was considered a price worth paying, because in reality there would be no objections in this country, and they would get away with it. The documents show this quite clearly; they only cared about being found out.'

'How did they get away with it?'

'By moving smartly and removing the population before anyone was aware of their existence. It's very shameful.'

The silence of most journalists for most of three decades also allowed them to get away with it. John Madeley, a freelance journalist and broadcaster, wrote a powerful, erudite report for the Minority Rights Group, *Diego Garcia: A Contrast to the Falklands*, which first alerted me to the plight of the Chagossians.[46] To show that the islanders had not been completely forgotten in Britain, Madeley described the astonishing lone campaign of George Champion, an English teacher from Kent, who set up the 1966 Society for Diego Garcians in Exile, and dedicated himself to explaining the crime to the British public.

Changing his name to 'Chagos', Champion made contact with Members of Parliament, American senators and the public. Once a month, he would stand outside the Foreign Office, holding a placard bearing only the words 'Diego Garcia'. People would stop and ask him who Diego Garcia was. 'Once they knew,' he said, 'they supported the cause.'[47] This reminds me of the courageous Brian Haw, who is currently camped in Parliament Square for the fifth consecutive year, displaying a small sign that says 'Stop Killing Kids. Let Iraq's Infants Live'.

A parallel conspiracy was under way in Washington in the 1960s and 1970s, also in high secrecy. The object was to keep the scandal of the depopulation from Congress, along with the aggressive nature of the proposed base on Diego Garcia. On December 14, 1966, a Foreign Office official alerted the Foreign Secretary to 'the American insistence that the financial arrangements must remain secret. The US government has, for cogent reasons of its own, chosen to conceal from Congress the substantial financial assistance which we are to get in the form of a remission of Polaris [nuclear weapon] dues.'[48]

The British were only too pleased to co-operate. A Foreign
Office cable to the Washington embassy promised that 'ultimately,
under extreme pressure, we should have to deny the existence of a
US contribution in any form, and to advise ministers to do so in
[Parliament] if necessary'.[49] The officials were terrified that 'if the
Americans, under pressure, reveal the existence of the financial
arrangement, then we should be in acute parliamentary and con-
stitutional difficulties'.[50]

This collusion demonstrates where elite loyalty so often lies –
not with the home country, its citizens or its democratic institutions,
but with a rapacious foreign regime seeking to occupy sovereign
territory for reasons it wishes to conceal from its own people.

Three years later, Foreign Secretary Stewart met the Prime
Minister of Mauritius, Seewoosagur Ramgoolam, whose government had accepted independence and a pittance of a bribe in
exchange for the 'detachment' of the Chagos. The subject of the base
came up. The minutes of their conversation record this assurance
from Stewart. 'Base', said the Foreign Secretary, 'is a misleading and
inaccurate word to use in this context. All that is involved
is a modest naval communications facility. It will in no way
constitute a base, as there are no plans to station operational forces
there, nor will the facility provide logistic support for such
forces.'[51]

Every word was false; the opposite was true. The 'modest naval
communications facility' which 'will in no way constitute a base'
today accommodates four thousand service personnel and support
contractors, two of the longest bomber runways in the world,
anchorages for thirty ships, two nuclear berths, space weapons
tracking domes, shopping malls, nightclubs, a golf course, tennis
courts, swimming pools and more. It is one of the four biggest
'expeditionary' American bases outside the United States.[52]

The administrations of President Johnson and President Nixon
kept these plans secret for more than a decade. Today, the National
Archives in Washington yield truths as scandalous as those hidden
in the London files. Documents describe the 're-location of former
copra workers' as a 'neat, sensible package', justified by the cover
story agreed with London that Diego Garcia 'has no permanent
population'.[53]

One of the authors was Jonathan Stoddart, who served in US embassies in Port Louis and London and in the State Department. In 2005, I arranged to meet him in a hotel in Washington. Now in his eighties, he said he had agreed to talk to me because of his strong belief in 'free and open expression'. I asked why he had written that there was no permanent population in the Chagos.

'The Foreign Office and the Ministry of Defence in London assured us those people were itinerant workers from Mauritius,' he replied. 'But, yeah, we heard all these stories.'

'Surely, you knew the truth as early as 1972.'

'What do you mean?'

'In 1972, the US Ambassador in Mauritius, William Brewer, wrote this to Washington: "It is absurd to state that Diego Garcia has no fixed population. There is no question that the island has been inhabited since the eighteenth century." Did you see that?'[54]

'Yes, I was aware of it. Bill Brewer was a graduate school class-mate of mine, and a very highly qualified foreign service officer. The problem was, the British were sticking to their line.'

'In one of your reports, you wrote that the US insisted that Diego Garcia be "swept" and "cleaned" of people. You also referred to the threat of bad publicity, so you were aware of the consequences of what you were doing. Did any of it trouble you?'

'I was troubled by the conflicting stories. Look, we sent a colleague, John Kelly, over there to see if there were any natives floating around on the island.'

'Were there?'

'He said no.'

'What year was that?'

'It must have been 1974.'

'But they had all been deported by then.'

'You know, I don't find this shocking. We have an expression for this in a democracy. It's called "CYA". Are you aware of that?'

'Remind me please.'

'Cover your arse.'

'Do you think the islanders should be allowed to go home?'

'Yes, if you can establish without question that ... wait a minute, that's a sort of loaded question.'

'CYA?'

'You've got to be pragmatic, John.'

A taxi took me across to midtown Washington, to the offices of Lehman Brothers, the investment bankers, where James Schlesinger is an associate. I had arranged to interview Schlesinger about the Chagos. As Defense Secretary under Presidents Nixon and Ford, then Director of the CIA, he was ultimately responsible for the American takeover of Diego Garcia and the building of the military base. The embodiment of what is known in the US as the 'national security state', Schlesinger is the hawk's hawk, with an abiding belief in imperial America. He is tall and has a granite-like, apparently impenetrable face that exudes the power of the mighty.

'During the 1970s,' I said to him, 'most countries bordering the Indian Ocean – twenty-nine of them actually – opposed the establishment of an American base on Diego Garcia. Was that opposition ever taken into account?'

'Well, they *publicly* opposed it, presumably because they had opposition among their own peoples. But these governments understood the Soviet threat following the 1973 Middle East war, and they said to us, "We have to oppose this publicly, but go ahead with the base."'

'In defiance of their own people?'

'They were being pragmatic . . .'

'When you became Defense Secretary, were you aware that the population of Diego Garcia had been forcibly expelled to make way for the base?'

'I was not aware of that.'

'But at that time, it was known to Congress, and Senator Henry Jackson said, "The whole episode stank with deceit and lies." Reading the official record in Washington and London, it's clear that the US and the British governments did a secret deal in the mid-1960s, and the key element was American insistence that the islands be depopulated.'

'That's not accurate.'

'It is accurate, because the record shows it to be, and the American Ambassador to Mauritius advised the State Department in writing that up to two thousand people had been living there since the eighteenth century.'

'I suggest that is not the case.'

'Well, it's there on the record. I can show it to you if you wish.'

'Actually, when this issue came up some years ago, I went back over the record, and I found no indication of what you are saying.'

'As a principle, do you think it's right to kick people out of their country to make way for a military base?'

'The notion of military necessity, I believe, usually takes priority, except in peacetime.'

'This was peacetime.'

'It was the Cold War, and we, and European governments, felt we were under threat.'

'What has that got to do with people living peacefully on their islands in the middle of the Indian Ocean?'

'My recollection is that the British government compensated the natives that they moved off to wherever it was . . . the Seychelles?'

'To Mauritius, most of them. I have seen them there; their lives have been wrecked and they have been barely compensated. Let me ask you this. Is there ever a time when people in power consider the consequences of the imposition of that power? In this case, it was disastrous.'

'How many people were involved?'

'Two thousand people, most of whom had roots going back to the eighteenth century.'

'Well, a fair number of them were external labourers.'

'That's been shown to be untrue and the episode hidden from history. What if something like this had happened to you and me? What if we were told we were about to be made instant refugees because someone wanted to put a military base in our country?'

'I suggest you look back on several centuries of the British Empire. This is modest relative to what else occurred; there was an indifference to natives.'

'No-one would argue with that, but haven't we moved on since then?'

'Sure, and people in the twenty-first century can look back and criticise, but that's the privilege of protected people.'

'Protected people?'

'Yes, people who criticise the past, even though the past has something to do with the liberties they enjoy today.'

'Aren't we meant to learn from the past: that if we find some great wrong has been committed, we say: not again?'

'Sure.'

'That's what happened. People's lives were devastated, and you were in power. Isn't this something that concerns you?'

'I missed the punch line.'

'The punch line is that if you take a decision in Washington and London and it devastates the lives of several thousand people on the other side of the world, shouldn't you be called to account?'

'This was a relatively small matter. If one goes back to British behaviour, for example, in World War Two, the attack on Dresden, the attack on the French Fleet, all under Winston Churchill, whom we so much admire, and rightly so, this is a very small matter that is being pinpointed now for reasons that I cannot ascribe to anything other than the quest for a certain publicity.'

'But the Chagossian islanders are not the Nazis, and from their point of view, it's a quest for justice.'

'And what is *your* motivation, if I may enquire? Purely the quest for justice, I'm sure.'

'Yes, it is. Do you not think these questions are valid?'

'I think the questions are based on a refusal to acknowledge the context of the times and to critique them when they have become far less relevant.'

'Dr Schlesinger, not for the Chagos islanders have they become less relevant. They're still barred from going home, and they're still not compensated.'

'I see. Well, I can only say I retain an open mind on whether this should have happened or not.'

Schlesinger stormed away, accusing me of not 'playing by the rules'.

In London in 1971, the latest big lie meant concealing the fact that the islanders had British nationality. That January, a senior official at the British High Commission in Port Louis cabled the Foreign Office prior to a meeting with the Mauritian prime minister, at which the Chagos were to be discussed. He wrote that he did not intend to raise the issue of the islanders' nationality, but that it was 'always possible that [he] might spot this point, in which case, presumably, we shall have to come clean'.[55]

The Foreign Office replied that it was not 'HMG's policy' either 'to advise "contract workers" of their dual citizenship', or to inform the Mauritian government, because British policy was a 'policy of concealment'.[56]

The policy of concealment ran almost to the end of the century, with all possible precautions taken to preserve it. A Foreign Office minute recommended to Foreign Secretary Douglas Hurd that 'no journalists should be allowed to visit Diego Garcia' and that visits by MPs should be discouraged in order to keep out those 'who deliberately stir up unwelcome questions'.[57]

In the late 1990s, however, a sarcophagus of official files at Kew had been cracked open. Armed with this extraordinary evidence, Richard Gifford and his legal team headed for the courts. In October 2000, Olivier Bancoult and a group of his compatriots, including Lizette Talate and Charlesia Alexis, flew to London to give evidence in a High Court action that challenged the legality of their dispossession.

While the case was prepared, they huddled together in a basement room in a cheap hotel; the Blair government contributed not a penny to their subsistence. Although the proceedings were conducted in a language none of them, except Olivier, understood, they each gave moving testimony of their vandalised lives and *La Lutte*.

The government had feared this, and in the three months prior to the hearing the Foreign Office mounted a disinformation campaign, led by Peter Hain, the former anti-apartheid campaigner now metamorphosed into the very model of a Blairite minister. 'The outer islands', Hain told the House of Commons, 'have been uninhabited for thirty years so any resettlement would present serious problems, both because of the practical feasibility and in relation to our treaty obligations.'[58]

A 'treaty' implied an agreement scrutinised by Parliament. There was no treaty: only a secret, criminal deal. The nature of the crime is spelt out in the Rome Statute of the International Criminal Court, which recognises forced depopulation as a crime against humanity.[59]

Moreover, it was demonstrably untrue that the islands had been uninhabited since the expulsion. Colonies of 'yachties' lived for months on the outer islands, and for more than twenty years four thousand American service personnel and foreign contractors had enjoyed living conditions on Diego Garcia that the US Navy described as 'outstanding' and 'unbelievable'.[60] Nevertheless, the Foreign Office commissioned a study of the 'feasibility' of the population returning to the islands. Not a single islander was consulted, and the world's leading scholar on the Chagos described it as 'a charade'.[61]

On November 3, 2000, in the High Court, Lord Justice Laws and Mr Justice Gibbs stunned the government. Citing the Magna Carta, which proscribed 'Exile from the Realm' without due process, they unanimously squashed the 1965 ordinance used to deport the islanders as unlawful. Referring to the governments responsible, the judges quoted Tacitus, 'They make a desert and call it peace,' and added: 'He meant it as an irony; but here, it was an abject legal failure.'

Olivier, Lizette, Charlesia and Rita at last could go home, it seemed.[62]

The press suddenly discovered the Chagos. 'Islanders going home after thirty years in exile', said the headline in *The Times*, and ' "Men Fridays" vexed Foreign Office'.[63] Olivier was photographed striding out of the High Court into the Strand, his arms held high in a victory salute. This picture, with the headline, 'Thirty years of hurt ends', hangs over the doorway of his lock-up in Port Louis, and still brings tears to his eyes.[64]

'It's something I will never forget,' he told me. 'When I came out of the court, I knew I had a victory. A small people had beaten a big power.'

Charlesia said, 'We were ecstatic. We thought the British had some feelings after all.'

Lizette said, 'Victory meant that I felt at ease for the first time, because I thought I would return to my motherland, and to the cemetery where my ancestors are. I thought I would see my lovely beaches again, and the beautiful sea, where we were born.'

The Blair government had other ideas. That afternoon the Foreign Office published a new immigration ordinance that banned the islanders from returning to Diego Garcia, where most of them had come from. Once again, 'treaty obligations' with Washington were cited.

However, the High Court judgement meant the government had no choice but to give the islanders British passports; and there seemed to be nothing to stop them returning to the outer islands. The first to test this were six Chagossian fishermen who set out in a small boat from Port Louis for Peros Banhos. 'When they landed,' said Robin Mardemootoo, 'it was so emotional for them to walk on their homeland and the land of their ancestors. But would you know, within five minutes, a British patrol boat found them and told them to leave? They said, "Wait a minute; here are our passports; this is our country; here is the High Court judgement; please read it." The British policemen said, "We're not going to talk to you; you have to get out." A hundred yards along the beach, a colony of yachties and sailors, most of them not British, played volleyball on the beach. No-one disturbed them.'

In June 2002, the Foreign Office published its 'study' of the 'feasibility' of the islanders returning home. This claimed that 'flooding, storms and seismic activity' would 'make life difficult' and that there would not be enough water, arable soil or fisheries to support the population. The cost of resettlement would be 'prohibitive'.[65]

Two international experts studied the 'study': Jonathan Jenness of Harvard University, an expert on resettlement of populations, and Professor David Stoddart, of Cambridge and Berkeley, the world's leading authority on the Chagos and coral reef islands.

Jenness noted that the Chagos had not experienced a single cyclone in thirty years of weather reporting; the last great storm was in 1891. 'To be frank,' he wrote, 'the Chagos is blessed with being free of major tropical storms. Most atolls don't have that blessing . . . The Chagos has a benign environment [where people] have lived for eight generations.' He described the official study as 'a distortion of the evidence at hand . . . and not objective . . . It is fatuous to imagine the islands cannot be re-settled.'[66]

David Stoddart first visited the Chagos archipelago almost forty years ago. No scientist knows them better. 'The Foreign Office actually tried it on with three so-called studies,' he told me. 'This made an impressive-looking volume. In fact, what they've produced is absurd. Page after page is devoted to establishing that the beaches are made of sand! They make much of the scarce water supply. I have published papers that show that these islands are among the wettest in the world, and the rain remains on the surface for three days. The whole enterprise is worthless, a waste of time, an expensive charade.'[67]

Cassam Uteem served as the first President of Mauritius for ten years from 1992. A courtly, eloquent man, he spoke to me as I have never known a former head of state to speak about a friendly government. 'I must remind you,' he said, 'this was done in violation of the United Nations Charter by using lies; I am not mincing my words: they were lies, damn lies. By throwing people out of their land, the British government knowingly led many of them to a certain death. No human being would treat another human being the way the British treated the Chagossian people. For a comparison, we have to go back to the days of slavery. And for this, Britain received a thieves' ransom; and still they refuse to obey the court and let people go even to the outer islands.'

I said, 'When you ask the Americans about this, they always say, "Well, ask the British." '

'This is very interesting. I went to the Foreign Office and was received by Baroness Amos, the minister responsible in the House of Lords. I asked for permission for the islanders to go and lay wreaths on the tombs of their ancestors. She replied, "We have no objection. On the contrary, we are going to help them. We are going to put at their disposal a ship. I assure you we ourselves are agreeable . . . but we don't know if the US is agreeable."

'I said to her, "So, Baroness, do you allow me to take the matter up with President Bush?" She said, "By all means." And this is what I did. I wrote to President Bush, asking him for authorisation for the Chagossians to visit their own islands and lay wreaths. The reply came back [from the State Department], "Yes . . . but the British are not agreeable." So that's the game. They are playing ping pong with the lives of the islanders.'

Baroness Amos prides herself on her Afro-Caribbean origins. She makes many liberal-spirited speeches, such as a major lecture in 2003 entitled 'Nailing the Lie and Promoting Equality', in which she 'identified with vulnerable minorities and the underdog'.[68] When I asked her for an interview, she initially agreed. When I said it was about the Chagos, she withdrew, via an underling.

In March 2003, Robin Cook resigned from the government in protest against the invasion of Iraq. I interviewed him the following year; he died in 2005. He told me he had first raised the scandal of the Chagos with Prime Minister James Callaghan at the 1975 Labour Party conference in Brighton.

'I was actually in his bedroom in the Grand Hotel and I said to him, "Look, Jim, I ask you every month the question of Diego Garcia and you never once told me there had been people living on the island." I vividly remember him spreading his hands on the bed-clothes and saying, "Well, Robin, you never asked the question." '

I said, 'That was cynical, wasn't it, when you consider what was done to the people?'

'Yes, it was. The episode was one of the most sordid and morally indefensible I have ever known.'

'Then why didn't you seize the opportunity to right the wrong when you became Foreign Secretary? After the High Court found in their favour, all you did for the islanders was grant them the nationality they had a right to anyway. You still prevented them from going home.'

'It was never a political possibility to return them. The Americans were there, and they had an agreement with us.'

'What if you had said to the Americans, "The highest court in our country has said a great injustice has been done and we have to give these people the opportunity to go home and reconstruct their lives."'

'Well, I did say that, more or less.'

'But you left out Diego Garcia.'

'Oh yes, because that was never achievable politically with the Americans.'

'That's where it all stopped?'

'Yes.'

In 2002, travelling with their new British passports, the Chagossians began to arrive in Britain, to bring their campaign to London and to escape the poverty of Mauritius. Flying into Gatwick airport, they staged a protest in the airport lounge, refusing to move for several days until they finally agreed to go to cheap hotels and a housing estate in Crawley, Sussex. 'If we were allowed to go back to the Chagos, then none of us would want to be here,' said Allan Vincatassin, their spokesman.[69]

The following year they were back in the High Court, this time seeking compensation. But this time, the spirits of the Magna Carta and Tacitus were absent as they faced a very different kind of judge, Mr Justice Ouseley, who from the bench referred to the British government as 'we' while describing the case as 'unmeritorious' and 'hopeless'.[70] He awarded the islanders not a penny, a decision 'welcomed' by Bill Rammell, the Foreign Office minister responsible for the Chagos. 'We have always maintained', said Rammell, 'that the proceedings [for compensation] were misconceived.'[71]

Five months later, Rammell made a stirring speech to the United Nations Commission on Human Rights in Geneva. 'I would like to recall', he said, 'the opening words of the Universal Declaration of Human Rights, which state that "recognition of the inherent integrity and of the equal and inalienable rights of all members of the human family is the foundation of freedom, justice and peace." In other words, without the observance of human rights by all states, freedom, justice and peace are fundamentally threatened.' He pledged to 'work to remove this threat'.[72]

Three months later, Rammell did the diametric opposite. Employing the same sleight of hand that the Wilson government had used to expel the islanders in the 1960s, he sent an order-in-council to the Queen for her rubber-stamped approval. This overturned the Chagossians' High Court victory of 2000 in its entirety and banned the islanders from ever returning home. 'Not in my wildest dreams', said Richard Gifford, 'did I think that the government would simply set aside the High Court judgement and act in such flagrant disregard.'

The order-in-council was tucked away on a list of innocuous royal decrees, between an amendment to the Royal Charter of the College of Optometrists and the appointment of four of Her Majesty's education inspectors for Scotland. No reasons for the repudiation of the court's ruling were given; the brief text referred dishonestly to the 'departure' of the islanders. A Privy Councillor simply read out the fate of thousands of Her Majesty's most vulnerable, abused and wronged subjects and, in that curious high-pitched voice, she said, 'Agreed!'[73]

That took place on June 10, 2004, election day in Britain, when the government reckoned no-one would notice, and the bad publicity would be minimal or non-existent. By and large, they were right. Two weeks later, just one Member of Parliament, Llew Smith, asked Rammell if any Chagossian had been consulted beforehand. The reply was an unadorned, ruthless 'no'.[74]

Rammell agreed to see me at the Foreign Office in King Charles Street, off Whitehall. I began by asking him why the British government had not complied with the High Court judgement and the United Nations and allowed the Chagossians to go home. He replied that the official 'feasibility study' showed that the islands were no longer habitable, that there were concerns about the sea level, flooding and fresh water.

I said, 'There are four thousand American service personnel and contractors, two bomber runways, each two and a half miles long, anchorages for a fleet of ships, living conditions the US Navy describes as "indispensable", "outstanding" and "unbelievable", and they want to extend their so-called lease beyond 2016. Are you asking us to believe these islands are really uninhabitable, even sinking?'

'No, no, of course they're inhabitable, but at a cost . . . and this cost is based on specific financial recommendations in the experts' report.'

'Here's a copy of their report,' I said. 'On page three, it says, "This report has not been tasked with investigating the financial costs of resettlement." Forgive me for saying so, but it sounds to me that what you've just said was made up.'

'If I say to you, Mr Pilger, that we have contingent financial liabilities, it means that if you have an earthquake, if you have a volcano eruption, if you have a tidal wave, the British taxpayer picks up the bill.'

'Mr Rammell, there isn't a snowball's chance in hell that there'll be an earthquake, a cyclone or a tidal wave in the Chagos. It is a totally benign environment. That's why the Americans have a huge base there and call the environment "unbelievable". Have you seen the living conditions of the Chagossians in Mauritius?'

'No . . . but I have no doubt that some people, as in many parts of the world, live in poverty. However, looking at the overall situation, the Chagossian community is now integrated in both Mauritius and the Seychelles.'

'They are clearly not integrated. I have seen this for myself, and former President Cassam Uteem has described how much they are not integrated. If you haven't been there, how can you be sure?'

'Please look what we've done for them. This government has legislated to give them British nationality.'

'But that was their right. Look at the compensation you've given them. Former President Cassam Uteem calls it peanuts. I've seen plenty of poverty in the world, and these people don't look to me in the slightest compensated.'

'The Chagossians have been given thirteen and a half million pounds at today's prices.'

'As you know, they've actually received no more than one thousand pounds per family, at the very most. That's why they are terribly poor and why they are disaffected from the population around them.'

'You can't manufacture money; you have to make choices about how you spend your money. As for repopulating the islands, the money would probably have to come out of aid we would give poor people elsewhere.'

'Does this government, do *you*, not feel any shame for what has been done to these people?'

'I'm not seeking to justify the decisions that were taken in the sixties and seventies.'

'No, I mean shame now. You have used the same archaic powers to ban them from going home.'

'No, I don't feel shame. But I do understand the historical attachment that the Chagossian community have to these islands, and we are prepared to support a visit to their ancestral graves.'

'Historical attachment? Let me ask you a personal question. What if you and your family were thrown out of your home, put on a ship, dumped on docks somewhere, destitute? How would you like it?'

'If I hadn't been compensated, I would be very angry . . .'

'Those leading this struggle are very spirited old ladies, whom you won't allow to go home to die. Isn't that shameful?'

'I am not going to be ashamed. As I've said, the money that would finance their move back could actually be spent on poor people.'

Rammell has admitted to Parliament that the cost of resettling the islanders is far from 'prohibitive'. It would be £5 million to set up and £5 million a year to maintain. As Richard Gifford points out, there is a wealth of income to be gained from the fisheries, and the European Union would support resettlement. That aside, £5 million is no more than the cost of maintaining a British embassy, such as that which flies the Union flag in Mauritius.[75]

When I was in Mauritius, the High Commissioner, David Snoxell, was being served by four tennis courts, lavish gardens, a full-sized swimming pool, a Jaguar car and a colony of staff, all paid for by the British taxpayer for whom Bill Rammell had expressed such concern.

Down the hill, no more than fifteen minutes' drive away, is the home of a family deemed unworthy of British taxpayers' money, according to the minister, even though they, too, are British citizens. I first glimpsed this family of Chagossian exiles in a 1982 television film, which compared their treatment with that of the Falkland islanders. In one sequence, the camera panned across fourteen people sleeping in shifts in one squalid room, with the baby in a cardboard box.[76]

Twenty-two years later, I found the same family living in the same squalid place. They still slept on the floor, the rain still poured in, the lavatory was still a hole in the ground, there was still no kitchen and they were still so poor they often went hungry.

I asked the father, Louis Onezime, what had changed since they were filmed.

'Nothing,' he said.

'I remember in the film your wife, a striking-looking woman, looking out the window.'

'She died after a heart attack. She was a young woman. Actually, she died of sadness.'

'She was very sad?'

'Very sad indeed. We were so happy in Diego.'

'Can you describe something of your life there?'

'Well, we had no need for money there. We had modest

possessions, but everything we needed. My wife was sad we had to leave all that behind, as well as our animals. We were even told to hurry up as the boat had to leave. Imagine running from where you were born and grew up, not knowing if you might ever see it again.'

'Do you suffer from the sadness your wife suffered?'

'Yes, I do. I am getting older, and my family is so poor one of my daughters must pay a fine because she can't afford to send her children to school. We eat only rice and bits of papaya from that tree over there. We buy green leaves whenever there are any in the shop.'

I asked Louis and his daughters if they had been compensated. They could remember a few debts being paid off for them 'years ago', and they looked puzzled at the question.

On January 14, 2005, Bill Rammell finally flew into Port Louis, to inspect the homes of Chagossians. Accompanied by a dozen policemen, he arrived at the Baie du Tombeau community centre at 7.30 a.m. Members of the Chagos Refugee Group, their supporters, and a few local and foreign reporters were waiting. The officials accompanying the minister had asked the police to keep the press outside, and baton-wielding officers guarded the door. 'No cameras,' they said. Chagossians crowded around the small, barred windows in order to witness the twenty-minute encounter.

Rammell opened the meeting by announcing that, although he was in favour of Chagossians visiting their homeland, unfortunately the Mauritian government had prevented the British from contracting a boat to take them. To his audience, this sounded like the London–Washington ping pong game.

Olivier Bancoult replied, 'You say, Mr Rammell, that you support our visit and its financing, but the only problem is the boat. Well, we have a boat.' He handed the minister a dossier on the boat, which was based in Dubai. 'It is ready to take us to the Chagos archipelago,' he said.

Taken aback, Rammell said he would 'consider' the dossier.* He then left hurriedly to visit Chagossian homes, where journalists were told by the police they were not welcome. Emerging to announce that the refugees lived 'no differently' from Mauritians, he said it was

---

* In April 2006, the British government allowed 102 islanders, led by Olivier Bancoult, to sail to the Chagos for a strictly conrolled twelve-day visit. As for their permanent return, 'it is not practical', said Foreign Secretary Jack Straw.

clear their poverty had 'absolutely nothing' to do with their enforced exile. Then he drove away, accompanied by police outriders.

There were two questions a persistent reporter had managed to ask as Rammell strode through the community. The first was about the tsunami of Boxing Day 2004, which, according to the *Guardian*, had been accurately predicted by the American base on Diego Garcia; but this vital information had remained the 'best kept secret in the US Navy', and one of the few places in the Indian Ocean the tsunami missed was the Chagos archipelago.

If Diego Garcia was British territory, why was this information not shared with the rest of the world, and did not the tsunami's wide berth of the islands make a mockery of the dire warnings in the British government's 'feasibility study'?[77]

The second question was about a report in the *Washington Post*, which alleged that Diego Garcia was part of America's gulag, and that 'al-Qaeda suspects' were held at 'Camp Justice' on the island, and tortured.[78]

Rammell fended off the first question, saying he would 'look into it', and denied outright that there were prisoners on this British territory. The *Washington Post* has repeated the allegation.[79]

As I write this, Olivier and Lizette and their compatriots have arrived in London for the High Court's long-awaited judicial review of the government's use of the royal prerogative to stop them going home. This is their last chance in the courts in Britain. The European Court of Human Rights will be next. Their case is being put by Sir Sydney Kentridge QC, a distinguished human rights advocate who represented Nelson Mandela and the family of Steve Biko in his native South Africa.

It is difficult to describe the determination of the islanders to win justice and freedom. This, and their refusal to be cast as perennial victims, are firm in my memory. I need think only of the tragedy carved in Charlesia's face and her pledge that 'we fight, and fight!'; and of Olivier standing over the graves of his brothers and sisters, whispering, 'No more!' I need only listen to their haunting songs, such as 'Afghanistan', which tells of bombers launched from their

paradise against men, women and children like them, and recall
their frequent expressions of generosity to the British, always
separating ordinary people from the elite, and a warmth of humanity
that comes only from people who lived as they once lived and who
have had to struggle almost unbearably to survive.

On my last day with them, Olivier, Lizette, Charlesia and Rita
took me to the monument overlooking Port Louis harbour that
marks where they came ashore and commemorates those who died.
They each threw stems of roses into the oily water. That evening, I
went with Charlesia and her grandchildren to the seashore. It was
dusk and a blazing sun descended on a horizon beyond which lay
the Chagos archipelago. Huddled together on the sand, they listened
as Charlesia sang:

> *When I was living on Diego, I was like a beautiful bird up
>   in the sky.*
> *Since I am here, I am living a worthless life.*
> *So give me your hand, my friend. We will cry and send our
>   message to the world that the military base is in our ocean.*
> *Yes, I have regrets in my heart.*
> *Look at my child who is growing –*
> *He does not know the native land of his mother.*
> *When we seek justice, don't beat us, Mr Policeman . . .*
> *When I was living on Diego, I was like a beautiful bird up
>   in the sky.*

2

The Last Taboo

An ideology that divides the world into those who
are worth more and those who are worth less, into
superior and inferior beings, does not have to reach
the dimensions of the German genocide to be
wrong.

Amira Hass, Israeli journalist

There was no such thing as Palestinians; they never
existed.

Golda Meir, Israeli Prime Minister

The pilgrims trudged up the Via Dolorosa, past a toothless vendor
of Pontius Pilate underarm deodorant ('Judge It For Yourself') and
Holy Sepulchre egg-timers. At each station of the cross, a Franciscan
friar led their prayers, and when they reached the Church of the
Holy Sepulchre, a smog of incense, sweat and drains descended
upon those able to elbow their way inside. Here, the countdown of
anguish was completed and ritual bells were fired like artillery at
heaven and the word was wailed forth that God was dead and had
not yet risen.

It was Easter 1968, my second visit to what the friars call the
Terra Sancta, the Holy Land, a term now bereft of meaning to all
but the devout. 'Arabs lived here,' the foreigners would whisper, and
it was even said they had lived here longer than anyone. But this
truth was now subversive, and 'the Arabs', so comprehensively
defeated in the 'Six Day War' ten months earlier, would themselves
barely whisper it lest they be roused in the middle of the night and
expelled from the city of their birth and their home given by the
Custodian of Properties to an American or a Dutchman recently
converted to Judaism. Officially, 'the Arabs' were now 'the demographic problem'; the word 'Palestinians' was used only by them.

In Israel, I had listened to those of a Jewish generation who
remained prisoners of their myths and fears and felt for them a

natural empathy, even admiration. Some had fought in a people's army, the Haganah, inspired by a humanism that was the stuff of legend in Western countries eager to relegate guilt in Europe and truth in the Middle East. As a young reporter I accepted such myths; I remain in awe of their stamina and an Orwellian lexicon of opposites that until recently has protected the epic injustice in Palestine.

In the preceding months I had stayed on a 'socialist' kibbutz and listened to how the land of Palestine, while it may have been in-habited by a few Arab nomads, was mostly desert, and one of the great feats of Zionist enterprise was to turn the desert green. The Jaffa orange, grown on kibbutzim like mine and exported to the rest of the world, was said to symbolise this proud endeavour against the odds – when, in truth, it confirmed the opposite. The orange groves and vineyards were stolen from Palestinian peasants who had been tilling the soil and exporting oranges and grapes to Europe since the beginning of the eighteenth century. The former Palestinian town of Jaffa is still called 'the land of sad oranges'.

It was only when my gracious Israeli hosts, driving along the corniche at Tel Aviv, reached the clock in the middle of a square that marked where Jaffa began, that they spat out the word 'Arabs'. Then, I felt something familiar. The unexplained hatred reminded me of South Africa, from which I had just been banned. As for the source of Israeli fears, they were like phantoms. The Palestinians were there but not there: employed as labourers and servants, but excluded from any context other than those inviting contempt.

Dan Hadarni, a photographer who had survived the Holocaust, travelled with me. A Pole and one of the 'human dust' of the Diaspora, he remembered, as a boy in Poland, the 'long black vans' of the Gestapo cruising the streets, and men in long overcoats getting out of them, enticing children to come for a 'joy ride'. The rear compartments of the cars were sealed and the windows were opaque, and when each joy ride began, gas would pour from nozzles under the seat; it would take no more than a block or two for half a dozen Jewish children to die. He had heard about the cars, so he ran fast when they came. Most of his family were gassed by the Nazis.

After he and I had driven the length of Israeli-occupied Palestine, and were returning to Jerusalem from the refugee camps at Qalandiyah and Aqabat Jabr, he said suddenly, 'I am full of confusion. I wish I had not seen what I saw today. It is better for an Israeli like me not to be confused, because then we are at our weakest. At the camp, I looked into a mirror: the people there were us, once again in the Diaspora; their bitterness was expressed with the words we used; their determination was our determination, which we grew up with in the ghetto. In my heart, I want them to be free, to go home, but I know I have to stop them.'

It was a bitterly cold and wet Easter. I had not worn a coat, and at Qalandiyah the wind spun off the large rocks on the bare side of the valley and carried the stench of the sewer that had overflowed and merged with the mud. Of the thousands of foreign Christians besieging Jerusalem, only two, a Canadian Lutheran couple, had driven the 10 miles across the valley, their Land Rover laden with blankets.

Some three thousand people lived in this camp, refugees in their own land, some within sight of homes that were no longer theirs, now incarcerated in dwellings of mud, sacking and corrugated iron. Water trickled brown, if at all, from communal taps, and there were communal lavatories and communal illnesses, such as madness, blindness and gastro-enteritis. Each person was issued 2,300 calories of rations per day, which would drop to 1,500 in the summer. These figures were calculated by the United Nations Relief and Works Agency (UNRWA) as precisely the amount a human being needed to survive, no more and no less, and precisely the amount the agency could afford on its minuscule handout from the 'international community'.

The main meal at Qalandiyah was a tin plate of gruel in which a variety of nutrients were said to be expertly balanced, plus a brick of bread and a vitamin pill. Children under fifteen were supposed to receive a supplement of protein – rice, powdered egg, a vegetable – but this seldom reached all of them as UNRWA's money frequently ran out; and those who managed to get the food would hurry back to the huts with it, where it was shared or put up for sale as the only defence against destitution. A quarter of the children were mal-nourished: a figure that has not changed for nearly forty years.

Two-thirds of Qalandiyah's men were unemployed; a generation had grown up who had never known work. They went nowhere. They walked up and down the camp's one undulating street. They huddled outside the administration block, listening to the broadcasts from Amman in which Palestinians throughout *their* Diaspora – in the Arab world, America, Europe, Latin America – sent messages to their families. These were inevitably followed by the melancholy songs of Oum Kalthoum, the beloved 'Star of the Orient', and the men hummed the refrains they knew word for word. Then they would walk some more or sit on small promontories jutting above the mud, which also served as places to scrub clothes and, when the weather allowed, to dry them. All of them exuded a listless humiliation, as if waiting for a deity to come to their aid while they watched their women suckle the next generation.

'I have seen only two children in shoes,' I said to Mohammed Jarella, a gentle, sardonic Jerusalemite who had come with me to Qalandiyah and who, like most of the UNRWA people, was himself a Palestinian.

'I have seen the same two,' he said.

'But it is very cold.'

'Yes, I can feel it.'

'Well, what are you doing about it?'

'Well, my friend John, I have our budget in my briefcase . . . here it is . . . you see, in this column is the money we have. In this next column is our expenditure . . . food for everybody and blankets for almost everybody. The two columns balance, you see. Three years ago we spent on food and roofs. In another three years . . . maybe we shall spend on shoes. That is our progress after twenty years.'

The highest hill above the camp rises in a mass of eroded lime-stone. As it began to rain, a lone figure walked down the slope towards us, with his son holding the tail of his long tattered coat. He extended his hand and gripped mine and did not let go. 'I am Ahmed Hamzeh, street entertainer,' he said in measured English. 'In Jaffa, I would play many musical instruments; I would sing in Arabic, English and Hebrew, and because I was rather poor, my small son would sell chewing gum while the monkey did its tricks. When we lost our country, we lost respect. One day a rich Kuwaiti stopped his car in front of us. He was one of those who came to Ramallah for the summer. He shouted at my son, "Show me how a Palestinian picks up his food rations!" I made the monkey appear to scavenge on the ground . . . in the gutter . . . And my son scavenged with him. The Kuwaiti threw coins and my son crawled on his knees to pick them up. This was not right; I was an artist, not a beggar . . . I am not even a peasant now. Never mind.'

'What do you feel about it now?' I asked him.

'Do you *expect* me to feel hatred? What is that to a Palestinian? I never hated the Jews. Frankly, I don't remember them much in Haifa . . . yes, I suppose I hate them now, or maybe I pity them for their stupidity. They can't win, because we Palestinians are the Jews now and, like the Jews, we will never allow them or the Arabs or you to forget. The youth will guarantee us that, and the youth after them . . . is that not the truth, Jarella?'

'My friend,' said Mohammed Jarella, 'I am here for the United Nations. I am meant to be neutral.'

'Neutral?' said Ahmed Hamzeh. 'What is neutral? Are you a Palestinian?'

'Yes, I am,' said Jarella.

'Then do I or don't I speak the truth?'

'You speak it.'

When he walked away, I noticed he was leading his son, who stumbled.

'It is trachoma,' said Jarella. 'In the early days it blinded hundreds of children in the camps. We have it under control now.'

The rain beat down. In the camp's one substantial building, concrete and unbearably cold as if the walls and floor were made of ice, a group of teenage girls was learning to sew. The faces ignored us; they had been pitied many times by foreigners. However, one girl followed my eyes, then without warning she stood up and began to shout. The girl beside her pulled at her apron and admonished her in whispers, but still she shouted, and sobbed, and her anguished voice reverberated in the freezing room.

Mohammed Jarella put his voluminous overcoat around her shoulders, as if to protect her from the cold. 'Ah, this is difficult,' he said, shaking his head. 'She is asking you why she can't go home. She is saying, "Why? Why?" She is sixteen and was born here. You know, this is the only place she has known; I doubt if she has even been to the mosque in Jerusalem. But she still believes this is not her home. In her imagination, she has a home elsewhere.'

Dan Hadarni and I drove on to Ramallah, a few miles away. With its Christian majority, Ramallah was at the matrix of the Holy Land seized from King Hussein's Jordan the previous June; already, there were voices in Israel claiming it as Israeli territory. To its six hundred thousand inhabitants, the West Bank of the Jordan was Palestine, or Falastin, the Arabic translation of the Roman Palaestina, although some Israeli historians insisted the Romans only used this name to wipe Judaea off the map. Whatever the biblical claims of convenience, the Palestinian Arabs had been the continuous majority here, living in flinty valleys terraced with olive and orange groves and vineyards over which minarets rose and people moved about like butterflies in the fields; only the oak forests were missing and, Jew and Arab were agreed, it was the damn Turks who cut them down.

In Ramallah, the big clock in Mukhtaribine Square was stopped at seven minutes past ten. On June 6, 1967, it was one of the first targets hit by shells a few hours before Israeli troops occupied the town as the prelude to their conquest of the West Bank. The streets were almost empty now. In a side road, a distraught family picked over the ruins of their house, blown up by the Israelis. It seemed a 'terrorist suspect' had slept there. The demolitions were a common sight in the towns and villages of the West Bank and Gaza. Palestinians were 'suspects' if they had previously been members of a political party, a trade union, a student society or a cultural association, all of which were banned.

If they uttered a word of protest against the occupation, they could be arrested; striking, or even closing their own shops during normal business hours, was forbidden. And before they were tried or even charged, their families and often their neighbours – people they might have barely known and innocent even in the eyes of the authorities – would be collectively punished. They would be bundled into the street regardless of the hour or the weather – women, children, the old, the sick – and marshalled to watch the destruction of their homes. This was to be their 'lesson'. It is not known if the Jewish soldiers who planted the explosives reflected upon the irony of their actions; few peoples had known more collective punishment than the Jews, merely for being Jews. Today, merely being a Palestinian made you 'suspect'.

Beneath the stopped clock in the square and outside a travel agent's where 'Israel' on the globe in the window had been carefully covered with Plasticine, a queue extended into the street. These were people going to America, where there was a Palestinian community of some five thousand. The Israelis allowed them to take out their money in foreign currency on condition that they signed a form declaring that their departure was voluntary and they would never return. Under international law, this was illegal, but both sides conspired in it, and most of the faces in the queue turned away when I approached them; their bitterness was touchable.

We drove south to Jericho, where a mile beyond the walls of the world's first city, now swept into a neat Neolithic pile, sprawled the world's largest ghost town: Aqabat Jabr, formerly a camp of twenty-five thousand refugees from Jerusalem, Nazareth and Haifa, all of whom had fled in a horrific stampede on the night of June 12, 1967, believing the advancing Jewish soldiers would slaughter them. By dawn the next day they had gone, all twenty-five thousand of them, across the Allenby Bridge to what was left of the Hashemite Kingdom of Jordan. All but one.

He was the mayor of the camp, and he approached me marching stiff-backed and with a broom on his shoulder as if it were a rifle. For these past ten months he had marched the empty streets, guarding the empty houses with his broom, shouting orders to no-one. The convulsion of that night, caused by the contagious fear, apparently had left him in this state.

Inside the mud-walled houses there had been no alteration since the night of June 12. The Israelis had left the camp as they had found it, returning only to sweep the streets for mines. In one house were a crib, unfinished basketwork, a table laid. In another a wedding album lay open, perhaps dropped in the scramble, and two shy faces peered up, smiling, and beside it, a copy of *First Steps in English Grammar* flapped its pages; doors opened and shut in the wind skidding off the scabrous hills; flies vibrated over cans of yeast which, said the label, were 'a gift of the American people, not to be sold or exchanged'.

*

In 'The Last Taboo', an essay published shortly before his death, the Palestinian-born Edward Said wrote: 'The extermination of the Native Americans can be admitted, the morality of Hiroshima attacked, the national flag [of the United States] publicly committed to the flames. But the systematic continuity of Israel's 52-year oppression and maltreatment of the Palestinians is virtually unmentionable, a narrative that has no permission to appear.'[1]

As I write this chapter, a crowd of world leaders is visiting the new Holocaust History Museum at Yad Vashem in Israel. 'The pilgrimage to Jerusalem of so many European leaders,' reported the Israeli journalist Amira Hass,

> shows that they are not deterred by the criticism of Israel – they are taking part in a media event that can only be interpreted as support for Israel . . . At best, the visit can be seen as encouragement to both sides to stick to the 'renewed peace process'. But encouragement for what? . . . For the separation barrier, whose construction is continuing with vigour, contrary to the verdict of the International Court of Justice? For the continuing mashing of Palestinian East Jerusalem and severing it from the rest of the Palestinian territory, in violation of the international demand that East Jerusalem serve as the Palestinian state's capital? Are the German foreign minister and the Dutch and Swedish prime ministers – after crossing themselves and proving they remember the Holocaust – planning to remind Israel that all the [Jewish] settlements, not only the outposts, are illegal? Will they demand that Israel evacuate them? Which of the participants in the ceremony will go to see the roads for Jews only and for Palestinians only? Will any of them protest the laws discriminating against Israeli citizens, only because they are non-Jews – Arabs – and threaten to impose sanctions until these laws are revoked?

She then addressed the 'fading memory' of the Holocaust. Memory is reclaimed, she wrote, not merely with memorial monuments and ceremonies. It is done mainly with an uncompromising rejection of the master race ideology, which divided the world into superior and inferior races . . . We [Jews] were placed at the bottom of the ladder in Nazi ideology. Would this ideology not have been criminal had we been ranked in the upper rungs?[2]

Amira Hass is one of a small group of remarkable Israelis who have made the Palestinians mentionable in Israel. In 1993, she did what no Israeli journalist had ever done: she went to live and report from among the people of the Gaza Strip, the 147-square-mile 'open prison' where a million and a quarter Palestinians are forced to live in almost destitute conditions.

To most Israelis, Gaza, like the occupied West Bank, is *terra incognita*, a breeding ground for terrorism and Islamic extremism. For three years Amira lived among Gaza's taxi drivers and farmers, doctors and housewives, activists and Islamic leaders. In a daily dispatch to her newspaper *Ha'aretz*, she illuminated a world in which ordinary people were denied basic personal and economic freedoms, justice and dignity; in which they were terrorised by the world's best-equipped soldiers and by unseen bureaucrats: the custodian of this, the controller of that. She described how a doctor in Gaza

> could not get permission to accompany his terminally ill mother to the hospital . . . she died alone. The doctor's brother was not allowed to leave the West Bank to attend his mother's funeral in Gaza . . . A young man from the Meghazi refugee camp got engaged to a woman from the Jelazun camp in the West Bank and was unable to visit her for five months. Another young man, whose fiancée was in Jordan, was denied a travel permit . . . A couple undergoing fertility treatment . . . received one permit for the day of their appointment – for the wife only.[3]

When I first met Amira, she was anxious to explain how evocative of the Jewish past Gaza was. 'My desire to live there', she said, 'stemmed from the dread of being a bystander.' She described the moment her mother, Hannah, was being marched from a cattle train to the concentration camp of Bergen-Belsen on a summer's day in 1944. 'She and the other women had been ten days in the train from Yugoslavia. They were sick and some were dying. Then my mother saw these German women looking at the prisoners, just looking. This image became very formative in my upbringing, this despicable "looking from the side".'

Amira's parents survived and came to Israel, 'naïvely', she said. 'They were offered the house of a Palestinian family in Jerusalem but refused it. They said, "We cannot take the house of other refugees."' Their moral determination has been passed to their daughter. For some of Amira Hass's readers, she is a traitor, and worse. 'I get messages', she said, 'saying I must have been a *kapo* [a Jewish camp overseer for the Nazis] in my first incarnation.'

In 2002, her book, *Drinking the Sea at Gaza: Days and Nights in a Land under Siege*, inspired me to return to Palestine and make a sequel to my 1974 documentary film, *Palestine Is Still the Issue*. I phoned her from London; she was in Ramallah, covering 'Operation Defensive Shield', Ariel Sharon's frontal attack on the West Bank towns in March and April of that year. We conducted our conversation as she crouched on the floor of a house with gunfire in the background.

'If I go out, the army will kill me,' she said.

'But you're an Israeli.'

'Makes no difference. Everybody here is a target.'

I arrived in the West Bank soon afterwards. The Israeli army had just attacked the refugee camp at Jenin, using fifty tanks, armoured bulldozers, helicopter gunships and F-16 fighter-bombers. Every day for a week, the F-16s had fired an average of 250 missiles against less than one square mile of shacks housing fifteen thousand people, half of them children. Fifty-four people were killed and hundreds wounded. The camp was defended by a few dozen men armed with rifles and crude booby traps. They killed twenty-three Israeli soldiers. This resistance, and its bloody cost for the invading army, sent Sharon into a fury. Describing the defenders as 'terrorists', he approved the demolition of the homes of four thousand people, some with the occupants inside.

Thousands of Palestinian men were rounded up and effectively kidnapped. Many Palestinians, according to Amnesty International, are 'systematically tortured'.[4] Israel, says Amnesty, 'is the only country on earth where torture and ill-treatment are legally sanctioned'. In Jenin, the homeless were again made homeless: for some of the elderly, it was the fifth time since the *Nakbah*, the 'catastrophe' of the establishment of Israel on May 14, 1948. There was little food and water, and no power and emergency medical help; foreign volunteers who tried to enter Jenin were fired at; Iain Hook, a 54-year-old Briton with UNRWA, was shot in the back and bled to death while the ambulance carrying him was delayed by the Israeli army.

In the Israeli media, there was outrage at accusations abroad of a massacre. The London correspondent of *Ha'aretz* wrote to the *Guardian* to complain, and definitions of 'massacre' were debated in the letters columns. That civilians were killed in cold blood, including children murdered by military snipers and a severely disabled man crushed in his home by a bulldozer despite a warning that he was inside (see page 75), was not debated. Such detail was too atrocious even for those whose reflex defence of Israel was once regarded as irrefutable.

While General Sharon's stated aim in attacking the West Bank was to 'smash the infrastructure of terror', his real aim was to mark indelibly the perimeters of his apartheid state and its colony. Would Jenin prove his undoing? For a moment, it seemed the 'international community' would stand up to Israel. In Geneva, the United Nations Commission on Human Rights began taking evidence; the first witness was the representative of Amnesty International, speaking with a public anger normally eschewed by that organisation.

'Grave breaches of the Geneva Conventions', he said,

> have been committed daily, hourly, even every minute, by the Israeli authorities against Palestinians. Israeli forces have consistently carried out killings when no lives were in danger. More than 600 Palestinian homes have been systematically demolished, making thousands homeless, the vast majority children . . . Amnesty delegates investigated the Israeli army's recent attacks on towns, including refugee camps. In each instance tanks had entered the area, rolling over cars, running over walls, breaking down house and

shop fronts . . . Heavy fire was used against densely-populated residential areas . . . electricity, water and telephones [were] cut off . . . In treatment apparently intended to hurt and degrade the population, Israeli soldiers who occupied apartments had systematically trashed them. [Troops] killed six medical aid workers, including two doctors. Ambulances, including those of the ICRC [International Committee of the Red Cross] have been consistently shot at.

He called for 'an end to the paralysis of the international community' in protecting lives in Palestine.[5]

The UN body, representing fifty-three governments, condemned Israel for 'mass killings' of Palestinians and 'gross violations' of humanitarian law, and affirmed the 'legitimate right of Palestinian people to resist'. This resolution was passed by forty votes to five, with seven states abstaining; most European Union states voted in favour. A stronger draft had equated the 'state terrorism' of Israel with the 'terrorism' of Palestinian suicide bombers. The removal of the words 'state terrorism' was not enough for the British government which, in voting against the resolution, demanded that more be made of Palestinian suicide attacks, which had 'provoked' the Israeli attack and 'set off the cycle of violence'.[6]

Britain is a principal architect of the historic disaster in Palestine. In 1917, with an eye to establishing a client state in the Middle East to watch over the Suez Canal and Britain's trade routes to India, the Foreign Secretary Arthur Balfour promised a 'national home for the Jewish people' in Palestine, adding that 'nothing shall be done which may prejudice the civil and religious rights of the existing non-Jewish communities'. Some historians regard it as the Zionist lobby's greatest victory.

Today, the Balfour Declaration invests the British government with a special responsibility to honour its commitment, and those of its predecessors since 1967, to support international action aimed at ending Israel's illegal occupation of the West Bank and Gaza. Statements by Tony Blair and his Foreign Secretary, Jack Straw, constantly give this impression. In 2001 and again in 2005, Blair held much-hyped 'international conferences' on Palestine in London. Both events produced nothing of value. They were public relations stunts that gave Blair, who has taken Britain to war more times than any other modern prime minister, spurious 'peacemaker' headlines. More importantly, they disguised the fact that British support for Israeli repression was secretly accelerating.

Understanding this deceit is vital in appreciating the scale of the injustice done to the Palestinians: what Nelson Mandela has called 'the greatest moral issue of our time'. In May and July 2001, the authoritative *Jane's Foreign Report* disclosed that Britain and France had given Israel 'the green light' to attack the West Bank. The Blair government was shown a top-secret plan for an all-out invasion and reoccupation of both the West Bank and Gaza, which were then administered by Yasser Arafat's Palestinian Authority under Israeli sufferance. The plan was to use 'the latest F-16 and F-15 jets against all the main installations of the Palestinian Authority [and] 30,000 men or the equivalent of a full army'. However, this plan needed 'the trigger' of a suicide bombing which would cause 'numerous deaths and injuries [because] the "revenge" factor is crucial'. This 'would motivate Israeli soldiers to demolish the Palestinians'.[7]

What had alarmed Sharon and his inner circle, notably the author of the plan, Brigadier-General Shaul Mofaz, the Israeli Chief of Staff, was a secret agreement between Arafat and Hamas, the Islamic organisation responsible for numerous suicide attacks, that these attacks should stop. Following September 11, 2001, Sharon and the Likud regime worried that a Middle East 'solution' would be a by-product of America's newly-minted 'war on terror', especially when George W. Bush blurted out a *non sequitur* that he had always backed the 'dream' of a Palestinian state. Something had to be done.

On November 23, 2001, Israeli agents assassinated the Hamas leader, Mahmud Abu Hunud. Twelve days later, the inevitable response came in co-ordinated suicide attacks against Israel. 'Whoever decided upon the liquidation of Abu Hunud knew in advance that would be the price,' wrote Alex Fishman, the well-connected intelligence writer of the Israeli daily *Yediot Aharonot*. 'Whoever gave a green light to this act knew full well that he was thereby shattering in one blow the gentleman's agreement between Hamas and the Palestinian Authority [which was] not to play into Israel's hands by mass attacks on its population centers.'[8]

On cue, within weeks the Israeli army attacked the Occupied Territories with unprecedented force. For Mofaz, who knew Arafat was striving for a negotiated settlement, this 'victory' would avenge what he saw as Israel's shameful withdrawal from Lebanon.[9] The result was all but the destruction of the Palestinian Authority and Arafat's political base. The Bush regime issued the usual anodyne statement about 'ending violence' and placed the responsibility on Arafat. 'Peacemaker' Blair said nothing.

The assault was brutal. When the UN Middle East envoy, Terje Roed-Larsen, was finally allowed into Jenin by the Israelis, he described what he saw as 'a sad and disgraceful chapter in Israel's history'. He said the Israeli army had prevented humanitarian aid, including food convoys, from entering the camp. Along with the foreign ministers of four European governments, he demanded an international investigation.[10] So unusually outspoken were the Europeans (less Britain) that Resolution 1405 was swiftly passed by the UN Security Council, establishing an investigative team of 'distinguished experts' with a brief to find out the truth about Jenin.

For thirty-five years, the Israelis had successfully manoeuvred Washington into ensuring that the only UN agency allowed into the West Bank and Gaza was the impoverished UNRWA, whose remit was strictly humanitarian aid. As the UN team prepared to fly out, Kofi Annan, the UN Secretary-General, met senior American officials and thereafter cancelled the investigation because of 'the Israeli government's refusal to co-operate'. That the atrocity had taken place outside Israel, in illegally occupied territory, was apparently not a factor.

It was the UN at its most craven, with Annan affirming his role as a placeman for the United States. The disgrace was illuminated the following November when Amnesty International published what it described as its most thorough investigation anywhere. Extraordinarily, the human rights organisation called on governments that were signatories to the Geneva Conventions to put on trial Israeli soldiers 'responsible for war crimes' in Jenin. These were: unlawful killings, using civilians as human shields, blocking medical help to the wounded, the torture of prisoners, and the wanton destruction of four thousand homes in which many died as they were bulldozed.

The case of Jamal Fayed, a 38-year-old severely disabled man, was cited. His family, said Amnesty,

> had shown [his] ID to the soldiers, who were preparing to demolish the house, to prove he was paralysed and could not get out of the home without their help. The soldiers refused to help and soon afterwards a bulldozer approached the house. The family yelled at the driver to stop. He didn't, and Jamal Fayed, still trapped inside, was killed.

Amnesty also described how two boys, aged six and twelve, were killed by Israeli tank fire as they went to buy sweets after the army had announced that the curfew had been lifted. The Israeli government ignored Amnesty, just as it had dismissed the United Nations.[11]

No other country on earth enjoys such immunity, allowing it to act without sanction, as Israel. No other country has such a record of lawlessness: not one of the world's tyrannies comes close. Israel is the undisputed world champion violator of international law – an international law founded as a consequence of the crimes of the perpetrators of the Jewish Holocaust.

Having been born in contempt of a UN Security Council Resolution (46) that required Jews and Arabs to 'refrain . . . from any political activity which prejudices the rights, claims or position of each community', Israel has since defied 246 Security Council resolutions and more than twice that number of UN General Assembly resolutions.[12] The right of Palestinians to return to their homeland, enshrined in UN Resolution 194, says one study, 'has been reaffirmed by the international community 135 times in the period 1948–2000. There is nothing like it in UN history, elevating this resolution from a "recommendation" to an expression of the determined will of the international community.'[13]

Israel has defied the UN each time. The wording of this resolution and others is strikingly similar to that of the Security Council resolution in 1990 demanding that Saddam Hussein get out of Kuwait. When he did not get out, he was attacked by an American-led force and his country's infrastructure crippled. When Israel regularly ignores UN orders to get out of the Palestinian lands it occupies illegally and brutally, it is rewarded with largesse and armaments from the United States and Britain. In one year, 2003, Israel asked the United States for $8 billion in loan guarantees. The Israeli official sent to Washington to negotiate this was Amos Yaron, who was the military commander in Beirut in 1982 when several thousand Palestinians were slaughtered in the Sabra and Chatila refugee camps. The funds were granted.

This acceptable lawlessness is woven into the fabric of Israel. There have been many Jenins. On the eve of the establishment of the Jewish state in 1948, the Irgun and the Stern Gang, Jewish terrorist groups, massacred 250 civilians, including more than a hundred women and children, in the Palestinian town of Deir Yassin. Twenty-five survivors were paraded around the streets of Jewish west Jerusalem before they were taken to a quarry and murdered, while other survivors were expelled from their homes.[14] Such atrocities were common – indeed, were regarded as essential in forcing the Palestinians to flee their land – although the Zionist leadership in pre-Israeli Palestine wanted the world to believe they were the work of 'dissidents'.

In 1948, a leading 'dissident' was Menachem Begin, a follower of the fanatical Zionist Ze'ev Jabotinsky who believed in the Jewish right to the entire biblical land of Israel 'from the Nile to the Euphrates'.[15] In 1941, Begin's deputy, Yitzhak Shamir, proposed that the Stern Gang co-operate with the Nazis to help defeat the British, sending a letter expressing its sympathy for the 'German conception' of a 'New Order in Europe' and offering to protect Nazi interests in the Middle East.[16] After the Irgun was outlawed, Begin established the Herut, an organisation denounced by Albert Einstein and other prominent Jews as 'closely akin in its organisation, methods, political philosophy and social appeal to the Nazi and Fascist parties'.[17]

Both Begin and Shamir went on to lead the Likud Party and become Prime Minister. In 1982, Begin launched a bloody invasion of Lebanon, which resulted in the deaths of eighteen thousand people, mostly Palestinian refugees.[18] Of the assault on civilians, including the continuous bombing of Beirut and the saturation bombing of all major Palestinian refugee camps in southern Lebanon, Begin said, 'Not for one moment would I have any doubts that the civilian population deserves punishment.'[19] He described Palestinians as 'two-legged beasts'.[20] As for the massacre in the Sabra and Chatila camps in Beirut, for which the Israelis were held responsible, Begin dismissed this shame as the anti-Semitism of 'goyim', a pejorative term for gentiles.[21]

The most famous 'dissident' is Ariel Sharon, at the time of writing still the current Prime Minister of Israel, though seriously ill after a stroke. In 1953, Sharon commanded Unit 101 of the Israeli army, whose 'mission' was to 'carry out special reprisals across the state's borders'. Its first operation, in August 1953, killed twenty refugees in Bureij camp, Gaza, including seven women and five children. On the night of October 14, Sharon laid siege to the village of Qibya. His orders from Central Command were 'to attack and temporarily to occupy the village, carry out destruction and maximum killing, in order to drive out the inhabitants of the village from their homes'. He passed this on to his men with these words: 'Objective: to attack the village of Kibiya [sic], occupy it and *cause maximal damage to life and property*, signed Major Ariel Sharon.' The emphasis in the original document is his. Sixty-nine civilians were killed, of whom the majority were women and children. As a result, the UN Security Council voted to record the 'strongest censure' of Israel.[22]

Like all the other resolutions, it was ignored – even though, extraordinarily, the US Department of State expressed its 'deepest sympathy' for the victims and demanded that those responsible for the massacre 'should be brought to account'.[23] Sharon was now notorious. In 1971, his troops destroyed some two thousand homes in the Gaza Strip, uprooting twelve thousand Palestinians and deporting hundreds into exile in Jordan, Lebanon and Israeli-occupied Sinai.[24]

In June 1982, General Sharon, now defence minister, ordered the invasion of Lebanon to destroy 'the terrorist infrastructure' of the Palestine Liberation Organisation, which was based in Beirut. This was a terrible, murderous episode. Laying siege to Muslim west Beirut, the Israelis cut off water, electricity and food supplies and bombed the city, using phosphorus shells and American-supplied cluster bombs in the warren of streets. During the first two weeks, an estimated fourteen thousand Palestinians and Lebanese were killed and twenty thousand wounded, the vast majority of them civilians. According to UNICEF, ten children were killed for every Palestinian fighter.[25]

By September, the PLO had decided to evacuate Beirut and, overseen by an international force, thousands of Palestinian fighters boarded ships that would take them to other Arab countries, while their women and children remained behind. With the evacuation complete, Sharon claimed that '2,000 terrorists' remained in the refugee camps; offering no evidence, he ordered the 'encircling and sealing' of Sabra and Chatila camps. On September 16, he allowed the Phalangists, who were fascists trained, armed and paid by Israel and with a history of brutality and hatred of Palestinians, into these two camps. They systematically murdered the elderly, women and children.[26]

The massacre took just under forty hours. The Phalangists were in constant communication with the Israelis, who could see into the camps from a watchtower and fired flares to light their clients' advance, while forcing escaping refugees back into the camps. The Israelis put the death toll at 700; other estimates rise to 3,500; the true figure is probably about 1,700.[27]

Robert Fisk of *The Times* was one of the first to enter the Chatila camp after the killers had left. He recalled the experience in his book *Pity the Nation*. 'Each time I took a step,' he wrote,

> the earth moved up towards me. The whole embankment of muck shifted and vibrated with my weight in a dreadful, springy way and, when I looked down again, I saw that the sand was only a light covering over more limbs and faces. A large stone turned out to be a stomach. I could see a man's head, a woman's naked breast, the feet of a child. I was walking on dozens of corpses which were moving beneath my feet ... families had retreated to their bedrooms when the militiamen came through the front door and there they lay ... many of the women had been raped, their clothes lying across the floor, their naked bodies thrown on top of their husbands or brothers, all now dark with death.[28]

The horror of Sabra and Chatila probably was the beginning of the end of the moral immunity which Israel had demanded and exploited in the West, especially Europe. Reading *Pity the Nation*, Fisk's reporting of the massacre, which was devastating for Israel, was all the more powerful for his dogged attempts to give the Israelis every chance to answer the charge sheet of their crime – a crime other journalists were prepared to gloss over, or excuse in some semantic contortion, even debating among themselves whether a massacre had actually taken place: a 'debate' that would find its echo following the 'mass killing' in Jenin twenty years later.

On December 16, 1982, a resolution by the UN General Assembly called the massacre at Sabra and Chatila 'an act of genocide'.[29] The following February an Israeli commission of inquiry, headed by Yitzhak Kahan, President of the Supreme Court, offered no evidence that a single terrorist was present in Sabra and Chatila when the camps were attacked.[30] The commission heard how Israeli forces had allowed the Phalangists to take away prisoners, who then 'disappeared', and it found that Ariel Sharon bore 'personal responsibility' for the massacre.[31]

All over the world, the pro-Israel or Zionist lobby's propaganda sought to control the damage by insisting that the Kahan Commission's report demonstrated the strength of Israel's 'democracy'; but the commission's findings changed nothing. Sharon was not disgraced in Israel. To many of his compatriots, he remained a hero. Begin, for his part, publicly threatened journalists who pointed out Israel's complicity in the massacre as the bearers of a 'blood libel' against all Jews.[32]

What's more, the commission failed to identify the obvious: that a crime against humanity had been committed. Even the word 'massacre' was sanitised into 'events' and, crucially, the term 'Palestinians' was never used. The sophistry had a serious purpose, of course. As a former prime minister, Golda Meir, had said, the Palestinians 'never existed'; they were merely 'the terrorists'.

This dehumanising runs through Israeli state propaganda and, with honourable exceptions, scholarship and journalism. By consigning a whole nation to 'the other', as Fisk pointed out in *Pity the Nation*, the Israelis are able to 'describ[e] their enemies as evil rather than hostile [so that] no sane individual would dare regard their political claims as serious'. Moreover,

> anyone who expressed sympathy for the Palestinians was evidently anti-Semitic – and therefore not just anti-Israeli or anti-Jewish, but pro-Nazi . . . If Israel called the PLO its enemy, then the Middle East dispute involved two hostile parties. But if the world believed that the Palestinians were *evil*, then the dispute did not exist. The battle was between right and wrong, David and Goliath, Israel and the 'terrorists'.[33]

At the height of the atrocities in Lebanon, Dr Schlomo Shmelzman, a Holocaust survivor, wrote a letter to the Israeli press, announcing that he was going on hunger strike until Israel stopped the killing. 'In my childhood,' he wrote,

> I have suffered fear, hunger and humiliation when I passed from the Warsaw Ghetto, through labour camps, to Buchenwald. Today, as a citizen of Israel, I cannot accept the systematic destruction of cities, towns and refugee camps. I cannot accept the technocratic cruelty of the bombing . . . I hear familiar sounds today . . . I hear 'dirty Arabs' and I remember 'dirty Jews'. I hear about 'closed areas' and I remember ghettos and camps. I hear 'two-legged beasts' and I remember *'Untermenschen'* ['subhumans'] . . . Too many things in Israel remind me of too many things . . .[34]

Qalandiyah camp is today the main Israeli checkpoint on the road from Jerusalem to Ramallah. I had been back in the 1980s and early 1990s, but returning once more in 2002 I recognised little of it. Surrounded by trenches fortified with coil upon coil of barbed wire, the tents had been replaced by sturdy hovels. The queue at the tap was unchanged; the roads and alleyways choke with dust in the summer and run to caramel in the rain.

At the UNRWA office I asked for Mohammed Jarella, but he was dead, and Ahmed Hamzeh, the street entertainer, had been 'taken away . . . very ill'. No-one knew about his son, who was surely blind now. Another generation kicked a punctured football in the dust and took their place behind the same sewing machines in the concrete administration block; they wore cheap trainers now.

In the zig-zag of sandbags, oil drums and breeze blocks at the military checkpoint, people stood in a conga-line, many jammed so tightly together their hands could barely swat the flies. Families held each other, the babies silent. The elderly appeared more at ease, perhaps because they had endured this over and over again. That said, I watched a frail old man fall in the crush; he was caught and held aloft by a young woman. There was no space for him to sit on the stones and gather himself, and pleas to a soldier nearby, who was bursting with acne beneath his helmet, came to nothing. He looked away, affecting the role of bystander.

My camera crew and I were in a van. The driver, a Palestinian, waited his moment, then leapt out and spoke to an Israeli officer; and we were waved through.

'What did you say to him?' I asked.

'I pretended to be an Israeli. My Hebrew is good.'

'How often do you do that?'

'Every day . . . I drive a taxi in Jewish west Jerusalem, picking up at the hotels. If my foreign Jewish passengers thought I was an Arab, they wouldn't hire me. I listen to them laughing about the "niggers" – that's us.'

It had been ten days since the Israeli army had withdrawn from its three-week occupation of Ramallah, the de facto capital of the Palestinian Authority. I have seen many places in the wake of an invasion, but this was different. The destruction was selective. Far from 'destroying the infrastructure of terror', its aim clearly was to destroy the infrastructure of organised society. Gross acts of vandalism and spite seemed systematic. I followed the route of a tank that had veered from one side of the road to the other in order to crush small family cars and flowerbeds and, one after the other, children's playgrounds, leaving swings and climbing bars mangled.

At the Aziz Shahen girls' school, ten tanks smashed into the playground and stayed there while snipers used the upper classrooms. When the children were allowed to return, they found everything trashed: their desks and chairs and textbooks and, as one girl pointed out, a tapestry in a broken glass frame saying 'Peace and justice in Palestine'. Irreplaceable musical instruments had been looted.

At the education ministry, soldiers had blown open the doors and gone to work on the computers, stripping them of their hard drives, which contained data for courses, examinations, graduation lists. Nothing was left. In the land registry office, all the records were stolen or destroyed, including deeds dating back to the Ottoman Turks. At the Peace and Love Radio Station, which broadcast to young people, the founder, Mutazb Seiso, said, 'It didn't take them long. The soldiers clearly had orders. They destroyed our transmitter, all our tapes, mini-discs, mixers: everything. We are finished unless we get help from abroad.'

At the Palestinian Cultural Centre I met the director, Liana Badr, an acclaimed novelist, in the street, wiping away 'my tears of rage'. The original manuscript of her book, *The Shadow of the Spoken Words*, lay scattered and torn across the floor of her office, from which the hard drive of her computer had been taken; it contained her fiction, plays, poetry. Almost everything else was smashed, or defiled; not a book survived with all its pages; not a master tape from one of the best collections of Palestinian cinema.

Day after day, the soldiers who camped here during the invasion vandalised them all: lifetimes of work such as the voluminous oral history, *Zetounat*, in which generations of Palestinian villagers described how the olive tree had been 'the source of light, fire, nourishment and healing' since ancient times and their efforts to save the hillsides of olive groves from Israeli bulldozers.

There were two toilets on each floor of the three-storey centre, yet the soldiers made a point of urinating and defecating everywhere else: on the floors, in flowerpots, even in drawers pulled out of desks. Someone had managed to shit into a photocopier. Shit-filled plastic bags and mineral water bottles filled with urine had been deposited where they would do the most damage: on open books and art objects, such as hand embroideries.

Upstairs, in the children's section, 'the department for encouraging children's art', almost everything had been urinated on. Four walls of children's paintings had been vandalised with gouache paints the soldiers had found, and smeared with faeces.

'This', said Liana Badr, 'is an entire art project, which was to be taken on a tour of schools. Look at it now, covered in shit and piss.'

Above it were scratched the candelabrum symbol of Israel, a Star of David and the words: 'Sons of bitches – you fuckers. I was born to kill.' A video recorder lay on its side, the inside torn out; beside it was a pile of pornographic tapes in Hebrew.

Where was the 'terror infrastructure' General Sharon said his soldiers were seeking? The Cultural Centre is situated in a residential district of elegant stone houses surrounded by gardens thick with cypresses and fruit trees. Tanks or bulldozers had systematically run over a row of cypresses. People living here told reporter Amira Hass that there had been so much shooting when the centre was first occupied that they assumed there had been gun battles with Palestinians. But no armed Palestinians ever appeared; it seemed that the soldiers were shooting at arbitrarily chosen targets as 'nightly entertainment'. 'One night,' she reported, 'the neighbourhood awoke to the sound of barking: they saw that someone had attached a speaker to a tape recorder and was playing a recording of barking dogs. Within a few minutes, all the dogs in the neighbourhood woke up and joined the racket. Very soon the barking reached more distant neighbourhoods.' The people fled.[35]

'This is the holy war of Sharon against terrorism,' said Liana Badr. 'It is against the memory and the culture of the Palestinian people. They know how we value learning and culture. In occupied Palestine, we have established sixty libraries for children. Compare that with Egypt, which has in total sixty-five libraries. Now we don't have anything to supply them; we have to begin again, and we are left with this feeling of humiliation; young men ate and defecated on our work, our memory, our art. Can you imagine the feeling this leaves? It is the feeling of rape.

'This culture, these works by our children, are our being. We have been raped; and all the while, the perpetrators are crying that they are victims, demanding the world's sorrow and perpetual silence about us while their powerful army demolishes our culture: our lives.'

Operation Defensive Shield left hundreds dead and wounded.

Many were shot when the army-imposed curfews were 'lifted'. Several times, Israeli government radio reported that the curfew had been lifted until six that evening, even as soldiers in the city were reimposing it at noon. At other times, army jeeps with loudspeakers drove through the streets at two in the afternoon telling people to return home within ten minutes, even though another announcement had 'lifted' the curfew until five o'clock.[36]

The psychological warfare succeeded. People did not know if they should risk going to the shops, work, school or university or stay in their homes. Weedad Safran, described in press reports as 'a grandmother in her 50s', lived alone and was hard of hearing. She is believed to have heard one curfew announcement, but not that which countermanded it. She decided to walk to the hospital to have a cast removed from her leg. She could barely hobble with a walking stick. She was shot dead by an Israeli sniper at the gates of the hospital.[37]

Dr Hamed Massri, a neurosurgeon at the hospital in Nablus, said two patients would have lived if ambulances had been allowed to reach them. They were Amar Ali Salamah, a carpenter, and Sakher Mohammed, a baker. The baker had been shot through the window of his home, where he bled to death before an ambulance was allowed to collect the body. That was not unusual.[38]

In Bethlehem, I met a former Palestinian UN official, Amjad Abu Laban, whose father had died at home from natural causes; because Amjad was refused permission to arrange collection of the body, he was forced to bury it in his small garden. 'Let me tell you what would have happened if we had tried to take him to the cemetery,' he said. 'On the eighth of March, a friend of mine, the director of a clinic, was driving to get medical supplies. He had done everything correctly. He had contacted the Israeli liaison officer. His car was well known to the army. He had even described what he would be wearing that day. He was told he could get the supplies. He was killed by a high-velocity bullet straight through the forehead.'

Palestinians see this violence as continuous and rarely acknowledged internationally for its murderous intent, its 'terrorism', and the disproportionate impact on their community, compared with Israel. Since the beginning of the second *intifada* in September 2000, an estimated 3,300 Palestinians have been killed by Israeli forces, more than half of whom were killed unlawfully, says Amnesty International. That is to say, they were not participating in armed clashes or attacks. Some 650 were children.[39] While I was in Ramallah, Qossay Abu 'Aisha, aged twelve, was playing in his garden when two Israeli soldiers shot him dead. A death like that occurs almost every day.[40]

Dr Mustafa Barghouti, the director of the Palestinian Health Policy Institute in Ramallah, studied an eight-month period to May 2001. He wrote: 'More than 500 Palestinians were killed and 23,000 injured. One third of the casualties were children; more than 60 per cent were shot while in their homes, schools or workplaces.'[41]

In 2003, the Palestinian Centre for Human Rights reported that 408 children had been killed since the beginning of the second *intifada* in 2000. As I write this, thirteen-year-old Iman al-Hams has just been shot by Israeli soldiers, despite having been identified as a little girl, wearing a school uniform. She had seventeen bullets in her body and three in her head. The PCHR describes victims like her as evidence of a shoot-to-kill policy and the deliberate targeting of children.[42] Yet the reputation of the Israeli army at home in Israel, and among many Jews abroad, is that of 'the most humanitarian in the world', in the words of Britain's Chief Rabbi, Jonathan Sacks.[43]

In 2002, Chris McGreal, the *Guardian*'s reporter in Jerusalem, revealed that the Israeli army had 'shot or blown up' fifty children under the age of eight in Gaza alone. The Israeli human rights organisation, B'Tselem, had obtained an internal military report confirming that the army had a policy of covering up its crimes. 'The message that the [army's] judge advocate general's office transmits is clear,' said the organisation: '. . . soldiers who violate the "Open Fire Regulations", even if their breach results in death, will not be investigated and will not be prosecuted.'

When challenged by McGreal about the killing of four children in Gaza, the Israeli commander made a rare admission: 'that his soldiers were at fault to some degree or other in the killing of most – but not all – of the children'. However, by the end of the interview he had changed tack. 'I remember the Holocaust,' he said. 'We have a choice, to fight the terrorists or to face being consumed by the flames again.'

McGreal asked the military spokesman who sat in on the interview if he could name the commander. 'No,' said the spokesman. 'He has admitted his soldiers were responsible for at least some of the killings. In this day and age, that raises the prospect of war crimes, not here but if he travels abroad he could be arrested some time in the future. Some people might think there is something wrong here.'[44]

What was striking about this encounter was not the commander's admission, however unusual, but his invocation of the Holocaust. I asked Mustafa Barghouti about this. 'What has it to do with us?' he said. 'Anti-Semitism has nothing to do with this region. Palestine was always a very tolerant society. For centuries, Palestinians, Jews, Arabs and Christians lived together with no big problems. This dilemma we face began when the Zionists decided they wanted a state at the *expense* of the Palestinians. The Holocaust has nothing to do with this; it was a European phenomenon. The word almost never heard in Israel is "injustice". It's as if the Jewish suffering can blank this out. So what has happened is that the very discourse of the injustice is reversed.

'This is very strange. I was at an international conference recently and the prevailing mood, even among people of liberal reputation, was that we, the Palestinians, have to apologise to the Israelis for being occupied by them. We have to apologise because we're forcing them to oppress us by just being here for thousands of years. We have to apologise to the Israelis who want to look civilised and democratic. It is as if the historical fact of our presence has forced them to oppress us, forced them to kill us: and of course killing our children is all part of this. They want us to apologise for being alive; and if this was a mistake, then it was God's mistake. Frankly, I don't think we have to apologise for God's mistakes, in the same way I don't believe we have to suffer because of a European crime, the Holocaust . . . Jewish blood is precious, but so is Palestinian blood. We two peoples are equally precious. I always say how sorry I am, not only for the seventeen hundred Palestinians killed in this *intifada* but also for the four hundred Israelis killed. All of us, Arabs and Jews, are the victims of this occupation.'

The belief that the army of occupation is 'the most humanitarian in the world' is remarkable. Written regulations that feign a

propriety of lawfulness and humanity are supplied to journalists by
military spokespersons – in the same way that British army information officers extol the sanctity of the Geneva Conventions, 'the
rules of proper behaviour', while their soldiers behave as brutally as
their colonial role demands.

In Jerusalem, I was handed an Israeli army document,
'Regulations for response to residents of the West Bank arriving at a
roadblock in urgent emergency medical condition'. This, an army
spokesperson assured me, was the product of a High Court of Israel
ruling and contravened by soldiers at their peril. It reads, in part:

> As a rule, the commander of a roadblock shall enable the
> passage of a person for the purposes of receiving medical
> care, even if he does not bear the necessary permit, if the
> case is one of an urgent emergency medical condition . . .
> in, for example, cases in which a woman on labor [sic]
> arrives at the roadblock . . . The commander of the road-
> block shall consider the possibility of accompanying
> a resident in urgent emergency medical condition with a
> vehicle . . .

Fatima and Nasser Abd Rabo live in a village near Jerusalem
that has a permanent roadblock. Residents cannot leave or return
without showing their permits. Theirs is a form of house arrest
common on the West Bank and in Gaza. When there is a curfew,
they simply cannot leave for any reason; their daughter, Arij, aged
five, cannot go to school; they dare not even go out onto their
balcony. The military will cut the electricity from time to time, and
they are left with candles. Archbishop Desmond Tutu came here,
and was struck by the similarity to the worst strictures of South
Africa's infamous pass laws.

'We hear our village has been designated "Zone A and B",' said
Fatima, as she sat in her kitchen with Arij on her lap. 'That means
it is Jewish land, and we cannot use it any more, and they want us
out. They have marked red lines to forbid us using it. They want
foreigners to have it; they told us that's what they are planning to
do.'

'How long have you lived here?'

'All our lives. We are not refugees. My parents and grandparents lived here.'

Fatima and Nasser had been trying for a second child and had undergone fertility treatment. During two years in Israeli prisons, Nasser says he was abused and suffered sexual problems. When Fatima became pregnant, he celebrated by borrowing enough to replace the tin sheeting on their home with a concrete roof. She described to me what happened on the night of October 22, 2001.

'It was seven o'clock, and I felt sharp labour pains, even though I was only seven months pregnant. Arij had been born two months premature, so we were apprehensive, and my husband asked a friend to take us to the hospital in Bethlehem in the truck he used for transporting chickens. When we drove up to the checkpoint, the soldiers looked at our permits and said we needed another document. I told them I was bleeding badly. All of us started arguing and they pushed my husband and hit him with the butt of a machine gun. He tried to placate them, then we decided to all stand quietly, hoping they would show us kindness.

'I had known in my heart that this would happen. When I was about to give birth to Arij, the soldiers at the checkpoint looked at me and laughed and said I was just fat . . . "Go home!" they said.'

'What did you do in this second crisis?'

'We went home and decided to try again when they had calmed down. We got a taxi this time, hoping they would allow it to pass. But still they refused. It was now about two in the morning. I was in the back seat and in final labour. One soldier looked in the window and imitated my moans. It was then that I had my baby; my mother-in-law cut the umbilical cord with a razorblade. I heard my son cry for the first time, and even then I thought about how happy I was [when I got pregnant] and how happy I was preparing for my son to arrive and looking forward to hearing his voice.'

With the baby wrapped in his jacket, Nasser told the taxi driver to drive back, and stop around a bend. From there, they set out for Bethlehem by foot, across the fields and rocky hillsides. It was cold. After an hour, they reached a road and flagged down a car, which drove them to the Holy Family Hospital. The baby was blue and in a critical condition. Seven hours later, he died from exposure. They called him Sultan and buried him near their home.[45]

Fatima spoke with the blunt eloquence of ordinary people who have struggled and learned somehow to live with their anger. Nasser, however, would not be interviewed. 'He is *too* angry,' she said.

'Why do you think the soldiers behaved that way?'

'Because it's normal. That's how they treat all Palestinians. They would rather help a dog than an Arab. Aren't you aware of this? Everybody in every country seems to know about us. Everybody is watching, but nobody is helping.'

From Fatima's home, which is built on a steep incline, you can see the modern Hadassah Hospital in Jewish west Jerusalem. She was the second woman in her village to lose her baby after being stopped by soldiers at a checkpoint. A woman in a nearby village lost hers in similar circumstances. A Palestinian Health Policy Institute survey over two years recorded the deaths of seventy-three babies at 'military checkpoints, barriers and trenches' and found that many women facing difficult deliveries had no choice but to give birth at home with no medical help.[46]

An ambulance makes little difference. During an eighteen-month period, the Israeli organisation Physicians for Human Rights monitored Palestinians seeking urgent medical care, such as women in labour and patients needing kidney dialysis and cancer treatment. It found 221 instances of ambulances being turned back at check-points, resulting in twenty-nine deaths.[47]

The Israeli army says that Palestine Red Crescent ambulances are used to transport explosives. In Israel, I found that people regarded this as a given. In fact, there has been *one* allegation that a bomb was found in an ambulance, and the Red Crescent has vigorously denied the authenticity of the reported incident, describing it as a conspiracy to discredit it. The Israeli human rights organisation B'Tselem says that 'despite repeated requests by human rights organisations and others, the [Israeli military] spokesperson has never provided any evidence supporting his claims that the Palestinians make "cynical use" of ambulances . . . documentation has never been disclosed'.[48]

From Geneva, the International Committee of the Red Cross, which normally remains aloof from such controversy, issued an extraordinary statement. There is, says the ICRC, an ongoing campaign of disinformation and slander against the Palestine Red Crescent Society. The ICRC has expressed on many occasions to members of the Israeli Government and Defence Forces its grave concerns about the repeated accusations against the PRCS that are being conveyed through the media. Despite numerous ICRC requests, the [Israeli military] has never presented any concrete evidence implicating PRCS members in acts of violence against Israelis when carrying out their missions . . . The accusations amount to a systematic propaganda campaign which threatens the entire humanitarian mission as they cast a shadow of suspicion and mistrust on those seeking to deliver badly needed assistance.[49]

On the day I visited Fatima, I arranged to meet Salim Shawamareh in a café near his home in Anata, an outer suburb of Jerusalem. I had been told: 'His story alone speaks for what others cannot imagine.' Salim has an Israeli ID card. This shows that he was born in Jerusalem and theoretically means that he has some protection from the brutalities of the occupation. In 1994, he applied for planning permission to have his land classified for agriculture. For this, he was told, he would have to pay $25,000, a fee that applied only to Palestinians. Over four years, he was refused permission three times, and twice he was told that two signatures were missing on a form where neither was specified.

'On July 9, 1998,' he said, 'my family and I were eating lunch when suddenly there was shouting, and the house was surrounded by soldiers. One of them said, "It's not your home now; it's our home. You have fifteen minutes to get out." When I challenged this, they arrested me, and started smashing the windows and throwing teargas inside, where my wife and kids were. My wife passed out; my kids were in a terrible state. Jeff Halper, the wonderful Israeli anthropologist who leads the Israeli Committee against House Demolitions, arrived and threw himself in front of the bulldozers. The soldiers beat up everybody; one boy lost a kidney; and my house was flattened. Seven years of working in Saudi Arabia, where I'd gone to save for a home, were wasted.

'I moved the family into a tent in the backyard, then I watched a miracle: Palestinians and Jeff Halper's people, Arabs and Jews together, rebuilt my home in twenty-three days. Hundreds came to help from all over Israel. It was finished on August 3. The very next day, my wife and I were woken at four in the morning with machine guns pointing at our faces. We were ordered out into the street where we watched our home destroyed for the second time. They destroyed the trees we planted. They even took the tent we'd been living in.

'Once more, I went to the Civil Administration where they said the house would not have been demolished if I had had the two missing signatures. But whose signatures? For two months, a lawyer tried to find out for me, with no luck. So, yes, we rebuilt my home again. It was finished on April 3, 2001. And at eight o'clock the following morning, the soldiers came again and destroyed my home again!

'Back at the Civil Administration, they kept moving the "zone" line. Was I in the zone meant only for Jews? I was never sure, because I was never told. Yes, we rebuilt it again, and the soldiers came again, this time with a tank. I couldn't stop my ten-year-old daughter running out in front of it, and the doctors say the shock to her nervous system was such that she's now going blind, a bit more every day. All my children don't sleep without wetting their beds and crying out with nightmares. That happens every night. What does this mean for me? It means that, as a father, I can't protect them, I am powerless. Now I must give up.'

When a friend of mine finally located the department that had dealt with Salim's case, he asked an official why this had happened. Was Salim a suspected 'terrorist'?

'No,' came the reply, 'he didn't come to us for planning permission.'

'But he did, three times.'

'We'll look into it.'

We heard nothing more, but were assured unofficially that Salim's house would not be demolished a fourth time. This, of course, was no guarantee. When I last heard, soldiers had begun bulldozing the homes of his neighbours. Since Israel occupied the West Bank and Gaza, an estimated eleven thousand Palestinian homes have been demolished. This is a 'strategy' learned from the

British who, as collective punishment for resistance to their rule in Mandated Palestine, demolished hundreds of homes.[50]

'Like every occupation before it,' wrote Amira Hass in *Drinking the Sea at Gaza*, 'Israel – despite having controlled the territories since 1967 – had still not learned that resistance and terror are responses to occupation itself and to the form of terror embodied by the foreign ruler.'[51] Most Palestinians would agree, though perhaps not with the proposition that Israel 'had still not learned' that its terrorism beckoned terrorism. Israel, they might say, deliberately drove the 'cycle' of terrorism and cynically exploited it, and Palestinian suicide bombing was no more than a consequence of this.

Edward Said addressed this in his essay 'Punishment by Detail':

> Suicide bombing is reprehensible, but it is a direct and, in my opinion, a consciously programmed result of years of abuse, powerlessness and despair. It has as little to do with the Arab or Muslim supposed propensity for violence as the man in the moon. [Ariel] Sharon . . . does everything in his power to create the conditions for [terrorism]. But for all its horror, Palestinian violence, the response of a desperate and horribly oppressed people, has been stripped of its context and the terrible suffering from which it arises.[52]

Suicide attacks are a recent phenomenon (as they are in Iraq, where they were unknown before the Anglo-American invasion). In the first *intifada* (1987–93), there was none. Palestinians defended themselves against bullets, tanks and helicopter gunships with small arms, mostly with slingshots. The first Palestinian suicide bomber struck in the Israeli town of Afula on April 6, 1994. This was in direct response to the Zionist fanatic Baruch Goldstein's mass murder of twenty-nine Muslim worshippers at the Cave of the Patriarchs in Hebron on February 25 of that year. 'Baruch wasn't a psychopath,' his widow Miriam told the Israeli newspaper *Yediot*

Aharonot. 'He knew what he was doing. He planned on doing what he did in order to stop the peace talks.'[53]

Thus began the 'cycle of violence'. Hamas, reported *Yediot Aharonot,* 'has distributed a circular in the [Occupied] Territories warning of five major actions in revenge for the massacre at the Cave of the Patriarchs.'[54] The suicide attack at Afula followed.

'Appalling and unjustifiable, like all lethal attacks on innocent civilians,' wrote the Palestinian journalist Sa'id Ghazali, '[suicide bombings] are a strange and shocking phenomenon, not only for Israel, but for the Palestinians, too . . . Waiting, complaining, begging, appealing and resisting for more than fifty-four years,' they had found a weapon that struck a kind of equivalence of fear.[55] They also handed Israel a propaganda weapon unlike any other; such a barbaric act, Israel's spokespeople would repeat incessantly, *proved* that the Palestinians were congenital terrorists.

As I climbed the stairs of breeze blocks, stepping over the exposed wires and curious children, I was confronted by a giant poster of the latest suicide bomber, whose family I had arranged to meet in the dusty warren of the Amari refugee camp near Ramallah. 'Suicide bomber' is a term unrecognised here; they know only 'martyr'. 'Wafa, Wafa,' chanted the children, pointing to the heroic image in the poster. A little girl stood beside it, hand on her heart. 'Me!' she said. The Palestinians had their first female martyr.

An attractive young woman of twenty-eight, Wafa Idrees was an inspiration to her family and friends. She was a carer devoted to helping people. As a volunteer 'first aider' with the Red Crescent, she was a stretcher bearer on the front line of Palestinian resistance. When the Israeli tanks came, and young men and boys confronted them with stones, she was there, witnessing 'terrible things', said a clinical psychologist who counselled her and other Red Crescent staff. 'The psychological effect on these very young people who are evacuating the dead and injured can be profound. They are taking away bodies that are quite literally in pieces.'[56]

Wafa was shot twice in the leg with plastic-covered bullets. She worked while injured, becoming more and more activist and angry. On Sunday, January 28, 2002, she hurried to work, telling her family she would see them that evening. Instead, she picked up 10kg of explosives in a rucksack, strapped it to her back and went to

Jewish west Jerusalem. Rushing into a lunchtime crowd in Jaffa Street, she detonated the bomb, killing herself and a bystander and wounding a hundred others.

'This was a surprise to all of us,' her eldest brother Khalil told me. 'We cannot comprehend that she did this. She loved life so much; she would care for the smallest creatures, such as little birds; and she was the one who would calm me whenever we disagreed; she was a peacemaker. Of course, we knew what was happening to her. She was under fire a lot of the time; she was shot twice and beaten up by the soldiers when she came to help the injured. She would watch someone's stomach being splashed out. She would watch people die who might have been saved if the Israelis had allowed her ambulance to pass the checkpoints; she would tell us ambulances were made to wait in a line of cars for one or two hours while a patient bled to death. She was deeply upset about pregnant women losing their babies at checkpoints, and mothers dying, too. Because she experienced all that, I can assure you my sister was not going to die for anything trivial.'

I asked, 'Would you have tried to stop her had you known what she was planning?'

'I am thirty-two years old and I have spent ten years in Israeli prisons because I have defended my homeland. So it is not that I don't have feelings for my people – I would sacrifice myself for Palestine – but the answer is, yes, I would have tried to prevent her in any way I could, because I couldn't let such a dear person do that; she was my only sister and I am full of grief that she left the house and did not return.'

Khalil and Wafa were born in a refugee camp. Their father died when they were children; their mother has a deformed leg caused by an Israeli bullet. As we talked (against a wall mural of a tropical island, like a dream place far removed from the camp), Khalil's four-year-old daughter, Milana, played at his feet; she wore a sunflower in her hair.

'As an activist, how do you deal with your sister's death?'

'If you are asking: do I want to avenge her death, frankly, yes. But I won't, because our aim is not to kill Israelis; it is to establish a Palestinian state and live in peace with Israelis and be friends and visit each other. Speaking personally, I don't ever want another

Israeli pulling a gun on me, and I don't want to pull a gun on any-one, ever again.

'Wafa, my sister, belonged to the Palestinian liberation move-ment [Fatah], the same movement that was involved in the peace process with the Israelis, including the Oslo Agreement that was supposed to lead to a Palestinian state within five years, and didn't. Sharon and his extremists have no interest in this: in real peace. Don't you know we are the only people in the world the United Nations says have a right to independence, who are *not* independent? We are unique in the worst possible way. Please, I don't want to be unique. I don't want Wafa's memory to be unique.'

'What has shocked people in other countries,' I said, 'is that suicide bombings are aimed not at Sharon and those like him, but mostly at civilians, people like those your sister killed. What do you say to that?'

'I want to say I am sorry for the killings, Israelis and Palestinians. But when I am sitting at home with my family and our house is being bombed, and I search the wreckage for loved ones – and this happens in every camp – then I will have a reaction *because* I am suffering; I will want the Israelis to suffer, too. Palestinians are not the first to feel like this, are they? The European media will always hear from the Israelis about their civilians being killed, but they do not see or want to see the everyday, overwhelming violence of the Israelis against us.

'With mere rifles, we face American Apache helicopters and American F-16 bombers. Why? Because we are on our own. A UN fact-finding mission wants to come here to examine the massacres ordered by Sharon, but the United States steps in and blocks them on Israel's behalf. So what can we do? How can we not feel completely isolated? How can we not feel despair? How can we not strike back? But what do we strike back with? All we have is our own bodies.'

'What does life mean to you now?'

'I will be frank with you: life has no meaning for me. I believe I have no feelings any more, knowing that any day now my house will be hit by rockets from the air. Even when I am driving, I search the sky for an Apache [gunship]. I have become a living martyr.'

The Palestinian poet Mahmoud Darwish, an opponent of all

kinds of attacks on civilians and a persistent voice for Israeli–Palestinian co-existence, wrote: 'We have to understand – not justify – what gives rise to this tragedy . . . Palestinian people are in love with life. If we give them hope – a political solution – they'll stop killing themselves.'[57] The following are lines from his poem 'Martyr':

I love life
On earth, among the pines and the fig trees
But I can't reach it, so I took aim
With the last thing that belonged to me.

For Rami Elhanan, an Israeli graphic designer, the sacrifice by a Palestinian of 'the last thing that belonged to me' caused the death of his fourteen-year-old daughter, Smadar. There is a home video-tape of Smadar that is difficult to watch. She is playing the family piano, and throwing her head back and laughing. She has long hair, which she cut two months before she died. 'It was her way of making a statement of her independence,' Rami told me with a smile. 'Her brothers used to tease her because she was such a good student. But she knew what she wanted. She wanted to be a doctor, and she loved to dance.'[58]

On the afternoon of September 4, 1997, Smadar and her best friend, Sivane, had auditions for admission to a dance school. Smadar had argued that morning with her mother, Nurit, who was anxious about her going to the centre of Jerusalem to buy books she needed for school. 'I was worried about the increase in suicide bombings,' said Nurit. 'But I didn't want to row, so I let her go.'

Rami was in his car when he turned on the radio at three o'clock to listen to the news and heard reports of a suicide bombing in Ben Yehuda shopping precinct. Three Palestinians had walked into the crowd and turned themselves into human bombs. There were nearly two hundred injured, and several dead. Within minutes, Rami's mobile phone rang. Nurit was crying. She had received a call from one of their son's friends, who had seen Smadar making her way into the Ben Yehuda mall shortly before the bombs went off. For hours, Rami and Nurit toured hospitals, looking for her. 'Finally,' he said, 'a policeman gently suggested we go to the scene of the bombing, where we were referred to a morgue.'[59]

Their 'descent into darkness', as Rami describes it, was also the beginning of an inspirational campaign for peace. I have not met anyone like Rami, and the interview I conducted with him in the sunny sitting room of his Jerusalem home moved me deeply. Sometimes, solutions to apparently intractable political problems seem closer at hand when there is a Rami Elhanan engrossed in them, saying the unsayable.

'It's painful to acknowledge, but it really is quite simple,' he said. 'There is no basic moral difference between the soldier at the checkpoint who prevents a woman who is having a baby from going through, causing her to lose the baby, and the man who killed my daughter. And just as my daughter was a victim [of the occupation], so was he.'

On the shelf behind him was a photograph of Smadar at the age of five, holding a placard. 'Stop the occupation,' it said. Rami calls her 'a child of peace'. Her parents were both brought up to believe that the establishment of Israel as a Jewish national homeland was an act of self-preservation. Rami's father had survived Auschwitz. His grandparents and six aunts and uncles perished in the Holocaust. Nurit's father, Matti Peled, a general, was a hero of the 1948 war. Rami describes him as 'one of the true pioneers of making peace with the Palestinians'. He was among the first Israelis to visit Yasser Arafat in his exile in Tunisia. Nurit herself has been awarded the European Parliament's peace prize.

Rami dates his own 'awareness of the truth we dare not speak' to his time as a young army conscript. The 1967 war had just happened and was not, he says, the 'divine intervention' it was portrayed as in Israel, particularly among the 'settlers' who built their illegal fortresses on newly occupied land. He describes it as 'the beginning of a cancer at the heart of Israel'. Later, as a soldier in the 1973 Yom Kippur war, he said he realised 'I had blood on my hands, too.'

Rami and Nurit are among the founders of the Parents' Circle, or Bereaved Families for Peace, which brings together Israeli and Palestinian families who have lost loved ones. They include the families of suicide bombers. They jointly organise educational campaigns and lobby politicians to begin serious negotiations. When I met Rami, they had just placed one thousand coffins outside the United Nations building in New York, each draped in an Israeli or Palestinian flag. 'Our aim', he said, 'is not to forget or forgive the past, but to find some way of living together.'

I asked him: 'How do you distinguish the feelings of anger you must have felt as a father at losing your daughter from the feeling of wanting to reach out?'

'Very simple. I am a human being; I am not an animal. I lost my child, but I didn't lose my head. Thinking and acting from the guts only increases an endless circle of blood. You have to think: our two peoples are here to stay; neither will evaporate. We have to compromise in some way. And you do that by the head, not by the guts.'

'Have you made contact with the parents of the suicide bomber who killed Smadar?'

'That was tried once; someone wanted to make a film about it, but I wasn't interested. I am not crazy; I don't forget, I don't forgive. Someone who murders little girls is a criminal and should be punished, and to be in personal contact with those who did me wrong, it's not the point. So you see, I sometimes have to fight myself to do what I'm doing. But I'm sure what I'm doing is right. I certainly understand that the suicide bomber was a victim the same as my girl was. Of that, I am sure.'

'Have you made contact with the parents of other suicide bombers?'

'Yes. Very warm and encouraging contacts.'

'What is the point of that?'

'The point is to make peace, and not to ask questions. I have blood on my hands, too, as I said. I was a soldier in the Israeli army . . . if you are digging into the personal history of each and every one of us, you won't make peace, you'll make more arguments and more blame. Tomorrow, I am going to Hebron to meet bereaved Palestinian families. They are living proof of the willingness of the other side to make peace with us.'

'Isn't the public mood in Israel quite different?'

'I have a friend who says that what I am doing is like taking water out of the ocean with a spoon. We [in the Parents' Circle] are very few, it's true, and the world is being led by very stupid people: that's also true. I'm talking about the American President and my own Prime Minister. To take this word "terrorism" and build every-thing around it, as they do, you only make more misery, more war, more casualties, more suicide bombers, more revenge, more punish-ment. Where does that go? Nowhere. Our task is to point out the obvious. George Washington was a terrorist, Jomo Kenyatta was a terrorist, Nelson Mandela was a terrorist. Terrorism only has mean-ing for those who are weak and who have no other choice, and no other means.'

'What has to be done to end this suffering?'

'We have to start by fighting ignorance. I go to schools and give lectures. I tell the children how the conflict began by asking them to imagine a house with ten rooms where Mohammed and his family are living in peace. Then, one stormy night, there's a knock at the door, and outside stands Moshe and his family. They are sick, beaten, broken. "Excuse me," he says, "but I once used to live in this house." This is the whole Arab–Israeli conflict in a snap; and I tell the kids that the Palestinians gave up seventy-eight per cent of the country which they are sure is theirs, so the Israelis should give up the twenty-two per cent that was left [following the 1967 war].'

He shows the schoolchildren maps of the offer Prime Minister Ehud Barak made to Yasser Arafat at Camp David before the 'peace process' broke down. The maps reveal that swathes of the West Bank were held back from the Palestinians and kept for Jewish settlers. 'This was the greatest secret of all,' he said, 'because Barak never allowed any [official] maps to be made. He was proposing something he knew the Palestinians would not, could not, accept.'

'What kind of reaction do you get: in schools, at public events?'

'I watch the faces of the kids when I show them the maps and tell them that we had seventy-eight per cent, and the Palestinians had twenty-two per cent, and that's all the Palestinians want now, and I *see* ignorance lift. You know, in Israel, the bereaved are said to be sacred. People give them respect because they have paid the price. I am due that respect, but of course there are people who don't want to hear what I say.'

Every 'Jerusalem Day' – the day the modern State of Israel celebrates its conquest of the city – Rami has stood in the street with a photograph of Smadar and sought to persuade people of his mission for peace. The last Jerusalem Day, he stood in front of crossed Israeli and Palestinian flags, and people told him it was a pity he wasn't blown up, too. 'That is the dimension of the problem,' he said.

'Will you do that this Jerusalem Day?'

'Yes, and I will be spat and cursed at by some, but I know that's only one part of the human equation; it's the other part we must solve, and I and other parents are making a start.'

'What is the price that a society pays when it runs a military occupation?'

'It's an unbearable price. The list begins with moral corruption. When we don't let pregnant women through checkpoints, and their babies die, we have reduced ourselves to animals and we are no different from the suicide bombers.'

'What do you say to Jewish people in other countries, like Britain: people who support Israel because they feel they must?'

'I say they should be loyal to real Jewish values, and support the peace movement in Israel, not the state at all costs. It's only pressure from outside – from Jews, from governments, from public opinion – that will end this nightmare. While there is this silence, this looking away, this profane abuse of our critics as anti-Jew, we are no different from those who stood aside during the days of the Holocaust. We are not only complicit in a crime, we ensure that we ourselves never know peace, and our surviving children never know peace. I ask you: does that make any sense?'

'But they might say the Jews are in danger of being pushed into the sea by the Arabs, that Israel must stand firm?'

'Pushed into the sea by whom? We are the most powerful power in the Middle East. We have one of the greatest armies in the world. In this latest operation [Sharon's attack on the West Bank in April 2002], we sent four armoured divisions against some five hundred armed people. It's a laugh. Who will push us into the sea? Who can push us into the sea? . . . The real issue is played out every day at the checkpoints. The Palestinian boy whose mother is humiliated in the morning will be a suicide bomber in the evening. There is no way that Israelis can sit in their coffee houses and eat and drink while two hundred metres away desperate people are humiliated and Palestinian children are beginning to starve. The suicide bomber is no more than a mosquito. The occupation is the swamp.'

The chairman of the Parents' Circle is Yitzhak Frankenthal, whose son Arik, a conscripted soldier, was kidnapped and killed by Hamas. His generosity of spirit was expressed in his address to a peace rally in Jerusalem. 'Let all the self-righteous who speak of ruthless Palestinian murderers take a hard look in the mirror,' he said.

> [Let them ask themselves] what they would have done had they been the ones living under occupation. I can say for myself that I, Yitzhak Frankenthal, would have undoubtedly become a freedom fighter and I would have killed as many on the other side as I possibly could. It is this depraved hypocrisy that pushes the Palestinians to fight us relentlessly – our double standard that allows us to boast the highest military ethics, while the same military slays innocent children . . . As much as I would like to do so, I cannot say the Palestinians are to blame for my son's death. That would be the easy way out [for] it is we who are unwilling to make peace with them. It is we who insist on maintaining our control over them. It is we who feed the cycle of violence . . . I regret to say it.[60]

Israel's dissidents are among the bravest I have met. Apart from the remarkable Mordechai Vanunu, who spent nineteen years in prison, mostly in solitary confinement, and who today lives under effective house arrest, most of those who take on the Israeli state remain in the community, where their punishment is often unrelenting. To many, they have betrayed not only their country but their family and their Jewishness and the memory of the victims of the Holocaust. Shopkeepers refuse to serve them; lifelong friends cross the road rather than speak to them. Without warning, they are shouted at and spat upon – like Rami with his flags.

At the time of writing, 635 Israeli soldiers have refused to serve in occupied Palestine. Hundreds have been sent to prison. Others have made public declarations that have worried the regime; they include paratroopers, tank officers and members of the Special Forces, Sayeret-Matka. In September 2003, twenty-seven air force pilots, including Brigadier-General Yiftah Spector, a hero of the

1967 war, announced they had refused to carry out 'illegal and immoral' raids 'on civilian population centres'. The majority are young conscripts who must serve three years with the military. Their organisation is 'Courage to Refuse'.

I spent an afternoon with one of them, former Sergeant Ishai Rosen-Zvi, an orthodox Jew. We met in a Tel Aviv park, away from unfriendly eyes. I asked him what had made him a 'refusenik'.[61]

'It took me longer than I wish to think. When I arrived in Gaza with my unit, I could see what we were doing was horrible, but I did my job; I felt uneasy and embarrassed, but I did my job. On leave, at home, I never talked about it; I became a kind of Jekyll and Hyde character. Then I began to realise I was on the wrong side of the checkpoint, the roadblock we had to man day after day. The real story of the occupation is there at the roadblocks. Your job there is nothing, you stand around, and you think that if you could phone home, you would say, "This is boring." Then it dawns on you what this nothingness really is. It is keeping thousands of people in frustration, in humiliation, in hunger, in anger.

'Imagine it. You are standing there and it's five in the morning, and you see their eyes – some of the people could be my grandfather – and you glimpse the humiliation and the hatred. You want to take them aside and say, "Look, I'm a good guy; I've got nothing against you." But of course that has no point. For them, you *are* the occupation. And *nobody* gives you their liberty for nothing.'

I said, 'The government insists the roadblocks are there to stop the suicide bombers coming.'

'The roadblocks were there thirty-five years before suicide bombing began. They are there to control, always control.'

'Did Palestinians waiting under your control ever want to debate this with you?'

'You have all the power; they have no power. You can, at any moment, take their ID, and then they have nothing, because without ID, they can be arrested at any time. So they take no risks; they don't debate; they may even be deferential, but that's not how they are in their hearts.'

'How do other Israelis regard you, people you meet every day, who know you are a refusenik?'

'Some look on me as an extreme leftist, which is funny, because

I am a religious person. For them, the whole question of morality doesn't come into it; they think I am twisted in the head. One of my best friends told me, "OK, it's a stupid war, but it's a war, and we've got to fight it." '

'And your family?'

'We don't talk about it, or we try not to. My wife is speaking all the time about other things, because it's *too* hard . . .'

'So you've done this on your own?'

'Yes. I am alone on this.'

'What is the price you've paid?'

'I am no hero, believe me. I am a hurt person; I am hurt when I am in the market and someone I don't know says, "I read in the newspaper what you've done. It's horrible. People like you are ruining our country." That is like a knife attack and I am plunged into a personal battle in my head and heart; how do I say it . . . ?'

'You mean you have to keep explaining it to yourself?'

'Yes, yes, and not just explain; I have to reassure myself. I have to say, "Ishai, you are *not* a traitor." It is hard saying this to yourself, on your own.'

'What do you say to those Jewish people abroad who associate criticism of Israel with anti-Semitism?'

'Well, this is a huge bluff. It is the worst kind of propaganda. Jewish people in Britain, all over the world, who play this game of bluff are perpetuating the occupation and all its horrors. They should not contribute to such a device that desecrates the memory of Jewish suffering, and use it to justify the oppression of another people. It is profane.'

'What would you like to say to your compatriots?'

'I would like to say they should think hard about patriotism, because criticising our government on this issue is the *only* patriotic thing we have left.'

The price of such critical patriotism can be very high. An elderly woman, Yaffa Yarkoni, holder of the Israel Prize, decided to speak her mind the day before Memorial Day 2002, a day when Israel remembers its fallen soldiers and her own patriotic songs are played on the radio. Since 1948, not a year has gone by without Yarkoni standing on a stage before an adoring audience and singing her most popular songs. At seventy-five, she was Israel's Vera Lynn, and when she spoke out, it was two weeks before a national tribute to her iconic place in the nation's mythology.

On Memorial Day 2002 she was due to give an interview on army radio, just as she had done every year. She was the singer of Israel's wars and her name was synonymous with volunteering for military service. Then Sharon launched 'Operation Defensive Shield' and his tanks blasted their way into the West Bank. Yaffa Yarkoni watched the television news and read the newspapers; she saw the demolished homes in Jenin and women crying in the rubble and lines of handcuffed Palestinians being marched through the streets. A photograph of an Israeli soldier inscribing numbers on the arms of Palestinian 'suspects' moved and enraged her.

At the army radio station, they were expecting her. She would appear in a programme entitled 'Volunteerism and Solidarity with the Soldiers'; she would say a few encouraging words for the troops, then they would play her song, 'Ha'amini Yom Yavo' – 'Have faith, the day will come'. When the interview began, Yarkoni was clearly not in the mood for any of this. She ignored the questions and instead talked about 'the absence of leadership' in Israel, and why she hoped her grandchildren would emigrate. Of the soldiers who refused to serve in the Occupied Territories, she said, 'It's their right to do what their conscience tells them to do.'

The switchboard jammed. A wave of incredulous hostility swept over her. That afternoon, she was asked to explain herself on another, popular radio programme. She said, 'When I saw [the soldiers] leading [the Palestinians] with their hands behind their backs, I said, it's like what they did to us and to children in the Holocaust.'

The principal of the school where she was due to speak that day phoned to cancel her appearance; when she stood up to sing at the Tzavta Club in Tel Aviv, she was booed and abused, and people walked out. Her business agents drafted an apology they hoped she would sign. They wrote that she sought 'the nation's forgiveness'. It backfired. The right-wing daily *Yediot Aharonot* reported that an apology had been 'forced' on Yarkoni, who, it claimed, had compared Israeli soldiers to Nazis. This falsehood was never corrected, and the tribute to more than half a century's 'heroic service' was cancelled. Like Rami Elhanan and Ishai Rosen-Zvi, she was abused in the street and called a 'Holocaust denier'. The editor of the mass-circulation paper *Ma'ariv* wrote: 'Yaffa Yarkoni has joined the new anti-Semites in Europe.'

She refused to back down. 'The [Occupied] Territories should be given back and that's it,' she told Yossi Klein, a sympathetic journalist on *Ha'aretz*. 'The writing of numbers on their arms . . . really shocked me. Isn't that what the Germans did?' She said she had received a message from a Holocaust survivor, thanking her for what she had said, because 'we should learn from the Holocaust not to abuse and humiliate other peoples'.

'With no regard for the trouble she could cause herself,' wrote Klein, 'Yarkoni raised questions that are not considered acceptable: Were the Nazis and their actions a unique entity or is there such a thing as "Nazi-like actions"? Are we, the Nazis' victims, capable of such actions?'[62]

For Jews, merely to raise these taboo questions requires a moral and intellectual courage, and imagination, reminiscent of Judaism's great humanists and reformers and revolutionaries. One such voice was Israel Shahak, survivor of the Warsaw Ghetto and Bergen-Belsen, professor of organic chemistry at the Hebrew University in Jerusalem and a founder of the Israeli peace movement.

In the 1970s I paid several visits to his small, cluttered flat in Tel Aviv. He would offer me a chair and sit on a pile of books, each sprouting sprigs of scrawled notes. His face was terribly scarred by Nazi tortures; his bifocalled gaze was unerring and his squeaky voice would rise, and rise, then burst into laughter. Two of his favourite words were 'unspeakable' and 'peace'.

'Peace!' he declared, rolling it around his tongue. 'Peace will come only when Jewish rights are no longer placed above human rights. That's *unspeakable!* We never had a Martin Luther or a Calvin who said, "Wait a minute, we've been wrong about some basic principles for thousands of years." If Israel is a democracy, why are we so afraid to change? Why are we locked in this perma-nent introspection? Only when people speak out for Jewish interests are they regarded as people who have seen the light.

'When Zola defended Dreyfus he was not regarded by Jews as a man who loved justice, but as a Jew-lover! Today [1974], you only have to look in the *Yearbook of Israeli Statistics*, and you can see that everything in Israel is classified in Jewish and non-Jewish categories . . . vegetables! melons! babies! . . . non-Jews, who happen to be the majority here, are *unspeakable!*'

I asked him if he believed Jews and Arabs would ever live together in peace.

'Yes!' he replied, 'but only if there is security for both of us. We will never have security if we think *only* as Jews.'[63]

In recent years, 'unspeakables' have been uttered by Israel's 'new historians', who have refused to accept the birth of the Jewish state as a miraculous coming. In Haifa I met Ilan Pappe, one of the most courageous of the revisionists. His scholarship has a disarming moral sense, as if he is making up for time lost by others. In *The Making of the Arab–Israeli Conflict, 1947–1951*, he challenges the claim by Zionist historians that the 1948 war with the Arabs, which led to the establishment of Israel, was fought to prevent 'another Holocaust'. He sets this 'myth of annihilation' against the ruthlessness of the Jewish leadership towards *any* Palestinian resistance to their expulsion from their homelands.

One of the most contentious issues about 1948 is the cause of the flight of hundreds of thousands of Palestinians from their homes in the months and weeks before Israel's declaration of independence. While Arab politicians and historians have long argued that this was a deliberate policy of ethnic cleansing, the Israeli 'patriotic version' maintains that Arab leaders ordered and encouraged the exodus from Palestine. The revisionists opened previously unseen Hebrew records and intelligence files that describe a detailed military plan for the conquest of Palestine, including a deliberate policy 'demanding the surrender of the [Palestinian] population' and the destruction of villages and their takeover by Jewish settlers. This was known as 'Plan Dalet', or 'Plan D'.[64]

In *A History of Modern Palestine*, Pappe says that massacres and atrocities, such as the murder of two hundred people at Deir Yassin, were 'not randomly committed, but part of a master plan to rid the future Jewish state of as many Palestinians as possible'.[65] This was the *Nakbah*, the 'catastrophe' mourned by Palestinians. 'Roughly 900,000 people', wrote Pappe, 'were expelled by force . . . Israel's creation was thus enabled by military power, ethnic cleansing and the de-Arabisation of the country.'[66] 'We should be merciless, and kill the women and children as well,' wrote Ben-Gurion's adviser on Arab affairs.[67]

Together with Amira Hass and other Israeli dissidents, Pappe has been viciously attacked. He has been called 'highly politicised' and 'another self-hating Jew'. Haifa University threatened to sack him after he defended one of his students whose research for a master's thesis revealed that two hundred Palestinians had been murdered by the advancing Jewish militia in Tantura, a town south of Haifa, in 1948. Having read the transcripts of more than sixty hours of evidence which his student, Teddy Katz, had taken from some forty eye-witnesses, Pappe was convinced of their authenticity. 'They include', he wrote, 'horrific descriptions of executions, of the killing of fathers in front of children, of rape and torture.'[68] However, Katz had made four minor mistakes and, even though he was awarded a top grade by the Middle Eastern department of the university, his degree was annulled. The episode got into the newspapers and Katz, a devout Zionist, was pressured to apologise.

Pappe also came under intense pressure. Supported by the threat of an international academic boycott, he kept his job. The Katz affair was a catalyst; Pappe's heresy had been his outspoken opposition to the occupation and, in particular, his debunking of the myth of the Oslo 'peace process' and why it had 'failed'.

This is Israel's most important contemporary myth. It says that Sharon's predecessor, Ehud Barak, offered the Palestinians the return of '90 per cent' of the Occupied Territories at Camp David in 2000 and that Yasser Arafat turned him down. Arafat's alleged rejection of this 'unprecedented act of generosity' became a catch-cry for renewed abuse of the Palestinians and Arafat, and the principal justification for 'Operation Defensive Shield' and the building of an apartheid wall.

There was no '90 per cent' offer. At Camp David, Barak promised a token military withdrawal from no more than 12 per cent of the Occupied Territories. He also made clear that Israel had no intention of giving back any part of Greater Jerusalem, which covers some of the best Palestinian land and is the administrative and cultural heart of Palestine. Most of the illegal settlements, which controlled 42 per cent of the West Bank and Gaza, would stay, leaving the Palestinians with fragments of their original homeland, or 15 per cent of pre-Israel Palestine.[69]

'In practice,' wrote Barak's chief negotiator at Camp David, Shlomo Ben-Ami, before taking up his negotiator's role, 'the Oslo agreements were founded on a neo-colonialist basis, on a life of dependence of one on the other forever.'[70] While Jews abroad lauded Barak's perceived munificence, many Israelis knew better, wrote Noam Chomsky. They understood that a dependent colony, 'a Bantustan proposal of the kind that South Africa instituted in the darkest days of apartheid', was being created. This would concentrate Palestinian life in three 'cantons' under Israeli control, virtually separated from one another and from the fourth canton, a small area of east Jerusalem. 'That is presumably the reason why maps were carefully avoided in the US mainstream.'[71]

Instead of the Palestinian capital returning to Arab Jerusalem, the centre of all Palestinian life was assigned to a nearby village, Abou Dis, which the Israelis used as a rubbish dump. Only a tiny proportion of refugees would be allowed back and the Palestinians would have to relinquish for ever their right of return – a right declared inviolable under the Universal Declaration of Human Rights. Not only would Israeli power prevail, but Israeli courts, reported *Ha'aretz*, would retain veto powers over any Palestinian legislation 'that might jeopardise major Israeli interests'.[72]

I asked Ilan Pappe about this. 'By the summer of 2000,' he said, 'the Palestinians were left with an offer of 10 per cent of what used to be Palestine: what I would call a stateless state with no genuine sovereignty, with no independent foreign economic or political policies, with no proper capital and at the mercy of the Israeli security services. In return for this, Arafat was asked to declare the end of the conflict, that there would be no more demands for independence.'

'President Clinton, the host at Camp David, presented himself as even-handed,' I said. 'Is it too strong to describe his role as a betrayal?'

'I don't think that's too strong. The term "peace process" belongs in an American dictionary; there was no genuine diplomatic effort for peace. [Clinton] accepted the Israeli concept of peace, which is to dictate to the Palestinians, and wrap it in the discourse of peace and present it to the world as a true peace effort. For a while, the Palestinians accepted this perception, and with the ceremony on the White House lawn in 1993 [with Clinton, Arafat and Israeli Prime Minister Yitzhak Rabin], the whole thing was staged in such a way that it was very difficult to object to it, because you would be labelled as "anti-peace". The truth was that they signed a document that did not relate even to one of the central issues about which they had been struggling for more than a hundred years.'

'Are comparisons of Palestinian gains with the bantustans of apartheid South Africa valid?'

'I must say that, from my personal point of view, [the analogy of apartheid South Africa] is something new and recent . . . but I think it helps clarify the situation. There is a clear policy of segregation and apartheid on the West Bank and Gaza. Towards the Palestinian minority inside Israel, about one million people, it is a more subtle version of apartheid, implemented at every level: legislative, legal, economic. Then there is the position of people like myself. We [who object] are totally alienated from our own society, which means that we are very much like those whites in South Africa that decided to join the ANC. Like them, we appear to run against everything that is cherished or sacred in the eyes of our own society. Like those whites who opposed apartheid, we have to be prepared to go to the very extreme: to ask others to impose sanctions on our own society because we believe there is no other way to change that which is fundamentally destructive to Israel and its neighbours.'

'What's the solution?'

'I think eventually we will have to have here one state. We may have to go through the stage of two states, therefore I don't oppose the idea of a two-state solution, provided people understand that should lead to a state that will be democratic and secular, which will contain a large number of refugees. This is the only way for the six million Jews and the six million Palestinians, who will be here in ten to fifteen years' time, to be able to live in this tiny area, between the River Jordan and the Mediterranean Sea. They may need separate political structures, a confederation, but it has to be a state of all the people.'

'Is that possible?'

'It's not possible in the short term. Such a solution is a utopia in the short term, but it is possible – and I say this with great sorrow – only after a calamity, I hope not a catastrophe, but some sort of event or development that would be an eye-opener. This is why I support sanctions against my own country; and I pay a high price for saying this. I explain to my friends and colleagues that I would rather pay an economic price than a price in human lives. This is very similar to the South African situation, where the ANC on its own could not have brought about an end to apartheid. There was the need for an orchestrated campaign of sanctions and, in the end, that worked.'

'How do you deal with the zealots in government: Sharon and the present Israeli establishment? They have such power.'

'They have a lot of power, and you can't work within that. This is where Europe is important. These zealots have a self-image of belonging to Europe and not the Middle East. They're wrong; Israel has a future only if it realises that it is part of the Middle East and not a bastion for European culture. Therefore, European pressure on them, that condemns Israel from a European perspective, can have an effect. Then there is the United States. Those like myself tend to think of America as a lost cause, but the American political scene is much more complex than meets the eye; and I don't think the Palestinians and their supporters have explored enough the avenues open to them there. They have allowed a vacuum, and that is why the Israel lobby is so strong, not because it is strong in essence, but because there is no-one there to oppose it.'

'What about the immunity that Israel still seems to enjoy in international affairs, and the power of the memory of the Holocaust?'

'Holocaust memory is central to the way Israel is treated and the way Israelis see themselves. The Holocaust allows Israelis to do anything: genocide even, and there is no internal criticism. Europeans, and the rest of the outside world, are not allowed to criticise Israel, so that anything between a genocide and a benign occupation is not open to criticism, and if you break that rule, you are charged with anti-Semitism.

'Then there is the very interesting manipulation of the Holocaust in the demonising of the Arabs, in general, and the Palestinians, in particular. It began with Begin likening Arafat to Hitler in 1982. Of course, you can dehumanise the Palestinians by comparing them to Nazis, and thereafter you are entitled to do to them things that very sensitive Israelis would protest against if they heard about it in other parts of the world.'

'Isn't this charge of anti-Semitism a deliberate confusion of valid criticism of Israel with the anti-Semitic attacks by far-right groups in Europe?'

'Anti-Semitism plays a very important role in the attempt by Israelis to manage criticism from abroad. At the same time, the European far right exploits the justified rage in European civil society about the Israeli occupation. Israel's manipulation of this is very cynical. What Israelis do is take the marginal phenomenon of anti-Semitism and claim that this is the main phenomenon. Some governments in Europe play along with this game: for example, the British government.

'Any attempt to have a concerted European policy opposed to Israeli policies as a genuine precondition for peace is thwarted by the British government – and by Germany. In Germany's case, it will take another generation for the Germans to be totally liberated in being able to separate the two issues of anti-Semitism and criticism of Israel.'

'Doesn't a lot of this come back to the fear in Israel that they will be "thrown into the sea"?'

'It's a genuine fear of Israelis and Jews alike. It comes from ignorance, first and foremost, and from manipulation by Israeli governments. It is a fear that was justified at the beginning of the Zionist project, because Zionist colonisation was rejected by the indigenous population and by the [wider] Arab world, and there was an attempt to end it. But that was sixty years ago and Arab governments and people alike have reconciled to the fact that there is a living organism here, which is Jewish society in Israel; nobody, either out of pragmatism or ethical consideration, refuses to contemplate it any more. What is important is that in the past fifty years, the victims have been the Palestinians, not the Israelis, and the victimisers have been the Israelis, not the Palestinians. The real danger today is not that the Jews will be thrown into the sea, but that the Palestinians will be thrown out of their homeland – there is, after all, the example of the millions who have already been thrown out.'

'Does war propaganda play a major role in Israel?'

'Yes. Look at the language used. Palestine is not Palestine; it's "the terrorist infrastructure". Because the Israeli army influences most of the media, all discussion of a war of liberation, even a guerrilla war, is avoided. You're not allowed to say in the Israeli media "guerrilla fighters". You're not allowed to say "occupation". You're not allowed to say "the West Bank" and the "Gaza Strip"; you have to say "Judaea" and "Samaria". This is all part of the distortion of the past and of the criminalisation of the other side. Ending the occupation would have a lot of popular support in Israel. But we are conditioned to see only "terrorists" and criminals, and an Islamic culture which tries to kill as many Jews as possible. After September 11, 2001, the Israeli media understood it could jump on the wagon and include the Palestinians in the "war on terror", justifying all sorts of connections that were unsubstantiated or just wrong.'

'Isn't it true that Israel is the only democracy in the Middle East and, for all its faults, is worth protecting?'

'First of all, it's a democracy for the Jews. In no way is it a democracy for the Palestinians who live in Israel and who make up twenty per cent of the population. The main test of any democracy is the way it treats a minority; and a state that imposes a very non-democratic suffering on an occupied area fails as a democracy. Yes, there used to be a game of democracy in Israel, but they've given up on that. Now it's a game that allows the government and the army to do whatever they want. They can discriminate against and kill Palestinians as they want. They can harass and intimidate people like myself who are non-Zionist Jews.'

'What is the price of speaking out?'

'As long as the game of democracy was played, the price was isolation. My promotion in the university was affected, and there was a mood that translated to threatening telephone calls. But I was never physically attacked, nor was I imprisoned for my views. I am worried now that there is a new game in town, starting with Sharon's election in February 2001, whereby people like myself will be treated without kid gloves. A certain group of Jews, like myself, who up to now were immune because of their colour, so to speak, should now be very careful, because I think we are about to be treated the same way as the Palestinians.'

'What's the effect of all this on Israeli society?'

'In the next ten or fifteen years, we shall have here a society of zealots, run according to the rules of a theocracy rather than a democracy, with a lot of violence, domestically and externally. It will become difficult to distinguish between the violence imposed on the Occupied Territories, on the Palestinian minority in Israel, towards people like myself and the overall violence of the society. There is an interesting study that shows the rise of domestic violence – of violence between couples and violence in the public space in Israel. People who serve in the army cannot liberate themselves from the mentality of force when they come home to civilian life.'

'Aren't the differences between the humane traditions of Judaism and the nationalism of Zionism confused regularly, almost wilfully?'

'Yes, and there is a world of difference. And it is this that helps me to keep regarding myself as a Jew and not a Zionist, and not to give in to anyone who says to me you cannot be a Jew because you are an anti-Zionist. Judaism is a universal approach to life. It ran contrary to every notion of nationalism; it was the Ten Commandments; it was making society a more reasonable place to live. Zionism took this universal message and narrowed it right down, as if what Judaism was about was a territory, a flag, a hymn; and although I don't absolve anyone from anti-Semitism, I believe this distortion of Judaism as colonialism created a new kind of anti-Semitism.'

It was dusk when I walked through the 'no man's land' of the military checkpoint between Israel and the Gaza Strip. The method of control here, sullen and efficient, contrasted with the mayhem of the West Bank, reminding me of Checkpoint Charlie, which separated East and West Berlin. The only human traffic seemed to be foreigners and officials. 'They've managed to make the Arabs disappear,' Avi Mograbi, the Israeli film-maker who made the mocking documentary *How I Learned to Overcome My Fear and Love Arik Sharon*, once said of Tel Aviv.[73] The same sleight of hand has been achieved at the gates of the most densely populated corner of the Arab world. The Israelis call this 'closure': put another way, they have walled in and locked up a million and a quarter people.

Once inside, I found myself consumed by a melancholia, as if I were a trespasser in a secret place of mourning. Skeins of smoke from wood fires hung over the same Mediterranean Sea that free peoples know; and the same fire-red sun descended on those who have never known freedom. Along beaches that tourists would regard as picturesque trudged some of the incarcerated of Gaza; lines of sepia figures became silhouettes, marching at the water's edge, through lapping sewage that poured from the Jewish 'settlement' at Netzarim. They struggled and leaned and often fell into the sand and stones.

Up on the embankment ran Gaza's only main road, Salah el Din, which once went all the way to Cairo. The Gaza Strip is barely 25 miles long and 3 miles wide, and this is its spine. Yet here it was severed by Israeli soldiers, forcing people and vehicles onto the beach. This was to ensure 'security' for the 'settlers' of Netzarim, who inhabited a parasitic oasis inside the Gaza prison, where they imagined they were in a place called Judaea. It was at the Netzarim checkpoint that twelve-year-old Mohammed al-Dura was infamously shot to death as his mortally wounded father tried vainly to protect him from Israeli gunfire. Iconic murals on walls pock-marked by bullets commemorate them.

Abu Raed al-Soltan, a farmer, stood on the other side of the road where we had agreed to meet. His daughter, Tagrid, was beside him and welcomed me in English. 'My father is not well,' she said. 'He finds what has happened almost impossible to believe.' The family, she explained, had had a small citrus orchard, which had brought her generation 'the first prosperity since before 1948'. She was the first girl to go to university. One morning in March 2002, her father had arrived at the orchard with his brother and found an Israeli tank crushing grove after grove. Their land had been declared part of the 'security zone' for the 'settlers'.

There was no warning; the soldiers shouted at them that if they continued to work the land, they would be in danger of being shot.

Pillboxes were built. 'My father was reduced to selling imported Israeli oranges in the market,' she said.

'How much does he make from this?' I asked.

'The Israelis have swamped the market. Ten kilos of oranges will bring less than a dollar. He supports a family of thirteen children, and he buys my books for university. He is very upset that I will have to drop out. He wants us all to be lawyers and doctors with the education he never had.'

She explained to her father what she had said, and he remonstrated. 'He wants you to know,' she said, 'he will sell his own blood to keep our family going.'

When we met, the only way they could reach the land was through a cemetery, al-Shuada, 'the martyrs' graveyard', where fighters of the Lijan al-Muqawwam al-Sha'biyyeh, the Popular Resistance, are buried. Suicide bombers are buried here, and their fresh faces look out from a ribbon of white headstones. Among these is buried the farmer's father, whose land was confiscated in 1948 in a similar, arbitrary way. The second time it happened he slept among the oranges and lemons, hoping his presence would ward off the bulldozers. He died soon afterwards.

Through a gap in the perimeter fence, we watched people working the land, overlooked by soldiers in a pillbox. 'They shoot when they feel like it,' said Tagrid. 'Now and then, before the dawn, tanks come and roll over newly planted land.'

'Why does your family keep it going in these conditions?' I asked.

'My father and my uncle are very determined. My uncle refuses to go to the market to sell Israeli oranges.'

As we watched, shots rang out, forcing us back behind the headstones. Just then the farmer's brother arrived, a large man so incandescent with anger that conversation with him was impossible. He strode into the field, shouted something at us, then turned and bellowed his rage and defiance at the soldiers in the pillbox. In 1974, I filmed an olive farmer in the grip of an almost identical experience. In more than a quarter of a century, nothing had changed.

Dr Mona El-Farra is a physician at the al-Awda hospital in Gaza's Jabalya refugee camp. She speaks rapid English, the words tripping ahead of her. 'I can catch [save] a life here,' she said, 'but I must be attentive; I must be quick.' Her passion is raising money for plastic surgery on children wounded by plastic bullets. I asked her to describe when this last happened.

'Three months ago,' she said, 'two tanks stopped in front of the hospital, and opened fire. Seventeen people were killed and eighty-eight injured, including children with terrible wounds. That happened a hundred metres away; it would have taken one minute to get them to hospital, but no-one was allowed through, and the medical staff watched people bleed to death in the streets. The paramedics, in their white uniforms, were fired on every time they sent out rescuers. In this hospital, we have lost one hundred and sixty medical personnel, injured or killed. We tried to get our people bullet-proof vests and were told this was not allowed; only international workers could have them.'

'Where were you born?'

'I was born in Khan Yunis, in the far south of the Gaza Strip. More than sixty thousand people live there now, in a refugee camp surrounded by settlers and tanks. They are the heartland of our suffering and resistance, and the world knows nothing about them. I want to show you.'

I drove with Mona to a road junction where a mile-long queue of traffic waited at a military checkpoint on the way to Khan Yunis: trucks carrying animal feed, flour and oranges; taxis with schoolgirls trying to get home. They would probably spend the night there: nothing moved in the heat and dust. The worried driver of a truck filled with live chickens poured water over the cages. In a few hours, unless the queue moved, he would begin to throw dead birds to the roadside.

Ahead was a set of traffic lights and a pillbox. When the green light flashed, it lasted only long enough for a dozen cars to pass. Sometimes it flashed in bursts of ten seconds. When the lights were not working, the soldiers fired shots in the air: one to begin, another to stop. No Palestinian could walk across, and no vehicle was allowed through with only a single occupant, for fear, say the Israelis, of a suicide attack. So local boys hired themselves out to lone drivers who wanted to avoid being shot at. Rubbish trucks were given priority, and people hid in the rubbish; the symbolism was lost on no-one.

Why was there this waiting and congestion? Not a single vehicle passed by on the intersecting road during the hour and a half I was there. It was a 'security road' for 'settlers' only; a Jews-only road.

Mounted video cameras surveyed the surrounding fallow land, which, before the settlers arrived, was lush with orchards and crops. 'See beyond that line of palms,' said Mona, 'see where the bridge is. That's where my home was. I have photographs of it, the day after the bulldozers came. It was one of twenty-six houses demolished at the start of the *intifada*. They came at eleven o'clock at night and uprooted the trees and destroyed our water well, then our house.'

'Who was in it at the time?'

'No-one. My mother was away visiting friends in Gaza City. She wasn't allowed to return to salvage anything. All the memories of our life were there. My childhood, my parents' childhood. Our history went back hundreds of years . . .'

'Where is your family now?'

'My mother is living in a hovel in Khan Yunis refugee camp. My sister is there, too. I cannot get a permit to visit them, or even to bring my sister, who is seriously ill, to hospital. I think about them all the time; I think of my life being controlled all the time. I can't even go to Jerusalem or Ramallah without a permit issued by the Israeli occupation army, and I have been refused this permit for eight continuous years now. During that time, my son was studying at Bir Zeit university on the West Bank. He was one hour and a half's drive away, and I could never go and see him.'

'What reason did the Israelis give you?'

'They would say, "We are not entitled to give you the reason." '

'Did they accuse you of being a terrorist?'

'They know I am a doctor! Think of the anger this causes. Think of how our young people feel. To go to school you need permission from the Israelis. To have an ID you need their permission. To get married, you need their permission. We live in an open prison – no, it's not open, because they have divided the prison into many small prisons. Blockaded streets become prisons; houses become cells. It's like a maze in a dream where you never reach the exit.

'For basic emergency medical supplies to reach this hospital, we waited five months. They were donated by friends in Egypt and impounded on the border, and they were allowed through only after they had spoiled in the Sinai heat. I am talking about urgently needed solutions, medications, painkillers . . .'

'Why do so many of the children have distended bellies?'

'Because they are desperately hungry. Before this siege of Sharon's, the Palestinian family was surviving, even doing OK. It's my job to talk to people and find out who is suffering, and I must be frank with you: starvation is everywhere. Families almost never see meat; if they are lucky, they will get one chicken every fortnight. They don't know fruit, and this is a land of fruit. The children get tea and sugar, and little else. Almost all of them are suffering nutritional anaemia. Most of the tap water is controlled by the settlers and what comes to us is undrinkable.'

In the *British Medical Journal* of October 2004, Dr Derek Summerfield reported on a field study of Gaza and the West Bank. He wrote that, over the previous four years,

> two-thirds of the 621 children killed at checkpoints, in the street, on their way to school, in their homes, died from small arms fire, directed in over half the cases to the head, neck and chest – the sniper's wound. Two-thirds of the children were under fifteen. Clearly, soldiers are routinely authorised to shoot to kill the children in situations of minimal or no threat. These statistics attract far less publicity than suicide bombings.

He cited a World Bank study showing that 60 per cent of the population of Gaza were barely subsisting at poverty level, and a study by Johns Hopkins and al-Quds universities that almost a quarter of infants under the age of five were acutely or chronically malnourished. 'The coherence of the Palestinian health system is being destroyed,' he wrote.

> The wall [currently being built across the West Bank by the Israelis] will isolate 97 primary health clinics and 11 hospitals from the populations they serve. Qalqilya hospital, which primarily serves refugees, has seen a 40 per cent fall in follow-ups because patients cannot enter the city . . . The checkpoint at the entrance to some villages closes

at 7pm . . . a man in a now fenced-in village near Qalqilya approached the gate with his seriously ill daughter in his arms, and begged the soldiers on duty to let him pass so that he could take her to hospital. The soldiers refused, and a Palestinian doctor summoned from the other side was obliged to attempt a physical examination and to give the girl an injection through the wire.

Dr Summerfield concluded his report by asking: 'How are we to affect this shocking situation, one which to this South African-born doctor has gone further than the excesses of the apartheid era?'[74]

While I was in Gaza, UNRWA food supplies to the majority of families in the refugee camps were suspended. 'The main warehouse is empty,' an official told me. 'We have appealed to the European Union for direct support; otherwise we'll soon have nothing.'

Israeli utility companies and, until their evacuation in September 2005, fewer than seven thousand Jewish 'settlers' controlled Gaza's resources, especially its water distribution. In the record high temperatures of summer 1995, the Israeli national water company, Mekorot, cut supplies to most of Gaza for twenty days because people had no money to pay their bills. The eight thousand inhabitants of the village of Ubaydiya were deprived of running water for eighteen months while the nearby Jewish settlements were 'flourishing in the desert'.[75]

Gush Qatif was one of ten Jewish settlements that surrounded Khan Yunis refugee camp, where Dr El-Farra could not visit her mother and sister. Following the 1967 war, when the Gaza Strip was captured by Israel, Moshe Dayan is said to have put his open hand in the sand and said, 'My palm is Israel, my fingers are Arab; we must take back the fingers.' Whether or not this story is apocryphal, it has become the quest. And Dayan was said to be a liberal. 'Jewish villages', he said in a lecture in 1969, 'were built in the place of these Arab villages. You do not even know the names of these Arab villages, and I don't blame you, since the geography books no longer exist. Not only do the books not exist, the Arab villages are not there either.'[76]

For ten years, Gush Qatif was surrounded by an electrified fence; there was a partially built wall, and fifteen army tanks were mounted on sand platforms and pointed directly into Khan Yunis camp. Palestinians whose homes faced the settlement would open their windows in the morning to heavy machine guns and army tank nozzles within 150 metres. Others lived in the rubble of their ruined homes.

'It is simply not enough to say that "Israel shells Khan Yunis",' wrote the Palestinian American journalist Toufic Haddad in *Behind the Lines*.

> The Israeli army uses heavy automatic machine guns that when fired at such proximity easily pierce through the shabby asbestos and cheap concrete of the refugee homes built by the United Nations Relief and Works Association in the late 1950s. Furthermore, Israel uses inflammatory tracer ammunition which causes fires to break out once the shelling begins. In one instance, 30 different houses were set ablaze in one night . . . Additionally, the shells lobbed into the camp from army tanks based in Gush Qatif and from navy vessels posted at sea, send hundreds of shards of shrapnel upon explosion liable to maim or kill all within a 30 meter radius . . . Israel has recently begun usage of a robotic-crane arm that extends to a position that overlooks the alleyways of the camp. At the end of its full extension is an armoured stronghold within which three Israeli soldiers equipped with heavy artillery fire upon the camp.[77]

Moshe Dann, an Israeli-American tour guide, agreed to take me to Gush Qatif. He wore a baseball cap, aviator glasses and a .45 calibre pistol. With Moshe at the helm we were waved through military checkpoint after checkpoint. When we passed a Palestinian family on their donkey, he said, 'Arabs,' as if pointing out the local fauna.

'Why do you think this land is disputed?' I asked.

'Primarily because the Jews, the Israelis, came to live here. The ironic thing is that the Arabs here have benefited tremendously from the fact that the Jews have built up the Gaza Strip. There is tremendous prosperity [among the Palestinians] as a result of Jewish settlement . . . Look at this bridge, this overpass, coming up ahead. Now that's very controversial . . .'

We were passing the junction where Mona El-Farra had taken me. Through the heat haze, I could just make out the endless queue of Palestinian vehicles, in the potholes and sand, watching us pass. Beneath the overpass was the rubble of Mona's family home.

'Why is it controversial?'

'This road can only be used by Jews.'

'Why?'

'In order to protect settlers from terrorists. They have to separate the communities; they have no choice. See these barriers; there used to be homes there. They had to be bulldozed to stop the terrorists.'

'Aren't these settlements provocations, dropped on Palestinian land, and joined by Jews-only roads?'

'Well, this situation is relatively recent. It's only since Arafat started his terrorist attacks on the Jews. There was really nothing we could do to prevent it, except to bomb the cities.'

'What would happen if the Jews moved out?'

'I think, in terms of raising their families, this is one of the best solutions for them.'

'How?'

'Economic co-operation is the best way to create peace. That's what's going on here: economic co-operation between Jews and Arabs . . .'

As we pulled up at the gates of Gush Qatif, I said, 'Moshe, there are a lot of angry-looking people standing around here with guns: an interesting model of economic co-operation.'

Two young settlers began screaming at us and waving their automatic weapons. 'There's a small problem,' said Moshe. 'Stay calm.'

'What are they saying?'

'Fuck off.'

David Reishe, a settler who had agreed to see us, was summoned and, after a tense wait, he arrived and spoke to the screamers. 'Drive through quickly,' he said. Faces scowled as we passed them.

Then another country unfolded. Sprinklers played on fresh green lawns and flowerbeds bloomed in row upon row of suburban cottages, many with swimming pools. Healthy children played in the quiet streets; a man trimmed his hedge; a woman strolled by with her twins in a baby buggy. We nodded greetings.

David Reishe, a gentle-faced man in his forties, introduced me to his family and friends, who laid out sandwiches and pitchers of orange juice on a long table. Their friendliness was disarming; I liked them. I was shown around.

'Ah, the Middle East sun!' said David, reaching for a cap to cover his pale white pate.

'We are both fair Europeans . . .' I said.

Smiling at the irony, he said, 'I was born in Haifa.'

'An Arab city . . .'

'Yes, Jews and Arabs lived there together.'

'But your parents came from Europe.'

'From Europe, yes . . . But I grew up with Arabs. You could say I was friends with Arabs until Arafat stirred up all this trouble.' It was as if the *Nakbah* of 1948 had not happened and Dayan had not spread his hand in the sand. Arafat, the devil incarnate, had obliterated all that, corrupting the docile Arabs, once happy on their donkeys.

Walking beside a 'security wall' three times our height, taking care to hurry past the gaps, David Reishe struggled to answer my questions, bemused at my failure to comprehend his constant point of reference: the Bible. 'Once you understand that everything that's going on today is determined by a bigger force than all of us,' he said, 'then you see the *obvious*.'

'What is the obvious?'

'OK, my parents came from Europe, but I'm here because it's *our place*. That's obvious. I cannot give back something that's not for me to give back; and no-one can give it back: no politician, no parliament. Ours is a movement that goes back three thousand years when Moses brought us here and we had the dream of building a temple in Jerusalem.'

'Isn't that a religious belief?'

'No, it's stronger than religion. It's something a lot bigger. I mean, maybe the feelings are the same as religion, but it's something we *believe in*. My kids are educated to believe it. On their side, the religious Palestinians feel the same. Ask the Hamas people. I understand what they are saying. They also have this belief. But it's not in our hands; it's not in theirs. It's bigger than all the people here.'

'Where will it end if there is no compromise and no justice for an aggrieved people? Perpetual conflict?'

'Well, life is full of conflicts. Maybe I'm saying something too strong. I mean, it's one zero game. We will fight. It's either us or them. One zero, and we'll win it.'

'Doesn't that mean that one side must always control the other?'

'Please don't ask me about politics.'

'But all this is about politics. If we're to speak about taking territory in the name of a faith, a belief, that's an extreme form of politics. Where does it end? Does it go all the way to Damascus?'

'Well, that's a good question. But listen, we're building the Jewish country, *all* the Jewish country right here. And that includes Jerusalem. We would like to give our cousins, the Arabs, everything, but we can't give them Jerusalem. There was never in three thousand years another country here. There was only one country, the Jewish country. The Palestinians never had any country, OK? Neither did the Turks nor the Romans.'

'Do you really mean that the Palestinians were not here?'

'Only as singles. There was no country: no king, no power. The true borders were written in the Bible. There are no other borders.'

'What about the large numbers of human beings who don't believe what is written in the Bible?'

'Well, I believe it, and I am responsible only for my view. Anyway, the Qur'an or any other Muslim book does not speak about a country here. Only terrorists claim a country on the other side. Ours is a war against them.'

'Are Jews terrorists, too?'

'No, once you are fighting for Jewish rights, you are not like that. It's different. *We* are different.'

As we spoke, we could see in the distance an area known as al-Muwasi, where twelve thousand Palestinians were completely enclosed by the perimeters of Gush Qatif. There was nothing like it anywhere in Gaza, or indeed Palestine. It was 'a concentration camp within [the] concentration camp [of Khan Yunis camp].'[78]

These were the people Mona El-Farra had spoken about: 'the heartland of our suffering and resistance and the world knows nothing about them'. Al-Muwasi was shut off from the outside world. For months at a time, no cars or carts were allowed to enter or exit. Residents could bring in only that which they could carry in their hands. Non-residents were banned, and the local schools and clinics were crippled because the only professionals in Gaza were elsewhere. Even the dead needed special permission to be buried in the main cemetery of Khan Yunis.

On January 15, 2001, after a settler was killed by the Popular Resistance – which had nothing to do with al-Muwasi – 150 settlers crossed the perimeter and went on a rampage, burning and firing their weapons into houses, as Israeli soldiers watched. Three days later, a leaflet in broken Arabic was circulated in al-Muwasi: 'Arabs of Muwasi, beware of the Jews and clear out to Khan Yunis.' This was a glimpse of what had happened during the *Nakbah*. I found it hard to imagine David Reishe doing this.

After the rampage, the Israeli Directorate of Governmental Properties ordered twenty families to evacuate their homes in preparation for their demolition. Only the intervention of human rights groups stopped the demolition of thirteen of the houses.[79]

Those tormented made repeated appeals to the International Red Cross and other human rights organisations to protect them, but to no avail. 'After all,' reported *Behind the Lines*, 'even the International Investigative Committee for Human Rights Violations in the Occupied Territories headed by the UN visited Khan Yunis . . . and came under Israeli military fire that injured five people, forcing the delegation's prompt retreat.'[80]

While I was there, Sharon threatened to attack Gaza as part of 'Operation Defensive Shield'. People built pyramids of sand in the streets, as if this would stop the tanks. The queues for purified water grew longer. Fear was masked by bravado: children pointed their wooden Kalashnikovs at the sky; young men swaggered with knives and a few with pistols. A wedding shop displayed a poster of an Israeli F-16 crashing in flames and the mythical Palestinian rifleman who brought it down.

In the centre of Gaza City is an incongruous cluster of high-rise blocks built with European Union grants to the Palestinian Authority during the years of the Oslo 'peace process'. They have dilapidated as quickly as the dream of Palestinian autonomy, leading to independence, has faded. I took a lift to the eighth-floor apartment of Lama al-Hourani, a Palestinian lawyer who grew up as a refugee in Beirut and returned to Gaza to marry. I found her rejoicing that she was pregnant with her first child after fourteen years, and terrified.

'People ask me when I am expecting the baby, and I say, well, it depends on Sharon. Will he allow me to continue my pregnancy peacefully? He even controls my fear, turning it up when he wants to. Waiting for his invasion is worse than the invasion itself. In these high buildings, we are a target for the F-16s. You hear them flying low right through the night. You hear them coming in and you wait to hear the missile. You hear them going round again, looking for the target, whatever it is. The first time they bombed in Gaza, all the children in my building started crying. The electricity was cut, we lit candles and I sang to the little ones.'

'Do you think it compares with the fear of suicide bombing?'

'It's the same.'

'How did you feel when you first saw on TV the carnage caused by a Palestinian suicide bomber in Israel?'

'I cried. I saw children and women terribly hurt. I used to call my Jewish friends in Israel and tell them I needed to talk to a Jew frankly, to feel that I was still a human being: that I still had principles. I don't agree with the suicide campaign, morally or politically; it doesn't help the Palestinians. But now my reaction is different. I still don't agree with it, but I don't cry any more; I have seen too much on our side.'

'Why don't you still cry for the women and children?'

'Of course, they should not be killed. But I don't cry. That is what the occupation has done to me, to all of us.'

'Do you ever talk to Jewish friends in Israel about the ironies – the fact that they, too, come from a background of humiliation, of home demolitions?'

'Yes, I speak to them about it, but they are so sensitive. They say, "Please don't compare it with the Holocaust." I say, why shouldn't I? You do many of the same things that were done to you . . . horrible things . . . walling us in, forcing us out. We have this now in Gaza. "Closure" they call it. Listen to their officials and you can hear the echo of their own history. They say, "Look, we are allowing them food supplies, and medicines . . . See how well we treat them." That's what Hitler told the world. But it wasn't true. Now they are doing what Hitler did: destroying our land, confiscating our property, putting us in concentration camps, even stamping numbers on our hands. They, the victims, have become the victimisers. It's very strange to see that. And please don't say I am anti-Semitic, because I am a Semite, too. We Arabs are Semites. If Hitler had come to Palestine, he would have done the same to us.'

'What upsets you most of all?'

'The fact that in 1988 we, the PLO, took the initiative and recognised Israel and, in effect, said they could have seventy-eight per cent of Palestine. Eighty per cent of Palestinians still agree with that compromise. All we asked for was to be recognised, too: that we, too, could have our own state on the remaining twenty-two per cent of the land. In Israel, those who said they believed in justice, the left, were never frank with the Israeli public, who continued to be fed on propaganda that we didn't recognise them.

'Even today, Israelis are ignorant of the huge compromise we made. In those days, the media concentrated on a few hijackings, just as they now give the impression we are all suicide bombers. They never explain the frustration and the sense of betrayal that caused these things. Who ever points out that, in the first *intifada*, when suicide attacks were unknown, Israeli snipers shot at the heads of children who were only throwing stones? This one-sidedness upsets me deeply. If I go to Europe, I need hours and hours to convince people of our position, but an Israeli can do it in five minutes.'

'What do you ask of the outside world?'

'I ask only that international law is upheld, and we have back our occupied lands: the twenty-two per cent. That's the only way to save my people from Israel *and* to save them from going to extremes . . . I've been working on having a child for fourteen years now; I don't want my child to want to go to a Jewish settlement and kill people at the age of ten. That's what's happening now. Our children, aged ten, twelve, thirteen, are wanting to kill themselves. You should see the mothers cry.'

'What will you teach your child?'

'I will teach my child not to hate the Jews, but, like all Palestinians, I will need help from the world.'

Forty per cent of Gaza's population are under the age of fifteen.

They are what Mohammed Jarella called 'children of the dust': that is, children of consuming poverty and big families who, having somehow survived their first few years, seem able to endure extraordinarily. Their wonderful childishness, their rowdiness and giggles and charm, belie their nightmare. Not only are 60 per cent of child *intifada* victims shot at on their way to school, or at home, or at play, but unseen violence ravages their inner selves.

Dr Khalid Dahlan, a psychiatrist, heads one of several children's community health projects in Gaza. He showed me the results of a recent study. 'The statistic I personally find unbearable', he said, 'is that 99.4 per cent of the children we studied, in camps exposed to constant attack, suffer trauma. Once you look at the rates of exposure to trauma, you see why: 99.2 per cent of the study group's homes were bombarded; 97.5 per cent were exposed to tear gas; 96.6 per cent witnessed shootings; 95.8 per cent witnessed bombardment and funerals; almost a quarter saw family members injured or killed; more than a third saw their neighbours killed or injured.'

Other research shows that almost all Palestinian children suffer unrelenting nightmares and 'night terrors', insomnia and bed-wetting. Young children face the dichotomy caused by having to cope with these conditions. On the one hand, they dream about becoming doctors and nurses 'so they can help others'; then this is overtaken by an apocalyptic vision of themselves as the next generation of suicide bombers.

They experience this invariably after an attack by the Israelis, when playground conversation turns to 'martyrdom', because 'not even the schools are safe'. For some boys, their heroes are no longer football players, but a confusion of Palestinian 'martyrs' and even the enemy 'because Israeli soldiers are the strongest and have Apache gunships'.[81]

Dr Dahlan invited me to sit in on one of his clinics. Thirty boys aged between ten and thirteen sat at tables arranged in a horseshoe. 'Each one', he said, 'is traumatised. Each one has acute anxiety or depression or a sense of loss and isolation. Many suffer from all three. Today the activity is free drawing. They will put on paper what is in their minds. I give them no subject: no suggestions. My object is to help them release their fear.'

After half an hour, the children produced pictures on the same theme: violence and war. They depicted Israeli F-16s bombing schools, tanks firing at children, ambulances at checkpoints and women crying streams of tears. One boy's page was coloured entirely black except for a blood-red scribble in the middle. 'We Palestinian adults', said Dr Dahlan, 'often feel that all this violence and fear has taken away our capacity and our right to protect our young, who no longer trust us to care for them: to keep them safe.'

Driving back along the beach road, I stopped near the checkpoint overlooking the Netzarim settlement. It is a ghostly strip, with the giant toothless faces of unfinished and bomb-damaged buildings collared in white, gusting sand. Several were planned as tourist hotels. Overlooking the sea is a carnival, a fun fair, empty and ruined. Riddled with bullet holes, the brightly coloured equipment hangs precariously on its rusted hinges, swaying and clanking in the wind. The ferris wheel leans as if falling slowly; dodgem cars lie blown on their side, surrounded by live 50-calibre shells, each of which holds enough explosive to extinguish a human form. The fun fair was the only one of its kind in Gaza; it became one of the most dangerous places in Gaza.

From behind a brick building announcing itself as 'The Wedding Hall' emerged a tall, thin and frightened man. This was the caretaker, Walid al-Derawi. As we spoke, he kept looking behind me, towards the road. 'Although I feel safer standing with a foreigner,' he said through my interpreter, 'we may be shot at.' He said that the carnival was built in 1997 and was so popular that the Palestinian Authority believed it could recoup its investment of a million dollars. On holidays, families would come at sunrise and queue joyfully.

'One day in summer 2000,' he said, 'bullets suddenly pinged against the whirling ride over there. Children screamed and there was panic. More bullets came in, and several people were injured. That was the end of it. After that, the settlers over at Netzarim, and the soldiers, used this place as a shooting gallery. For a week or two, couples still came to get married in the Wedding Hall, but the snipers waited for them, then opened fire.'

Leaving Gaza, I was rewarded with a spectacle of Palestinian flags fluttering from inside the walled compounds of Jabalya camp.

Children are responsible for this, I was told. No-one tells them to do it. They make flagpoles out of sticks tied together and loose power lines and one or two will climb on to a wall and hold the flag between them, silently. They do it when there are foreigners around, and they believe they can tell the world.

Dori Gold is a senior foreign affairs adviser to Israel's prime ministers, notably Ariel Sharon. A former ambassador to the United Nations, he runs a 'think tank' in Jerusalem, the Centre for Public Affairs. He travels a great deal to the United States, where he promotes Israel in lecture tours. Television viewers around the world will recognise him as one of Israel's fluent, American-accented government spokesmen.

I arranged to interview him in his office overlooking a leafy street of whitewashed suburban villas. He is an avuncular, self-assured figure with refined, rehearsed arguments. He began by talking a great deal about Israel as part of the 'democratic Western alliance', standing shoulder to shoulder as equal partners in a 'war on terror'. He compared what he called 'Israel's regional difficulties' with the hardship of Britain during the Blitz.

I said: 'Israel is the fourth most powerful military nation in the world, certainly the regional superpower. It can deal with any military threat. Isn't the real cause of your people's insecurity the fact that you run a military occupation that holds captive another people?'

'That argument doesn't hold up,' he replied. 'Yes, up until 1993, the Palestinians were under us. But then we withdrew our military government and established a Palestinian Authority under Yasser Arafat. The Palestinians were no longer under Israeli military occupation, although it's true they didn't have an independent state, either. The only reason Israeli forces returned to the West Bank in September 2000 was because of the *intifada* that Arafat imposed on us. Had there been no *intifada* there would have been complete Palestinian self-government.'

'A lot of Palestinians did not want the kind of self-government that was a de facto colony of Israel. They knew that all Israel had to do was roll its tanks across the green line. So wasn't the intimidation of an occupation always there?'

'A military occupation is very carefully defined in the Hague Conventions of 1907. It means you have a military *government* . . . one reason why Palestinians speak about being under an occupation is because they have to face the charge that they are engaging in terrorism. When a young Palestinian straps dynamite to himself and walks into a crowded Israeli café, killing thirty Israeli teenagers, that is called terrorism. You don't need to be a lawyer to figure that out.'

'What about Israeli terrorism?'

'You have to be very careful with the language . . . Terrorism means deliberately targeting civilians. That's what IRA terrorism was all about in Northern Ireland. That's what happened on September 11, 2001; and that's what happens to Israeli schools, coffee shops, malls. Israel does not engage in terrorism. Israel specifically targets, to the best of its ability, Palestinian terrorist organisations.'

'How do you explain an Israeli sniper deliberately shooting an old lady hobbling along with a cane, trying to get to hospital for chemotherapy treatment? We'd be here all day citing other examples. Isn't that terrorism?'

'Unfortunately, in every kind of warfare, there are cases of civilians who are accidentally killed. Terrorism means putting the cross-hairs of the sniper's rifle on a civilian deliberately.'

'That's what I've just described.'

'No. I can tell you that did not happen.'

'It did happen just the other day and in front of the world's press. You see, that's the problem with your argument that terrorism exists only on one side. Don't you see that?'

'If you mix terrorism and counter-terrorism, if you create some kind of moral obfuscation, if you get muddled and say, well, the Americans and British operating in Afghanistan hurting an Afghan civilian are engaged in terrorism, then you will pull the rug out from beneath the entire Western alliance.'

'What rug?'

'The rug of keeping our societies safe.'

'Aren't you aware that many people in Western countries regard the bombing of Afghan civilians, *any* civilians, as terrorism?'

'Mr Pilger, do you regard the bombing of civilians by accident by the British as terrorism?'

'By accident?'

'I said "by accident" because I don't believe British troops would ever put civilians in danger deliberately.'

'That's a very touching belief.'

'Touching?'

'Britain has a rapacious imperial record in the Middle East, in your own country, and yes, I do regard the bombing of civilians as terrorism.'

'Mr Pilger, the reason I don't believe that would happen is that the British government is a democracy and has to be accountable.'

'May I ask how you justify your soldiers' violent behaviour at checkpoints, where they frequently humiliate people: the very kind of humiliation the Jews suffered?'

'I don't know what you're referring to . . .'

'I interviewed a woman who was not allowed through a checkpoint to hospital and lost her baby as a result. There are many similar cases.'

'I have seen with my own eyes the Palestinian Red Cross [sic] and ambulance carrying a young suicide bomber with a suicide belt around his body.'

'Where?'

'I have referred to it in writing. Please check the record.'

(I checked the record. In August 2001, Dori Gold told Agence France-Presse that four Palestinians had jumped from a Red Crescent ambulance in Nablus after shooting at Israeli troops. The four men were shot dead. Later, in an unusual admission, an army spokesman said the men had not been anywhere near the ambulance. 'There was a mistake in the field report of the event,' he said.[82])

I said: 'The checkpoint deaths have been verified by respected Israeli human rights organisations, such as the Physicians for Human Rights.'

'Checkpoints will end the moment that terrorism ends.'

'You must be aware that the overwhelming majority of civilians killed are Palestinian, that sixty per cent are killed in their workplace, at school or at home.'

'I haven't seen the data. There are many NGOs [non-governmental organisations] operating here, and some are funded by all kinds of strange organisations.'

'But there is a clear pattern in these killings, which, if it was happening to Israelis, you would call terrorism.'

'You know, Winston Churchill used to say: don't confuse the arsonist with the fireman. Yasser Arafat imposed a war of terrorism on Israel, and Israel responded. You have to understand there is a propaganda battle going on and it's no less intense than the actual warfare on the ground. We all have a responsibility to be aware of lies.'

'Does Amnesty International lie?'

'What do you mean?'

'Amnesty has documented Israel's use of "systematic torture and almost total impunity for unlawful killings of Palestinians, collective punishment, the use of human shields, people imprisoned without trial, the demolition of homes". Are they simply putting out propaganda?'

'Well, every case has to be examined and we have to respond.'

'But have they got it wrong?'

'I know of terrible abuses of human rights on the Palestinian side . . .'

'Have they got it wrong about Israel?'

'We have a system of laws. We have a justice system and a Supreme Court, which protects Palestinians . . .'

'Then why are so many Palestinians in prison without having been tried for any crime?'

'I tell you, we apply the law in this country.'

'Article 49 of the Geneva Convention says that no state is allowed to put its own civilians as settlers into occupied territories. That's the law of nations, and Israel has defied it. Isn't that correct?'

'Article 49 of the Geneva Convention was intended to deal with situations like the Nazi occupation of eastern Europe, not the case of Israel allowing Israelis and [other] Jews to live on the West Bank.'

'Mr Gold, that can't be right, because in October 2000 the United Nations Security Council called on Israel to respect the Geneva Convention, and the vote was unanimous.'

'We have a dispute over this question. We say it's a distortion to apply the Geneva Convention, which dealt with Nazi conditions in Europe, to the situation here.'

'In the UN General Assembly, the vote against Israel on this issue was one hundred and fifteen to two. Is the whole world wrong?'

'Look at what the General Assembly votes against! It even voted against the United States proceeding with a missile defence programme!'

'Are you saying that was foolish?'

'What I'm saying is that the General Assembly includes countries from the Non-Aligned Movement, so you're sharing your position with Zimbabwe, Cuba and Yemen.'

'That's only three countries, and I'm not sharing my position with anybody. The United Nations is the arbiter of international law, Israel is a member of the UN and the Security Council has delivered two hundred and forty-five resolutions about Israel's behaviour and the General Assembly's score is over five hundred. Isn't that an amazing record?'

'Here's the real question: does this attention of the Security Council and the General Assembly to Israel reflect the enormity of the problem here, or the politicisation of the UN system?'

'Doesn't it reflect, on the basis of Israel's record, that you are a rogue state?'

'The answer is this: did the signatories to the Fourth Geneva Convention ever meet to discuss the Soviet invasion of Czechoslovakia, and the Soviet invasion of Afghanistan, and Vietnam's invasion of Cambodia?'

'Are you saying the world has ganged up on Israel?'

'I'm looking for a fair standard. If the signatories to the Geneva Convention ignore so much and meet only when Israel builds condominiums in east Jerusalem, something is wrong with the functioning of the international community.'

'When will Israel agree to negotiate with the Palestinians, not for a colonial annexe but for a homeland as secure and independent as Israel itself?'

'Prime Minister Sharon has said he would accept a Palestinian state.'

'What kind of Palestinian state?'

'Do you want Israel to concede the terms of that negotiation in this public interview? Or is it better to agree the general principle?'

'What about the general principle of a state as independent as Israel?'

'We don't need a string of adjectives . . .'

'How can negotiations begin if the principle of an independent state is not a precondition?'

'Negotiations must not have preconditions.'

'But you already have preconditions. What about all those tanks and F-16s aimed at Palestine?'

'And what about the Palestinians?'

'Yes, they have suicide bombers, and they have some small arms and kids with slingshots . . .'

'No, no, no, no. That is not a proper comparison. The Palestinians have an alliance with the Arab states.'

'Can I ask you: have you yourself ever seen and experienced what life is like in a refugee camp?'

'Absolutely. And the camps should have been dismantled years ago, especially in Syria and Jordan, and the refugees brought into those societies. We took refugees from all over the Arab world: Jewish refugees. We integrated them into Israeli society.'

'What gives an American or a Russian the right to settle here when a Palestinian has barely any rights at all?'

'After centuries of anti-Semitism against the Jewish people, the international community recognised that the Jews have a right to a Jewish state in this, their historic homeland.'

'But didn't Israel come about at the expense of the Palestinian people who had nothing to do with the medieval traditions of Christianity, the source of anti-Semitism, and who weren't part of the Nazi project? They were simply the indigenous population.'

'A bargain was struck after World War One and confirmed by the Allied powers, that the Jews would have their state in this area and the Arabs would be free from the yoke of the Ottoman Empire. The Arabs got their states. All we want is a Jewish democratic state living in peace.'

'But should the Palestinian people pay the price for this by losing the very thing that the Jewish people asked for – a homeland?'

'We are willing to create a Palestinian self-governing entity. Some might call it a Palestinian state . . .'

'Mr Gold, you used the words "We are willing to create". What right have you to create somebody else's homeland?'

'We are being asked to negotiate that. We are willing to make a contribution.'

'The other day, I interviewed the father of a fourteen-year-old Israeli girl who was killed by a suicide bomber. He said the only way to stop the violence was to deal with the cause, not the symptoms. And the cause was an end to the occupation. Has he got a point?'

'He has a point that he is right to raise. But most Israelis voted for Prime Minister Sharon and we have a unity government that encompasses ninety per cent of the Israeli body politic. We believe that symptoms do matter: that terrorism must be eradicated. There is no grievance, no sense of deprivation that can possibly be articulated by strapping dynamite to a young Palestinian . . . nothing justifies that.'

'When those famous Israelis, like the late Prime Minister Menachem Begin, committed acts of terrorism just before the birth of Israel – such as blowing up the King David Hotel and killing ninety-one people – you could have said the same of them. What's the difference?'

'We have a new understanding now. After September 11, the world got a wake-up call. We have to remove this scourge [of terrorism] from the earth, whether you are talking about the struggle here or in Northern Ireland or Sri Lanka: all those places where terrorism has been used. The three democracies [Israel, the US and Britain] must make a global commitment to eliminate this threat from the world. Period.'

'Does that include state terrorism?'

'No country has the right to target civilians. We risk the lives of Israeli soldiers in counter-insurgency operations, so that we do not have to cause any damage, any losses on the Palestinian side. Twenty-three Israelis died in Jenin so that Palestinian civilians could live.'

'Are you serious?'

'All militaries today call in air strikes, use artillery, use all kinds of weaponry that we refuse to use. In the operation in Jenin, we took the decision to send in ground forces. Our soldiers died so that we wouldn't call in air strikes . . .'

'That's an incredible statement. The Israeli military attacked the refugee camp at Jenin with tanks and planes and armoured bulldozers that demolished homes with people in them.'

'I repeat: Israelis died so that Palestinian civilians could live.'

Tanks destroying Palestinian homes so that Israelis might feel secure; fairgrounds echoing to the sound of target practice rather than laughter; sprinklers drenching lawns in Jewish fortresses while the refugee camps run dry: I experienced many such dizzying inversions of the natural order on my journeys to the West Bank and Gaza to make a documentary film entitled *Palestine Is Still the Issue*. It was the second film to carry the title; the first I made twenty-eight years earlier.

The truth itself about Palestine has been inverted for so long, and so successfully, by Israel's friends in foreign governments and promoters in the media and elsewhere that any attempt to break Edward Said's 'last taboo' is met with orchestrated smear and disinformation.

The second film – whose interviews and research form the basis for this chapter – was broadcast in September 2002 on the independent television network in Britain and in other countries. It cast the conflict in Palestine as an historic injustice, which is the taboo.

In broadcast journalism in Britain and other Western countries, the Israeli occupation of Palestine is reported, at best, as a 'conflict' between two warring factions, each possessed of right and wrong and responsibility. Tim Llewellyn, a former BBC Middle East correspondent, calls this 'the tyranny of spurious equivalence'.[83] With exceptions, the media coverage is a variation of the state propaganda of both Israel and its Western backers.

The second *Palestine Is Still the Issue* showed the daily humiliation and cultural denigration of the Palestinians, the victims, and featured Israelis and Palestinians who were not stereotypical and expressed a desire for justice and reconciliation. Israel's leaders were called to account, as was Yasser Arafat; I described the Oslo 'peace process' as 'a classic colonial fix in which Arafat and his elite got the trappings and privileges of power while the mass of the people got what an Israeli journalist called the "autonomy of a PoW camp" '.

The official Israeli position occupied a significant part of the film; the longest interview was with Dori Gold, speaking for the Sharon government. Finally, virtually every word and frame was subjected to a forensic legal examination both for accuracy and to ensure compliance with the balance and fairness regulations in the UK Broadcasting Act.

The film was broadcast at eleven o'clock at night when most of its potential audience had gone to bed. Still, a million and a half people watched it, and many others read about it. Of the fifty-odd films I have made, only those on Cambodia and East Timor generated a greater response. Several thousand emails arrived at Carlton Television, the ITV production company. Most of those that were critical of the film came from the United States and other countries where it had not been shown. Many were abusive to an unusual degree. I was described variously as a 'demonic psychopath', 'a purveyor of hate and evil', 'an anti-Semite of the most dangerous kind'. My murder or that of my family was considered 'not a bad idea'.

Many of the emails were strikingly similar, having come via an organisation in New York called Honest Reporting. An investigation by the *Guardian* in February 2001 followed a similar blitz of accusations of 'anti-Israel bias' against the paper's Middle East correspondent, Suzanne Goldenberg (herself a Jew). This revealed that Honest Reporting, with subscribers all over the world, was a prime mover of the hyperactive outrage that seems to distinguish the pro-Israel lobby. It drafted complaints, provided generic material and coached people on how to attack allegedly 'anti-Jewish' work they had not seen.

Honest Reporting is run by a fanatical Jewish group called Aish HaTorah, which, reported the *Guardian*,

> verge on the colourful in their antics. Founded by Rabbi Noah Weinberg, who complains that '20,000 kids a year' are being lost to Judaism by marrying out, Aish invented speed-dating – eight-minute sessions in cafés to help New Yorkers find compatible Jewish partners. They're widely

regarded as right-wing extremists. And they're certainly not people entitled to harass the media into what they call 'objectivity'.[84]

The vociferous campaign did not stop at the internet. A letter from the Board of Deputies of British Jews, which describes itself as 'the representative body of the British Jewish community', repeated the wording supplied by Honest Reporting. Carlton's switchboard operators and duty officers were roundly abused and threatened; I received a number of death threats at home. The angry voices often bore English middle-class accents. A Jewish doctor in Cheshire said he was 'left wondering how much of Arafat's personal fortune has been transferred into John Pilger's personal fortune'.[85]

Farce intruded. Michael Green, the Jewish chairman of Carlton, publicly attacked his own company's film. In an interview with the *Jewish Chronicle*, he described *Palestine Is Still the Issue* as 'a tragedy for Israel as far as accuracy is concerned' and said he 'intended to make sure there is a programme that shows the Israeli point of view'. Having been alerted by the Israeli Embassy and the Conservative Friends of Israel, he had seen the film before it was broadcast and was 'extremely unhappy with it'.[86] Green had told no-one in Carlton's production department that he had seen the film or was unhappy with it. Neither did he have the right to commission a 'balancing' programme – that was the responsibility of the ITV network.

The next day, under the headline 'Carlton rebukes own chairman for attacking documentary', the *Independent* published a statement by Carlton's Director of Factual Programmes, Richard Clemmow, and Executive Producer Polly Bide. 'Carlton stands by John Pilger's programme and its accuracy,' it read.

The film went through the normal channels of editorial scrutiny prior to completion and senior executives at both Carlton and the ITV Network Centre approved its transmission. Michael Green's opinion is his own. He had no involvement in the programme or its transmission. The film sought to give a voice to people in the Palestinian and Israeli communities who are seldom heard.[87]

I wrote to Green asking for an explanation for his attack on my film. I received no reply. The day his *Jewish Chronicle* interview appeared, his assistant paid a visit to the company's press office and instructed staff to say that Carlton had received only complaints about the film. When it was pointed out that at least half the responses had praised the film, the assistant's reply was that Green had demanded that the company say they were all negative. Asked what inaccuracies Green had identified, he replied that 'this was Michael's opinion'.[88]

The press officer who looked after my films was Laurelle Keough, a feisty compatriot of mine. Green called her to his office on high in the Carlton Communications building in Knightsbridge. 'What newspapers do you read?' demanded the chairman (which Laurelle interpreted as a question about her politics). 'What do you think of Pilger? Isn't it true that everyone is hostile to this film?' She replied that this was not true and she asked him to substantiate his charges, which he declined to do. An Israeli government document subsequently turned up on her desk with a compliments note from Green. Shrill in tone, it dealt in generalisations.

As the head of a public broadcaster, Green's intervention was unprecedented in British television, and it had an immediate effect. I received more personal threats, including death threats. The Carlton chairman had not only provided inflammatory ammunition to an unjustified, orchestrated campaign against the film, but ensured that the positive public reaction was overshadowed. After two weeks, a majority of the emails, letters and phone calls received praised ITV for showing the film, complaining only about the late hour of its transmission.

This included a significant Jewish response. The distinguished London literary agent Jacqueline Korn (who is my agent) wrote to Green:

> That people should write disgustingly objectionable and threatening letters to John Pilger, both Jews and funda-mentalist Christians from the Mid-West, and make threatening and abusive phone calls to members of staff at Carlton, seems to me quite evil and as far removed from any moral sense as anything could be . . . it is about time

that Jews in the Diaspora stopped being so defensive . . . I find your position in all of this extraordinary.[89]

The playwright Harold Pinter described the film as 'both powerful and balanced, and necessary'. The actress Miriam Karlin wrote to the *Guardian*: 'Did the Board of Deputies and the Israeli embassy only see parts of the programme which made them feel, quite rightly, uncomfortable? We believe that three of the Israelis interviewed represented the best of Israel, humanity and true Judaism.'[90] The film's historical advisers, Ilan Pappe of Haifa University and Nur Masalha, Director of Holy Land Studies at the University of Surrey, wrote that it was 'accurate, balanced and admirable'.[91]

I was commissioned by the *Guardian* to describe the episode in a piece for its opinion pages. The day after this was published, and without consulting or alerting me, the paper ran a piece attacking both the film and the article under the headline 'Massacre of the truth'. The author was Stephen Pollard, a trenchant Zionist.[92] Such is the power of the pro-Israel 'lobby' – which, I should add, is not the 'Jewish conspiracy' that Zionists often use to invoke the red herring of anti-Semitism.

After itself receiving 116 complaints, the Independent Television Commission, the official body regulating commercial television in Britain, decided to investigate – even though 553 viewers had written to the commission praising the film. Of all my films, including those that have drawn fire from governments, *Palestine Is Still the Issue* has been the only one subjected to an official inquiry. For two months, the producer Chris Martin, Carlton's senior lawyer Stephen Rudoff and I toiled on a defence, the equivalent of a thesis.[93]

We replied in detail to the charge that the film had been 'highly selective of, if not distortive of [historical] facts'. We agreed that it had challenged what is known as the 'Israeli and patriotic version of history', which underpinned the great injustice done to the Palestinians. This was perhaps the most important part of the film; for no other modern state has been established by means of the expropriation and expulsion of an entire people.

The objections concentrated on my commentary that, in the

months and weeks before the establishment of Israel in May 1948, the Palestinians 'were expelled from their homes or forced to flee in a blitz of fear and terror'. This directly contradicted the 'patriotic version', which denied there was a wholesale expulsion and maintained that Palestinians fled their homes at the urging of Arab leaders.[94]

I have dealt with this in earlier pages, acknowledging the work of a group of 'new' Israeli historians who have opened previously inaccessible Hebrew archives and government files. These reveal that the flight of the Palestinians was the consequence of a tactic planned and executed by the Haganah (Jewish army) *before* the Arab states reacted to the declaration of the State of Israel – specifically 'Plan D', which aimed at gaining control of principal Palestinian towns. Avi Shlaim, professor of international relations at Oxford and author of *The Iron Wall*, wrote: 'Palestinian society disintegrated under the impact of the Jewish military offensive that got under way in April [1948] . . . by ordering the capture of Arab cities and the destruction of villages, [Plan D] both permitted and justified the forcible expulsion of Arab civilians.'[95]

We produced evidence that 369 Palestinian towns and villages were depopulated or destroyed prior to Israel's declaration of independence.[96] Drawing on official records, the Israeli historian Benny Morris documented massacre after massacre of Palestinian civilians, in such places as Deir Yassin, al-Dawayima, Eilaboun, Jish, Sfasaf, Majd al-Kurum, Hule Sasa and Lydda. In Lydda and Ramle, the scene of total expulsions, the authorised accounts refer to 'ethnic cleansing'. A Jewish brigade was ordered: 'Flight from the town of Ramle of women, the old and children is to be facilitated. The males are to be detained.'[97] Arriving at the scene, David Ben-Gurion, Israel's first Prime Minister, was asked by General Allon, 'What shall we do with the Arabs?' Ben-Gurion, wrote Morris, 'made a dismissive, energetic gesture with his hand and said, "Expel them."' The order to expel the entire population 'without attention to age' was signed by Yitzhak Rabin, a future Prime Minister.[98]

Morris reported the feelings of guilt that some expressed over this strategy. The Mapam Party co-leader Meir Ya'ari said,

Many of us are losing their [human] image . . . How easily they speak of how it is possible and permissible to take women, children and old men and to fill the roads with them because such is the imperative of strategy. And this we say . . . who remember who used this means against our people during the [Second World] war . . . we are appalled.[99]

In *Palestine Is Still the Issue*, I had said, 'In 1967, Palestinians once again fled their homes during the Six Day War when Israel occupied the remaining 22 per cent of Palestine, describing this as an act of self-defence.' This was described by complainants as wrong and offensive. That the Arab states attacked first, they said, was 'a matter of historical record'. Although Zionist propaganda had made much of six hundred thousand Jews pitted against five Arab states, the historical record offers a very different interpretation. Arab League armed forces, representing the five countries, had mustered merely twenty thousand men. Their heaviest armour consisted of twenty-two light tanks and ten ancient Spitfire aircraft. The Jews had fifty-two thousand active fighting troops, many of them highly mobilised, and a thirty-thousand-strong home guard, along with the Irgun, a 'special operations' or terrorist group.

The historian Patrick Seale wrote that the Egyptian army was far from threatening, with most of it bogged down in a civil war in Yemen. President Nasser, for all his bluster, had no wish to invade Israel. This was demonstrated by his decision to send only two divisions into Sinai, which he knew would be no match for the Israelis. It was a myth that the Arabs attacked first. While there was a single attack by Jordan, this came after 'so-called "pre-emptive" Israeli action'.[100]

On the Syrian border, it was Israel that invaded the demilitarised zone. In *The Iron Wall*, Avi Shlaim wrote that the war was 'unleashed by [Israel] issuing a series of threats . . . to occupy Damascus and overthrow the Syrian regime'.[101] In his classic text-book *A History of the Modern Middle East*, William L. Cleveland wrote that 'the legend of a defenceless new-born Israel facing the onslaught of hordes of Arab soldiers does not correspond to reality'.[102]

In January 2003, the Independent Television Commission announced that it rejected all complaints against *Palestine Is Still the Issue*. The commission praised the film's 'journalistic integrity', the 'care and thoroughness with which [the film] was researched' and the 'comprehensiveness and authority' of its historical and other factual sources.[103]

The judgement was a landmark, accepting not only that a documentary film about the *justice* of the Palestinian cause was 'balanced' within the terms of the Broadcasting Act, but also that it sought to redress an overall imbalance in the television coverage of Palestine and Israel.

Included in our submission was a study by Glasgow University's pioneering Media Group, which concluded that the public's lack of understanding of events in Palestine and their origins was actually compounded by television news reporting: in other words, the more people watched, the less they knew.

Viewers were rarely told that the Palestinians were victims of an illegal military occupation; the term 'Occupied Territories' was almost never explained. Only 9 per cent of young people interviewed by the researchers knew that the Israelis were the occupying force and that the illegal settlers were Jewish; many believed them to be Palestinian. The selective use of language by broadcasters was found to be crucial in maintaining this confusion and ignorance.

For example, words such as 'murder', 'atrocity' and 'savage, cold-blooded killing' were used only to describe the deaths of Israelis. 'The extent to which some journalism assumes the Israeli perspective', wrote Professor Greg Philo, 'can be seen if the statements are "reversed" and presented as Palestinian actions. [We] did not find any reports stating that "the Palestinian attacks were in retaliation for the murder of those resisting the illegal occupation".' The study concluded that news on British television reflected 'an overwhelming bias towards the policies of the State of Israel'.[104] It was a glimpse of the truth and of why the injustice in Palestine endures.

The BBC is subjected to 'unremitting' pressure from Israel and its friends, says former BBC Middle East correspondent Tim Llewellyn. The corporation's management 'is by turns schmoozed and pestered' by a 'skilful embassy and by Israel's many influential and well-organised friends'. This is 'productive, especially now that accusations of anti-Semitism can be so wildly deployed'. He describes

> an inbuilt cultural tendency in broadcasting newsrooms, easily exploited, to see the world in terms of "them" and "us" . . . The carnage in an Israeli shopping mall is somehow more evocative and impressive in news terms than the bomb that devastates the shabby apartments in an Arab slum. The words broadcasters so often use to explain those images stand in the way of them, as if to try and block them or ameliorate them, rather than tell of the horror they signify.[105]

The day after I returned from Palestine, I watched on the main BBC news a report from Gaza, which had been attacked by Israeli F-16 fighters and helicopter gunships. The casualties included children from three families. Standing in the blood-spattered rubble of an apartment, a BBC reporter described the attack as part of 'Israel's war on terror'. No irony resonated in his voice as he inverted the evidence all around him.

Shortly afterwards, the BBC's *Correspondent* series broadcast a report about the siege of the Church of the Nativity in Bethlehem, in which several hundred Palestinian fighters had taken refuge. 'The Israelis were determined not to damage the building,' began the narrator. 'The international press were cleared from Manger Square, but we were allowed to stay and observe the Israeli operation.' With this privileged access unexplained, the film introduced its star, an Israeli colonel who had 'guaranteed medical treatment to anyone wounded'. He spoke fluent English and was seen saying a cheery hello on his mobile phone to friends in London.

Without evidence or challenge, he described the Palestinians inside the church as 'killers' and 'terrorists'. His stated right to 'arrest' the foreign peace protesters who were also in the church drew no query from the BBC producer with him. And as the sun set behind his fine profile, the good colonel was given the film's last word. 'The issues' between Israelis and Palestinians, he said, 'were personal points of view.'

When the credits revealed that the film was actually made by an

Israeli production company, I phoned Fiona Murch, the executive producer of *Correspondent*. She assured me that there had been a BBC producer on location. Had he asked 'real journalistic questions', she said, the Israeli company, Israel Goldvicht Productions, would not have won the 'trust' of the Israeli army. That was the way of 'fly on the wall', she said. '[The film] was breaking a stereotype; it was about a good, decent man.'

I asked her why no reference had been made to the illegal occupation of Bethlehem and the rest of the Occupied Territories, and why no Palestinian was interviewed. She said I ought to have seen an earlier *Correspondent* film, which 'had Palestinians in it'. It is impossible to imagine the BBC employing a Palestinian production company to make a film that broke the stereotype and showed the 'good, decent men' who defended their homeland against the often brutal occupiers.[106]

This is not to suggest the BBC *never* looks critically at Israel. The reports of Jeremy Bowen from Israeli-occupied Lebanon come to mind. (The Israeli government refrain is that the corporation is permanently 'biased' against them.) But these are exceptions, and getting rarer. In 2001, a bold edition of *Panorama* examined the well-documented part Sharon played, as defence minister, in the massacres in the Sabra and Chatila refugee camps in Lebanon in 1982. The Israeli reaction was apoplexy, including threats of legal action, all of which came to nothing, except perhaps for the immeasurable effect on BBC managers; no comparable programme has since been made.

Orla Guerin, a BBC correspondent with a maverick's reputation as fearless and candid, came under intense scrutiny by the Israelis. From time to time, she showed the true suffering of the Palestinians. Like the *Guardian*'s Suzanne Goldenberg, she was the recipient of a stream of hate mail and the BBC of 'official' complaints whenever her reports suggested that the Palestinians were victims of an occupation. It was striking to observe the gradual change in her approach.

On May 12, 2005, I watched her report on Israeli Independence Day which, to Palestinians, is a day of grief as they remember the horrors of the *Nakbah*. She made no mention of the *Nakbah* and she interviewed no Palestinians. Illegal Jewish settlers in Gaza were given generous airtime in which to complain about 'being thrown out of our homes' should Ariel Sharon go ahead with his plan to 'disengage' from Gaza. Over close-up images of Sharon crying at a flag-waving event, she said: 'The next few weeks will be traumatic for him [Sharon] and his people.'

So 'embedded' is the BBC that at times it appears to be trying to compensate for any fleeting recognition of the Palestinians as peace-makers. On June 7, 2005, BBC radio news reported that British officials were to meet the Islamic organisation Hamas at 'low levels . . . mayors not implicated in the violence'. Most of the report was devoted not to the significance of the meeting (Hamas had agreed to be part of a Palestinian ceasefire) but to an Israeli government official repeatedly complaining about 'dealing with terrorists'. Not a single Palestinian was interviewed.

The report was an example of how secret history is kept secret, for no mention was made of the fact that the Israelis themselves had actually helped to set up and fund Hamas as part of 'a direct attempt to divide and dilute support for a strong, secular PLO by using a competing religious alternative', in the words of a former Middle East CIA official. His and other evidence is in documents obtained from the Israel-based Institute for Counter Terrorism.[107]

What Peter Beaumont of the *Observer* calls the 'psychological harassment' of journalists is matched by physical threats, and worse. Year after year, the Foreign Press Association in Jerusalem documents the intimidation, wounding and murder of its members by the Israeli army. To my knowledge, no foreign journalist has been deliberately harmed by the Palestinians. In a period of eight months as many journalists, including the CNN bureau chief, were wounded by the Israelis, some of them seriously. In each case, the FPA complained. In each case, there was no reply.[108]

Shortly before he died, Edward Said bitterly reproached foreign journalists for their 'destructive role' in 'stripping the context of Palestinian violence, the response of a desperate and horribly oppressed people, and the terrible suffering from which it arises'.[109] Some journalists will argue that the nature of their job is ephemeral and historical meaning is not their remit. But Jean-Paul Sartre was surely right when he wrote that 'historical conditioning exists every minute of our lives'. It makes no sense to suggest that journalism, unlike any other human activity, is devoid of consequence and absolved of responsibility. Just as the invasion of Iraq was a 'war by media' – caused perhaps as much by the neglect, silence and complicity of journalists as it was by politicians – so the same can be said of the one-sided 'conflict' in Palestine. In both cases, the consequence is the spilt blood of thousands of innocent human beings.

Censorship by omission, conscious or not, plays a major part. The *intifada* has almost never been reported in the 'mainstream' as a legitimate war of national liberation, an uprising against oppression, like any other. Real causes are omitted, like the overriding strategic importance of Israel to the United States and the related repression of a pan-Arab movement capable of challenging Western control of Middle Eastern oil, and the use of Israel as a testing ground for new American weapons and as a channel to anti-democratic clients the US is (or was) reluctant to support publicly.

In 1981, Yacov Meridor, chief economic co-ordinator of the Israeli Cabinet, said,

> We are going to say to the Americans, 'Don't compete with us in South Africa, don't compete with us in the Caribbean or in any other country where you can't operate in the open. Let us do it.' I even use the expression, 'You sell the ammunition and equipment by proxy', and this would be worked out with a certain agreement with the US where we will have certain markets, which will be left to us.[110]

Israel helped apartheid South Africa to develop nuclear weapons, and was a 'conduit' for American arms despite a UN embargo. The South African military used Israeli Uzi and Galil weapons, and its armoured vehicles were modernised by Israel. Israeli *kibbutzim* even manufactured helmets for the apartheid police. 'Israel is a source of inspiration for us,' said Prime Minister B. J. Vorster.

In Central America, Israel and the CIA armed and trained the Nicaraguan Contras, and the Guatemalan death squads, and the fascist military in El Salvador. Between them, they left at least a hundred thousand dead. Little of this was reported. It took the bravest of whistleblowers, Mordechai Vanunu, to tell the world that which correspondents in Jerusalem knew: that Israel had developed one of the world's most formidable nuclear arsenals.

The 'Oslo Accords' in the 1990s are an exemplar of the misreporting and omission of the real aims of Israeli and American power in Palestine. The 'peace process' was never about peace, but principally about greater Israeli control of the Occupied Territories, given international respectability. In 1997, Israel Shahak wrote, 'A tacit understanding exists between Israelis and Palestinians who attended the secret negotiations [in Oslo] to the effect that no autonomy in the West Bank and the Gaza Strip can possibly materialise even if the Oslo Accord mandates it.'[111] In 1995, one of the 'architects of peace', Shimon Peres, reassured the Israeli public: 'The deal kept the following in Israeli hands: 73 per cent of the lands of the [occupied] territories, 97 per cent of the security, and 80 per cent of the water.'[112] Many Palestinians understood this and suspected the collusion of Yasser Arafat and his elite, who would receive unaccountable petrodollars from the Gulf states and at least $100 million from the US for a 'security' apparatus that had all the trappings of a pampered palace guard that also acted on Israel's behalf.

Orchestrated by an American president eager to be remembered for something other than his affair with Monica Lewinsky and whose Zionist connections would help him pay off his debts, the 'peace process', wrote John Steinbach,

> provided perfect cover to implement the policy formulated by Ariel Sharon in 1977 called the 'Matrix of Control'. This called for the establishment of strategic hilltop settlements throughout the West Bank, to be connected by 'bypassing roads' and reserved for the exclusive use of settlers [and the Israeli army] ... the Matrix of Control was the tail that wagged the entire Clinton 'peace process'. It brought Israel seven years of feverish settlement activity (the number of settlers more than doubled during the years of the 'peace process') and enabled the construction of a web of Israeli army forts and twenty-nine highways, on which Palestinians were banned, funded by the Clinton administration.[113]

Only when the Oslo project was near completion, with the West Bank already transformed into a series of South African-style 'bantustans' (ghettoes is probably more accurate) and Israeli military control assured, did Prime Minister Ehud Barak present his 'generous offer' to Yasser Arafat at the final meeting in Camp David in July 2000 (which I have dealt with earlier in this chapter). The only new land he offered consisted of stretches of desert next to the Gaza Strip that Israel used for toxic waste dumping. The rest was a maze of settlements and military bases, which meant that a cantonised Palestine would have no direct access to its international borders and its citizens would continue to be subjected to more than three thousand Israeli military orders that overrode any Palestinian legislation.[114]

The absurd claim that Barak had offered '90 per cent' of the West Bank was reported without challenge across the Western world. Typical headlines were: 'Israel agrees to quit West Bank' and 'Israel ends Jews' Biblical claim to the West Bank'. When Barak finally walked out, he accused Arafat of 'rejection bordering on sabotage'. This was echoed by Clinton and became the official truth and the media's truth; it was also false.

'The facts do not validate that claim,' wrote Clinton's chief negotiator, Robert Malley, two years later.

> True, the Palestinians rejected the version of the two-state solution that was put to them. But . . . Israel rejected the *unprecedented* two-state solution put to them by the Palestinians [that provided for] a state of Israel incorporating some land captured in 1967 and including a very large majority of its settlers; the largest Jewish Jerusalem in the city's history; preservation of Israel's demographic balance between Jews and Arabs; security guaranteed by a US-led international presence.[115]

The omission of this truthful account from the American and British media, together with the demonising of Arafat (for the wrong reasons), laid the way for the election of Sharon in 2001 and the implementation of the plan he had called 'Greater Israel's next stage'. In 2004, he announced that Israel would 'disengage' from

Gaza and dismantle the settlements there. Hey presto, the war criminal was a peacemaker! 'I'm backing Sharon', said the headline over an article by the *Guardian*'s liberal Zionist Jonathan Freedland, who anointed Sharon 'the unlikeliest standard bearer for those who yearn for progress in the Middle East'.[116]

The opposite was true. Sharon's closest adviser, Dov Weinglass, who had invented the 'disengagement plan', disclosed that its aim was to distract attention from international criticism of Israel's construction of a wall across the West Bank, which the International Court of Justice had ruled illegal. 'It is designed to freeze the peace process,' he said, '[and] prevent the establishment of a Palestinian state [together with] discussion about the refugees, the borders and Jerusalem.' The settlements would be relocated rather than dismantled, so that the annexation of the West Bank and the apartheid wall would be approved by the Bush regime. 'Effectively,' he said, '[it means that] this whole package that is called the Palestinian state, with all that it entails, has been removed from our agenda indefinitely. All with a [US] presidential blessing and the ratification of both houses of Congress.'[117]

And that is what happened.

For three weeks in August and September 2005, the Israeli government and its promoters successfully distracted much of the world with a theatrical display called 'disengagement'. Given saturation television coverage, night after night, 'settlements' of messianic zealots, many of them foreigners and many wailing and disporting themselves for the cameras, their children told by their parents to wrap themselves in prayer shawls and sob and shriek defiance, were removed from Gaza.

'Those who claim, genuinely or dishonestly,' wrote Jonathan Steele, 'that the world's media are biased in favour of Palestinians had their argument collapse this week.' In making their 'painful sacrifice' for peace, as Sharon called it, the 'settlers' were evicted by Israeli soldiers given 'sensitivity training' to ensure their actions caused minimal 'pain'. Proper notice was given, transport was provided, generous compensation was paid in advance and new government-subsidised homes awaited them in Israel proper.[118]

Some 8,500 'settlers' were removed. By contrast, in the first ten months of 2004, as many as 13,350 Palestinians were made homeless by giant American-supplied armour-plated bulldozers. No warning was given; families often had no time to go upstairs and gather precious belongings. If they did not move immediately, the loudspeakers woke them up in the middle of the night; they risked being arrested or shot. There was no round-the-clock television coverage of this, indeed, hardly any coverage at all; no compensation was paid.[119]

Sharon was congratulated by George W. Bush for his 'historic and courageous actions', and for his 'boldness' by the chairman of the Democratic National Committee, Howard Dean, a liberal.[120] Blair said something similarly effusive, as did most of the editorials in the American and British press. However, warned Jonathan Freedland in the *Guardian*, if there were more evictions of 'settlers' from the West Bank, 'Sharon would be a hero no more'.[121]

He need not have worried. There was, effectively, no 'disengagement'. Up to mid-October 2005, at least 5,500 more 'settlers' had been moved to the West Bank than were removed from Gaza. Secretly, Israel has expanded its presence in the Occupied Territories, seizing more land than it gave up in Gaza. At the same time, Palestinian east Jerusalem is being surrounded by a frenzy of Jewish home-building. A new municipal boundary extends 45 miles into the West Bank, cutting off fifty-five thousand Palestinian families. Through this will run the apartheid wall which Israel is building in defiance of the International Court of Justice, dividing families, people from their places of work, children from their schools.[122]

For Sharon, wrote Jeff Halper, head of the Israeli Committee against House Demolitions, 'it's a done deal. [He] has finally fulfilled the task with which he was charged thirty-eight years ago by Menachem Begin: ensure permanent Israeli control over the entire Land of Israel while foreclosing the emergence of a viable Palestinian state.'[123]

Having rejoiced in the departure of the 'settlers', the people of Gaza are still being cut off from the outside world. According to James Wolfensohn, the former president of the World Bank and special UN envoy to the region, Israel is 'almost acting as though disengagement had not happened'.[124] The Israeli army, reported the Israeli news agency, 'is to build another security fence around the Gaza Strip. In the end, the system will comprise three fences, state-of-the-art electronic and optical sensors as well as remote control machine guns. This system should be completed in less than a year for a total cost of $220 million [paid for by the US taxpayer].' The writer Israel Shamir described this as 'entombment'.[125]

An Israeli geographer, Arnon Soffer, who advises the government on the 'demographic threat' posed by the Palestinians, told the *Jerusalem Post*, 'The pressure at the border will be awful. It's going to be a terrible war. So, if we want to remain alive, we will have to kill and kill and kill. All day, every day.'[126]

Since the settlers' departure, a new terror has begun. The Israeli air force is attacking the people of Gaza by releasing deafening 'sound booms' that cause widespread fear, induce miscarriages and traumatise children. Flying at low altitude after dark, aircraft create sonic booms that send shock waves across the territory and sound like earthquakes or huge bombs. The UN refugee agency said the majority of patients at its clinics were under sixteen and suffering from anxiety attacks, bedwetting, muscle spasms, loss of hearing and breathing difficulties. At Gaza's Shifa hospital, the number of miscarriages had increased by 40 per cent.[127]

One sonic boom was unintentionally heard in Israel. 'It was like a heavy bombardment,' reported *Ma'ariv*, the Tel Aviv daily. 'The noise that shook the Israeli skies was frightening. Thousands of citizens leapt in panic from their beds . . .' For this error, the military was forced to apologise to the Israeli public – while continuing its terrorism of Gaza.[128]

There was no apology for the murder of Iman al-Hams, a Palestinian schoolgirl aged thirteen who lived in Gaza's Rafah refugee camp. On November 15, 2005, an Israeli military court acquitted an army officer who had shot Iman seventeen times after he had been warned she was just a child and 'scared to death'. Having shot her as she walked away, the officer, who was not identified, 'confirmed the kill' to his soldiers, then emptied an entire magazine into her head. On a tape recording, he 'clarifies' why he killed Iman. 'Anything that's mobile, that moves in the zone, even if it's a three-year-old, needs to be killed,' he said. At no point had his troops come under attack. The court acquitted him of minor charges such as 'conduct unbecoming an officer'.[129]

As I have been writing this, two events have again placed

Palestine back on the front pages. First, Ariel Sharon suffered a
stroke, giving rise to a wave of propaganda to rival that of the
settlers' exit from Gaza. Overnight, Sharon was beatified. The man
whom the Kahan Commission said bore 'personal responsibility' for
the Sabra and Chatila massacres, who had already achieved infamy
in the massacre at Qibya, the man who destroyed Lebanon and
deliberately ignited the second *intifada*, was now the embodiment of
'peace' and 'hopes hanging by a thread'.[130] For Jonathan Freedland
of the *Guardian*, whose heart did 'plummet' at the news that Sharon
was mortal, Israel had 'lost its grandfather'. For behind that murderous
front was actually a dear old chap busily planning 'greater progress –
the partial ending of the occupation and the dismantling of illegal
settlements – than at any time for four decades.'[131]

In response to these fevered inanities, Karma Nabulsi, a
Palestinian, wrote of Sharon:

> His fate for us was a Hobbesian vision of an anarchic
> society: truncated, violent, powerless, destroyed, cowed,
> ruled by disparate militias, gangs, religious ideologues and
> extremists, broken up into ethnic and religious tribalism,
> and co-opted collaborationists. Look to the Iraq of today:
> that is what he had in store for us, and he has nearly
> achieved it.[132]

While Sharon lay in a coma, a majority of Palestinians dismayed
his backers by voting for Hamas to run their 'Authority' on the West
Bank and in Gaza. Washington and the European Union immediately threatened collective punishment of a people who had
exercised the very democratic rights Bush had claimed he was
bringing to the Middle East. The irony is ephemeral; the West and
Israel will have to deal with Hamas, which, aside from its closet
affair with the Israelis, has long offered a negotiated, long-term
truce.[133] On February 27, 2006, the Hamas leader, Ismail Haniyeh,
said, 'If Israel declares that it will give the Palestinian people a state
and give them back all their rights, then we are ready to recognise
them.'[134] This ground-breaking statement received minimal coverage
beneath headlines of the latest American, European and Israeli
threats.

From Gaza, Dr Mona El-Farra emailed me: 'We continue to struggle against this great injustice, and with the support of all people who are struggling against injustice, we might be able to succeed. I think so. I hope so. Please, don't forget us.'

In 1983, the Palestinian artist Mona Hattoum exhibited in London an extraordinary installation she called 'The Negotiating Table'. When I saw it twenty years later, I was reminded that the injustice done in her country was like a spectre: unmoving and watchful, regardless of the manipulations and deceit of the oppressors and their backers. 'The Negotiating Table' links deception with truth, illuminating both. This is how the artist herself describes it:

> The room is dark, lit only by a light bulb over a table on which the artist lies motionless. Empty chairs surround the table. Her body is bloodstained, covered with entrails, wrapped in plastic, and her head is firmly covered in surgical gauze. On the soundtrack news reports about civil war and speeches of western leaders talking about peace can be heard.

The droning, insincere, incessant voices of Western broadcasters and politicians, one merging with the other, clip upon clip, produced an unforgettable heightened reality. Art succeeded where journalism had failed; I don't believe anyone looking at this, transfixed as I was, would fail to grasp how the injustice in Palestine has been perpetuated.

I understood immediately the inhuman effect of the wall Sharon is building like a snake across the Occupied Territories. I recalled Palestinian villages I had seen on the Israeli side of the wall. Each is now surrounded by a separate, ring-like wall, making it an island and stranding the villagers in a kind of concentration camp. There is a tunnel through which they have to go to reach the rest of the West Bank. In the tunnel there is a portcullis, which the Israeli government can bring down at any moment, trapping them. The designers of the wall say this is more 'cost-effective' than the kind of manned checkpoint that trapped Fatima and caused the death of her baby.

I would add to Mona Hattoum's spectral work the voice of the unnamed author of this press release issued by the Department of Trade in London:

> Israel is a remarkable success story for British taxpayers. Although the country is only about the size of Wales, UK exports to this lively market have grown steadily. British exporters feel at home in Israel, and Israelis are very well disposed towards British business people. Moreover, our two prime ministers are in regular contact and have a good working and personal relationship. They brief each other and consult on recent political developments regularly.

A significant section of the British Labour Party once supported justice for the Palestinians. The massacres at Sabra and Chatila in Lebanon in 1982 reinforced this support, and Ariel Sharon was reviled for his part in the crime. This worried the Israelis, and in the 1990s a high-ranking official, Gideon Meyer, was posted to the London embassy with instructions to make contact with the new Labour leader, Tony Blair. Meyer invited Blair to dinner with Michael Levy, a London businessman with close links to the Israeli establishment. They got on extremely well. 'We both play to win, there are no prisoners,' said Levy of his tennis partner.[135] It was not long before Blair and his wife, Cherie, were flying first-class to Israel, all expenses paid by the Israeli government.

Levy returned disaffected members of the Jewish community to the party and raised the sort of money that would free the leadership from dependence on the unions, and Blair moved New Labour away from the Palestinians and sided with Israel. Front-benchers like Robin Cook, then the shadow Foreign Secretary, were obliged to clear their statements on the Middle East with Jonathan Powell, a former Foreign Office official who became Blair's chief of staff. One of Blair's first acts as Prime Minister was to reward Levy with a peerage and make him his 'special envoy' to the Middle East. Thus the British government accredited a passionate Israel supporter as its representative: an absurdity Mona Hattoum would appreciate.

On September 11, 2001, an arms fair was held in London's Docklands, backed by the Blair government. Many public events were cancelled that day, out of respect for the victims in the Twin Towers, but not this showcase for the latest weaponry. The Israelis had a whole pavilion there; one Israeli company, Raphael, exhibited its Gil-Spike missile, which had a proven record of use against civilians in south Lebanon and the occupied Palestinian territories and which the British Ministry of Defence wanted to buy.

The following year, Britain doubled arms exports to Israel *after* the Sharon regime had broken a written assurance that it would not use British military equipment in the Occupied Territories. BAe Systems was allowed to export vital military components for American-made F-16 aircraft and Apache helicopters, in which Israeli pilots frequently attack civilian areas.[136] Arming Israel, secretly and deceptively if necessary, was now British policy.

In April 2004, Baroness Symons, minister at the Foreign Office, replied to an article of mine in the *New Statesman* which said the government had licensed torture equipment for export to Israel. 'I can confirm that this was not the case,' she wrote.

The last public accounting of arms exports approved by the Foreign Office, the *United Kingdom Strategic Export Controls Annual Report* for 2002, confirms that a category of arms exports known as PL 5001 had been licensed for sale to Israel. This category includes 'leg irons, gang chains, electric shock belts, shackles, handcuffs' together with 'specially designed' equipment for riot control vehicles. As Amnesty International has reported frequently, torture is common in Israel's political prisons.[137]

Britain's arming of Israel is tiny compared with America's. F-16 fighters, Apache and Blackhawk gunships, a variety of missiles and other equipment: indeed, almost everything new on America's high-tech military drawing board seems to reach Israel. *Ha'aretz* noted in spring 2005 that the Pentagon's proposal to supply the

Sharon regime with a substantial number of bunker-busting bombs 'prompts concerns about a unilateral strike against Iran'.[138] Thanks to Washington, Israel's military is now the fourth largest in the world, with an air force more than double the size of the Royal Air Force and the French air force combined.

Israel's weapons of mass destruction are another taboo. American and other Western leaders never mention them. Developed under American sponsorship, chemical and biological weapons, including nerve gas, are manufactured at a top-secret research institute at Nes Ziona, near Tel Aviv.[139] With between 200 and 500 thermonuclear weapons and an advanced delivery system, Israel has supplanted Britain as the world's fifth largest nuclear power and may rival both France and China in the size and sophistication of its nuclear arsenal.[140] 'Arabs have the oil, but we have the matches,' boasted Sharon.[141]

The prime responsibility for this lies in Washington. The struggle in Palestine is an American war, waged from America's most heavily armed foreign military base, Israel. In the West, we are conditioned not to think of the Israeli Palestinian 'conflict' in those terms, even though the evidence is overwhelming. This is not to understate the ruthless initiatives of the Israeli state; but without F-16s and Apaches and billions of American taxpayers' dollars, Israel would have made peace with the Palestinians long ago. Instead of normality, its assigned role has been clear: the destruction of Arab secularism and nationalism.

The American and Israeli 'projects' have become virtually indistinguishable. When Israel attacked the Jenin refugee camp in 2002, US 'observers' were there. Two years later, when the US attacked Fallujah in Iraq, its marines used Israeli-instructed techniques, such as bulldozing homes and firing wire-guided missiles from helicopters and 'specially armed tank rounds to punch holes in buildings without totally collapsing them, as in Jenin', wrote John Cooley.[142] Television pictures of Iraqi prisoners hooded and trussed might have been taken in Palestine following an Israeli sweep. Methods of interrogation are shared: American abuses at Abu Ghraib prison in Iraq closely resemble those reported in Amnesty's reports on Israel.

The asymmetry of American 'aid' to the 'Israeli–Palestinian conflict' is revealing. With a population of six million, representing

0.1 per cent of humanity, Israel receives nearly 10 per cent of America's 'aid' budget – for arms and war equipment alone. This figure is due to rise to $2.4 billion by 2008. According to the Congressional Research Service, the same 'aid' budget includes $28 million 'to help [Palestinian] children deal with the current conflict situation' and to provide 'basic first aid'. So America arms and equips the Israelis, who bomb and shoot the Palestinians, who are then given American 'first aid'.[143]

Strategically, US and Israeli planning are almost identical. It was distorted Israeli intelligence channelled through a special unit in the Pentagon (the 'Office of Special Plans') that formed the basis for the Bush administration's lies about Iraq's non-existent weapons of mass destruction. Following the invasion, Sharon urged the United States to turn to Iran. In 2006, an attack on Iran is a real possibility, with Israel having taken delivery of some five thousand American 'smart air-launched weapons', including five hundred 'bunker-buster' bombs.[144]

For those inspired by the great international movement that helped to bring down apartheid in South Africa, the parallels with Israel, however imprecise, offer a way forward. 'Apartheid is a crime against humanity,' said Nelson Mandela. 'Israel has deprived millions of Palestinians of their liberty and property [and] perpetuated a system of gross discrimination.' The claim that Israel is a democracy is not dissimilar to the fiction shared by white South Africans. Elections, a parliament, courts of justice, even a certain freedom of speech were, and are, said to be the necessary trappings. Like the apartheid state, which enshrined racist white supremacy behind a democratic façade, the Israeli state is based on Jewish supremacy.

Jews in any country can come to live as full citizens in Israel while the indigenous population is denied the right of living in its homeland. Non-Jews are restricted in how much land they can own and where they can build their homes. Eighty per cent of land owned by Israeli Arabs has been confiscated. Along with Jews-only roads, there are now Jews-only leisure facilities, including beaches. 'More than 1,100 were detained, including children on school trips,' reported the *Guardian*, since 'the operation to create Jewish-only beaches'.[145]

Since 1948, the Israeli Supreme Court has dismissed all cases that deal with equal rights for Palestinians who are citizens of Israel, who comprise 19 per cent of the population (as distinct from Palestinians whose homes are in the Occupied Territories, or who were driven there). Forty-two per cent of these Israeli citizens live below the poverty line and are discriminated against in employment and education. It is a crime publicly to question Jewish supremacy in the state, and those who do so are prevented from standing for or holding public office.

On May 15, 2005, the Israeli parliament voted to extend racist amendments to the Law of Citizenship and Entry, preventing the reunion of up to twenty-one thousand families of Palestinians with Israeli citizenship and Palestinians from the Occupied Territories. According to the Adalah Legal Centre in Israel, the amendments 'create three separate ethnic tracks for citizenship in Israel: a track for Jews, a track for Arabs and a track for foreigners'.[146] As a result, families are permanently separated: wives from husbands, children from parents, some only a few miles from each other, kept apart by the razor wire, by guns at arbitrary checkpoints and now by a 'Berlin'-style wall. During Christmas 2005, for the first time, Bethlehem was walled off, its people corralled, its streets almost silent.

This systematic separation of families was a feature of South African apartheid, which United Nations sanctions and a worldwide economic, cultural and academic boycott helped to overcome. What country other than Israel would have enjoyed a complete absence of such international opprobrium while oppressing another people over four decades? And why, whenever there has been a call for a boycott of Israeli universities, has the cry of 'academic freedom' gone up from those who have never spoken out about Palestinian freedom? Why, whenever there has been a call for a boycott of Israeli cultural institutions, has the cry of 'artistic freedom' gone up from those who have said nothing about the systematic smearing of shit on children's paintings at the Cultural Centre in Ramallah, the trashing of original manuscripts, the theft of musical instruments, the prevention, day after day, of children going to school?

Why, whenever there has been a call for a boycott of Israeli sporting teams, has the cry of 'keep politics out of sport' gone up from those aware that Palestinians are often denied a real football to kick in the dust of their prison camps? Why, whenever there has been a call for a boycott of Israeli products, has the cry of 'freedom to trade' gone up from those who have remained silent while thousands of the same children, their societies wilfully cut off from any trade, suffer acute malnutrition?

'While there is this silence, this looking away, this profane abuse of our critics as anti-Jew,' said Rami Elhanan, the Israeli father who lost his daughter to a suicide bomber, 'we are no different from those who stood aside during the days of the Holocaust. We are not only complicit in a crime, we ensure that we ourselves never know peace, and our surviving children never know peace. I ask you: does that make any sense?'

3

Shining India

Starvation is the inevitable result of globalisation
and its policies, which have transformed food from
a basic need to which everyone has a right into a
globally traded commodity.

Vandana Shiva

The crows beat their wings against the bay window, waiting to
ascend and dive. Their cries are incessant; it is their apocalyptic
swarm that is different in India. They dance in the black rain as the
monsoon envelops Bombay, hovering above the sea with its
putrefied flotsam of sewage and fish entrails; they perch on a billboard image of young businessmen, who are light-skinned and
joyful and celebrating their ownership of a mobile phone that
features a TV screen. The young businessmen and the fat crows
overlook a pyramid of rubbish, which is inhabited by a scabrous dog
and darting rats (with an eye to the crows) and by a tiny human
being, her sari glued to her by the rain, digging methodically with
her hands.

Bombay is India's richest city. It handles 40 per cent of the
country's maritime trade; it has most of the merchant banks and two
stock exchanges and a population density rising to one million
humans per square mile. Delight and shock are simultaneous
responses. Raise your eyes and the magnificent gothic edifices of the
British Raj seem hardly real: the Rajabai Clock Tower, which once
chimed *Rule, Britannia!* on the hour; and epic indulgences, the
greatest railway station in the world, through which a million
workers pass each day, with its stained-glass elephants overlooked
by a British lion and an Indian tiger sculpted by the students of John
Lockwood Kipling, father of the poet who was born here; and the
Prince of Wales Museum (it is still called that on the streets, just as
Bombay's new name, Mumbai, is all but ignored), with its
collections that whisper a cultural history few Westerners know,

its perfect dome dominating the Crescent Site that leads to the Gateway of India, which was built to welcome the British emperor and oversaw his exit.

In Victoria Garden, the rain sheets down on Prince Albert on his steed, and people walk as if in an exercise yard, round and round, past the incredulous reindeer and the listless tigers. An ice-cream van plays 'Things go better with Coke' in Hindi. Nearby is what is called the 'rail roads' district, which foreigners rarely see; it says nothing has changed. People here have fled their land tenancies in utter hunger. Once, the city offered work in and around its textile mills, but these have been replaced by 'ITES parks' (call centres and other IT 'enabled services').

The conditions these latest refugees live under are barely describable: an extended family of twenty is squeezed into a packing case, the sewage ebbing and flowing in the monsoon; in the dry season it stays. Fat crows wait, as ever, or ride on umbrellas; skeletal dogs chew at nothing. Yet glimpse inside this stricken Lilliput and there is new-pin neatness, clothes wrapped in plastic and the children in vivid colours. It is both haunting and humbling, always, to see such dignity: that of a poor man, wrote Nissim Ezekiel in his poem 'Island', 'taking calm and clamour in his stride'.[1]

But why should they? I met a man from Bengal who has been saving weeks for the equivalent of six pounds, which would buy him a shoeshine stool; he discussed his predicament with me; he asked for nothing. He, and they, are aliens to the beaming faces on the billboards, and the question is always the same: why should such a rich and resourceful and culturally wise society, with its democracy and memories of great popular struggle, live like this? When I was last in Bombay a generation ago, I asked the great Bollywood film director Raj Kapoor why poverty was so resistant in India.

'Outsiders misjudge us,' he replied. 'We are a dynamic society. But most of us are forced to live a life preordained by powerful groups for their benefit. The point is, they need the poverty, which is very good for their enrichment, for raising political hopes, for passing out food parcels, so to speak, and for reinforcing divisions of religion and caste. However, all that is distraction: just as my movies are distractions. When people fully understand this and act, things will change in India.'

Two years earlier, in 1971, I had put the same question to Prime Minister Indira Gandhi. She and the Congress Party had just been re-elected by a huge majority. Her campaign had been one of promises, and the poor voted for her. 'After independence,' she said, 'I realise that somewhere along the way our direction changed. We had a choice. Either we bought foreign goods or we helped the industrialists grow rich. So now we have a middle class and we have poor people who know they are poor. That is the beginning of our great change.'

The 'great change', apart from her disastrous imposition of martial law followed by her own assassination, never happened. Rather, it happened in the 1990s, when the steady enrichment of 'the industrialists' under Congress governments gave way to a strain of imperial capitalism, designed in England in the late eighteenth century. In *The Discovery of India*, written in 1944, Jawaharlal Nehru foresaw this latter-day version of the 'corruption, venality, nepotism, violence and greed of money of these early generations of British rule in India [that] passes comprehension'. It was, he added, 'significant that one of the Hindustani words which has become part of the English language is "loot" '.[2]

He was referring to the East India Company, or the 'Honourable East India Company' as it was known in the imperial legends taught to my generation. We were not to know that it would be the model for the multinational corporation and the 'global economy'. Today, a revisionist respectability is being awarded it by popular histories and exhibitions at the British Library and the Victoria and Albert Museum. Yet, like modern India itself, this most rapacious arm of empire and pioneer of modern consumerism, observes the historian Nick Robins,

> has more profound and disturbing lessons to teach us. Abuse of market power; corporate greed; judicial impunity; the 'irrational exuberance' of the financial markets; and the destruction of traditional economies . . . none of these is new. The most common complaints against late twentieth and early twenty-first century capitalism were all foreshadowed in the story of the East India Company two centuries ago.[3]

The East India Company's 'CEO' was Robert Clive. 'Clive of India' looted, literally, Bengal's treasury of all its gold and silver and loaded it onto a fleet of more than a hundred boats. The 'profit' to the company was £2.5 million (more than £200 million today), of which Clive's cut was £234,000 (£20 million). The 'multinational' was born, conceived by a breed known as speculators, who in 1784 drove up the price of food beyond the reach of India's poor. 'Estimates vary,' wrote Robins, 'but up to ten million people may have died of starvation.'[4] In a country which, in the seventeenth century, was the 'agricultural mother of Asia and the industrial workshop of the world', where the weavers of cotton enjoyed a higher standard of living than their counterparts in England, life under British rule became a lesser commodity.[5]

On December 12, 1876, *The Times* confined its report of a cyclone that killed an estimated quarter of a million Bengalis to the following: 'The calamity is not likely to give rise to much material distress among the people. Government relief centres have been opened [but] no large sums of money will be spent and care will be taken to leave everything as far as possible to private trade.' Of the legacy of empire, Nehru wrote prophetically: 'Entangled in its meshes, we have thus struggled in vain to rid ourselves of this past inheritance and start afresh on a different basis.'[6] Today, the legacy has new life in the modern imperial cult of 'neo-liberalism'.

With the rise of the Hindu nationalist BJP-led government in the 1990s, India was shorn of Nehru's paternalism, and the divided society described by his daughter was licensed by the International Monetary Fund. The barriers erected by the Congress Party to protect Indian industry and manufacturing were demolished. Coke and Pizza Hut, Microsoft and Rupert Murdoch entered what had been forbidden territory. The slogan 'Shining India' (or 'India Shining') was invented by an American advertising firm, Grey Global Group, for the same class of illusionists who now celebrate Clive of India and his looters: Shining India would catch up China as an economic power, the Indian middle classes would grow rich and poverty would be eradicated.

Indeed, the official 'truth' in Delhi at the close of the twentieth century was that the number of Indians living in absolute poverty had fallen by as much as 10 per cent. In his landmark study *Poverty and Inequality in India: Getting Closer to the Truth*, Abhijit Sen reveals that the Indian poor actually increased, and that for them the 1990s was a 'lost decade'. In 2002, those in absolute poverty made up more than a third of the population, or 364 million people. 'Inadequate nutrition is actually far more widespread than either hunger or income poverty,' he wrote. 'Half of Indian children are clinically undernourished and almost forty per cent of adults suffer chronic energy deficiency.'[7] India is home to more people living in poverty than any other country in the world.[8] 'It is better to be a poor person in Botswana or the Occupied Territories of Palestine than one in India,' wrote the *Hindu* journalist Palagummi Sainath.[9]

For the poor, denied the few 'safety nets' of the old era, life was harder. For most of the rest, little had changed. In India's most modern city, 40 per cent of the population have no access to safe drinking water. 'The food and water in Bombay', wrote Suketu Mehta in *Maximum City: Bombay Lost and Found*,

> are contaminated with shit. Amoebic dysentery is transferred through shit. We have been feeding our son shit. It could have been in the mango we gave him; it could have been in the pool we took him swimming in. It could have come from the taps in our own home, since the drainage pipes in Bombay, laid out during British times, leak into the fresh-water pipes that run right alongside. There is no defence possible. Everything is recycled in this filthy country, which poisons its children, raising them on a diet of its own shit . . . In other countries, there is a kingdom of the sick and a kingdom of the well. Here, the two are one.[10]

Certainly, India's growth rate has leapt above 6 per cent, but this is about capital, not labour, about liberated profits, not people. The hype about a high-tech India storming the barricades of the first world is based largely on myth. This is not to diminish India's rise to pre-eminence in computer technology, with its computer-literate generation in Delhi and Bombay and Bangalore, and distinguished alumni (such as the inventor of Hotmail); but this new technocratic class is tiny and, looked at from the peaks of India's struggle for freedom, it becomes an almost melancholy curiosity.

The famous call centres (known in India by their Orwellian moniker, Business Processing Outsourcers, or BPOs), where educated Indians affect knowledge of British and American 'lifestyles' and speak in American accents and call themselves 'Jerry' and 'Sonia' in order to service the likes of American Express, employ only about 245,000 people. For those reaching higher, the most ruthless meritocracy in the world awaits them. Out of the two hundred thousand applicants for places in the network of elite universities that make up the Institute of Technology, only forty succeed.[11]

Since 1993, the so-called consumer boom in India has embraced, at most, 15 per cent of the population, for whom the new prosperity has meant the acquisition of basic modern living amenities, rather than cars and mobile phones. For the majority of Indians, the 'global market' has a meaning familiar to the majority of humanity. As the billboard images of role models with white skin and good teeth have gone up, so already fragile public services have deteriorated. According to United Nations figures, India spends less than 1 per cent of its gross domestic product on health and, in the health services available to most people, ranks 171st out of 175 countries, just ahead of Sudan and Burma. Yet spending on private health, which only the well-off can afford, is among the highest in the world.[12]

Indian newspapers reflect this gulf in striking ways. The *Indian Express* presents a searing investigation into appalling hospital conditions, then trumpets India's inclusion in a facile 'best countries in the world' list drawn up by the American magazine *Newsweek*, based entirely on the country's 'neo-liberal reforms'.[13] *The Times of India* reports that Maharashtra's Director of Health is off on 'a plum assignment' with the World Health Organisation. He will be absent for four months, conducting a health survey in South-East Asia. During 2003–4, in his domain, some nine thousand tribal children – the very poorest – died from malnutrition and a lack of medical care. The state's Acting Chief Justice has criticised him for 'negligence' of duty. 'The deaths are common,' the Director replies, 'and I have done enough in the past ten years.'[14]

There is much about this story that explains why the majority of Indians shocked their betters by voting out the BJP-led government in 2004. With its $100 million 'Shining India' campaign, the government saturated the media with messages and images of consumerism: the young men with good teeth and the cleverest mobile phones became symbols of a 'feel-good factor', another Americanism. The absurdity of this became apparent when people tried to translate it into a native Indian language. 'Good' became *gur* (cane sugar) in Hindi, and farmers would ask: 'What is this sugar that is made from "feel"?'[15]

A majority of Indians voted against this version of corporate globalisation, which the BJP had blended with its communalist and xenophobic *Hindutva* ideology. The peasant farmers driven to contemplate suicide by the spiralling rise in the price of food grains, whose availability had fallen to a level lower than that recorded in the great Bengal famine of the 1940s, the women who carry water great distances and whose children die unrecognised by the state, the youths with no hope of work, let alone a mobile phone that takes pictures, voted for *swadeshi*: economic justice that affirms basic needs and the right to human dignity. Although aimed at a fundamentalist regime whose economic 'reforms' had reinforced their poverty, their votes were an angry scream against an elite that has made them all but invisible since independence.

Like Indira Gandhi, her daughter-in-law Sonia Gandhi led the Congress Party to its unforeseen victory by speaking against poverty, though rarely against the elitism that controlled and entrenched it. When she stepped aside as the new prime minister, the man who replaced her, Manmohan Singh, made it clear there would be 'no rollback' of the 'new market'. India, rejoiced *Newsweek*, 'is headed in what the smart money believes is the right direction'. The magazine offered a glimpse of this 'right direction' by devoting two pages to an attack on India's pharmaceutical industry for having produced life-saving drugs cheaply. The 'exposé' lauded the new government's decision to obey the World Trade Organisation and 'spell an end to quick and cheap generic drugs' for the poor.[16]

This has meant a gold rush of foreign companies conducting clinical tests on poor Indians. Given the rise of the cost of research in the West, India is suddenly a profitable location. Offering a poor person $100, a small fortune, for using an untried drug, makes a mockery of the spirit of informed consent. 'Third world lives are worth less than European lives; that is what colonialism was all about,' said Srirupa Prasad, a professor of medical history and bioethics.[17]

In its election campaign, the Congress Party used the slogan 'What did the common man get?' It is a question the party of freedom might ask itself. For example, since the beginning of 2005, the Congress-controlled Maharashtra state government has demolished ninety thousand homes of Bombay's poorest, adding three hundred and fifty thousand to the street population. The city's authority has announced its intention of making Bombay 'the next Shanghai' by 2010. This is known as 'Vision Mumbai' and is the invention of the American consultants McKinsey.

The people made homeless lived in Ambujuradi and Bhimchaya, on the edge of a mangrove belt. They had been moved there in 1992 from another slum demolished in a previous scheme. They are the people on whose backs modern Bombay was built. The new middle classes have depended on them as cheap builders, cheap cleaners, cheap nannies, cheap messengers. 'There is no alternative,' said the state chief minister, Vilasrao Deshmukh, apparently unaware of the notorious echo in his words. 'Many people will be inconvenienced and will have to make sacrifices.'[18]

My first sight of India was in the summer of 1966, an inferno. The monsoon had failed completely and the yellow heat had turned unyielding farmland to dust. Crows perched on the walls of the mission hospital at Nasirabad, a hamlet in the state of Rajasthan, which was officially in 'a situation of great need': the euphemism for an extreme drought beckoning famine. Unable to sleep in the heat, I listened to human noises, thin and distant, laments rather than cries for help. Who were they? A woman facing the loss of her first-born? Another drawing her sari over an empty breast, while her baby clawed blindly at it? A fatalist decreeing that his people's miseries be atoned for by his own death? Or simply someone who was hungry and who was dying?

There was no water, except that left muddy and polluted at the bottom of the few remaining wells, and that brought by camel and lorry. People came to Nasirabad like nomads to an oasis, and at night they lay outside the hospital: leather heads in fiery red turbans, brown mites with bent backs and limbs as wide as the pigtails that hung down their backs, their hands torn from heaving on a rope for half a pail of brackish liquid. No-one begged. Supplicants out of desperate need, there was a grace to their wretchedness as each accepted four ounces of wheat, which was said to be enough to exist on.

Twenty miles to the south were several villages that had not been abandoned. A light shower had fallen during the night and people had been up since four o'clock scooping the puddles into clay water carriers, the indispensable *matkas*. Most of the water was given to two valuable goats while families prepared to walk three miles to another village which had a working well; they would make this journey in temperatures reaching 42 degrees Centigrade three times a day. All the men had a tell-tale hump on their left shoulder: a purple misshapen swelling caused by lifetimes of carrying *matkas*. 'Does it ache?' I asked one of them. 'Head hurts, feet hurts,' he replied, 'but not this; it's dead.' The boys had the beginning of the hump. In good times, they said, when the rain came, they lived on *roti* and chilli paste and water; without water, the youngest had begun to die. 'What do you want to be when you grow up?' I asked a twelve-year-old. 'A soldier of India,' he replied, drawing his bent body to attention and saluting.

More than 70 per cent of Indians live in villages and depend on agriculture. The conditions I found forty years ago have not changed. Not only is malnutrition rife among the minorities, the 70 million tribal people and 150 million Dalits (untouchables), but the 'lost decade' has laid waste the lives of small farmers of *all* ethnic groups. Almost every day the newspapers carry a village suicide story. In the Guntur district of Andhra Pradesh, reported the *Indian Express*, fifty-five farmers had taken their own lives in two months.[19] 'The suicides are our hidden scandal,' the environmentalist Vandana Shiva told me. 'They are an epidemic, running into many thousands. Governments dare not admit the true figure.'[20] Debt, often owed to moneylenders at interest rates of up to

120 per cent, is aggravated by the neo-liberal 'free market' in the patenting of seeds and natural fertilisers by foreign bio-science companies: 'the piracy of our life source', as Shiva calls it.

'All across India,' she writes, 'farmers are pushed into debt, destitution and suicide as they are sucked into the global markets for costly seeds and chemicals. These global markets increase production costs by 100 per cent, while imports of highly subsidised, artificially cheap products force the crash of prices for indigenous products in a skewed market.' The 'liberalisation' of seed imposed by the World Bank has forced farmers into buying expensive hybrid seeds and chemicals they cannot afford. 'Pollinated seed varieties that can be saved and replanted', writes Shiva, 'are instead replaced by hybrid seeds that must be purchased every year from [foreign] corporations.'

She cites two cotton-growing regions where suicide levels are at their highest: Bhatinda in Punjab and Warangal in Andhra Pradesh. In both regions, 'opening up the market' for seeds has pushed farmers into terminal debt.

> Not all the indebted farmers took the ultimate step of suicide. Bobby Ventaka Reddy, for example, fell deeper into debt as spurious seeds and chemicals ruined his crops year after year. Continuously harassed by moneylenders, he heard of a broker who helped farmers to earn money by selling their kidneys ... this was a better option than suicide, so he took it.

The surgery has left him weak and unable to work. While the government will not admit it, thousands of 'globalised' Indian farmers sell their kidneys in order barely to survive.[21]

But people are not still; alternatives exist. Since the nineteenth century, mass movements in India have demonstrated that the Indian poor need not be weak, embodying Shelley's rallying cry: 'ye are many / they are few'. It was the unarmed masses that forced the British out, and their organisations remain the touchstone of progressive political life, from the million-strong all-female Self Employed Women's Association (SEWA) to the socialists who run West Bengal. Elected in 1978, the popular communist government has introduced and administered Operation Barga, which keeps track of and registers every one of the state's 2.3 million share-croppers. Each tenant farmer is sought out and his rights are explained to him, and the government's political organisation in his village ensures that he can get long-term loans and is not intimidated by landowners. Operation Barga is regarded throughout India as a success, especially as rice production in the state has soared.[22]

The antithesis of this is to be found on the fringes of the cities, which offer an apocalyptic warning of what happens when people are driven off their land. The Indian countryside is not overpopulated; its population density is less than the Netherlands. But its cities, the likes of Bombay and Calcutta, seem about to explode.

As my plane approached Calcutta, the progress of events during the five months since I was last in Bengal was clear. It was November 1971. Beyond Dum Dum airport's sprawl of permanently in-complete terminal buildings lay a city of refugees that had grown almost to the size of Calcutta itself. Three million more had come from East Bengal (then East Pakistan), the equivalent of Birmingham erected virtually overnight. They lived in large water pipes awaiting installation, in tents or huts, or under corrugated iron, hessian and straw. The cholera epidemic that had broken out among the first arrivals had been contained, and the children were now dying from common diseases like chicken-pox. It was the eve of the war between India and Pakistan that created Bangladesh.

Satire was close at hand. Calcutta, which lives at night in an unrelieved brown haze caused by smoke from thousands of little wood fires mingling in the humidity with unchecked industrial filth, had been ordered to 'brown out' in the event of an aerial attack by Pakistani forces. Civil defence units in soup-plate helmets and *lungis* toured the streets announcing an air-raid warning practice during which, they said, 'everybody must stay indoors and remain in the face-down position until the siren has ceased to operate'. The fact that a third of the population had no doors to stay inside, let alone roofs to stay under or walls to stay between, apparently had not occurred to the relevant authorities.

I set out for Flower Street in Taltolla, the poorest, most crowded district. Flower Street was a microcosm of Calcutta. Most of the people there lived under the sky and without work, sanitation, education or adequate nutrition. The water pipes, which Messrs Jessop & Co. had laid beneath Flower Street a century earlier, had long passed their life expectancy and had burst and were surrounded with sewage. The street's only water pump was inscribed, 'WASTE NOT, WANT NOT – 1914'.

My friend Dudley Gardiner worked in Flower Street. A rumbustious tank of a man, Dudley was a former sergeant-major in the Royal Fusiliers who had come to Calcutta after taking part in the 1956 Suez invasion, which he saw as an attack by a rich country on a poor country and which so distressed him that he set out to make his own amends. Every day, in his battered Land-Rover, he brought essential supplies to people in Flower Street. 'Call it *political* charity if you like,' he would say, gruffly.

Dudley had an uncommon view of Calcutta. He saw it as a vivid expression of humanity and its citizens as immutable heroes; merely to survive in such a place was, he argued, heroic. He never saw himself in the same light. My memory of him is standing over a disabled boy called Pabul Ran, whom he fed in the street where the boy lay and lived, his umbrella at the ready to ward off pariah dogs and the sky assault of crows. 'He was born on my birthday and I've been feeding the little bastard ever since,' he said. 'The bloody trouble is, when I go, he'll go.'

Dudley suffered from a blood disease which caused gross swelling of his legs and he suffered in the heat. When I called at his home, which was a room bare except for a bed, a chair and a few snapshots from his army days, the door was bolted. Someone came up the stairs and said he had been ill and had been taken away; he did not know where. I left a note under his door and walked to the corner of Flower Street, where Pabul Ran, the little bastard, lived. But he was not there either.

I shall always appreciate Dudley's sense of history. The heroism of people, he said, had been 'passed down' since Clive of India began stripping *Sonar Bengal* – Golden Bengal – of its 'inexhaustible riches' and since the Victorian trading masters established on the banks of the Hooghly an Asian Manchester, where people who previously had had enough to eat were enticed off their land so that fortunes in manufacturing could be made on their labour.

Clive of India's heirs could be glimpsed less than half an hour's drive away. The Tollygunge Club, which had been considered slightly but significantly inferior to the Calcutta Club until the latter 'went native' after independence, was preoccupied with preparations for the Ladies' Rose Bowl swimming competition and the brains trust in the writing room and the poolside dance and bingo. The times had not mitigated the exclusiveness of the club, whose membership now included local Congress politicians aspiring to be the new Raj. Maoist guerrillas had hurled a bomb at the gymkhana horses, which was bad enough; then one of the bombers turned out to be 'that agreeable little wallah' who had held aloft an umbrella on the green for the members. Naturally, all the 'umbrella boys' had to go.

Now and then, an Indian Army brigadier would appear on the terrace of the club or in the foyer of the Grand Hotel, which faced the *maidan* and from which it was possible to discern the pear shape of the Empress Victoria rising through the filthy haze. I found these former KCIOs – King's Commissioned Indian Officers – exotic hybrids. They strutted and spoke as Sandhurst and its Indian off-shoots had taught them, and they commanded sanitised nations within the nation: vast military cantonments in which hunger and disease did not exist. India has more than a million men under arms in three brigades, thirty divisions, thirty-five squadrons and forty-six warships, consuming almost half the national budget. Since independence, arming India has been an article of faith for the former Raj. Tony Blair's government spent almost six years persuading Indian politicians to buy sixty-six Hawk fighter jet air-craft, worth billions, in a country where, as Abhijit Sen wrote, 'half of Indian children are undernourished'.

Walking along Chowpatty Beach, the concave figures huddled beneath rattan and hessian are barely noticeable. The property rising above them is worth more than in London or Paris. The speculators call it 'brown gold'. This is where the rich and the upper echelons of the new middle class live. On some days, they seem an illusion made real by the advertising directed only at them and by a press that sends more than four hundred reporters to cover a fashion show, yet all but ignores the agricultural crisis that affects 70 per cent of the population. At dinner parties, people speak longingly of the authoritarian rule in Singapore, Malaysia and China. Democracy, they believe, 'causes disunity and waste in India'.[23]

Down below their apartments is where the Quit India movement once held its great freedom rallies; Laburnum Road is nearby, and the house where Gandhi lived and learnt spinning and devised his great non-violent movement. Today, it is a museum; there is a letter from the Mahatma to Hitler, urging him to mend his ways, but no sign of my favourite Gandhian quotation: 'First they ignore you, then they fight you, then you win.'

At the Oxford Book Store in Churchgate, I attended the launch of a book by the Mahatma's grandson, Rajmohan Gandhi, a biography of Ghaffar Khan, the inspirational 'Muslim Gandhi' and opponent of Partition. 'India is in many ways a violent country,' he told me. 'The fact that we have democracy today is largely due to the non-violence of the freedom movement.'

Democracy perhaps, but freedom waits.

4

Apartheid Did Not Die

We, the people of South Africa, declare that our country belongs to everyone and that all our people shall share in the wealth.
> *Freedom Charter, African National Congress*

Just call me a Thatcherite.
> *Thabo Mbeki, President of South Africa*

If the ANC does not deliver the goods, the people must do to it what they have done to the apartheid regime.

> *Nelson Mandela*

A watchtower stood silhouetted against Table Mountain, lit by spokes of early morning sunlight; gulls floated on the wind and two ostriches strolled beside the gently rolling surf. Beneath us was the summit of an ancient mountain long submerged in the brackish waters at the tip of Africa, a place of limestone and granite and twenty-two shipwrecks. 'Apparently that's the quarry where they worked,' said the Afrikaner helicopter pilot as he banked, unaware that one of 'them' was sitting next to him. Kathy – Ahmed Kathrada – looked down and nodded, his dark glasses covering eyes damaged by the glare of the limestone where he and Nelson Mandela and Walter Sisulu and other dangerous men had wielded a pick, year upon year, decade upon decade.

On March 21, 1960, a massacre changed almost everything in apartheid South Africa. When police shot dead sixty-nine people in the town of Sharpeville, an 'armed struggle' was declared by the African National Congress and the Pan African Congress; house arrests followed and the leaders went underground. The eventual arrest of Mandela, Sisulu and Kathrada, together with Govan Mbeki, Denis Goldberg, Raymond Mhlaba, Elias Motsoaledi and Andrew Mlangeni at the Rivonia farmhouse, the ANC's secret head-quarters, led to the 'Rivonia treason trial'.

On June 12, 1964, they were found guilty of sabotage against the state (even though the armed struggle was barely in its planning stage) and sentenced to life in prison. The following day, all but Goldberg, who was sent to a prison with a whites-only section, were flown to Robben Island to begin their sentences. 'It was a bitterly cold winter's day,' recalled Kathy as we landed on the same asphalt strip thirty-three years later. A sign on an arch says 'We Serve to Work', and when Kathy first saw it, it reminded him of *Arbeit Macht Frei* ('Work Makes you Free'), which he had seen on the gates at Auschwitz.

'I was thirty-four years old and the only non-African. [He is of Indian descent.] For this reason, I was the first to be issued with a prison uniform. Race determined every action. I was given the regulation shirt, jersey, canvas jacket, trousers, socks, shoes. It was so cold; yet Mandela and the others were given short trousers, no socks and, as a special favour, shoes instead of the rubber-tyre sandals normally given out to Africans. But they *had* to wear short trousers, and there could be no concession, not even in winter. The rationale of apartheid was quite simple: Africans were regarded as children. And that's still true. You'll find, in whites' homes, they talk of their garden boy and their kitchen girl.'

He led me along the battleship-grey corridors, which were silent except for the sound of the wind and the ocean and our footsteps echoing on the buffed floor. 'We Serve With Pride', said another sign. Kathy shook his head. 'This is it,' he said, turning the key in the door of what looked like a stone closet, five feet by five feet. We entered and the two of us all but filled it. 'I slept on that floor for the first fourteen years. I had no bed, just a raffia mat. That's all. I got a bookcase and eventually I was allowed to make a table.'

'How long were you in this cell?' I asked him.

'Almost eighteen years . . . with the light always on, always burning bright.'

'It was never off?'

'Never.'

'Did this place always stay a cell, to you, through all those years?'

'No. I was in it often twenty-three hours a day and I suppose I gave it a bit of me. I tried to give it colour. I used to order Christmas wrappings and paste them on the wall and all over my bookcase: anything but the grey. Life is not grey.'

'What did you miss most of all?'

'The presence and sound of children, their laughter, even their crying. I didn't have children myself . . . The system understood this longing, and the comfort of even a suggestion of normality, and when the warders brought their families, we were made to turn our backs. That was hard.'

'How did you get news?'

'In the first few years, we were allowed one letter and one visit every six months, and the letter had to be not more than five hundred words. My first letter was withheld from me because they objected to the contents. Eighteen years later, I was finally given it, and the objectionable part was: "There has been a change of government in Great Britain. Harold Wilson and the Labour Party are now in power." That was considered dangerous. More than anything, they feared us having information.

'In 1976, I needed medical treatment that was only available on the mainland. Once off the ferry, the route our car took, I was told, was to avoid newspaper posters. At the doctor's surgery, we sat in the waiting room, and to the horror of my guards, other patients arrived and opened up their newspapers. They were told to put them away, and some refused, of course, and so the warders formed a human wall around me so that I couldn't read the headlines.'

During a raid on his cell, the warders found a photograph of a white woman, Sylvia Neame. The senior warder, Lieutenant Fourie, declared, 'Kathrada is an Indian and I can see no reason why he wants a photo of a European woman . . . He is not allowed to be in possession of a photograph of a European woman in his cell.' He tore it up and threw it at Kathy's feet. Sylvia Neame was Kathy's lover. Under apartheid, intimacy between the races was a crime. She, too, was a member of the resistance and later imprisoned.

He took me to Mandela's cell and I stared in awe at its confinement; then we walked out into the sunshine and laughed about idle things and reflected on what Kathy called the 'amazing luck' of the white population as the beneficiaries of a generosity called 'reconciliation'. I wondered how it was possible for him to emerge from a quarter of a century of incarceration (only two years fewer than Mandela) as a sane, rounded, tolerant and humorous human being.

He said the influence of Gandhi had taught him to avoid bitterness; in a letter from prison, he had written, 'Unfortunately, my nature will not allow me to harbour hatred for anybody, no matter how deeply he may have wounded my feelings.'[1] When I asked him how he endured, the three reasons he gave were the inner strength he drew from his loved ones, his communism and, above all, the struggle he shared with his Robben Island comrades.

'I'll give you an example,' he said. 'When one of us became demoralised, we were never alone. The senior people, Sisulu and Mandela, regardless of their own personal problems, were always there to help those of us in need. They would bring toothpaste and soap to those who had run out of money. When an epidemic of influenza hit us, Mandela and two or three others cleaned and emptied our latrine buckets, brought us water and food. Once, I had a bad back, I couldn't move and empty my bedpan. The others just appeared, Mandela and the rest, and took it and cared for me and saw that I was all right.'

In his letters from prison, Kathy refers affectionately to Mandela and Sisulu as 'the geezers', because they didn't approve of the pop culture that interested him. 'You see,' he wrote in 1988, 'the geezers are generally mission-educated men . . . They tend to be rather strait-laced, which immediately restricts conversation to kosher subjects, absolutely forbids the telling of "rude" jokes, as well as the use of four-letter expletives – even in anger!'

Mandela's self-control and reluctance to show emotion, especially after visits by Winnie or old friends, exasperated Kathy. 'We are convinced (and told him so)', he wrote, 'that if he were to be called to the office and told that he would be released, he would return to the cell and tell us after an hour or two as if it is simply one of those everyday things.'

I asked him how the geezers regarded him. 'Not once was there a show of ill-feeling toward me,' he said, 'because, as a non-African, I was treated slightly better by the system than they were. I had slightly better food: more sugar and a quarter loaf of bread, whereas Mandela and the others were not allowed bread. After protests for a year or two, African prisoners were allowed to purchase bread at

Christmastime. That is how struggle in prison works. After three or four years, we succeeded in equalising clothing, so the African prisoners could wear long pants. Equalising food took longer – over a decade actually – but eventually we succeeded. In our way, we were continuing the fight against apartheid.'

The exercise yard at Robben Island has a long wall, which Kathy touched almost reverentially. 'Before this went up,' he said, 'we had a garden here. It took years to get permission for it, and it was a real gain, particularly as it played such a part in the writing of Mandela's autobiography, which was written on the island, secretly and illegally. Mandela would write ten or twelve pages at a time, give it to me for my comments, and to Walter Sisulu for his comments, then he would do the final version, and hand it over to another ANC prisoner, Mac Maharaj, to transcribe into small handwriting. Mac was brilliant at that, and would reduce six hundred pages to fifty pages or less, which he concealed, and I won't go into where. As for the original, it was buried in the garden in plastic containers. The idea was that as soon as Mac was released after twelve years, he would take the copies to London and send me a signal to say it had arrived safely with the publishers. Then we could destroy the originals.

'But all of a sudden they started building this wall, and one Sunday morning, there was Mandela and me and one or two others digging furiously to rescue the originals. We got some of it before we were caught. Our offence was that we had abused the privilege of study, and our books were taken away and our studies suspended.'

'For how long?'

'Four years.'

He spoke as if years were months, even weeks. Meeting Robben Islanders like Kathy, and glimpsing their life, is to understand how the struggle against apartheid in South Africa and around the world drew such strength from their example of moral and physical courage and limitless ingenuity. For this reason, Robben Island became known as the 'university of the struggle'. It was also a hell-hole.

Johnson Mlambo, 'a twenty-year-stretch man', wrote a fellow prisoner, 'was made to dig a pit big enough to fit him. Unaware of what was to follow, he was still digging when he was suddenly overwhelmed by a group of convicts. They shoved him into the pit and started filling it up . . . When they had finished, only Mlambo's head appeared above the ground. A white warder, who had directed the whole business, urinated into Mlambo's mouth. The convicts tried to open his tight-locked jaws, but could not . . . The warder pissed and pissed . . . When [he] had finished . . . vicious blows of fists and boots rained around the defenceless head sticking out of the ground.'[2]

Humiliation and brutality, at once systematic and arbitrary, exemplified apartheid, as I soon found out as a young reporter on assignment to South Africa in the 1960s. On my first day I was taken to a bar in Johannesburg, typical of the smoky, sweaty, almost sinister, wood-panelled holes-in-the-wall where the clientele consumed vicious varieties and quantities of local brandy. Everyone was drunk; most were legless. A formidable native journalist and muck-raker, Meish Levin, had taken me to this place: to 'initiate you, man'. Meish, who hated apartheid, had distinguished himself a few weeks earlier by walking up to Johannes Vorster, the State President, at Jan Smuts Airport and shouting, 'You're nothing but a fucking Nazi, man!'

Once inside this rotting place, we were snared by a barfly who insisted on telling us about his Scottish heritage, which apparently made him superior to 'the Boer'. He also wanted us to know how well he treated blacks. 'You don't buy that bullshit of the kaffir being badly off, do you?' he said, and without waiting for an answer, he shouted to the Greek landlord, 'Hey, Nick, bring out your kaffir!'

A black man, of indeterminate old age, emerged, and the barfly crooned at him, 'Here, boy, get me some Rothmans from the machine over there.' The old man got the cigarettes and handed him the change, which the barfly threw on the floor. 'That's yours, boy,' he said, 'all of it! See my friends, see how good we treat kaffirs!' The old man went down on his knees and scooped up the change.

The year was 1967. I flew down to Cape Town on a South African Airways aircraft whose blinding tangerine and gold

Lizette Talate, a Chagos islander, whose family 'died of sadness' following their expulsion by the British government.

A United Nations Palestinian refugee camp following the birth of Israel. 1948.

A Palestinian youngster, Gaza. 2002.

Israel's apartheid wall separating the Palestinian town of Ram from an Israeli road. 2006.

South African boxer Ronnie van der Walt, whose career was ruined when the apartheid regime 're-classified' his race from 'white' to 'coloured'. 1967.

John Pilger interviews Nelson Mandela, Cape Town. 1997.

Jonathan Shapiro ('Zapiro'), *Mail & Guardian*, Johannesburg. 2000.

South Africa's new black rich, Durban Derby. 2005.

Kabul's buses, scrapped by Western-backed warlords. 2005.

Dr Sima Samar is sworn in as Afghanistan's first Women's Affairs Minister.
She was soon hounded from office and today fears for her life. 2001.

US soldiers give orders to Afghanis outside Bagram base, near Kabul. 2005.

Afghanistan has more uncleared landmines than any country. 2001.

The 'new' India. 2004.

upholstery matched the Bavarian-style hats of the stewardesses. The woman sitting next to me asked what I thought of South Africa, as many whites did, especially those who regarded themselves as liberals. 'Isn't it a beautiful country?' she said, not bothered whether I replied.

The taxi from Cape Town airport was driven by a thin, tooth-less man who chain-smoked and had the sallow skin and hollow eyes of South Africa's poor whites. 'No view like it in the world, eh?' he said, with a touch of menace, as Table Bay spread before us. 'See Lion's Head? And that shape out there, that's Robben Island, where we keep the terrorists.' Mandela and Kathy had barely begun their quarter of a century in the limestone quarry.

Cape Town reminded me a little of Sydney, where I had grown up: its face turned towards the ocean and the wind, the bleached, surfy, apparently relaxed way of the whites, many of them 'trying to get a colour up' on fine beaches, from most of which people whose colour was already up were banned. The difference from Johannesburg, I was told, was that some people with 'mixed' on their birth certificates lived almost as whites. They broke the law every day by sitting in whites-only seats on buses, attending whites-only cinemas and even cohabiting with whites.

For those who found this continuing round of deceit too much and wanted to put the final official seal on their honorary white status – those who, in a poignant local expression, decided to 'try for white' – there was an incredible apartheid institution called the Race Classification Board: incredible, that is, to outsiders, but both credible and vital to those who had thrown their life's gambling chips on white. If they could convince a tribunal of three that their appearance was white and they were generally accepted by 'the public' as white, the Board might exercise its power to alter the race classification on their identity card. The prospect was a lifetime of privilege, or humiliation. Black-skinned people, of course, need not apply.

A few weeks before I arrived, the South African parliament had passed the Population Amendment Bill, which tightened apartheid by requiring, in an appeal for race reclassification, not only 'appear-ance and acceptance' but also 'proof of descent'. Only a fool tried for white now, for the new law said that 'coloured' descent meant 'coloured' for life, no matter the 'whiteness' of one's skin. With typically meticulous devotion to detail, the legislators of apartheid made the amendment cover the 353 people then waiting for their race to be 'reclassified'.

This obsession with race was the dark heart of apartheid, and its victims were the saddest people. I came to meet one of them, a boxer called Ronnie van der Walt, who had received a letter from the Ministry of the Interior that was to change his life. The letter began, 'In terms of the Population Distribution Act, you are hereby classified as a Coloured Person.'

Ronnie van der Walt was a local hero, the welterweight who had beaten Willie Ludock, the South African champion and leading contender for the world title. He was widely tipped to be the next champion. And he was an Afrikaner; his name and language were the products of Afrikanerdom; he was the proud grandson of Johannes van der Walt, one of South Africa's greatest wrestlers. He had gone to whites-only schools, fought on the lucrative whites-only circuit – 'coloured' boxers, no matter how good, were lucky to get the equivalent of £5 a fight – and, most important, he regarded himself as a white man invested with the Afrikaner's ingrained sense of exclusivity. Naturally, he was a lifelong supporter of Dr Hendrik Verwoerd's National Party.

To official eyes that had followed his career and the rapid rise of his popularity, however, Ronnie van der Walt was suspect. He was swarthy, as my taxi driver was and as many Afrikaners are: the result, more often than not, of prolific sexual contact between their white settler ancestors and Hottentot and Khoisan in Cape Town and blacks in the isolated farming areas. That aside, someone in the boxing world probably bore Ronnie a grudge, and this was a sure way to get rid of him. On the day he received the letter from the ministry, a copy of which had gone to the Cape Boxing Control Board, he was due to fight in a tournament at Cape Town's Green Point Stadium. His name was promptly deleted from the programme and posters with his picture were torn down.

'We had to do it,' the secretary of the Board, Sydney Beck, told me, 'or Ronnie would have been fined or gaoled. The law says coloureds and whites can't step into the same ring and Ronnie, the poor bastard, is now a coloured.'

I met Ronnie and his wife Rachel in their Dutch colonial farm-house, eight miles from the city. The walls were full of Ronnie in his glory: Ronnie after this knockout, Ronnie receiving that trophy. And there was an oval portrait of grandfather van der Walt, his face very stern and very white. 'I apologise for my red eyes,' said Ronnie. 'To be honest, I've been anxious and confused for months, ever since I received a letter from the Race Classification Board.' This had summoned him to Room 33 in the Old Training College Building and instructed him, in a handwritten 'PS', to 'bring your wife and children'.

'I saw two men at different times. They tried to be polite, but it was difficult because they asked me questions like, "Who are your friends? Are they white?" One of them said, "All right, then, what are your fans? Aren't they your friends?" I said some of them were, but, man, I can't help it if coloured people like to watch a good fight. Why shouldn't they? The second man walked round Rachel, my wife, and the kids, peering at them from every angle like you do when you buy an animal. He said nothing, just peered. Then he whispered, "Don't worry, I'll do my best for you." The children didn't understand, of course, but, I tell you, we all cried when we got outside.'

To Ronnie, the shame of being declared a coloured man meant wearing a hat for the first time in his life, wide-brimmed and pulled down over his eyes. 'In the bus today, I compared my bare arm with the man in the seat next to me. If I'm black, I must be dreaming . . .'

The van der Walts' ordeal in Room 33 was mild compared with that of others summoned before the Board's Star Chamber. Theirs was also one of the few cases which, because of Ronnie's standing in the sporting world, reached the press. Even when a case went to the Supreme Court for further appeal, no names were published and the hearings were secret – out of respect, claimed the government, to people who, in their desperation to be classified white, were forced to renounce everything of which their ancestors might have been proud. Such professed humanitarian concern was charlatanry; the proceedings in Room 33 were secret because, as Meish Levin put it, 'it's there that apartheid presents its arsehole'.

After transacting a bribe, I was smuggled into the Old Training College Building in Queen Victoria Street, and to the second floor where I took a seat at the back of Room 33. Here was apartheid's horrific quackery on display, its moral and intellectual mutation made to appear normal with 'procedures' and 'guidelines' and decision-making based on 'criteria'. Laid out like a magistrate's court, with a witness box and tables for counsel representing the 'applicants' and the Ministry of the Interior, it was presided over by three officials, whose dour, fraudulent respectability was expressed in an exaggerated courtesy that was both bizarre and brutal.

The first family to be ushered in was a middle-aged man, his wife and their two sons, aged ten and eight. They were *veld* Afrikaners and their case was not uncommon: the youngest son had been born with negroid features and, although he had been registered at birth as white and baptised in that citadel of apartheid, the Dutch Reformed Church, the whispers in the town had reached such a pitch that the principal of the boy's school was moved to write the following to his parents: 'I can no longer ignore the concerns of other parents and, with the authority invested in me by the Education Department, I must inform you that your son must be withdrawn from this school until the status of his European race has been made clear.'

The 'magistrates' began their interrogation, asking the boy's father, 'To your knowledge, did your father or grandfather cohabit with a Bantu?' (Bantu: the apartheid term for African.) The reply was barely suppressed anguish, becoming outrage when the mother was asked, 'Have you ever gone with a Bantu?'

'Have I what?' she cried.

'Have you ever been impregnated by a Bantu?'

'Stop this! What are you saying?'

'Madam, we have to establish if there has been some intrusion into your genes?'

'Genes? I don't know what these genes are . . .'

The questioning lasted three-quarters of an hour and the couple called on the Lord to help them. Then the three officials stepped down from the bench and called to the son to come forward. One of them produced a comb, which he ran through the boy's hair, over and again, after dipping it in a clear solution in a labelled bottle. When he had finished, he lifted the boy's eyelids and peered at the whites of his eyes, and inspected his gums. Finally, he ran both hands round the base of his skull. The three muttered solemnly among themselves and concluded the proceedings by thanking 'everyone concerned' and wishing them 'all the best'.

In the lunch break, I asked the father what he would do if his son was classified coloured. 'What can I do,' he replied, 'but make him a house servant or something like that, otherwise he won't be able to live with us, will he?'

Three months later, the Board upheld the family's appeal 'on the basis of descent' and the son retained his white classification. However, such were the whispered stigma and hostility that the family had to move away from the place where all of them had been born.

Ronnie van der Walt also lodged an appeal with the Board, and his friends began to prepare a case they hoped would prove his white descent. They were aware, however, that Rachel, his wife, had 'mixed' ancestry that could be traced. So even if Ronnie was classified white, he would no longer be allowed to live with his wife, because they would be contravening the Immorality Act, which prohibited cohabitation between people of different racial classification. With his fight career ruined, Ronnie did not wait for the appeal hearing and took his family to live in Britain.[3]

Apartheid had what its apologists would call 'anomalies'. The most vivid anomaly was District Six, in the centre of Cape Town. Perched between the foot of Table Mountain and the Atlantic, District Six was a maze of winding streets and cobbled lanes, with tenement versions of the flat-roofed 'Cape Dutch' houses of the late eighteenth century. More than fifty-five thousand Asians, Africans, mixed-race 'coloureds' and whites lived there, generally speaking in harmony. It was a vibrant legacy of the original Cape Town which for centuries had been home to sailors from Portugal, farmers from Holland and England, labourers from India and the Malay states, and native Africans. Those of mixed race, the so-called coloureds, were as much the boast as the product of District Six: such, it was said, was the tolerance at the centre of institutionalised intolerance.

'People who never really knew District Six dismissed it as a slum,' wrote Brian Barrow in *The Spirit of District Six*:

They never cared about the quality and vivacity of the people who were its life blood. They would reinforce their beliefs with invidious remarks about dirty streets, peeling walls and drug trafficking. They saw the district only from the outside without ever caring about its soul. This approach had the seeds of inevitable tragedy because the spirit of District Six was in the hearts and minds of its people . . . While so many other South Africans found pride and esteem in their cultural bonds with Europe and other parts of the world, the people of District Six were quite happy to be uniquely themselves and, in doing so, they fitted the definition of 'South Africans' more genuinely than anyone else.[4]

I was taken to District Six by Basil D'Oliveira, then the greatest all-rounder in English cricket, who had grown up there and learned his cricket in the streets and dusty playgrounds. Dolly, as he was known in District Six and in England, was staying in his boyhood home with his wife Naomi and two children. Seven years earlier, he had accepted an offer from Middleton Club in the Central Lancashire League, knowing he would never play for South Africa because of his race. He became a sensation, batting, bowling and fielding his way into the heavy type of Fleet Street's sports pages: hitting a century in twenty-five minutes and two hundred in sixty-five minutes. Having applied successfully for British citizenship, he was selected to play for England against the West Indies.

When I met Dolly in Cape Town, the apartheid regime and the Marylebone Cricket Club were embroiled in secret 'negotiations' over whether he could tour South Africa for England in the 1968 Test series. This was a critical time for the growing campaign to boycott South African sport, at the centre of which was a modest, highly talented cricketer with a message that was all the more powerful for its understatement. 'I am not saying anything,' he would say. 'I am just trying to play cricket with the best of the world.'[5]

During the English winter of 1966–7, Dolly had returned to District Six to coach young coloured players, 'to give back to my people what they gave me and maybe help the best get out,' he told me. We first met in the lounge of my hotel in the city centre. Something was clearly wrong. His good-looking confidence had gone; he seemed terrified. 'I've got out of the habit in England,' he said. 'I've made a mistake. We're breaking the law. If they catch me here with you I could end up in prison.'

We were about to leave when a waiter came to take our order. He was an African, and, recognising Dolly, he slapped him on the back. 'Listen,' he whispered, 'I'll serve the great Basil D'Oliveira even if it means risking my job. What'll it be, man? A beer?' Sitting with a white in a whites-only hotel was one thing; drinking alcohol with him was pushing his luck. Dolly ordered a fruit juice, but continued to glance over his shoulder. 'I'm sorry,' he said, 'I never thought I would feel this again.'

We almost ran the few blocks to District Six, as if to safety. We entered at Harrington Street, the Jewish quarter with its nine synagogues, passed Vernon Terrace, lined with its great palms whose seeds had been brought by pilgrims from Mecca, and the curry shops, and shops with curtains of sausages, and hawkers, and the Grand Canyon Barbershop, and the Moravian Chapel and the Muir Street Mosque, in which hung the inscription: 'Enthusiasm is the vehicle of my life . . . Sorrow is my friend . . . Knowledge is my weapon.'

And children. Streets of children, most of them shouting, 'Dolly, Dolly, the wonderman! Play with us, *please*, man!' A bat and an old tennis ball materialised, and the man who had recently struck forty-six runs – 6, 6, 6, 6, 6, 6, 4, 6 – from an eight-ball over batted one down the hill, which was expertly fielded by a man in a fez. The throng followed us to St Joseph's, where Dolly had gone to school, and the headmaster, Mr Finnan, greeted us. 'Just in time for prayers, Basil!' he said. 'Have you heard? They're going to pull down the school next. The whites are taking over. Everything is going out to the sand flats . . . out of the way.'

In 1950, the Group Areas Act categorised people by race and made it illegal for those of different races to live in the same area. District Six remained an unspoken exception. In 1966, the Housing Minister, P. W. Botha (later State President), declared it a 'whites only' area. The announcement at first was not taken seriously by many residents, who said, 'They'll never do it. Where would they put people like us?' The officials who appeared in the streets, surveying and studying plans, became the butt of increasingly faint-hearted jokes. The blackest joke was that they came from the 'Department of Community Development'.

The first bulldozer arrived soon afterwards and the last left in 1980. Every house and shop and playground was turned to rubble. People fought back, many refusing to leave their homes until they were forcibly evicted and 'removed' to the windswept, sandy peninsula between Table Mountain and the 'Hottentot's Holland' mountains that define the hinterland. As if to mock their expulsion, they were allowed to take the street names with them. All that was left standing was the Moravian Chapel, two churches and a mosque.

Basil D'Oliveira flew back to England after his winter in District Six and was selected for the England team to play Australia for the Ashes. Immediately after scoring 158 in the final Test, he was told he was to be left out of the Test side to tour South Africa in 1968. It was a decision that spared the apartheid regime the 'embarrassment' of having to ban him from his homeland rather than allow a coloured man to play cricket with whites. A BBC investigation subsequently produced compelling evidence that the British establishment, exemplified by the MCC and its chairman, the former Tory prime minister Alec Douglas-Home, had colluded with the apartheid regime to keep Dolly out of the side while maintaining that 'sport should be kept out of politics'.[6]

On my return to London, I received a letter from the South African Embassy banning me from the country 'for the indefinite future'. No reason was given. Eight years later, an embassy official phoned me to say he would like to meet. His name was Christopher van der Walt, Ronnie's name. It is a common surname among Afrikaners, but how ironic. We met three times, during which he told me how much he loathed both apartheid and the 'old Boer guard'. He assured me that young, enlightened Afrikaners, like himself, were taking power. Then he came to the point. 'Journalists like you who have been naughty in the past,' he said in the curiously coy South African way, 'should have a go and apply for a visa. And when you get your visa, I shall give you a list of names of the right people, the *enlightened* people, to interview.' He said I would not know South Africa from the 1960s. 'The situation has changed *out of all recognition.*'

I was awaiting a reply to my visa application when Soweto, led by its schoolchildren, rose up against its oppressors. The reaction, on June 16, 1976, was a massacre. The *Rand Daily Mail* published 499 names of black people known to have been killed. Most of them were shot by the police, some were children as young as four years old and, as at Sharpeville, many had been shot in the back. The wounded were thrown into heaps by the police together with the dead, and deliberately left to die.

The uprising flared again throughout South Africa in the 1980s and protests spilled over from the townships. Strikes and boycotts were met with brutal, politically ineffectual states of emergency. South Africa was becoming a state of siege; the apartheid regime began to panic. White privilege, which conferred one of the highest standards of living on earth, was at risk, especially as English-speaking capitalists decided secretly to get out of bed with the white supremacists, whose rapidly growing status as international pariahs was becoming bad for business. A series of meetings, both clandestine and well-publicised, between white businessmen and ANC leaders in exile would be critical in turning the 'struggle' to the advantage of white business and beckoning the ANC's embrace of the ideology of international capital, neo-liberalism.

On February 2, 1990, F. W. De Klerk, who had taken over from P. W. Botha as State President, announced, 'The prohibition of the African National Congress, the Pan African Congress and the South African Communist Party . . . is being rescinded.' Soon afterwards, Nelson Mandela was freed. In 1994, millions of South Africans queued, some for several days, to vote in the country's first-ever democratic elections.

It was the end of the forced, 'legal' division of people by the colour of their skin, leaving intact the equally rigid division of people by economic means. 'We, the people of South Africa,' the ANC's Freedom Charter had declared in 1955, 'declare that our country belongs to everyone and that all our people shall share in the wealth. The land shall be shared among those who work it. There shall be houses, security and the right to work . . . '

*

After an absence of thirty years, I returned in October 1997. The South African Airways stewardesses now included a 'coloured' face and they no longer wore tangerine Bavarian-style hats. When my passport was inspected by a black woman who bade me 'Welcome to South Africa', there was a pinch-me effect. It was a time of hope and talk of a 'rainbow nation', along with mounting concern about the direction of the liberation government.

For a few miles, as you leave Cape Town airport, the N2 high-way gently rises and falls, and at each peak a wall has been built that was not there during apartheid. I was told it was to protect tourists and businesspeople from the 'eyesore' of a landscape of shanties. This concern for the sensitivities of foreigners became known as 'Operation Shack Attack'. What is unusual about Cape Town is not its physical beauty but the way many whites present it to the rest of the world as a European garden city with little connection to Africa. It is as if the majority of the population does not exist, which in many respects under apartheid they do not. Little had changed.

The *Property Times* is a supplement of the *Cape Times*. It reads as if Cape Town were Surbiton or Melbourne. It describes 'sheer luxury' on the beach at Clifton and overlooking Hout Bay and 'delightful duplexes' at Pinelands; and 'after all, life begins at 50' in Helderberg Village, with its croquet lawns, swimming pools and four restaurants. The 'opportunities cry out' from the exclusive golf-course estates and resorts along the Cape Garden Route ('Nature's Valley is the top rater') to the mock Tudor houses of Constantia, above Cape Town, one of the richest places on earth.

At the Brit & Boer in Constantia, there are few Boers to be seen; the voices are from the Home Counties and occasionally the Thames estuary. They deny they are *soutpiels*, the Afrikaans slang meaning saltdicks: those with one foot in Africa and the other in Britain. Their racism is expressed, as ever, in code: 'civilised' and 'cultural' and 'criminal elements' and, after a few drinks, 'boys', meaning African men.

Up the road lived Sir Mark Thatcher – before he ran into some bother funding a *coup d'état* in Equatorial Guinea. I stopped outside his gate, on which was a written warning that I would be shot if I tried to enter. A transplant of thatched Devon was visible, then large men with wires in their ears came running.

Thatcher was sold this edifice by Pam Golding, who runs Pam Golding Estates, South Africa's poshest real-estate chain. She showed me over a mock Tudor mansion nearby, which she was hoping to sell for £2,500,000.

'Will you get that?' I asked.

'Oh, yes. Buyers, particularly from England, like something with character.'

'Does it have servants' quarters?'

'Yes . . . staff quarters we call them now . . . they're at the back, tucked away: no problem. Quite a few gardeners are needed, actually a team. The gardens have been likened to Kew, you see. They've been created so that a little bit of England took root here.'

'Has life changed for you and your clients since the end of apartheid?'

'Well, we're very much aware of disadvantaged people and everybody is doing their best to become one rainbow nation. It's certainly changed from a business point of view. When sanctions were applied, it was pretty tough in this country.'

'Tough?'

'Tough in business. We were isolated. Since the ANC has been in power, business has looked up and it's booming. I think people are forgetting about the baggage of the past.'

'What has changed?'

'Attitudes. There is no doubt that firms want affirmative action to work: you know, bringing in black executives, sharing our experience with them.'

'What about sharing the wealth, redistributing it?'

'Yes, well . . . it's not . . . I mean, the joint ventures are very interesting because there's a getting-together, and there is wealth among black people, definitely.'

'Do you ever see the other side of Cape Town, you know, the Cape Flats and the shanties?'

'Seldom . . .'

'You must marvel at the contrast of a vast mansion like this, and the wretchedness of people's homes not far away.'

'I don't know about marvel . . . look, one day, Utopia would be that everybody has their own little house and their own little piece of ground, but it's going to take time. There's a definite plan in place.'

'You sold Mark Thatcher his house . . .'

'Oh, yes!'

'What kind of house is it?'

'It's a very lovely house; it's what I would call a top executive house. It's thatched, yes, but not what we call in this country over-the-top. Actually, it has a sort of . . . a bit of an African flavour. But of course it's a luxury property. The thing is, he wanted something *sensible . . . and* I was particularly pleased to meet Baroness Thatcher.'

'She has been a great friend of you people in South Africa, over the years, hasn't she?'

'Oh, yes, she is fantastic and we have welcomed her to our Mount Nelson 100 Club dinners. It's a club of women like myself, busy people . . .'

'You didn't by any chance sell Earl Spencer his house, did you?'

'Yes I did! It was also thatched in the English style and very laid back. I think he's exceptionally happy there.' (A few months later, Spencer's wife divorced him and got the house.)

'Are we in Britain losing some of our important celebrities to South Africa? Is that something we should be worried about?'

'I don't think so at all. I think people come for the season; they love Cape Town and they buy and they invest . . . I mean, take this house . . . yes, it's eighteen million rand, but it's right up to English standard. It's all imported: all the oak, the beautiful doors.'

'Do people long for the good old days before 1994?'

'Oh no, we're *thrilled* to be part of the world again! We can go anywhere, to Europe, wherever, with the weight off our shoulders, the stigma gone . . .'

On the way to Clifton Beach, Robben Island shimmered in the distance. 'This is Cape Town's Riviera,' said Pam. She wanted to show me her 'prize property', which overlooked the gently rolling surf. The entrance on the street, which faced Africa, was a phalanx of iron bars. It was full of grotesque black and gold lacquered furniture.

'Now this house is fantastic,' she said. 'Your beach is your garden. It will go for eighty million rand, at least.' (In 2005, a similar house went for 150 million rand.)

Up to 1995, many of the foreigners who bought places like these used 'FRs': financial rands that were sold cheaply on the money markets in the 1980s by a regime desperate to attract investment and circumvent sanctions. They meant that property was automatically discounted by up to a third, making buyers the beneficiaries of apartheid twice over. Since then, the depreciation of the rand against sterling has again made South African property seem a bargain. Moreover, the owners' wealth and privilege are now guaranteed by the new democracy, which offers legitimacy: the lifting of the 'stigma'. For the residents of Clifton and Constantia, life is unchanged. On our tour, several of the majority population were to be seen: servants on their way to and from the fortresses of wealth.

'Do you know,' said Pam Golding, 'this house is actually wind free? *And* the Oriental furniture comes with it. Just put your Porsche in the garage and, hey presto, you have an *absolute* bargain, a real yuppie pad, right here in the jewel of Africa.'[7]

I thanked her and drove down the hill to the city centre, along De Waal Drive, which skirts a wasteland I did not recognize the day I arrived. It is a strange place, as if an earthquake had struck there long ago and the land had never been reclaimed. This was District Six.

The Moravian Chapel, the mosque and the two churches still stand, and there is a featureless building that is a technical college. Otherwise, the unruly lines of the foundations of houses and streets and playgrounds remain, covered in grass, like an undisturbed archaeological site. Having been cleared of its community, District Six remained for many years a ghost town. Try as it did, the regime could not sustain the interest of white 'developers', who found their plans stalled in numerous court challenges. There was something defiant here, in the stubble of people's homes and lives, as if spirits were on guard.

Certainly, defiant voices rose from behind Table Mountain, where they had been dumped, which the writer John Matshikiza called 'the dark side of the moon': places called Langa (the sun) and Nyanga (the moon), and Athlone, Manenberg, Guguletu, Khayelitsha and Mitchells Plain. This was the Cape Flats, where streets bore the old names of District Six – Hanover Park, Tyne Court and Lavender Hill – and atomised families, many in 'temporary dwellings', were buffeted by the north wind and a permanent state of fear and siege and alienation.[8]

The Flats bred poverty, serious drugs and crime. The names of its gangs are now infamous: 'The Americans', the 'Hard Livings' and the 'Sexy Boys'. Their authority is such that Cape Town's unsuccessful 2004 Olympic bid team asked them for 'support' in keeping the peace when the Olympic Committee visited. For many people, the police are discredited by their behaviour during the apartheid years when they used gangs to mete out punishment beatings.

Thus a once-lively culture has become a derivative shell of itself. The Flats could be east Los Angeles, with its murals eulogising dead American gangsta-rappers and 'don't mess wit me' graffiti and woman-hating rap music and American ghetto-speak, like 'yo' and 'mudder-fucker'. The journalist Hazel Friedman wrote that 'the legacy of District Six, like Sophiatown in Johannesburg [an expelled black community], might have been cultural integration in the face of apartheid. The legacy today is of blood and tears with pretty little to die for and plenty to die from. If little else, there remains a culture of aspiration . . . to get out at any cost.'[9]

On December 10, 1994, the year of democracy, former residents of District Six opened the District Six Museum in the Central Methodist Mission in the centre of Cape Town. On the floor is a giant map on which residents have written, and still write, their names on the spot where they lived. Alongside, in a bundle on the floor and hanging from a first-floor gallery, is a linen scroll on which they write their comments. 'The gates of memories never close,' wrote Edna Brown. In the 1970s, a city official was given the job of taking the old tin street names out to Table Bay and dumping them in the Atlantic; instead he kept them in his home, and when the museum plans were announced, he revealed his haul, and the rusted signs now hang over the map along with Langston Hughes's verse:

Hold fast to dreams
For if dreams die
Life is a broken-winged bird
that cannot fly

At the museum, I met Noor Ebrahim, a Muslim who was classified 'coloured' because his grandfather was Indian and grandmother Scottish. 'District Six was a vision of what South Africa might have been,' he said. 'That's why they destroyed it. I cried the day the bulldozers came.' He was moved to Athlone on the Flats in 1975 and took his racing pigeons with him. That evening, as he recalls in his memoir, *Noor's Story*, there was no sign of his birds. After a sleepless night, he drove to Caledon Street in District Six, where 'I saw a sight which shook me to my core: my pigeons, all 50 of them, were congregated on the empty plot where our home had stood.'[10]

After 1994, the restoration of District Six was delayed by acrimony among the people themselves, who divided between former tenants and property-owners interested in gentrification, and former residents and the descendants of those removed. In one sense, it was apartheid's last stand.

On February 11, 2004, the first two new residents of a reclaimed District Six, octogenarians Ebrahim Murat and Dan Mdzabela, were handed the keys to their new houses in Chapel Street by President Thabo Mbeki. It was thirty-eight years to the day since P. W. Botha had declared District Six for whites only and the very idea of returning seemed, for most, an implausible dream.

Some 3.5 million South Africans were forced from their homes and land between 1960 and 1982. This is a conservative estimate. Most still await justice and restitution for this most enduring crime of apartheid. Tens of thousands of children died as their families were dispossessed and wrenched apart. 'South Africa had its own Final Solution,' Michael Lapsey, an ANC activist and Anglican priest, told me. His hands and one eye were blown away by a security police letter-bomb.[11] Verwoerd, Vorster and Botha sent a whole African nation to a gulag that was hidden from the rest of the world and remains largely hidden from history. Botha has never been prosecuted for his crimes and, at the time of writing, is living out his life in comfort.

The apartheid regime's 'removals' policy reached its nadir with the terrible farce of the 'bantustans', the so-called 'tribal homelands', where 'separate development' could proceed with the fake trappings of self-government. In 1970, the Bantu Citizenship Act established ten 'bantustans' in the most infertile and wretched parts of the country. Most people sent to these 'homelands' had no connection with them; at the same time, their South African citizenship was cancelled. The ultimate goal was the transfer of the entire black population from South Africa.

The 'bantustans' were not merely dumping grounds. Like the native reserves set up in 1913 and 1936, they were designed to provide the cheapest possible labour. Their existence – four were designated 'foreign countries' – allowed white industrialists to pretend they had no responsibility towards their black workers, who, hey presto, were now 'migrant workers'. Not even the most miserly sick pay and pensions, let alone medical care and schools for their children, were now necessary. 'The central lesson from this crucial aspect of apartheid,' wrote Patrick Bond in *Talk Left, Walk Right*, 'was that capitalism systematically looted the "bantustan" areas.'[12]

East of Cape Town, in a former 'bantustan' known as Ciskei, is Dimbaza. In December 1967, the first seventy families were dumped here. More than ten thousand people were to follow, mostly women and children packed into trucks like animals. They arrived at night and faced a windswept hillside, without water, power, shelter. One of them was Stanley Mbalala, who was twelve years old. He told me he remembered a forest becoming firewood during the first winter. People lived in tents and some built wooden huts with zinc roofs and dirt floors. Later arrivals had boxes made from asbestos and cement that were so hot in summer and cold and damp in winter that the very young and old perished in them. In 1969, a spokesman for the Chief of Bantu Affairs Commissioner's Office explained the policy: 'We are housing redundant people [in Dimbaza]. These people could not render productive service in an urban area.'[13]

Physically, Dimbaza is remarkable. In the centre is a children's cemetery, as if an entire community has been arranged around the graves of its young, mostly of infants aged under two. There are no headstones. There are plastic toys among the weeds and the broken glass of shattered flower holders; emaciated cattle graze there. I tripped over aluminium pipes embedded in pieces of broken concrete, which served as headstones. On one of them is scratched, 'Dear Jack, aged six months, missed so bad, died 12 August 1976'. Most died from preventable illness like diarrhoea, or they starved to death. At least five hundred children are buried here, or were.

Stanley told me that in the 1970s heavy rains washed away many of the graves, and little skeletons appeared at the bottom of the hill. 'There has never been the money to make anything of this sacred ground,' he said.

In 1978, this rural concentration camp became, in the words of the regime, a 'showcase of investment opportunity'(cheap labour); and factories were laid out like a grandstand surrounding the children's graveyard. Since then, most of them have closed down and most people are unemployed. Stanley, the survivor, lost his job in 1996, two years after he gained the vote.

I first learned about Dimbaza in 1972 after reading *The Discarded People*, by Cosmas Desmond. A fiercely independent voice who spoke for South Africa's homeless and landless, Cosmas was then a priest on secondment from Liverpool in Britain. He chose to stay and left the priesthood; it was not long before he was arrested for his activism. Today, he continues to challenge, as he says, 'the shibboleths of power, whoever is in charge'.

In March 1969, Cosmas set out to find the gulag. He travelled twenty-four thousand miles, criss-crossing South Africa and entering a 'hidden world . . . the labyrinth of broken communities, broken families and broken lives which is the South African government's removals policy'.[14] At first, he had difficulty locating what were called 'resettlement camps'. 'One of the most distressing features [of the journey]', he wrote, 'was the ignorance, apathy, fear and suspicion of so many of the white people to whom I spoke. Often, the white clergy, for example, were not even aware of the existence of resettlement villages within their parish; others knew about them but saw nothing wrong.'[15]

In 1968, the first of almost thirteen thousand people were dumped at Limehill in Natal (now KwaZulu-Natal). Like those at Dimbaza, according to the regime, they had 'become, for some reason or another, no longer fit for work or superfluous in the labour market'. In *The Discarded People*, Cosmas described his shock at seeing Limehill:

> . . . a wretched and desolate place. There is not enough water and not enough land for even a meagre subsistence farming. There is no industry and no work within daily

reach. The inhabitants struggle against disease on the edge of starvation. It is impossible to say whether the physical degradation or the mental torture of living in such a place is the more terrible.[16]

The regime lied about an outbreak of typhoid, even denying that anyone had died in the 'transfer of volunteers'. In one month, wrote Cosmas, thirty-three people died from gastro-enteritis alone. He photographed sixty new graves in the cemetery; most were of children. 'I saw the emaciated, fevered children and their heart-broken parents, yet officially there was no cause for alarm or action.'[17]

Thirty years later, I travelled with Cosmas back to Limehill. We drove through countryside that seemed a giant quarry; in the distance were the silhouettes of wrecked cars and women filing across the saddle of a hill, carrying water from where cattle drank and defecated. The small shadows we passed on the road belonged to stunted children and their mothers, walking, carrying. In the 'new' South Africa, undernourishment and malnutrition are widespread. Almost half the population lives in poverty, with twenty-two million people described as 'desperate' and '5.3 million South African children suffering from hunger'. According to the United Nations Development Programme, all the indicators of poverty and unemployment have shown significant increases since 1995.[18] Limehill is an emblem of this, as it was of apartheid.

The ANC government guarantees a child support grant of 180 rand a month to poor children under the age of fourteen. This was increased from 160 rand which, according to the Alliance for Children's Entitlement to Social Security, was only enough to buy a small packet of sugar, beans, salt, mielie-meal, powdered milk, a brick of margarine, a loaf of bread, a jar of peanut butter, four small cans of pilchards, a packet of soy mince, one apple, one orange, one onion and one potato, every month.[19]

For children to qualify for this grant, they must have a birth certificate. Many rural children have no birth certificate and the cost of getting one – of having affidavits sworn, of travelling to the nearest welfare office – is beyond the income of many mothers, who are usually lone carers. And most cannot read the application form, let alone complete it. They are the successors to the 'discarded people'.

In July 2003, the party journal *ANC Today* announced that 'MASSIVE PROGRESS [*sic*] has been made in building a democratic state, tackling poverty and neglect, setting the economy on a sustainable growth path, entrenching safety and security, and placing South Africa at the forefront of Africa's development and equitable global relations . . .'

Charles Meth and Rosa Dias of the University of KwaZulu-Natal cite this claim in their landmark study of poverty in South Africa. On the contrary, they say,

> about four million people joined the ranks of those in poverty over the period 1999–2002. [This is] almost two-thirds as much again as the population increase over the three years. Such an outcome is not unexpected, given the large increase in the number of unemployed . . . Government claims to have made 'massive progress in tackling . . . poverty and neglect' look a little weak in the face of this massive rise in human misery.[20]

It was raining when Cosmas and I arrived at Limehill, and the rain clattered into pots and pans that lined the streets of mud. People waited in a long queue for their turn at a water standpipe; many had given up and gone to where they could fill their buckets with contaminated water. There was no sanitation, and the power came and went.

A big man of energy and frustration, Sabelo Molefe, met us at the Limehill Advice and Resource Centre. He wore a T-shirt that said, 'Let's talk!' For a year he ran his office from a public payphone. 'We are supposed to be free,' he said, 'but where is the spirit of freedom? Victims of forced removals should be treated uniquely. Even the apartheid regime in its last years promised free water and housing. Now the people here are caught in a vice; the government won't give them legal title to their homes, and without it, they can't borrow from the banks. So their poverty is assured. That's not what they voted for.'

These are the people to whom Mandela said on his release, 'Your hopes and dreams are about to be realised.' For South Africa's rural poor, who are the very poorest, hopes and dreams were systematically set aside. The ANC constitution says that land restitution must date from the Land Act of 1913, which took away most of South Africa from the majority of its people and gave it to whites. Blacks were allotted just 7 per cent of all agricultural land – in a country where barely 13 per cent was arable. Another 6 per cent was added in 1936. White farmers then held more than 86 per cent of farmland. In the first decade of democracy, less than 4 per cent of white-owned agricultural land was given back.[21]

'What the constitution did was entrench the right to private property,' said Cosmas. 'Those owning the land were given the right to hand it on, to sell it or to hold on to it. Blacks have the right to buy land, but they have to find someone willing to sell it to them, quite apart from having to find the money. That means that fewer than sixty thousand white farmers continue to own the country's best land. Actually most of them don't really own it, because their properties are mortgaged to the Land Bank, which is basically the government. If the government foreclosed on them, the land would be handed over. But the government says, No, we need these people to produce . . . In fact, most of our agriculture comes from just three per cent of arable land, which is owned by a tiny group of extremely wealthy white commercial farmers. That's how the system was under apartheid, leaving rural blacks imprisoned in poverty.'

Driving down the mountain, away from the land of the very poor, we could see the land of the very rich. The hunched, scabrous terrain that surrounded Limehill gave way to a vast white-owned garden, as if we had been spirited to the lush green fields of southern England.

In September 2005, a comprehensive study was presented to the South African parliament that compared the treatment of landless black farmers under apartheid and today. During the final decade of apartheid, 737,000 people were evicted from white-owned farmland. In the first decade of democracy, 942,000 were evicted. Almost half of those forcibly removed were children and almost a third were women.[22] A law meant to protect these people and put an end to peonage, the Security of Tenure Act, was enacted by the Mandela government in 1997. That year, Mandela told me, 'We have done something revolutionary, for which we have received no credit at all. There is no country where labour tenants have been given the security we have given them . . . where a farmer cannot just dismiss them.'

The law proved a sham. Ninety-nine per cent of evictions never reached the courts. Some white farmers continue to abuse their black workers with the impunity that apartheid gave them. In 1997, I asked one farmer, Wayne Kretzman, who then had 920 hectares in Natal, why the evictions continued. 'These people have alternative work,' he said, 'but they don't want it. I give them a year's notice before I evict.'

'Why do you evict?' I asked.

'They must pay the rent of the accommodation they get, and if they don't pay, you have to get rid of them.'

'But their accommodation is basic, to say the least. Why do you charge them rent for this when their wages are so low?'

'I pay the going rate. It's not my problem if they can't afford these things.'

'There is now a law against summarily evicting people.'

'Look, it's easier to evict today than it ever was.'

I found Mfenda Geza living with his family of eight in a shack with Spar cardboard boxes as walls and a dung floor and an open stove in the middle. He described his journey from feudalism. 'I was employed by the father of the white farmer,' he said. 'I was there almost forty years; the graves of my family are on the hillside. When democracy came, I decided to better myself, for my family's sake. I went back to school and was at last able to read and write properly. I contacted the Food and Allied Workers' Union, and it was when I was elected as a councillor on the transitional rural council that the trouble started. We were all thrown off; we can't get the farmer even to reply to lawyers' letters.'

In the report to parliament, a rural woman says, 'My husband was killed and I had to leave because the farmer did not want women without husbands or fathers who could not work.' Another woman says, 'The white farmer wanted my kids to look after his goats and sheep and I refused, so he beat me and said I had to get off the farm.' One of the report's authors, Marc Wegerif, said, 'The dispossession of black South Africans has continued unabated in post-apartheid South Africa . . . consolidating farm ownership in fewer hands.'[23]

The ANC's Freedom Charter states, 'Restriction of land ownership on a racial basis shall be ended and all the land divided among those who work.' When the ANC came to power in 1994, the 'priority' of land restitution was allocated 0.3 per cent of the national budget. In 2005, it is still less than 1 per cent.[24] When Zimbabwe's president, Robert Mugabe, attended the ceremony to mark Thabo Mbeki's second term as president of South Africa, the black crowd gave him a standing ovation.

'There was considerable surprise and great consternation in some quarters,' noted the writer Bryan Rostron, 'yet this was probably less an endorsement for Mugabe's despotism than a symbolic expression of appreciation for an African leader who, many poor blacks think, has given those greedy whites a long-delayed and just come-uppance.'

It was also a warning.[25]

Johannesburg sunsets are spectacular: they glow furnace-red, then an orange is painted in broad brush strokes across the vast African sky. 'They're like that because of the pollution and dust,' say the residents. The bitter-sweetness of the 'new' South Africa is ever present in humour that is at once self-mocking and heartbreaking, if it is humour at all.

When I met Edith Venter, a Johannesburg 'socialite', she was visiting her couturiers, The Boys, in the Rosebank Mall. For the 'trying on', she wore jewellery estimated to be worth £100,000.

'I was nominated Best Dressed Woman of South Africa and, you know, people wait to see what I'm wearing because there's always something different,' she said.

I enquired, 'You don't have one of those Imelda Marcos wardrobes, do you, you know, with all the shoes?'

'Yes, I do, yes, I do. I have all the dresses and all the shoes. I have the lot.'

'So another world record has gone?'

'Absolutely.'

'Why is it difficult to find any white person who supported apartheid?'

'We were all there . . . and a lot of people supported it, but to find them, you're going to look under every bed and under every bush, every rock. Yeah! . . . Personally, I didn't support it. I always felt uncomfortable.'

'Do white people know how black people live now?'

One of The Boys interrupted: 'We know but we don't go! I mean, *are you crazy?*'

'Actually,' said Edith, 'you will find a lot of black people, who can afford it, have now moved into the whites' areas, which is fabulous for them.'

Houghton is fabulous for them. It is one of the richest suburbs in Johannesburg, and is memorable for its walls: long, high, white walls that bring to mind Breyten Breytenbach's remark about 'painting our windows white to keep the night in'. The ubiquitous servants hurry to and fro; as in Constantia, there are no white people on the streets. The walls are topped with razor wire, which is claimed as a South African invention, and display signs: 'YOU HAVE BEEN WARNED – 24-HOUR ARMED RESPONSE'. Behind them are Alsatian dogs as big as wolves.

It was an early spring evening in St David's Road, and the grass was glistening from the spray of many sprinklers as the first guests arrived. Chauffeur-driven Mercedes and BMWs with black faces in the back converged on a garden party at number 50. The guests were mostly men in business suits, both white and black men who seemed to know each other and affected an uncertain bonhomie across the old racial divide. The party was given by an organisation called BusinessMap which, according to its brochure, gives 'guidance on . . . Black Economic Empowerment'.

The guest of honour was Cyril Ramaphosa, former secretary-general of the National Union of Mineworkers and the man who held the microphone for Mandela when he told the black nation on the day of his release, 'Your hopes and dreams are about to be realised.' The principal negotiator of the ANC's 'historic compromises', Ramaphosa is now a multi-millionaire businessman. When I arrived at Johannesburg airport, there was a large poster with a picture of him grinning and the words: 'Cyril invites you to share our interest in beer, food, property and newspapers.' This was a share issue for a company called New Africa Investments, which soon after Cyril issued his invitation lost more than half its share value.

Cyril's message on the lawn in Houghton was that black people needed to 'empathise with their former opponents'. Now empathising with rich white businessmen, for his metamorphosis he had received an accolade from Baroness Thatcher: she who once described Mandela and the ANC as 'terrorists'.

Cyril is a champion, some would say the embodiment, of 'Black Economic Empowerment', or BEE, which he describes as a 'philosophy' for the new South Africa. What this means is the inclusion of a small group of blacks in the country's white corporate masonry, which continues to dominate economic life. From banking to mining, manufacturing to media, white-owned companies, since democracy, have taken on black 'partners', the most prominent of whom are former liberation heroes, known as 'the struggle aristocracy'. Thus, the same black faces pop up in boardroom photographs. This co-option has allowed white and foreign capital to fulfil its legal obligations under new corporate charters and, more importantly, to gain access to the ANC establishment.

When a tender for a major development project is proposed, or a merger is announced, it is often a black executive at the top table who appears to be taking the initiative. The rewards are substantial. When Standard Bank cut in Cyril Ramaphosa and another millionaire and ANC power-broker, Saki Macozoma, the pair netted millions in equity. 'Two people who are already very wealthy have got themselves a nice little stake in South Africa's biggest bank without, apparently, having to put down any cash,' reported *Business Report*. 'And depending on the dividend stream from their Standard Bank shares over the next fifteen to twenty years, they may not ever have to pay anything at all.'[26]

In November 2005, Nicky Oppenheimer, chairman of De Beers, the world's largest diamond producer, announced the sale of 26 per cent of the company to a black empowerment group, Ponahalo Investment Holdings. 'De Beers is here to make a profit,' he said, 'but we must benefit the people and communities where we operate.'

The people who will benefit lavishly are half a dozen ANC luminaries, including Manne Dipico, chairman of Ponahalo and a former premier of Northern Cape province, whose slice is 343 million rand, Moss Mashishi, a leading figure behind South Africa's Olympic Committee, and Cheryl Carolus, the former South African high commissioner in London.[27]

For the first five years of democracy, seldom a week passed without a magazine or newspaper celebrating beneficiaries of the 'empowered' class. They ranged from Ramaphosa, now one of the richest men in South Africa, and his brother-in-law Patrice Motsepe, a mining magnate, and Motsepe's sister Bridgette, also a mining tycoon (she is married to an ANC government minister), to the lesser known, such as 'business whiz' Tumi Modise, described as 'South Africa's most brazen and outspoken capitalist'.

There is Tumi in the glossy pages of *Femina* leaning on her white Mercedes outside her Avant-Garde Cleaning company. The problem with her fellow blacks, she says, is that they have 'no work ethic'. She pays only the minimum wage to her female workers, and is proud that her 'street fighting' toughness sees off the unions.[28]

Thabo Mbeki is an economist, trained at the University of Sussex. Before he took over from Mandela as president, he told me that BEE was an 'essential goal' of the new South Africa. But for whom? I asked. 'There has to be a gradual process,' he said. 'For example, I think major corporations understand that it's in their own interest that a genuine independent black business class should emerge, in much the same way that they helped empower Afrikaner political power by bringing Afrikaners into the [British-dominated] economy.'

I said, 'Didn't that arrangement merely help to unite the white minority in oppressing the black majority?'

'Yes, okay, I understand that. Let's say the de-racialisation of the South African economy is going to take time . . .

I said I had met a black businessman who told me that a white-run company had hired him to get tenders from the government. He described himself as the black ham in the white sandwich. 'Isn't this process you mention about personal enrichment and black tokens?' I asked.

'That certainly is happening. We have the same solid block of white faces coming to see Nelson Mandela. So they need a black face. That's how co-option works, and it will have to change. We need time, you see.'

That was in 1997, and time has seen co-option and enrichment spread right across the new black elite. 'The Left Goes Right into Business' said the headline above yet another glossy magazine's gallery of former 'struggle comrades' who 'bring new values and insights to the corporate sector, shifting its ethos and developing new ways for business to negotiate the rapids of South Africa's economic transition . . . The same verve that cracked apartheid is now helping business crack the growth conundrum.' This uneasy reference to the past matched the slightly sheepish poses of those who, in their new designer suits and striped executive shirts, lamented how 'difficult it was to cross the line between activism and business'. They spoke about inspiring the poor to 'work towards their goals'.

One who also speaks about 'goals' and 'leading by example' is ANC secretary-general Kgalema Motlanthe, who lives in a 'six-figure mansion' in the Blue Valley Golf and Country Estate where, says its website, 'reflections of cobalt skies, elegant Tuscan estate homes and limpid dams and streams' abound. Indeed, it is no less than a 'secure, serene haven' with its own 'Gary Player-designed golf course'.[29] The estate is 'gated' and surrounded by 'rapid-response security' and dogs.

There is the salutary story of Mamphela Ramphele. When she was appointed to a senior position in the World Bank, she was described as 'epitomising black empowerment'. A 'renaissance woman' from the heart of the struggle against apartheid, she was banished for seven years as a Black Consciousness activist and the comrade/lover of Steve Biko. In 1999, she was co-opted to Washington. 'It is historic to have an African appointed to the post of managing director,' said the president of the World Bank.[30]

In South Africa, her appointment received a chorus of praise in the media and academic world. She had been vice chancellor of the University of Cape Town, where she had carried out a series of retrenchments among low-paid workers: action the World Bank would admire. Was it out of respect for her distinguished past that no-one said publicly what her new 'empowerment' actually meant?

The notorious history of the World Bank in South Africa and throughout the continent is documented. Run by the richest governments and dominated by the US Treasury, it makes clear there is 'no alternative' for Africa other than a rapacious 'free market model'.

In 1950, within two years of the formal declaration of apartheid, the World Bank was supporting the white supremacist regime with huge infrastructure loans. For example, energy loans supported electric power only for business and white people. The Sharpeville massacre in 1960 was no deterrent; soon afterwards a loan of $45 million was granted. From its support for the mass-murdering Mobutu in Zaire to its demand that Africans must pay the 'odious debt' of their World Bank-supported tyrants, the Bank has been a principal agent of Africa's oppression. As for its 'development' projects such as privatised water supply, even by its own internal evaluation, the Bank considers 51 per cent of its African ventures to have failed.

In the year Mamphela Ramphele was appointed, 1999, a World Bank consultant to the South African government declared that wages of the poorest workers in the public sector were too high and recommended that they not be paid at all and instead given 'food for work'.[31] None of this interrupted the accolades. A friend of Ramphele told the *Sunday Independent*, 'It's an affirmation of the BC [Black Consciousness] ideal that we can get to the top of the world if we are determined to.' Like Cyril Ramaphosa's directorships and the grand, 'Tuscan' homes of the Blue Valley Golf and Country Estate, joining Africa's institutional enemy is the 'top of the world'.[32]

Long before democracy, magazines like *Ebony*, *Tribute* and *Enterprise* celebrated the tastes and interests of a black bourgeoisie whose two-garage Soweto homes were included on tours for foreigners the regime sought to impress. Like the ANC government today, the apartheid regime in its last decade understood the value of a black 'middle class' as a buffer in a brutally unequal system. Of course, there never was a 'middle' – and that has not changed.

Faced with a growing popular resistance in the mid-1980s, P. W. Botha offered black businessmen generous loans from the Industrial Development Corporation. This allowed them to set up companies outside the 'bantustans'. In this way, a black company like New Africa Investments Limited was able to buy part of Metropolitan Life from the Sanlan corporation. Within a decade, Cyril Ramaphosa was deputy chairman of what was effectively a creation of apartheid.[33]

According to the ANC, the wealth 'generated' by the newly empowered would 'trickle down' and 'create jobs'. The opposite happened. As black capitalists proved they could be as ruthless as their former white masters in labour relations, cronyism and the pursuit of profit, hundreds of thousands of jobs were lost in mergers and 'restructuring'. Between 1995 and 2000, as the black 'empowered' moved into white enclaves of wealth and privilege, unemployment almost doubled and the majority of South Africans fell deeper into poverty.[34] While the gap between the wealthy whites and newly enriched blacks began to close, the gulf between the black 'middle' class and the majority widened as never before. The new apartheid was one of class, not race, although some would say it was merely furthering class divisions that had long existed within all the races.

In the early years of democracy, much of the inspiration for the new cronyism came from Mandela himself, who formed close personal relations with powerful white businessmen, regardless of whether they had profited during the apartheid years. The South African writer Mark Gevisser chronicled this, often drily, describing how Mandela fostered and clearly enjoyed the company of 'the captains of industry': from Harry Oppenheimer, the mining magnate, who had opposed one-man-one-vote, to Raymond Ackerman, the head of the retail giant Pick 'n' Pay, whose 'generosity [to Mandela] played a significant role in getting the president to effect a speedy resolution to the 1994 Pick 'n' Pay strike soon after he was elected'.

Mandela's immediate aim was to get money for the ANC and his charities. With the president at his side, the electronics multi-millionaire Bill Venter, the former husband of Edith, described his company as having been 'consistently committed to both human rights and the empowerment of disadvantaged people'. The occasion was the opening of a library named after the great anti-apartheid fighter Bram Fischer, to which Venter had given money. Fischer's daughter, Ruth Rice, commented: 'It was all a bit off; all this stuff about this great philanthropist Bill Venter . . . It left me wondering where he had been fighting, and why I hadn't heard of him.'

As for Mandela, wrote Gevisser, he

> set himself up as a father-confessor of sorts for the private sector: unlike soldiers or politicians, however, businessmen don't need to 'fess up – they just need to cough up . . . It's very canny indeed . . . kids get schools, rural folk get clinics and big business gets a salve to its conscience, a boost to its corporate responsibility portfolio, a brush with greatness and a photo to prove it . . . After Bert Wessels of Toyota gave an ANC official a cheque for 250,000 rand following Mandela's appeal to the business sector to help the party gear up for elections, the cheque was returned to him at a business lunch, by Mandela himself. It was apparently not big enough.

This, wrote Gevisser, 'carries great risks: Mandela may not be for sale, but that doesn't mean big business won't try to buy him'.[35]

In October 2005, the funeral of the mining magnate Brett Kebble in Cape Town illuminated the shadows of 'black economic empowerment'. Kebble, who was murdered, probably by a hit man, had set up numerous BEE front companies. More than a billion rand in deals were funded by his mining company, JCI, from which Kebble resigned shortly before he was killed. At the time of his killing, both JCI and another of the companies he controlled, Randgold Resources, were suspended by the South African stock exchange and large numbers of shares were reportedly 'missing', according to the Johannesburg *Mail and Guardian*.[36]

Kebble was doing deals with or on behalf of important people in the ANC, including the 'investment arm' of the ANC Youth League. Members of the League formed a guard of honour at his funeral; his coffin was flag-draped and the national anthem reverberated through the magnificent St George's Cathedral. Famous and newly enriched faces from the 'struggle aristocracy' were there. President Mbeki was represented; the Western Cape Premier, the Mayor of Cape Town, the Speaker of Parliament, a clutch of MPs and a former ANC Chief Whip and convicted fraudster were there, along with members of the white elite, not least the property doyenne Pam Golding, she of the thatched Tudor castles of Constantia and Camps Bay. Outside, black fists were raised, and people called out Kebble's name as '*umlungu wethu*': 'our white man'. It had all the drama of a 1980s funeral of a fallen resistance hero, reported the *Mail and Guardian*, the T-shirts and berets having been replaced by the accretions of the new bourgeoisie: Gucci dark glasses and suits to match and, for the women, expensive black hats.[37]

In the 1970s, the ANC declared: 'It is a fundamental feature of our strategy that victory must embrace more than formal political democracy. To allow the existing economic forces to retain their interests intact . . . does not represent even a shadow of liberation.'[38] In 2001, George Soros told the Davos World Economic Forum: 'South Africa is in the hands of international capital.'[39]

In the South African winter of that year, Henrietta Mqokomiso stood outside her home in Alexandra township in Johannesburg. It was dawn and bitterly cold. She and her children knew what was coming. Three yellow crosses were painted on her door, which meant that, in a few hours, her house would be demolished: a house that had precious electricity, water, a bathroom and a toilet. Along with thousands of others, she would be forcibly removed to a barren plot, where, if she was lucky, there would be a shack with no power, no water, no bathroom and no toilet. 'Apartheid was better than this,' she said.[40]

Forced removals, the signature of apartheid, are common again in South Africa. Henrietta was told that her street was to be 'upgraded'; no other explanation was given to her. If her removal was part of a scheme to clear slums along the polluted Jukskei river, the bleak alternative she was given was no justification. She was not consulted and there was no appeal; and the river remains polluted.

This kind of brutal treatment, at worst, state vandalism, is not very different from that which drew the West's opprobrium to Robert Mugabe in Zimbabwe – but not to South Africa, where foreign capital investment has returned to the record levels of the apartheid years. The modest 'new beginning' Henrietta expected when she stood for almost two days waiting to vote for Mandela and the ANC did not materialise. She says she is poorer and less secure now than she was under apartheid, a view often heard in the townships.

While average white household income has risen 15 per cent, according to government statistics, average black household income has fallen by 19 per cent: a descent from one level of poverty to another. Power and water bills have risen so fast they now consume almost a third of the income of the poorest families.[41] Unable to pay, an estimated ten million people have had their water and electricity cut off. In 2004, the Landless People's Movement accused the government of reneging on its 'liberation pledge' to redistribute 30 per cent of the country's agricultural land from sixty thousand white farmers to the rural and urban poor. Little more than 2 per cent of land had been transferred in the decade since liberation.[42]

'Just call me a Thatcherite,' said Thabo Mbeki at a press conference in June 1996, at which the two-year-old ANC government presented its economic strategy, known as Growth, Employment and Redistribution, or GEAR.[43] Behind a façade of 'wealth and job creation' was, in all but name, a World Bank 'structural adjustment programme' in thrall to an orthodoxy known as the 'Washington Consensus', which had devastated the economies of poor countries all over the world, notably in sub-Saharan Africa.

Public services would fall in behind privatisation, often in 'public–private partnerships'; foreign investment would receive generous 'tax breaks'; low tariffs would entice foreign imports; low inflation would preside over low wages and high unemployment (known as 'labour flexibility'); controls on capital flight would be lifted and the rand would be subjected to the vagaries of the 'market'. Above all, the rules and disciplines of the institutions set up by the United States and its collaborators – the World Bank, the International Monetary Fund, the World Trade Organisation – would be imposed. Tariffs were lifted at a rate faster than that urged by the World Bank, and the Bank's 'recommendation' that the government devote a quarter of its budget to paying off apartheid's debt was, said Finance Minister Trevor Manuel, 'non-negotiable'.

It was as if the ANC aspired to be whiter than white in its

relations with the rulers of the world. As for the democracy at home, neither the national executive committee of the ANC, nor parliament, nor the unions, nor the public was consulted. Old allies were shunned or treated to we-know-best truculence; the ANC's partners in a 'Tripartite Alliance', the Congress of South African Trade Unions (COSATU) and the South African Communist Party (SACP), were shown only the section headings of democratic South Africa's first economic plan.

'We seek to establish', said Manuel, 'an environment in which winners flourish.'[44] Having metamorphosed from long-haired biker and Cape Flats activist to the very model of a born-again capitalist, Manuel boasted of a deficit so low it had fallen almost to the level of European economies, with minimal public spending to match and a dedication to 'economic growth', the euphemism for a profit-inspired economy.

There was something surreal about all this. Was this a country of corporate hustlers celebrating their arcane deals in the voluminous business pages: of Harvard-trained technocrats breaking open the champagne at the latest credit rating from Duff & Phelps in New York? Or was it a country of deeply impoverished men, women and children without clean water and sanitation, whose infinite human resource was being repressed and wasted, yet again?

One of my favourite cartoons of South Africa's great political artist Jonathan Shapiro is of a black child in a township slum reading the financial pages to his mother, who is attempting to wash their clothes in a filthy pit. 'You'll be glad to know', he says, 'that according to analysts, the economic fundamentals are in place.'[45]

How did this happen? 'I think the reason behind the ANC leadership going for the IMF approach is because they are ashamed that most of their people live in the third world,' said the Africa analyst Peter Robbins. 'They don't like to think of themselves as being mostly an African-type economy. So economic apartheid has replaced legal apartheid with the same consequences for the same people, yet it is greeted as one of the greatest achievements in world history.'[46]

In its early years, the ANC government was subjected to an 'ideological barrage', as the writer Hein Marais describes it, with 'incessant' pressure from the United States to accept the message of a 'plethora of research projects launched by the IMF and World Bank'.[47] A seduction of the ANC and its allies was well under way. 'Why did "pacts", "compacts", "accords", "social contracts" and the like occupy so much of the Democratic Movement's energy in the early 1990s?' asked Patrick Bond in *Elite Transition*. 'How did mediocre hucksters of neo-liberalism flatter and cajole so many formerly tough-minded working-class leaders and progressive thinkers into abdicating basic principles?'[48]

At first, a few spoke out. Mary Metcalf, the education minister in Gauteng province, wrote, 'The only benefit of the discredited system we inherited is the opportunities it provides for radical change.' She described schools that were 'built deliberately without toilets' and 'with no access to running water within walking distance'. For every four teachers, there was only one classroom, and no library, no laboratory, no staffroom, no desks. 'What is difficult', she told me, 'is that these historic distortions are being addressed in impossible conditions of financial austerity . . . that make the provision of acceptable conditions for teaching and learning an absolute impossibility.'

Financial austerity – 'neo-liberalism' – was now policy. South Africa's liberators had inhaled the hot air of corporate-speak, and within three years of taking power, the ANC government was being invited to the top table at Davos and to G-8 meetings, where its 'macro-economic achievements' were offered as inspiration to the rest of 'developing' humanity. And from GEAR came another awful acronym, NEPAD, the New Economic Partnership for African Development. Ordained by Bush and Blair, this was dreamt up at Davos as the ANC government's contribution to the spread of 'neo-liberalism' throughout Africa.

At home, the people in the townships had not forgotten. The ANC's 'unbreakable promise' was the Reconstruction and Development Programme, or RDP. This was one of the 'solemn pledges' in the manifesto of the first democratic election. Based on the Freedom Charter, it was regarded by millions of South Africans as honouring a declaration of rights that had been a beacon for the removed, the detained, the tortured and all those fighting the apartheid state.

In April 1996, shortly before GEAR was announced, the RDP office was quietly closed down and its budget transferred to the finance ministry and the office of Thabo Mbeki, the deputy president. 'Sadly, it's out of date,' a ministry adviser told me. Two years later, the United Nations Development Programme described GEAR as basically 'no different' from the economic strategy of the apartheid regime a decade earlier.[49]

The African visionary Amilcar Cabral wrote that for Africa's new bourgeoisie to serve the people, they would have to commit 'class suicide'.[50] That is to say, they would have to turn their backs on the seductions of power: the Mercedes in the driveway, the directorships, the 'Tuscan' homes in the Blue Valley Golf and Country Estate, the fawning of white technocrats in thrall to capitalism's latest super-cult. They would have to think of their own people first, and not as agents of forces beyond their control, but as true representatives.

Frantz Fanon had this in mind when, in *The Wretched of the Earth*, he warned of the danger of liberated Africa's new middle class

> discover[ing] its historic mission: that of intermediary. Seen through its eyes, its mission has nothing to do with transforming the nation: it consists, prosaically, of being the transmission line between the nation and a capitalism, rampant though camouflaged, which today puts on the mask of neo-colonialism. The [new] bourgeoisie will be quite content with the role of the Western bourgeoisie's business agent, and it will play its part without any complexes in a most dignified manner. But this same lucrative role, this cheap-jack's function, this meanness of outlook . . . is in fact beginning at the end.[51]

Was it simply a matter of the ANC having been in exile so long it was willing to accept power at any price? Although there were those who had flirted with radical change, it was mission Christianity, not Marxism, that left the most indelible mark on the ANC elite in exile and prison. Certainly, Mandela never seemed to spell out a coherent vision, not like a Cabral or a Nehru. Even the revered Freedom Charter, a 'rights of man' document, was an expression of hopeful liberalism rather than a blueprint to transform a repressed society. It was the Black Consciousness Movement that inspired many people in the townships to confront the bullets and tear-gas: people who, since 1994, have been forced back into the shadows.

Dramatic and hopeful as the events of February 1990 were – F. W. de Klerk's lifting of the ban on the ANC, followed by Mandela's release from prison – they raised worrying questions for many in the resistance. What exactly was the deal struck between the ANC leadership and the fascist Broederbond which stood behind the apartheid regime? What had Mandela and Mbeki and the other exiles in Zambia offered? What role had the Americans and international capital played?

In 1985, apartheid suffered two disasters: the Johannesburg stock market crashed and the regime defaulted on its mounting international debt. The chieftains of South African capital took fright; and in September that year a group led by Gavin Relly, chairman of the Anglo American Corporation, met Oliver Tambo, the ANC president, and other resistance officials, in Mfuwe, Zambia. Their message was that a 'transition' from apartheid to a black-governed liberal democracy was possible if 'order' and 'stability' were guaranteed. These were euphemisms for a capitalist state in which social justice would not be guaranteed.

A deal was put together in high secrecy between November 1987 and May 1990, when ANC officials led by Thabo Mbeki (who had attended the Lusaka meeting as Tambo's political secretary), met twenty prominent members of the Afrikaner elite at a stately home near Bath, in England. Around the fireplace at Mells Park House, they drank vintage wine and malt whisky. They joked about eating 'illegal' South African grapes, then subject to a worldwide boycott. 'It's a civilised world there,' recalled Mof Terreblanche, a corpulent Afrikaner stockbroker and close friend of De Klerk. 'If you have a drink with somebody and you argue and you sit, and you sit and talk, and have another drink, it brings understanding. Really, we became friends.'[52]

So secret were these convivial meetings that none but a select few in the ANC knew about them. Mbeki feared that his plans for a deal – he preferred 'historic compromise' – would be rejected as a sell-out by those of his comrades facing the full fury of the regime in the townships. This was understandable as the prime movers behind these meetings were those who had underpinned and profited from apartheid – such as the British mining giant Consolidated Goldfields. The company picked up the bill at Mells Park House, where it was clear that the most important item to be decided around the fireplace was the economic system that would accompany 'democracy'.

At the same time, Mandela was conducting his own negotiations. In 1986, he was moved from Robben Island to Pollsmoor prison, where he was given three rooms and the opportunity to receive and entertain people in privacy. A white chef and a wine list were provided. Later, he was moved to the chief warden's house at Victor Verster prison, which had a phone, a fax and a swimming pool.

The regime's aim was to split the ANC between the 'moderates' they could 'do business with' (Mandela and Tambo, together with Mbeki) and the majority who made up the UDF and were fighting in the streets. Mandela's principal contact with the regime was Neil Barnard, an apartheid true believer who ran the National Intelligence Service. Barnard and his colleagues called Mandela 'the Old Man'; a relationship of mutual opportunism, if not dependence, developed, with Mandela constantly offering reassurances that whites had nothing to fear from black liberation. He went so far as to phone P. W. Botha on his birthday.

On July 5, 1989, Mandela was given a suit and tie and shiny shoes and taken to meet the '*Groot Krokodil*' (Big Crocodile) himself, as P. W. Botha was known. This was the man who had caused more suffering among the South African people than almost any of the *verkramptes* (extremists; literally, 'narrow ones'). After small talk, Mandela asked for the release of political prisoners; Botha refused. However, the Big Crocodile did something that mattered a great deal to Mandela. He stood and poured the tea. 'I came out feeling', said Mandela later, 'that I had met a creative, warm head of state who treated me with all the respect and dignity I could expect.'[53]

Botha's successor, De Klerk, met Mandela on December 13, 1989. He did not pour the tea. Contrary to the myths about him,

De Klerk was no liberal or reformer. During the 1980s he had rejected even Botha's evolving position and argued against the very idea of blacks in parliament; a black president was anathema to him. At a public meeting in 1987, recalled Patti Waldmeir, the *Financial Times* correspondent, De Klerk 'urged whites to report people of other races living in segregated white areas – even though government largely turned a blind eye to informal integration by then. He fought to keep blacks out of white universities. And he repeatedly stressed his commitment to "group rights" – the guiding principle of neo-apartheid.'[54] It was 'group rights' that the white negotiators demanded at Mells Park House.

What was forcing 'pragmatism' on De Klerk were the signals from Washington. American companies pumped 40 per cent of the oil that powered apartheid, and supplied the computers that ran the police state and the trucks and armoured vehicles that attacked the townships. At the United Nations, the US had protected South Africa by vetoing hostile Security Council resolutions. And when the regime developed nuclear weapons, Washington winked.

Although the Reagan administration had given the white supremacists every benefit of the doubt – a policy known as 'constructive engagement' – the American business establishment decided in the mid-1980s that the regime was becoming a liability; provoking a people's uprising in the most important market in Africa was 'counterproductive'. Declassified US files make this clear. On October 24, 1985, a top secret report of a White House meeting describes the urgent need to set up a 'US Corporate Council on South Africa' that would co-ordinate business pressure on Pretoria to 'move more rapidly away from apartheid'. Full-page newspaper advertisements were agreed; in thinly veiled language, they would say that Washington had decreed that apartheid was now bad for business.[55]

In 1985, the Chase Manhattan Bank recalled its South African loans and announced it was 'divesting'; others followed. The US Congress passed the Comprehensive Anti-Apartheid Act. When De Klerk came to power in 1989, capital was haemorrhaging at such a rate that the country's foreign reserves would barely cover five weeks of imports. The declassified files leave no doubt that De Klerk and the Broederbond were on notice to rescue capitalism in South Africa.

At 4.16 p.m. on February 11, 1990, Mandela walked free. He had wanted an extra week in prison to prepare himself, but De Klerk said no. He was bundled out. When he stepped out onto the balcony of Cape Town City Hall, he reached for his spectacles and realised he had left them in prison. Wearing his wife's glasses, and with Cyril Ramaphosa supporting him, he spoke to millions in South Africa and around the world. 'Now is the time to intensify the struggle . . .', he said, warning the regime that if its orchestrated violence continued, 'the people will not hesitate to fight back'. It was a proud and angry statement and perhaps the most militant speech Mandela ever made.

The next day he appeared to correct himself. Reassuring the white establishment he was 'not a communist' and that majority rule would not result in 'the domination of whites by blacks', he repeated his earlier description of De Klerk as 'a man of integrity'.[56] This upset many in the resistance; and when word spread that he and Mbeki had been secretly negotiating for more than two years, there was widespread disappointment and dismay. This turned to anger when it was revealed that Mandela had written to P. W. Botha offering special constitutional protection for whites.

'Do you recognise,' I asked Thabo Mbeki, 'that many people saw this as a betrayal?'

'Had we not made the historic compromises,' he replied, 'there would have been a bloodbath and a great suffering across the land.'

He was referring to the threat from the 'far right'. Did such a threat ever exist? The rout of an armed group of AWB (Afrikaner Resistance Movement) fascists as they retreated from their farcial 'invasion' of Bophuthatswana prior to the 1994 elections indicated the emptiness of the threat. Certainly, it turned out to be far less important than the more expert and sinister machinations of de Klerk and his colleagues. As for the averted 'great suffering', while it is true there was no civil war, the political decisions made by Mandela, Mbeki and their fellow 'moderates', relegating the needs of the poorest, have allowed the continuation of suffering by exclusion: apartheid by other means.

The black majority were misled. The ANC had promised that, once in government, it would honour the spirit of the Freedom Charter. The Reconstruction and Development Programme was adopted as official policy before the 1994 election. The liberation government, Mandela had pledged, would take over the mines, banks and monopoly industries and 'a change or modification of our views in this regard is inconceivable'.[57] However, on his first triumphant travels abroad, he spoke very differently to audiences of businessmen.

'The ANC', he said in New York, 'will reintroduce the market to South Africa.' With Mandela's reassurances, foreign capital, led by American companies, surged back into southern Africa, tripling its stake to $11.7 billion.[58] The unspoken deal was that whites would retain economic control in exchange for black majority rule: the 'crown of political power' for the 'jewel of the South African economy', as Professor Ali Mazrui put it.[59]

Over the course of three years, half a dozen critical decisions were made by a small group around Thabo Mbeki (who was advising Mandela), Finance Minister Trevor Manuel and Trade Minister Alec Erwin. These were: in 1992, to drop nationalisation, which had been an ANC pledge reiterated by Mandela: in 1993, to endorse the apartheid regime's agreement to join the General Agreement on Tariffs and Trade (GATT), which effectively surrendered economic independence and, in the same year, to repay the $25 billion of apartheid-era inherited foreign debt, grant the Reserve Bank formal independence, and accept loans from the International Monetary Fund; and in 1995, to abolish exchange controls which allowed wealthy whites to take their capital overseas. Incredibly, Finance Minister Manuel later allowed South Africa's biggest companies to flee their financial home and set up in London.

When I met De Klerk in London in 1998, I asked him if the ANC's fears of a civil war were justified, and about his own role in the state terrorism that sought to sabotage the 1994 elections.

He makes good use of the cigarettes he chain-smokes. He stubbed one out and lit another, and seemed to be smiling. He began a series of brief sentences with the words 'I deny . . .' and 'I knew nothing . . .'

He denied he knew anything about the murderous, covert operations confirmed by two cabinet committees which he chaired. He denied knowing about the death squads of Vlakplaas, the head-quarters of a South African Gestapo, even though one of its

commanders, Dirk Coetzee, had publicly confessed. He denied
receiving a letter from Coetzee alerting him to assassination orders
given in his name.

'How could you know nothing?' I asked. 'You were at all the
meetings, you were privy to all the planning, all the documents. You
were the President of South Africa.'

'I knew nothing,' he interrupted.

'About any of it?'

'Any of it.'

Smoke and silence. Finally, he said, 'I remind you; I have been
awarded, with Mr Mandela, the Nobel Peace Prize.'

'Mandela regards you as duplicitous,' I said. 'He can barely
speak your name.'

He shrugged and took a drag. 'That is for him . . .'

'Mandela says you were no more than the head of an illegal, discredited, violent minority regime.'

'You must understand there is a difference between illegal and
illegitimate.'

'You described "separate development" [apartheid] as an
"idealistic mission".'

'That is a complex issue . . . and I believe history has moved
forward. We are now at peace.'

'Didn't you and your fellow white supremacists really win?'

His expression changed as if a secret truth had been put to him.
He waved away the smoke.

I said, 'You ensured the white population had to make no substantial changes; in fact, many are better off, and white corporate
power has never been stronger.'

Smiling, he replied, 'It is true that our lives have not fundamentally changed. We can still go to the cricket at Newlands and watch
the rugby. We are doing okay . . .'

'For the majority, the poverty has not changed, has it?'

He clearly warmed to this implied criticism of the ANC and agreed
that his most enduring achievement was to have handed on his regime's
economic policies, including the same Reserve Bank governor, the same
finance minister in the post-1994 'government of national unity', the
same corporate brotherhood. He spoke about blacks who 'now live in
big houses' as the beneficiaries of 'affirmative action'.

'Isn't that the continuation of apartheid by other means?'

'You must understand, we've achieved a broad consensus on many things now.'

Driving into the black township of Msobomvu in the Eastern Cape the view ahead was spectral. Burning drums on the roadside spread skeins of ash, and neat pyramids of tyres and hubcaps were guarded by silent men. Litter, cascading from a truck, fluttered with the dust. The sense of separation from the 'new' South Africa of the shopping mall seemed complete. Children in pressed school uniforms smiled; those a few years older did not.

'Many people here have no reliable source of survival,' said Charity Kondile, very precisely, 'and no expectation of justice in its various forms.'

Charity is a schoolteacher. She lives opposite the school in a house that is more solid than many in Msobomvu, although it perches on the side of a hill given to earth movement in heavy rain. We sat on big comfortable chairs in her small sitting room, and she made tea. On the shelf were photographs of her children, mostly of Sizwe, her son, in black-and-white and faded colour. He looked like so many young men on melancholy display in their mothers' sitting rooms, long lost in the 'struggle'.

Sizwe Kondile was twenty-four when, some time between May and July, 1981, he was never seen again. As an ANC activist, he had been taken to Jeffreys Bay police station in the Eastern Cape where, the security police claimed, he had tried to jump from a window with his hands cuffed behind his back. Captain Dirk Coetzee said that a colleague had told him 'they had brought in a doctor friend [to look at Kondile]. He told them there was blood on the brain and that if they wanted to avoid a second Steve Biko case, they would have to do something about it.'

Coetzee described how he and colleagues from the Vlakplaas 'special unit' had driven Sizwe to Blomfontein and 'made a show' of intending to release him. They tied him to a tree and used 'knock-out drops' on him so that they 'did not have to look him in his eyes' when they murdered him. 'I supplied the drops and we put them in his beer or cold drink,' said Coetzee. 'Two drops would anaesthetise you, eight drops could kill you. Kondile seemed confused and disorientated. He fell flat on his back. One of the men shot him in the head with a Makarov pistol fitted with a silencer.'

He spared no detail. The body, he said, was burned for seven hours on a pyre of wood and tyres. 'The buttocks and upper parts of the legs had to be turned frequently to ensure they were reduced to ashes.' At the same time, he and his colleagues ate barbecued meat and drank brandy and beer. 'It is easier to eat while the bodies, which take seven to nine hours, burn. In every field workers' vehicle was a *braai* [Afrikaans for barbecue], meat and liquor. The jobs were unscheduled, but after each one we always had a *braai*. When a soldier is in war, he must eat.'[60]

Coetzee said this in front of Charity Kondile one summer's morning at a hearing of the Truth and Reconciliation Commission. As usual, a hymn had opened the proceedings and Archbishop Desmond Tutu had said a prayer. A big white candle was lit, evoking the Christian liturgy and symbolising 'the bringing of truth'. Then the names of those among the killed or tortured or disappeared whose cases would be examined that day were read out. At the end of her testimony, Charity was asked, as all the witnesses were, if she could forgive the perpetrators of their crimes. She remained silent.

Twenty-one thousand witnesses gave evidence at the commission's hearings. Those who had committed crimes on behalf of the apartheid state were granted amnesty if they could persuade the commission their actions were politically motivated. Of seven thousand who sought amnesty, a third were successful. Captain Coetzee was one of them. Although convicted of the murder of another activist, he is free today.

'Whether people told the truth or not,' wrote the historian Tom Lodge, 'or whether or not [the victims] could feel themselves reconciled to their former tormentors, the TRC was a crucial agency in reconstructing the South African state's moral authority, in remaking the body politic.'[61]

Charity Kondile has yet to see evidence of the 'state's moral authority'. A form of sacrament was offered her, but no compensation. The paltry sum of 30,000 rand (£2,700) went to the mother of Sizwe's child. There was no justice. 'What does re-

conciliation matter to me and my family?' she said. 'And reconciliation for whom? Who makes the sacrifices? How is it possible for the
victims of a form of genocide to reconcile with their oppressors, who
don't even have to express their regrets?'

Although the notion of a confessional was powered by Desmond
Tutu, the politics of a Truth and Reconciliation Commission came
out of the deals Mbeki and his colleagues struck around the fireplace
at Mells Park House and Mandela's secret meetings in Pollsmoor
prison. 'Reconciliation' was the apartheid regime's escape clause.

I asked Charity what she would say to Mandela and Tutu, who
insisted that criminal justice was not necessary, that amnesty and
reconciliation were 'enough'.

'One has the feeling', she replied, 'that if Mandela's son had been
killed in the way our children were killed or Archbishop Tutu's son
had been killed, they wouldn't be talking like that. They have every
right to forgive their own torturers and jailers, but they have no right
to forgive and protect Sizwe's killers and deny his family justice.'

'What is justice to you?'

'Justice is bringing the murderers to court, trying them, convict-
ing them, punishing them. I don't want them hanged. That is not the
point. That is not justice: that is retribution.'

'What did you feel seeing Coetzee tell his gruesome story at the
hearing?'

'I felt angry, of course, but I thought to myself, "You are
pathetic." All that stuff about fighting communism. Pathetic.'

'Have you ever confronted him?'

'At the amnesty hearing he wanted to meet me and "look me in
the eye", he said, and say a pathetic sorry. Without justice, that was
an insult. I am not sitting with the murderer of my son, who is going
free . . . This is a man who said that while he was burning the body
of my son, the flesh was smelling good and they were having beers
at that time. This was tantamount to cannibalism, even
Satanism . . . We *might* get some reconciliation in this country if
there was true justice for the victims of criminals like this, and social
justice for all of us, because we were all victims.'

'How do you remember Sizwe?'

'He was a highly principled young man, one of those who didn't
give us any trouble in the family. He didn't like anything that was

corruption, he always wanted to go straight. He was soft spoken, a thinker. He would say he should go to the front, you know, the frontline of our struggle, to help make us free. For nine years, I didn't know what had happened to him. I looked at the faces in the street; I was always searching, hoping. I went to where I thought he had been killed and took some earth; and I was so happy to hear from his friends that he had said the two most important people in his life were his mother and sister. You are never sure, and when something terrible happens you hang on to that. It's not justice, but it heals the heart.'

Shortly after I met Charity, I was sent a tape of a programme shown on television by the South African Broadcasting Corporation, called *People of the South*. The 'celebrity guest' was Dirk Coetzee, introduced by the show's host as 'the honourable assassin'.

'So Dirk,' said the host, 'welcome, welcome.'

'Thank you very much. Thank you for the honour of being on your show. I appreciate it.'

'Dirk, our honour entirely. What would you say to a young man thinking of a career in the police force? You know, he's saying to himself, "Mmmm, I want to be a copper".'

'I'd say, well, it's adventure, it's adventure that turns one on . . .'

'Adventure, eh? Well, thank you, Dirk!'

Dirk Coetzee was given amnesty for the murder of six people. Not only is he free; in 1995, he was re-employed by South Africa's National Intelligence Agency. He retired in 2003 and at the time of writing, he is working for a private security company in Pretoria – a black empowerment company. His unctuous host on TV was Dali Tambo, son of the late Oliver Tambo, president of the ANC.

At Vlakplaas, Coetzee's deputy killer was Joe Mamasela, who publicly boasted that he could 'remember killing forty-four people'. He, too, is free, having worked for the attorney-general's department until his retirement, on a pension.[62]

On October 8, 1997, I took a taxi to the Truth and Reconciliation Commission hearing in the centre of Cape Town. It was the day of the generals and could not be missed. In order to qualify for

amnesty, applicants had to make a full disclosure of their crimes and
show they had been acting with authorisation: that they were 'only
taking orders'. Yes, but surely apartheid's generals *gave* the orders.
Through a crooked smile, the taxi driver said, 'You enjoy yourself in
church, man.'

Major-General Joep Joubert was the first to take the stand. He
had a prize fighter's flattened nose and the sheepish eyes of an
untoward child. As head of South Africa's special forces, he was a
killer of distinction. His victims were not soldiers, but civilians and
activists. He sought amnesty for the murder of ten youths near the
Botswana border, a Bantustan cabinet minister Piet Ntuli, and ANC
activist Dr Fabian Ribeiro and his wife Florence: thirteen people in
all.

'I was authorised,' he said, 'to send troops out to kill perceived
enemies of the state by the then Chief of the Defence Force,
Lieutenant General Jannie Geldenhuys.'

'How was this authorised, general?' he was asked.

'One evening at a function I explained the plan in broad terms
to General Geldenhuys. He told me he thought it was good.
I accepted it like that. With that remark [he] authorised implementation . . . The principle that people should be "eliminated" was
"accepted" at the highest level.'

'Does eliminate mean kill?'

'I think we should be very careful when we look at the word
eliminate. I can eliminate a person by arresting them. I can neutralise
a person by arresting him. Each case must be dealt with on its merits.
If you could eliminate a person by not killing him then you could
arrest him. I don't think the generally accepted term "eliminate"
means kill.'

Next was General Johan Coetzee, the former police
commissioner, who brandished two Afrikaans dictionaries which, he
said, showed that 'eliminate' meant 'removed' to a place of
detention. He reckoned his subordinates might have 'misconstrued
the meaning', because they did not have dictionaries 'to understand
these type of things'.

Next was General Johan van der Merwe, who put it all down
to 'an unfortunate choice of words' and did not know if the word
eliminate was meant to 'convey a subtle message'. He agreed that

people had been killed, alas, because the word was understood by 'subordinates' to authorise murder.

This 'debate' went on for most of two days until Brigadier William Schoon took the stand. The brigadier was regarded as an 'authority' on the meaning of 'eliminate', having run Vlakplaas, the death squad headquarters of Dirk Coetzee and Joe Mamasela. Breaking ranks and the semantic impasse, he said, 'Words like "eliminate" and "take out" . . . referred only to killing people.'[63]

General Joubert was granted amnesty for the murder of thirteen people.

One telling argument intruded on this farce. It came from a notorious security police spy, Craig Williamson, who took part in a series of terror bombings, including the 1982 bombing of the London offices of the ANC, and numerous political murders. Why, he asked, should the perpetrators of apartheid's crimes shoulder all the blame? 'Our weapons, ammunition, uniforms, vehicles, radios and other equipment,' he replied,

> were all developed and provided by industry. Our finances and banking were done by bankers who even gave us covert credit cards for covert operations. Our chaplains prayed for our victory and our universities educated us in war. Our propaganda was carried by the media and our political masters were voted back into power [by whites] time after time with ever-increasing majorities.[64]

None of those on Williamson's list sought amnesty, because the 'reconciliation process' did not require it. The Truth and Reconciliation Commission's terms were defined so narrowly that the ANC's 'historic' political compromise became an historic moral compromise. Not only was Dirk Coetzee allowed to brag about his 'adventures' on television and disingenuous generals to drone about the meaning of 'eliminate', most South African whites and their institutions were allowed to pretend, like good Germans, that they had opposed apartheid all along. With her nice sense of irony and £100,000 necklace, Edith Venter said as much.

'No serious examination was made of the system that gave rise to some of the most horrific, racist social engineering of modern times,' wrote Terry Bell in *Unfinished Business: South Africa, Apartheid and Truth*. 'Instead, there was a concentration on a proportion of the individual victims who came forward and on their immediate torturers, killers and persecutors. This narrowly focussed litany of bloodshed and brutality often obscured more than it revealed. Apartheid was presented as a caricature . . . [not] a crime against humanity.'[65] And yet the Afrikaner Broederbond 'made the nature of the apartheid administration probably unique'. It included most of the leading government politicians, the generals, judges and senior police officers in apartheid South Africa. The Broederbond was not even approached to appear before the commission.[66]

The message of the 'reconciliation process' was that the perpetrators of state crime would be held neither accountable nor responsible, and their impunity was protected. 'Imagine that a truth commission had been appointed in the Soviet Union after Stalin and this commission had said nothing about the Gulag,' wrote Mahmood Mandani, the author and academic. 'What credibility would it have had? The South African equivalent of the Gulag was called forced removals [whose] 3.5 million victims comprise faceless communities, not individual activists. They constitute a social catastrophe, not merely a political dilemma. Were these removals not gross violations within the terms of reference set by the law?'[67]

The rural concentration camps at Dimbaza and Limehill, where tens of thousands of children perished, were the product of policies carefully constructed by Broederbond fanatics, yet, as Bell points out, 'the records of the [Broederbond] remained intact. Its motto, "Our strength lies in secrecy" was rigorously followed; this ensured that, unlike state records, its history, which is the underlying history of a system known as apartheid, was never under threat.'[68]

On June 9 and 10, 1998, Dr Schalk Janse van Rensburg gave evidence to the Truth and Reconciliation Commission about the Roodeplaat Research Laboratory, of which he was a director. This was a top secret, military-run organisation that developed lethal toxins for use against 'South Africa's enemies'. The laboratory manufactured cholera organisms, anthrax to be deposited on the

gummed flaps of envelopes and in cigarettes, and walking sticks that
fired fatal darts that would feel like a bee sting. The following is
from the transcript of his evidence:

Jerome Chaskalson (for the commission): Why don't we
have a look at one of the lists of the Roodeplaat projects?
Document TRC-30 may be a useful place to start.

Van Rensburg: [This] is a list of 163 projects commenced by
the laboratory in 1985, 1986, and from 1990 onward. Of the
163 projects, 66 per cent concerned potentially lethal toxins.

Chaskalson: Can I refer you to another document . . . On the
first page of this list we have three beer bottles with botulinum
and three beer bottles with thallium. We've got sugar and
salmonella, we've got some whisky and paraquat, we've got a
baboon foetus, we've got cigarettes with B-antheral, we've got
five coffee chocolates with B-antheral, some peppermints with
aldicarb, peppermint chocolates with cyanide, whisky with
colchicines – and the list seems to go on. Would you consider
this to be a list that could have been used for some form of
scientific research, or is it a list of murder weapons?

Van Rensburg: Undoubtedly a list of murder weapons, no
value for research whatsoever.

Chaskalson: Doctor, are you aware that at least two of the
substances on this list cause acute heart failure and also have
the dubious merit of not being traceable?

Van Rensburg: That was a very highly sought-after merit . . .

Chaskalson: Can you elaborate as to why you say that?

Van Rensburg: [Our] most frequent instruction . . . was to
develop something with which you could kill an individual
that would make his death resemble a natural death, and that
something was to be not detectable in a normal forensic
laboratory . . . There was an incident of a black dissident
whose shirt was laced, probably with paraoxon or one of the
nerve poisons. This was their standard way to get rid of those

fellows. He lent his shirt to his friend and his friend died. [There were also] plans to contaminate medication used by Mandela with heavy-metal poison, thallium. Dr Basson [Wouter Basson ran the programme] mentioned that if you give just the right dose, you can cause what appears to be an outbreak of meningitis or encephalitis. And in doing so, he mentioned in passing that he had given some thallium – actually he said 'we' – to Steve Biko.

Van Rensburg said he was ordered by Dr Basson to develop a vaccine to make blacks infertile. This was his major project, which was 'population control' to combat a 'black tidal wave'. The 'big dream' at the laboratory was to develop a race-specific biochemical weapon, a 'black bomb' that would kill or weaken blacks and not whites. The reason, he said, was fear of 'insurrection and communism'. He had taken the job in the laboratory in the belief that his work would protect South African soldiers defending their country against communists.

'Within two weeks of joining,' he said, 'I realised this is not defensive work; this is offensive work. It was a shock to me. There was an incident in which they claimed to have murdered a young white conscript who was an ANC supporter by simulating a snakebite.'

He was asked why he did not leave. 'If you let the side down,' he replied, 'you're dead, right? So what do you do? You try and leave quietly and hope they don't kill you.' He said he was eventually fired 'after being confronted by Basson about my liberal views' – but only after he had risen to be director of the laboratories.[69]

Van Rensburg was waiting to hear if he had been granted amnesty when I arranged to visit him on his farm in Mpumalanga province, formerly part of the Orange Free State. The nearest town is Standerton, whose Pietretief Street is named after a Boer general killed by Zulus; the great siege of Blood River happened not far from there. In the Hotel Toristo, the 'private bar' is for whites only; there is no need for signs. There are three pawnshops and a bold, permanent sign on a bridge: 'Jesus loves you'.

Van Rensburg's farm overlooks land that sweeps down to the River Vaal. 'Once, if the blacks came over that hill, they were shot,' he said, as a half-joke. 'Now, white farmers are murdered all around here.' This reminded me of the 'black tidal wave' he had mentioned at the hearings. A large, quiet man, he described the Truth and Reconciliation Commission as 'a superb way to clean the country of unpleasant undercurrents, grudges, grievances, rumours, imagined and unimagined feelings'. He was clearly hopeful.

'Did you find giving evidence traumatic? You were very frank.'

'Yes, it was like mixing a pudding with a cloud off my shoulders [*sic*]. You know, we'd been hiding . . . There was a real threat of assassination and death.' The 'we' was himself; he used the first person plural a great deal, like others seeking amnesty for crimes.

'Did you try and warn any of the potential victims?'

'I tried to get to Bishop Tutu, and tell him, but it was difficult . . .'

'What was to happen to Tutu?'

'They got into his home and tried to lace his food, but then he got wind of something and he would not accept laced food that was given to him on an aircraft. He pushed it aside, and said, "I'm not happy with that." '

'Why did you work at the laboratories?'

'There was the carrot of an annual [salary] agreement, the travel card and all that. [He had pointed out a Mercedes in his garage, which had come with the job.] And maybe I'd be working on the cause of cancer.'

'But you became the director, overseeing all that was going on there.'

'Well, I was Director of Laboratory Services . . .'

'One of your colleagues who gave evidence said you agreed with him on most of the work being devoted to making murder weapons. You also told the commission you were part of a programme aimed at black fertility.'

'You find my position hard to reconcile?'

'Yes.'

'Well, if I had walked out and said "yah" to the world, I'd be dead now.'

'How does it seem to you now, living under a black government, which was the nightmare of your organisation?'

'A contradiction, yes, a contradiction . . . you must remember, I knew blacks as a child; I played with them; I knew them to be as human as I was.'

Dr Schalk Janse van Rensburg was eventually refused amnesty. Although he had admitted making toxins that killed people, he told the commission he never knew exactly who was killed by them. The commission's rules were that amnesty could be granted only in specific cases of human rights abuse. It is possible that one day he can be charged as an accomplice to murders; but that is unlikely. He gave evidence for the prosecution in the trial of his former boss, Dr Wouter Basson, the head of the apartheid regime's chemical and biological programme, who denied all wrongdoing and was acquitted. Regardless of a parade of witnesses and apparently boundless evidence, it was ruled that he could not be tried for murders committed outside the country, notably in Namibia. Known as 'Dr Death', Basson is now a 'motivational speaker' and in demand by groups such as the South African Council for Businesswomen.

Near the end of its life, the Truth and Reconciliation Commission held what were called 'institutional hearings'. The first invited leading members of the judiciary to give evidence. Not a single judge turned up. 'I must express my distress,' said Archbishop Tutu. As he was about to move the proceedings to the next stage, a young anti-apartheid campaigner, Paula McBride, took the witness stand and delivered a *J'accuse* for which no-one was prepared. Having married the activist Robert McBride on death row in the 1980s in an attempt to save his life [he had bombed a bar in Durban, killing two people], she knew something about apartheid, the law and judges.

'The judiciary,' she said, 'enforced every aspect of apartheid from the most petty and degrading to the most murderous and genocidal. They sent people to jail for walking the streets of their own country without a pass; for using "white" facilities; for loving someone of the wrong colour; for trying to live, or set up business outside of ghettos and bantustans. They sent people to the gallows, knowing full well they had not had a competent defence. They gladly accepted statements that had obviously been secured through torture . . . They upheld the grand theft of the homes and lands of black people. They punished opponents of their system – for *theirs* it was – with the harshest array of cruelties . . . Yet, even up to now, they have managed to preserve and propagate the absurdity that they were somehow above it all – impartial.'

Noting that leaders of the liberation movement had been subpoenaed to appear before the commission, she asked, 'Why are the judges not being subpoenaed by the Truth and Reconciliation Commission to account for what they have done in our history?'

Tutu and the shaken commissioners met during the lunch adjournment to discuss her challenge. 'No decision was reached,' reported the *Guardian*, 'but it is believed that sentiment was in favour of confronting the bench if it proved necessary.' However, no subpoenas were issued, and there was no confrontation.[70]

Some seventy companies, business organisations and individuals made written submissions. The words of some reflected their contempt of the commission. The Chamber of Mines, representing the most voracious, ruthless, profitable and lethal industry in the world, summed up a century of mining in South Africa in just six-and-a-half pages. Mining had been 'largely instrumental' in developing South Africa, said the document, providing employment for people from 'deep rural areas' and 'contributing to economic activity in those areas'.

Black people in the gallery shook their heads; someone said, 'Shame.' The places where South Africa's miners come from, such as the Transkei and neighbouring Lesotho, remain the most forsaken, impoverished on earth. Tens, perhaps hundreds, of thousands of miners and their families are racked by the effects of untreated and uncompensated occupational diseases.

'Since 1960, the wages of black employees have increased in real terms by 492 per cent,' said the Chamber of Mines document. In fact, up to the late 1970s, miners were paid less, in real terms, than they were in the nineteenth century. Missing from the six-and-a-half pages was any mention of the sixty-nine thousand miners killed on the job, which was described merely as inherently 'dangerous'.[71]

For the Chamber of Mines, not much had changed in eighty-five years. In 1912, its president declared, 'What is wanted is surely a policy that would establish once and for all that outside special reserves the ownership of the land must be in the hands of the white race, and the surplus of young men instead of squatting on the land in idleness . . . must earn their living by working for a wage.'[72] The following year, the Land Act drove Africans into 'native reserves' where they were to be a cheap source of labour for the mining industry and agriculture. The mining 'houses', such as the tentacular Anglo American, pioneered the prison-like compounds that all but enslaved the workforce, taking away the miners' humanity and devastating their families and communities.

Once apartheid was legalised in 1948, Anglo American's power was unstoppable. The relatively small South African economy had four main pillars: the three insurance-based groups and Anglo American, which, with its shares often accounting for half the dealing on the Johannesburg stock exchange, was apartheid capitalism's 'final arbiter'. To the world, the company promoted itself as an opponent of apartheid, and various charities and foundations were established to demonstrate this 'liberalism'.

During the 1960s, the South African economy boomed, regardless of worldwide opprobrium following the Sharpeville massacre in 1960. Gross domestic product rose by 9.3 per cent, more than in any country in Europe or North America. It was Anglo American, with its vast international influence, that did most to staunch the withdrawal of foreign investment in the wake of Sharpeville and effectively rescue apartheid.[73]

Within South African society, the company is royalty. It was founded by Sir Ernest Oppenheimer, father of Harry and successor to the 'randlords' who sucked the gold and diamonds out of Johannesburg; the family seat is Brenthurst, fifty manicured acres in the wealthy, walled northern suburbs of Johannesburg. 'Their births, marriages and deaths', wrote the authors of *South Africa Inc.*, 'are an endless source of media fascination.'

> During the 1950s, Johannesburg newspapers would solemnly announce: 'Mrs. Harry Oppenheimer will leave Johannesburg for London on Friday, January 18 . . . to take her two children back to school.' Johannesburg whites will long remember Mary's first wedding in 1965, when a riot

took place among the thousands of people fighting for a glimpse of the young bride, fresh from her debutante season in London. There were 500 bottles of champagne for the 1,000 guests, not one of whom was an African . . . Harry's present to his son-in-law was a Maserati sports coupé, the first such car in Africa.[74]

Now it was 1997. Sitting at a long white-clothed table in Johannesburg's Carlton Hotel, where the Truth and Reconciliation Commission was meeting that day, was Anglo American's triumvirate: Nicky Oppenheimer, Harry's grandson, Bobby Godsell and Julian Ogilvie-Thompson. They looked relaxed, even bemused. Godsell told the commission that mining has been a 'creator of wealth which benefited many'. In an accent from the era of pith helmets, Ogilvie-Thompson described Anglo American as 'a torch bearer' against apartheid. '*Surely* no one wants to penalise success,' he said. 'Do you *really* think South Africa would have been better off if Ernest Oppenheimer had gone to Australia?'[75]

This same imperviousness was evident in my interview with Michael Spicer at the time of the hearings. Spicer was Executive Vice President of Anglo American. Under apartheid, the company felt no compulsion to explain itself publicly. With democracy came 'public relations', and the gaunt, unsmiling Spicer was put in charge.

'Oh, it's *you*,' he said. 'Had I known it was you, I wouldn't have agreed to this.'

'There was no conspiracy, Mr Spicer. Your secretary was given my name. Shall we begin? . . . It has been estimated that the human cost of every tonne of gold mined is one life and twelve serious injuries . . .'

'Those are statistics of great concern . . . all mining has risk, South African mining has the most risk. What one has to do is mitigate the risk and that requires a number of interactions: technical interactions, human interactions and, I think we would gladly accept now, management/employee interactions, which may not perhaps have always been there to the degree that was desired.'

I quoted an industry report that said, in one year, Anglo American had the highest gold-mining fatality rate in South Africa.

'I can't find any response from the company,' I said. 'Would you like to respond now?'

'Highly regrettable . . . highly regrettable . . . My final word is that we are concerned about mine safety, we are working with the union, we are doing all we can . . .'

I quoted the government mining engineer, Mr Bakker: 'In almost every accident, one can find underlying causes. There is a lack of management, supervision and training, and [there is] negligence: a lax enforcement of standards.' I asked if he had it wrong.

'No, I think that's certainly part of a much broader issue.'

'What do you mean? What's your company's response?'

'I've given it to you . . .'

'Research has shown that a third of all miners are suffering a serious occupational disease, and end their working life with very little compensation.'

'The amounts have been increased.'

'By how much? Can you give me an example?'

'I don't have the figures, no . . .'

'Don't you find it extraordinary that someone in your position in a mining company is unable to answer a simple question about miners' compensation?'

'I don't find that extraordinary at all.'

Contrary to his reformist reputation, Harry Oppenheimer, according to his official biographer, Anthony Hocking, 'never subscribed to the view that apartheid was morally wrong. In his view, it was at root an honest attempt to cope with overwhelming racial problems.' In 1967, the South Africa Foundation, a business organisation to which Oppenheimer belonged, took out a full-page newspaper advertisement imploring South Africans to stop apologising for apartheid and instead 'substitute a tone of confident self-assertion which publicised *the opportunities* of apartheid' (original emphasis).

When Oppenheimer retired in 1982, his successor, Gavin Relly, said that he, like Oppenheimer, did not favour 'one man, one vote' as that 'would simply be a formula for unadulterated chaos at this point in time in our history'.[76] He supported as 'necessary' the imposition of vicious states of emergency by the apartheid regime in its attempts to stem a popular uprising.[77]

As the 1980s progressed, and the old methods of repression were failing, Anglo American directors privately discussed their fear that the company would be 'remembered as the I. G. Farben of Apartheid', an allusion to the German company that used slave labour during the Third Reich and the part played by German business in underpinning the Nazis.[78] Today, having removed its share base to London, Anglo American has never been richer. In October 2005, the company announced that its shareholders would receive profits amounting to $1 billion.[79]

South African mining companies have greeted democracy by sacking half their labour force, many of the men stricken with diseases such as silicosis and tuberculosis, the result of the hot, silica-filled, dusty and insanitary conditions in the gold mines. The fortunate have been compensated with a pittance. In most cases, their ability to walk and breathe has quickly diminished to the point where they begin to choke. Most cannot afford an oxygen tank and die in their forties. Many of the families are too poor to pay for a burial.

No research into the health of miners has ever been made available by the companies, if undertaken at all. A 1997 study by the late Professor Neil White at the University of Cape Town found no significant reduction of dust levels in the gold mines in fifty years, and a silicosis epidemic without equal anywhere in the world.[80]

Richard Spoor, a lawyer who has led the fight against the companies for compensation, estimates that five hundred thousand gold miners have been abandoned penniless after contracting silicosis.[81] 'The mining houses knew perfectly well that their mines were killing and maiming workers on an industrial scale,' he wrote.

> [This] required that black people be dehumanised so that they could be killed and maimed without evoking outrage. Racist ideologies fomented and given currency by the mining industry helped bring this about. It also required that, in collaboration with the apartheid state, the industry should devise a statutory regime without cost or legal consequence ... which conferred civil immunity on employers.[82]

In the early years of democracy, when nationalisation and other promises of the Freedom Charter were still being spoken about, the names of black empowerment 'partners' were added to the boards of the mining companies. Their function was not merely to schmooze the new black government, but also to mask a regime of impunity. Today, death from occupational disease is classified as 'natural' in South Africa – unlike in Britain, where an inquest determines blame, and compensation follows. The government has shown no real interest in justice for the miners, as if it is an embarrassment.

'Although thousands of workers die every year as a direct consequence of their exposure to excessive levels of dust in the mines,' wrote Spoor, 'no inquest has ever been held into one of these deaths, no formal enquiry has ever been held into the cause of any one of these deaths and no employer has ever been prosecuted for exposing his workers to harmful quantities of dust in the workplace. These circumstances make a mockery of our constitution.'[83]

This story has a sinister postscript. In 2002, the Mineral and Petroleum Resources Act became law, giving the government the power to grant mineral rights regardless of land rights. This means that mining companies no longer need to spend huge sums acquiring new mineral rights. As long as a business-friendly minister approves, the companies can mine anywhere free of charge, effectively making all of South Africa 'up for grabs' by the same businessmen who drove people off the land a century ago.[84]

Swathes of South Africa were turned into the equivalent of Chernobyl. In the Northern Cape, asbestos tailings discarded by the mining companies – Gencor, Gefco and the British multinational Cape plc – poison the air, water and food of countless people, not least the men who once worked in the asbestos mines. Typically, a dump of asbestos tailings overlooks a village near Postmasburg, where the prevailing wind delivers disease. One microscopic fibre can cause mesothelioma, a cancer that attacks the lining of the lungs, or other parts of the body, and kills very painfully. Children are especially vulnerable. The disease can take up to thirty years to manifest itself, so the effects of 'unrehabilitated' dumps like the one near Postmasburg will be felt indefinitely.

In 2002, after it was taken to court in London, Cape plc agreed to pay out a total of more than £7 million to seven thousand victims over ten years. The company has since breached the agreement, citing financial difficulties, and most of the victims have received nothing. Moreover, the South African government waived all claims against Cape requiring it to clean up the environment. In 2003, Gencor and Gefco agreed to a settlement; while promising to contribute to a government clean-up fund, the company also won a waiver on all further claims for removing asbestos dumps and cleaning up the environment.[85]

No company has offered reparations: not in mining, nor in any industry. Appearing before the Truth and Reconciliation Commission, an Afrikaner business group proposed that a fund be set up; this was the only practical offer from the South African 'private sector' to right the wrongs of the past. Other suggestions were short-lived. Professor Sample Terreblanche, an economist, proposed a wealth tax that would 'lift' the majority made poor by apartheid. He said only a modest 0.5 per cent tax on incomes over two million rand was needed. This was described in the press as 'controversial' and not heard about again.[86]

In any case, said Finance Minister Trevor Manuel, the liberation struggle was not for money, and compensation was not necessary because government policies were 'uplifting' the poor. He noted that some of those who had gone before the Truth and Reconciliation Commission seeking compensation were 'Oscar contenders'.[87]

Most people who poured out their grief before the commission asked for nothing but justice. A few sought no more than a gravestone or a wheelchair. The commission directed that some twenty thousand victims should each receive a single payment of 30,000 rand, the equivalent of £2,700. With that, epic crimes were swept aside and millions of South Africans were denied justice. Like the judges who enforced apartheid, not one multi-billionaire businessman applied for amnesty, no doubt confident none would be required. They were right.

However, a group of victims of apartheid is taking action in an American court against companies they say aided and abetted gross human rights violations in South Africa in defiance of United Nations sanctions in the 1980s. They are suing the companies under

America's 200-year-old alien tort statute, which allows foreigners to bring human rights claims in American courts. What is striking about this case is that the South African government is astonishingly backing the companies against the victims.

In 2003, President Mbeki and his justice minister, Penuell Maduna, asked the court to drop the case on the grounds that it would deter 'much-needed foreign investment and delay the achievement of the government's goals. Indeed, the litigation could have a destabilising effect on the South African economy as investment is not only a driver of growth, but also of employment.'[88] The former chief economist of the World Bank, Joseph Stiglitz, replied on behalf of the claimants that this argument had 'no basis', because 'those who helped support that system, and who contributed to human rights abuses, should be held accountable . . . If anything, it would contribute to South Africa's growth and development.'[89]

At the time of writing, the court action is proceeding and the government's attacks on the claimants have become hostile and vitriolic. A senior official in Mbeki's office, Frank Chikane, a former liberation theologian, said, 'I have seen [apartheid] victims being organised by interest groups who make them perpetual victims. They will never cease to be victims because they [the "interest groups"] need victims to advance their cause. I think it is a dehumanising act.'[90]

As if that was not enough, those seeking justice for the horrors of apartheid were ticked off by Nelson Mandela himself, now a defender of the 'rights' of international capital. At an event attended by leading businessmen and hosted by South Africa's richest man, Nicky Oppenheimer (Harrow, Oxford and Anglo American), Mandela gave his name to a new foundation, 'Mandela Rhodes', and used the occasion to deride the court case in New York as 'outside interference'. Bereft of irony, he said of Africa's most rapacious imperialist, 'I am sure that Cecil John Rhodes would have given his approval to this effort to make the South African economy of the early twenty-first century appropriate and fit for its time.'[91]

As the Truth and Reconciliation Commission approached its final hearing, Archbishop Desmond Tutu pleaded to businessmen, journalists and others. 'Please, I beg you to take this last opportunity to rid yourselves of the burden of the past,' he said.[92] None replied. By concentrating on perpetrators – those who took orders instead of those who gave them and benefited from them – Tutu and his fellow commissioners effectively let off the white population of South Africa, the undisputed beneficiaries of apartheid. Their exclusion allowed them to be horrified by the confessions of the hit men and torturers and to feel betrayed and violated by the system they supported, even to cast themselves as victims.

The Truth and Reconciliation Commission was never meant to bring about reconciliation and justice itself. That 'unfinished business' is the state's responsibility, which the ANC government has given every sign of abandoning in favour of its new business 'partners'. Faced with official and institutional hostility, the commission worked hard and often courageously under extreme pressure. Denied proper funding, it could deploy only twelve investigators; yet its outstanding achievement is to have publicly exposed and discredited apartheid, so that no-one can now say they 'didn't know'. This was due to a parade of brave people stricken by the brutalities of the system, yet prepared to speak out, and to the tireless Desmond Tutu and his fellow commissioners and terrier-investigators, like Jan Ake Kjellenberg and Piers Pigou, and to a remarkable summary of the hearings called *Special Report* which the South African Broadcasting Corporation put to air every Sunday night between 1995 and 1997.

The presenter of *Special Report* was a blunt, eloquent journalist, Max Du Preez, whose native tongue had produced the word 'apartheid' and who refused to allow his white viewers to escape complicity; he pointedly referred to them as 'you'. When he himself gave evidence to the commission, he was unsparing of his colleagues. 'If the mainstream media had reflected and followed these [death] squad confessions, and revelations,' he said, 'the government would have been forced to stop the torture, the assassinations. It would have saved many, many lives.'[93] In trying to make moral and political sense of the crime of apartheid, voices like those of Max Du Preez, Charity Kondile, Desmond Tutu, Paula McBride and many others had to compete against forces eager to promote a cosmetic, 'reconciled' order in South Africa. The result was a diminished truth.

In the 'new' South Africa, as in the old, the symbiotic relationship with Britain has a special place. It was British capital that 'opened up' South Africa in the nineteenth century and laid a foundation of racial division and white supremacy. With apartheid legally enforced in the 1950s and 1960s and the black resistance progressively crushed, British investment rose correspondingly, doubling between 1956 and 1970.[94]

At Sharpeville in 1960, two British-supplied Saracen armoured vehicles mounted with machine-guns were used against peaceful protestors. Sixty-nine people were killed and hundreds wounded. After a brief pause, foreign investment poured into South Africa, with British companies accounting for 61 per cent. Profits were huge. In the eight years after Sharpeville, the return on investments was 12 per cent, a third more than throughout the rest of the world.[95] By the end of the 1980s, despite a United Nations embargo, British investment in South Africa accounted for as much as 50 per cent of all foreign investment in that country.[96]

With democracy, it was business as usual. The week the Truth and Reconciliation Commission opened its hearings into the collaboration of business with apartheid, nine foreign companies tendered for the contract to supply South Africa with arms and military equipment worth £3 billion. The orders were for fighter aircraft, helicopters, battle tanks, ships and submarines. South Africa has no external enemies. It has, however, poverty described as 'desperate', with more than five million hungry children, and a health system unable to cope with epidemic disease, such as AIDS and tuberculosis.[97]

The British arms industry won the choicest tender for a dozen Hawk aircraft, for which the ANC government agreed to pay £17 million each – twice the price quoted by an Italian aircraft builder and 'by far the most expensive option', according to a British parliamentary report.[98] In keeping with its policy of arms sales to the 'third world', the government of Tony Blair offered the ANC a

South African 'Marshall Plan' to 'compensate' for the exorbitant cost of the aircraft, with BAe Systems agreeing to a 'package of industrial participation'. This comprised a £270 million scheme to make power-plant parts, a £93 million titanium plant and a £16 million 'industrial park'. In addition, BAe and its Swedish collaborator, Saab, promised to generate £1.3 billion worth of foreign investment.

In January 1999, Blair flew to South Africa, paid a fulsome tribute to Nelson Mandela and told people in a poor township, 'The whole world wills you to succeed.'[99] The unpublicised purpose of his visit was to put pressure on the South African government to buy the Hawks at their inflated price and accept the 'package'. He succeeded. The ANC's then Minister of Trade and Industry, Alec Erwin, hailed the deal 'as a clear demonstration of South Africa's . . . ability to leverage economic benefits from the state's procurement of goods and services'.[100]

The £270 million power plant scheme never happened and the £93 million titanium plant is unlikely to happen. 'Without these two projects, BAe had virtually no industrial participation package,' says the parliamentary report. The £1.3 billion foreign investment has yet to be 'generated', although a Swedish firm, Swedish Match, has bought into two tobacco companies in South Africa, including a firm making a chewing tobacco called 'Taxi', about which there are health concerns.[101]

The ANC government was suckered and is today immersed in a scandal of the kind that accompanies almost every major British arms deal. Bribes of more than £160 million were paid, as revealed by the *Guardian* and confirmed by Blair's then Trade Secretary, Patricia Hewitt. Known as 'commissions', these are legal under British law. Following allegations that he had taken a bribe of £500,000, Joe Modise, the South African Defence Minister, announced that he was retiring because of ill-health.[102]

The bank assigned to finance the British 'package' is Barclays, which famously profited from apartheid (and the slave trade). At the time of writing, the South African parliament is examining the default clauses in the Barclays loan agreement, which appear to cede control over much of the country's economic life to the bank, the British government and the International Monetary Fund.

How could this happen? The answer may lie in all those ANC pilgrimages to the World Bank and IMF in Washington, all those 'presentations' at Davos, all those ingratiations at the G-8, all those paid-for tours of 'private finance initiative' (PFI) projects in Britain, all those foreign advisers and consultants coming and going, all those pseudo-academic reports with their 'neo-liberal' jargon and all that atmosphere in which 'winners flourish'.

Through its Department for International Development, a euphemism, Britain has shown the ANC government how to deal with its poor. 'DfID' is required by British law not to spend money other than for the purpose of poverty reduction. It breaks this law constantly, for it is, in reality, a privatising agency. In 2004, the minister, Hilary Benn, admitted giving £6.3 million to the Adam Smith Institute, an extreme right-wing lobby group, for proposals to 'reform' the 'public sector' in South Africa.[103] DfID funds the 'British Investment in South Africa Promotion Scheme'. This promotes 'business-to-business' links between British and South African companies, which have little to do with the reduction of poverty.[104]

Local authorities and non-governmental organisations in South Africa have learned that in order to secure British 'aid', they must demonstrate a preference for the private sector. Thus, the ANC-run Johannesburg City Council has assigned its 'business partners', the British company Northumbrian Water and the French company Suez, to install pre-paid water meters in the black townships of Orange Farm and Phiri. People there are so poor they cannot afford the cost of a regular water supply, which has soared since the end of apartheid. When pre-paid meters were installed in KwaZulu-Natal, the poorest drew their water from the rivers, and cholera infected a hundred thousand and killed 260.[105]

On his return to South Africa, where he was born and grew up, Peter Hain, the Blair government Cabinet minister and former anti-apartheid campaigner, said, 'Where South Africa was once the reactionary pariah of Africa, now it is the radical and progressive model [pursuing] visionary leadership and modern economic policies.'[106]

Shortly after Hain said this, thirty-five prominent Afrikaner businessmen, all of them underwriters of the apartheid regime, wrote an open letter in support of the ANC's 'modern economic policies'. At the same time, Pik Botha, the old regime's longest-serving foreign minister, who travelled the world defending the racist system and its atrocious wars and the terrorism against ANC activists, announced he was joining the ANC. 'I think I can associate myself', he said, 'with the ANC's fundamental principles [such as] the protection of private property.'[107]

On my wall in London is my favourite photograph from South Africa. Always thrilling to behold, it is of a lone woman standing between two armoured military vehicles, known as 'hippos', as they rolled into Soweto. Her arms are raised, fists clenched, her thin body both beckoning and defiant of the enemy. It is May Day, 1985; the uprising has begun and she is an emblem of her people.

The photographer Paul Weinberg described to me how he was crouched in a ditch as a column of hippos invaded Soweto. People fought back with stones, facing rubber bullets and live ammunition. 'There in the ditch beside me,' he said, 'was this bird-like woman, who pulled out a bottle of gin, took a swig, then went over the top and marched straight into the moving line of vehicles. It was one of the bravest things I've seen.'

When I returned to South Africa after an absence of thirty years, I discovered that much of this spirit of resistance had survived. Among people I met in the townships, it was expressed by those, dignified and resolute, forming a human wall around the house of a widow threatened with disconnection of her electricity, and in people's rejection of demeaning government 'RDP houses' they called 'kennels'. It was expressed by Rose Mkhangeli and twenty-five other women who built their own modern houses with their own hands. 'These are our dream,' said Rose. 'The first time I flushed my toilet I was frightened!'

Today, it is expressed in the pulsating mass demonstrations of the 'social movements' and allied organisations that are among the most numerous, sophisticated and dynamic in the world. They are the Anti-Privatisation Forum, the Soweto Electricity Crisis Committee, the Education Rights Project, the Landless People's

Movement, Jubilee South Africa, the Coalition against Poverty, the Treatment Action Campaign, the Centre for Civil Society, the Concerned Citizens Forum – to name a few. Although some may wax and wane, their political value can be measured by the way they have forged links with the international human rights and anti-capitalist movement that, together with independent trade unionists, expresses that amorphous power called 'public opinion'.

What South Africa has in abundance is a force called *ubuntu*, a humanism that is never still, having survived the brutalities of indus-trialisation and apartheid and now the dismay of renewed economic apartheid. *Ubuntu* is a subtle concept from the Nguni languages that says a person's humanity is expressed through empathy and solidarity with others: through community and standing together. A Xhosa proverb is '*Ubuntu ungamntu ngabanye abantu*' – 'People are people through other people.' Steve Biko called it 'authentic black communalism'.

This is not to deny it is idealistic and that it carries the usual frailties, most of them the product of poverty; but the evidence of its resilience seems, to me, almost everywhere in South Africa. In its embrace of a rigid order, the ANC has underestimated and under-valued the imaginative genius in its own people.

As we walked through Limehill, where the 'discarded people' were dumped, Cosmas Desmond mentioned 'something far greater than survival against the odds'. He said, 'People here have come through changes in climate, colonisation, apartheid, and they've emerged with an essence of humanity and skills of life that we barely know about. And yet, the elite in South Africa, white and black, assume the people here know nothing, because they have no respect for that which is *African* and no understanding that we can learn so much from the African experience. They confuse knowledge and wisdom. The West has a lot of knowledge; Africa has a lot of wis-dom. Each needs the other, though what are we without wisdom?'

The generosity is astonishing. I failed to meet a black South African who dreamt of revenge: of persecuting whites, as whites had persecuted blacks. Yes, crime is a huge problem, not surprisingly, given the great state crimes that devastated whole generations and have gone unpunished, and not excusing the heists and crimes of greed. Behind their walls and dogs, those whites who neither expected nor deserved so painless a transition from the atrocities of apartheid have yet to appreciate the second chance they have been given.

To listen to young white medical students bitterly complaining about their legal obligation to spend two years in a rural clinic is to test tolerance. South Africa's doctors were complicit in apartheid. One of the doctors who saw the fatally injured Steve Biko and did nothing was struck off only years later, then allowed to practise. Pathologists who supplied reports that allowed coroners to reveal nothing about people tortured to death have continued to draw their pensions.

Mbuyi Ngwenda was thirty-six when he took over as general secretary of the National Union of Metalworkers of South Africa. Like many of the black trade union leaders, he was born in the impoverished Eastern Cape. He won an apprenticeship as a fitter-and-turner at Volkswagen, and joined the union and both the ANC and the South African Communist Party. A resistance fighter in the 1980s, he was imprisoned and tortured. When we met, I liked him instantly. I remarked on his reputation as a 'firebrand' and a 'snappy dresser'.

'Well, I'm a townboy,' he said, laughing. 'I guess you have to look the part. I am a firebrand, *certainly*, for the wealth and education of this country being shared among all of us. What is freedom if we don't have that? These terms are so foolish. What I want, and the majority of people want, is the gates to their economic prison to open. Life is hard, but it shouldn't be this hard. We have fought and we've endured, and now we have our right to dignity.'

'What if this government doesn't deliver dignity?'

'First, we have to convince the people in power that they are mistaken: that taking on an economic structure that excludes the majority and rewards a few is wrong. So we'll keep talking and debating and arguing and, if that fails, we'll rise: peacefully but with such power we can't be stopped. Actually, nothing can stop us now.'

On March 10, 1999, Mbuyi Ngwenda died after a sudden illness. He was thirty-nine.

South-west of Johannesburg, the slag heaps rise like Mayan monuments. The white miners' houses are neat, their gardens trim; their black servants come and go. The black miners' compounds resemble late Victorian prisons, where twenty men share a room and one tap. At the Carltonville pit-head, Franzi Baleni, the National Union of Mineworkers' representative, began his day by calling around to find out how many men had been killed or injured overnight. 'Last night, there were no fatal incidents,' he said. 'On Friday two people were killed. It was negligence. Work was allowed to go ahead in the faulty seam above, causing a rock fall. The company wants every man to produce another ninety tons. If we don't, the jobs are lost. If we do, lives are lost.'

'Is South Africa free yet?'

'We are half free.'

The phone rang. He spoke to a union official about an injured miner. Shaking his head, he hung up and leaned forward. 'Actually, a quarter free.'

From the highest point in Alexandra township, I could see the glass peaks of Sandton City, Johannesburg's wealthiest shopping and residential municipality. 'Alex' supplies Sandton's servants, gardeners, chauffeurs, security guards. Down the road was the African Children's Feeding Scheme malnutrition clinic. It is not known how many malnourished children live in Alex as the population shifts between half a million and eight hundred thousand, depending on when and where there is work.

'There are people in Sandton who never knew Alex existed,' said Mzwanele Mayekiso, 'even though we're only a mile or two apart. They thought Alexandra was a place in the Middle East somewhere.'

Mzwanele was a leader of the National Civic Organisation, which fought apartheid as part of the United Democratic Front. He has since studied in the United States. I asked him what he had learned from being in America.

'I learned that we in South Africa are the model for a global apartheid: I mean, right here – Alex up against Sandton: very poor and very rich side by side, but really a world apart. Look at American cities. They're like Jo'burg now, and Jo'burg is becoming more and more like them. Detroit is almost identical, with the black majority tied down by poverty in ghettos, and the whites in their glass mountains and gated suburbs, and a few rich blacks allowed on the golf course. That's a lot more effective form of apartheid than the Boers dreamt up. Behind the rainbow and reconciliation slogans, we've been slotted into the new world order.'

In August 2001, more than five million workers, students and poor people went on strike and filled the streets of the major cities for two days. There has since been an explosion of community uprisings across South Africa, with people again torching their shacks and squatter camps and local government buildings. In 2005, the Congress of South African Trade Unions formed a new movement, said to be inspired by the United Democratic Front, which led the uprising against apartheid. However, the unions are reluctant to let go of their official 'alliance' with the Mbeki government; and while their leaders face both ways, they prevent the emergence of a party to challenge the single-party and single-ideology state that South Africa has become. If there is no challenge, frustration will grow in one of the most politicised populations in the world.

This is not to suggest that people fail to recognise the achievements of the ANC government, such as water and power connections, child support grants and the passage of enlightened legislation like the Choice of Termination of Pregnancy Act, which made abortion legal and has saved thousands of lives. Since 1994, as freedom of speech and association have flourished, calcified assumptions and attitudes have changed. All that is undeniable and admirable.

But the most basic freedom, to survive and to survive decently, has been withheld from the majority of South Africans, who are aware that had the ANC invested in *them* and the 'informal economy' by which most barely survive, it could have actually transformed the lives of millions. Land could have been purchased and reclaimed for small-scale farming by the dispossessed, run in the co-operative spirit of African agriculture. Millions of houses could have been built, better health and education would have been possible. A small-scale credit system could have opened the way for affordable goods and services for the majority. None of this would have required the import of equipment or raw materials, and the investment would have created millions of jobs. As they grew more prosperous, communities would have developed their own industries and an independent national economy.

Roger Ronnie is one of South Africa's most outspoken union leaders. As general secretary of the huge South African Municipal

Workers' Union, he has campaigned against the return of apartheid-era evictions and the takeover of the water supply by foreign companies. When we met at my hotel in Cape Town, he said, 'Next door is where my home was. I was six years old when my family was forcibly removed and sent down the N2 highway to a slum near the airport. The moment we were gone, a shopping mall was built.'

'What recompense would you accept?'

'I don't want anyone to apologise for their sins. I want true reconciliation, which is the redistribution of wealth from those who benefited under apartheid to those who suffered. The more things have changed, the more they have stayed the same. Look at the way the police and the whole machinery of the state are coming down heavily on townships. People have not forgotten that apartheid and capitalist exploitation were two sides of the same coin. Because of the loyalty of people to the democratic government, it may take up to ten years for the sense of alienation and betrayal to come home. But it will come home.'

Steve Biko's memory remains a touchstone. As I write this, it is twenty-eight years since he died, after having been abducted and driven hundreds of miles, naked and in a coma, from a police cell in Port Elizabeth to another in Pretoria. His death intensified the oil and arms embargo against the apartheid regime and rallied young people all over the world. On a wall in Tembisa township, in large letters, are his spine-tingling words: 'You are either alive and proud or you are dead, and your method of death can itself be a politicising thing. So if you can overcome the fear of death, which is irrational, you're on your way.'[108]

Reading again Biko's interview with Donald Woods in 1976 – eighteen years before an elected black government – I am struck by his prescience. 'For the white man,' he said, '[one man, one vote] would be the greatest solution! It would encourage competition among blacks, you see, and it would eliminate the most important ground for critique from abroad of the present regime. *But it would not change the position of economic oppression of blacks. That would remain the same*' (original emphasis).[109]

*

A memorial to Cecil Rhodes stands at the base of Table Mountain in Cape Town. Coated in graffiti and seagull droppings, it is surprising it is still there. Long before the Boers declared racism official policy, Rhodes planted the roots of a more durable form of apartheid. 'I prefer land to niggers,' he declared. As prime minister of the Cape in the late nineteenth century, he was the driving force behind the Glen Grey Act, which established the first 'native reserve' and prepared the way for the 1913 Land Act that took South Africa from most of its people and confined them in pools of cheap labour. 'We must adopt a system of despotism,' he wrote, '. . . in our relations with the barbarians of Africa.' Rhodes was, above all, a businessman, and the 'British' business he helped build in southern Africa produced an undreamt-of balance sheet of profit, and suffering.

That was not how Rhodes was seen by imperial historians. For well over half a century, he was a celebrated hero of English liberal beneficence, initiating such good works as the elite Rhodes Scholarships. He was the exemplar of those English Christian gentlemen who oversaw a piracy across the world while 'taming' and 'reforming' the natives 'towards the standards of European civilisation'.

This was how the *Manchester Guardian* expressed its liberal view on May 26, 1948, the eve of the National Party victory, after which apartheid was legalised:

> The Bantu [African] cannot be confined to the Reserves, because these are neither big enough nor fertile enough to maintain them. They cannot be excluded from the towns, because they are needed there; South Africa's industry cannot grow without them . . . The one inescapable fact that dominates the African continent is the slow – often painfully slow – but ultimately irresistible movement of the African peoples towards the standards of European civilisation.

Thus, the English-speaking bourgeoisie in South Africa (and Britain) could cast the Boers as 'irresponsible' zealots and themselves as bearers of an enlightened 'non-racialism'. It was a myth very much alive when I first arrived in South Africa in the 1960s. The revisionist historian Timothy Keegan describes it as a 'liberal humanitarianism [that] turned out to be a shallow, tawdry, deceptive thing'.[110]

The tarnished legacy of Rhodes helps explain the passion aroused by the part played by white liberalism in South Africa. A liberal icon very different from Rhodes is Alan Paton, the author of *Cry, the Beloved Country*, published in the tumultuous year of 1948. Paton was leader of the multi-racial, though white-dominated Liberal Party. 'South Africa will eventually reject the Liberal Party,' he predicted, 'but accept its policies.' He was probably right, as liberalism has determined the limits of South African democracy.

Cry, the Beloved Country sold fifteen million copies and was considered 'the single most important force' that brought what was known politely as 'Dominion misrule' – racist oppression – into international disrepute. Yet in Paton's world, the liberation of black people offered no African renaissance, but rather white redemption. African women would sing and clap over their daily chores; rich men, like Sir Ernest Oppenheimer, were benign white elders; and capital punishment was the answer to black crime.[111]

The Alan Paton Centre stands in the grounds of the University of KwaZulu-Natal in Pietermaritzburg, where he lived. There is a hush; pleasant women offer cups of tea and brochures of coming events. In a replica of Paton's study, his walking jacket is slung across his chair, and on the wall is his favourite cartoon, entitled 'The Gentleman of the Lamps'. This depicts two express trains about to have a head-on collision. One is 'Black Power' and the other 'Afrikaner Nationalism' and Paton is waving lamps, trying to make them stop. It is the quintessential liberal position.

Helen Suzman gave the Alan Paton Lecture on the fiftieth anniversary of the publication of *Cry, the Beloved Country*. The foremost liberal of the apartheid era, she was for thirteen years the lone Progressive Party MP in the whites-only parliament. 'Liberalism', she said, 'evoked vehement negative responses among those struggling for liberation in South Africa. Many people accused me of giving legitimacy to an illegitimate government simply by sitting in parliament. My answer was that I used parliament to best advantage by putting probing questions which provoked answers that, I might add, were freely used by my critics.'

She eulogised Paton, who, like herself,

> was also on the receiving end of criticism from people in the liberation struggle, especially for his uncompromising opposition to the use of violence in the anti-apartheid campaign and to economic sanctions and disinvestment . . . Had he been alive in 1995 and observed the wild enthusiasm of the entire nation at [democratic] South Africa's success in world rugby, he would have thought that his 'one hope for our country' had indeed come to pass – as he put it in *Cry* – 'that is when white men and black men desiring neither power nor money, but desiring only the good of their own country, come together to work for it'.[112]

The World Cup rugby final in 1995, which South Africa hosted and won, was white South Africa's celebration of the ending of its international pariah status. Nelson Mandela presided, wearing an ill-fitting Springboks jersey, for many the symbol of white supremacy. It seemed an unnecessary, almost embarrassing gesture. But many liberals approved in the spirit of Paton's notion of powerful whites and impoverished blacks 'desiring neither power nor money' and coming together for 'the good of their own country', no matter that the country is still dominated by injustice.

Liberals were a vital, courageous part of the liberation movement. In 1983, I made a film about Helen Suzman and described her as South Africa's 'voice of decency'. She was tenacious; in one period of 104 days, she made 66 speeches, moved 26 amendments and put down 137 questions, in the cause of social justice – in a 'parliament' that was otherwise a forum for fascism and its collaborators. She also brought hope to Mandela and the other prisoners she visited, and she was unrelenting in letting the world know of the iniquities of the oppression in South Africa.

I asked her then how she dealt with the charge of hypocrisy that said that liberal privilege helped to shore up apartheid. 'I do what I can do,' she said, 'but it's limited. I'm a privileged white. I could have left, but I decided to stay. People who think that the revolution is coming live thousands of miles away. We won't get a complete change of regime. That's not going to happen.' She was right.

Biko was unsparing of liberals. To them, he wrote, apartheid was an 'eyesore spoiling an otherwise beautiful view', an eyesore they could 'take their eyes off' whenever they wanted to.[113] That was true of those South Africans who muttered darkly about the iniquities of the 'Nats' (the ruling National Party) and otherwise remained silent and complicit. It was not true of those who, like Suzman, fought the regime skilfully and bravely.

When I first went to South Africa, I asked to see Lawrence Gandar, editor of the now defunct *Rand Daily Mail*. Gandar had been a solitary voice raised against apartheid in signed editorials, which his successor, Raymond Louw, described as 'exhorting white South Africans to make the inevitable, ineluctable choice. Whites could not have the best of both worlds, enjoying the fruits of economic integration and ignoring their political obligations. They had to make a choice.' The *Rand Daily Mail*'s exposé of the appalling conditions for blacks in South African prisons reverberated around the world, earning him and the reporter, Benjamin Pogrund, an eight-month trial that ended in fines and a suspended jail sentence for Pogrund.

The black journalist Thami Mzwai wrote of Gandar: 'From one's high school days, the *Rand Daily Mail* had a special place in the hearts of the black community. It was the first paper to regard them as human beings. It fought for them. Its blend of inspirational and aggressive writing was the talk of the times.'[114] In contrast, many of the *Rand Daily Mail*'s white readers resented the light he shone in their eyes, as did key members of the board of SA Associated Newspapers, which owned the *Mail* and eventually sacked him as editor.

When I met Gandar, he was editor-in-chief, a powerless position. I asked him how an outspoken journalist endured such a state of fear as South Africa. His opaque face looked and looked at me before saying: 'You wait until the door is opened and they push you through it. You never open the door for them.'

Donald Woods is the most famous of this group. A fifth-generation white South African who spoke Xhosa, Woods grew up as a believer in apartheid. After hearing an especially hypocritical debate in parliament, he was incensed, and realised apartheid was a 'great obscene lie'. As editor of the *Daily Dispatch* he met, was challenged by and befriended Steve Biko, whose champion he became. Perhaps as only a liberal might, he sought tirelessly to persuade members of the regime to speak to Biko.

When Biko was kidnapped and killed, Woods's outrage led to his own 'banning' for five years, which prohibited him from writing and from being in the company of more than one other person. He eventually escaped to London and a movie, *Cry Freedom*, was made about him and Biko. When we met in Johannesburg in 1998, he helped me to understand the reluctance of great liberals to criticise the ANC government, 'their' government. 'I could never imagine it,' he said, 'and sheer delight has got in the way of my critical eye.'

Biko's complaint was that white liberals had the presumption to speak for blacks. '[They] acted as the spokesmen for the blacks,' he wrote. 'But then some of us began to ask ourselves, "Can our liberal trustees put themselves in our place?" Our answer was twofold: "No! They cannot," And: "As long as the white liberals are our spokesmen, there will be no black spokesmen." '[115]

The World was an irrepressible black paper, based in Soweto, which declared beneath its masthead: 'Our own, our only paper'. *The World* invited the regime's fury when it backed the Soweto children's uprising in 1976, and columns like 'Joe's Burg' mocked the attempt to impose Afrikaans on schools. At the Truth and Reconciliation Commission hearings into the press, black journalists angrily complained that their work and courage went unrecognised.

Hugh Lewin, a celebrated white journalist and author, told me he understood the bitterness of 'forgotten' black journalists. 'They are right,' he said. 'Those on *Drum* and *The World* established a very strong tradition of not being pushed around, no matter the risks. That survives today among black journalists, some of whom have a very healthy disrespect for politicians and authority. They don't trust the black government; they've never trusted governments and see no reason to trust this one.'

Lewin was both a journalist and a resistance fighter, one of the white members of the African Resistance Movement, a group largely forgotten today. He was caught and spent seven years in the notorious Pretoria Central Prison as a political prisoner. His memoir, *Bandiet* (bandit), a classic of the anti-apartheid struggle, touched me deeply.[116] He describes black Death Row prisoners singing through the night before a hanging, and the humiliation of having to sit, day after day, in a circle, sewing rotten mailbags with tarred string, then trying to rub the tar off their hands with ice-cold water. He rarely saw visitors.

On his release, he went into exile for twenty-one years. When he returned to South Africa, he joined the Truth and Reconciliation Commission, whose work he came to admire. 'It allowed us to forgive, though not as a gesture of reconciliation,' he told me. 'Reconciliation was for Desmond Tutu, not me.'

He reminded me of Max Du Preez, whose weekly *Special Report* of the commission's hearings told white South Africans that which many of them did not want to hear. Max is highly critical of the 'white' press under apartheid. 'They did not pursue the stories we broke,' he said, 'and they left us to take the rap. They could have saved lives.' Max and a group of Afrikaners and others published *Vrye Weekblad* ('Free Weekly'), whose fearless exposés connected figures in the regime with its death squads.

That *Vrye Weekblad* was an Afrikaans newspaper made it especially dangerous, and endangered. For four years, it was one of the most read and most persecuted newspapers anywhere. Its offices were bombed, staff received daily death threats, and the regime showered it with criminal and civil prosecutions. The end came when an accused senior policeman sued for defamation and won on appeal. Ordered to pay damages, the paper was forced to close in January 1994, a few months before South Africa's first democratic elections.

In 1999, Max publicly declared himself an 'African' in a book entitled *Pale Native*.[117] The response of several black compatriots was fury, as if his Afrikaner bloodline could never be forgiven. A few years later, I asked him if he still regarded himself as an African. 'Of course,' he replied. 'My skin colour has nothing to do with it.'

*

The Groote Schuur Estate sits on the slopes of Devil's Peak near Cape Town. Originally a granary attached to one of the earliest Dutch farmhouses, it was rebuilt in the late seventeenth century as a mansion and furnished as an extravagant folly; seven gilt-embroidered, eighteenth-century standing clocks chime eerily in rooms that are kept dark. In 1893, the house was bought by Cecil Rhodes, then Prime Minister of the Cape, who ordered enough period furniture from Maples in London 'to fill it up'. 'No Victorianism!' he ordered. 'I like it big and barbaric.' Rhodes remains a presence today. The sweeping staircase is fixed with wooden replicas of the Zimbabwe bird he kept in his bedroom, where nothing has been altered since he slept there and a cabinet displays his death mask.

When I first came to South Africa in the 1960s, Johannes Vorster, Nazi admirer and former assistant commandant of the *Stormjaers* or stormtroopers, was ensconced in the prime minister's residence at Groote Schuur. Now, as I waited at the gates, it was as if the guards had not changed. White Afrikaners all of them, they checked my ID with the confidence of men in secure work. In Afrikaans, '*Bevil is Bevel*' loosely translates as 'We were only taking orders.' One of them carried a dog-eared copy of *Long Walk to Freedom*, Nelson Mandela's autobiography. 'I've almost finished it,' he said. 'It's very eenspirational.'

Mandela had just had his afternoon nap and looked sleepy; his shoelaces were untied. Wearing a bright gold shirt, he meandered into the room where Mrs Vorster and Mrs Botha and Mrs de Klerk had held tea parties with the bone china that is still on display. 'Welcome back,' he said to me, bursting into a smile. The sheer grace of the man makes you feel good. 'You must understand,' he said, 'that to have been banned from my country is a great honour.'

The township hero of the 1950s, the aristocrat, the boxer, dancer, ladies' man and lawyer all seemed evident. To a woman waiting to see him, he said, 'Aren't you married *yet*?' Her protesting, 'But I *am* married!' was lost in his laughter. When I asked him how it felt to be regarded as a saint, he replied, 'Saints aren't allowed to trip up. That's not the job I applied for.'

He is well used to deferential interviews. Several times, I was ticked off – 'You completely forgot what I said' and 'I have already explained that matter to you'. He would brook no criticism of the ANC and listed the government's achievements: the constitution, the supply of water to more than a million people, the building of clinics, the free health care to pregnant women and children. He quoted an array of statistics about inflation, deficit and economic growth, 'which is up, and going up'.

I asked, 'Weren't there two kinds of apartheid and the more entrenched kind was economic, which hasn't changed?'

'You must remember that the best way to introduce transformation is to do so without dislocating any aspect of our public life. We do not want to challenge big business that can take fright and take away their money.'

'But what about the rich getting richer and the poor . . . ?'

'As for poor people, here's an example for you. There is no country where labour tenants have been given the security we have given them, where they now have a right to the land they occupy, where a farmer cannot just dismiss.'

'But they *are* evicting them, regardless of the new legislation. For most tenant farmers, little has changed.'

'No, no, that's an exaggeration. We have set up a process and proper structures . . . '

'The Freedom Charter said the people of this country would share in all its wealth. Is that still possible?'

'Why not? They are beginning to share in that wealth. You now have blacks, coloureds and Indians involved in companies that command billions in assets, something totally new in this country. You see in Johannesburg many blacks now buying properties in the wealthy suburbs.'

'Many?'

'Compared with before . . .'

'A government minister called the ANC's policies Thatcherite, complete with privatisation and deregulation . . .'

'You can put any label on it you like; you can call it Thatcherite but, for this country, privatisation is the fundamental policy.'

'That's the opposite of what you said before the first elections, in 1994.'

'There is a process. You have to appreciate that every process incorporates change.'

'Where is there a country that has satisfied the needs of the majority, the poor people, with policies similar to South Africa's?'

'Why do we have to compare ourselves with any part of the world? We need not even compare ourselves with Western countries, because they are lagging behind countries in the Middle East, like Saudi Arabia, where students enjoy benefits I have not seen anywhere in the world, where they study free and are even paid three hundred dollars a month for studying free. You don't find a thing like that in the West.'

'Saudi Arabia has an appalling human rights record. It has extra-judicial executions, torture and political prisoners – like you were.'

'What does "human rights record" mean? I don't share the view that narrowly defines human rights. Does a country [like the United States] have human rights when a large section of its people are poor and are ill and can't afford medicines? You mustn't think only of countries that have the vote.'

'Reconciliation has been your constant theme. Do you reflect on the fact that not a single leading figure in the old regime – from the military, business, judiciary – has shown any genuine remorse for apartheid?'

'That's going too far. The Dutch Reformed Church was publicly commended by Archbishop Tutu for apologising. You have individuals, like Leon Wessels, and a city mayor and some others who have apologised generally. What the public wants is for those on high to confess they authorised the crimes of apartheid. That has not been forthcoming . . . and yes, it's a tragedy that de Klerk has avoided accepting responsibility for what he authorised.'

The ambiguity of Mandela is expressed in his dealings with other governments. As the first liberation president, he ordered a ridiculous and bloody invasion of tiny Lesotho. He allowed South African armaments to be sold to Algeria, Colombia and Peru, which have notorious human rights records. He invited the Indonesian mass murderer General Suharto to South Africa and gave him the country's highest award (Suharto had given money to the ANC in exile). He recognised the brutal Burmese junta as a legitimate government, even though the plight of its legitimate leader, Aung San Suu Kyi, who is under permanent house arrest, reflected his own struggle. When I asked him about this, he replied merely that apartheid was 'unique' – which contradicted his unswerving support for the Palestinians and the parallel he draws between Israeli apartheid and South African apartheid.

Yet his government led the international anti-landmine campaign to victory at the United Nations in 1997. In retirement, he has been more outspoken than he was as president; his sense of injustice seems more acute, as though he feels free at last to spend his moral inheritance. In 2002, he made a dramatic political gesture that showed disapproval of his successor's apparent indifference to the AIDS disaster; he embraced an AIDS activist, Zackie Achmat, who was HIV-positive. Many South Africans have died of AIDS without their families admitting the cause. He also revealed that three members of his own family had died of AIDS. 'There is no shame,' said Mandela, putting his arm around Achmat.[118]

Perhaps no international figure has alerted the world to the dangers of the Bush regime as Mandela has. Although he later back-tracked somewhat, he said that Bush is 'introducing chaos into international affairs'. (When Bush did not return one of his calls, he called Bush senior and asked him to 'do something' about his son.) He described Dick Cheney and Donald Rumsfeld as 'dinosaurs who do not want [Bush] to belong to the modern age . . . it is a tragedy what is happening, what Bush is doing in Iraq. What I am con-demning is a president who has no foresight, who cannot think properly, who is now wanting to plunge the world into a holocaust.' His description of Tony Blair as 'Bush's foreign minister' was finely timed; Thabo Mbeki, his successor, was about to visit Blair in Downing Street.[119]

When my interview was over, Mandela leaned forward and asked if I thought he had been 'too soft' on Indonesia over East Timor. I said yes, he had been too soft. 'It's a dilemma,' he said. 'They helped the ANC during our struggle.' Walking with him to the door, past Mrs Vorster's bone china and Cecil Rhodes's wooden Zimbabwe birds and the seven standing clocks, I said, 'You must at times be struck by the irony of your situation.' He gripped my forearm. '*All* the time,' he said. As he climbed into his silver

Mercedes, he had still not tied his shoelaces, and his small grey head was barely visible in a bevy of white men with paunches and huge arms and wires in their ears. One of them gave an order in Afrikaans and the Mercedes and Mandela were gone.

Denny from King Taxis drove me to Soweto. 'I don't like being here,' he said. 'It is a place of tears and blood.' Soweto is 20 miles from Johannesburg, which the city council considered the minimum 'respectable distance' from the white suburbs. An outbreak of bubonic plague in 1904 was used as an excuse to herd blacks out of the city and on to a 'native' location in the scrub of a farm called Klipsruit.

We drove through Kliptown, past the Wonderful Hair Salon and Nana's Liquor Store and patches of stubbled ground on which second-hand clothes were spread for sale. It was here that the Freedom Charter was presented to the people of South Africa on June 26, 1955. More than seven thousand people watched 2,884 ANC delegates adopt the Charter, then intone it as a prayer, seeking 'for our people . . . their birthright to land, liberty and peace [robbed] by a form of government founded in injustice and inequality'.

On the approach to Soweto, an army watchtower stood empty, the barbed wire cut and strewn, rusting, in long grass. It was on this road that the thin woman had stood between the armoured 'hippos', her fists clenched. When I said to Denny this was surely a place of heroes, he shook his head and said, 'Tears and blood . . .'

I had arranged to meet Sifiso Mxolisi Ndlovu at his old school, Phefeni Senior Secondary, where South Africa's greatest black uprising began. In 1976, Sifiso was one of the organisers of a student boycott of Afrikaans as a teaching language. The regime had decreed that English would be replaced with what Sifiso called 'the language of the oppressor'. The Deputy Minister of Bantu Education, Dr Andries Treurnicht, told the white parliament, 'Why should blacks be allowed in schools if they do not want to be taught in the language chosen by the Government?'[120]

Sifiso met me at the gates of the school, which was surrounded

by coils of barbed wire 'to keep out the criminals'. Diagonally opposite is the flat-roofed house where Nelson and Winnie Mandela lived
in the 1950s. For £1.70 you can look around and inspect grainy
family photographs and read the Christmas cards Nelson sent his
children from Robben Island.

'I was fourteen,' said Sifiso. 'The older boys were excluded from
the pilot programme [to impose Afrikaans], so all those in the
boycott were very young. It soon spread to the other schools and a
march was planned for June sixteenth. We made signs that said, "To
hell with Afrikaans". We were angry, but we were light-hearted as
well. We didn't want a confrontation. We wanted to be heard.'[121]

By eight o'clock on that morning, as many as ten thousand
children were marching from Orlando High School. Ahead were
hundreds of armed police. The regime had known nothing like this.
Exuberant boys and girls sang and 'toy-toyed' (danced), their arms
linked. 'Away with Afrikaans!' they shouted over and over. The
police opened fire and forty children were killed in the first volley.
Among them was Hector Pietersen, who was thirteen. There is a
famous photograph of his body being carried by an anguished
friend, with his sister running alongside. This became the symbol of
a resistance that would suffer many more years of 'tears and blood'
in a struggle for freedom not yet won.

5
Liberating Afghanistan

The people there are dead because we wanted them
dead.
*Pentagon spokesman on the bombing of a village
that killed 93 civilians*

Traffic jams are a sign of prosperity and this is
what my government has managed to achieve.
*Harmid Karzai, US-installed President of
Afghanistan, 2003*

Kabul has contours of rubble rather than streets, where people live
in collapsed buildings, like earthquake victims waiting for rescue.
They have no light or heat; their apocalyptic fires burn through the
night. Hardly a wall stands that does not bear the pockmarks of
almost every calibre of weapon. Cars lie upended at roundabouts.
Power poles built for a modern fleet of trolley buses are twisted like
paperclips; the buses are stacked on top of each other, reminiscent
of the pyramids of defunct vehicles erected by the Khmer Rouge at
the dawn of 'Year Zero'.

There is a sense of Year Zero in Afghanistan. On the edge of
Kabul, my footsteps echoed through the once grand Dilkusha
Palace, built in 1910 to a celebrated design by an English architect,
whose circular staircase and Corinthian columns and stone frescoes
of biplanes lie in ruins. From its cavernous, bombed-out shell
emerged reed-thin children like small phantoms, offering yellowing
postcards of what it had looked like thirty years ago: a vainglorious
pile at the end of an Afghan Champs-Elysées. Beneath the sweep of
the derelict staircase were the blood and flesh of two people blown
up by a bomb the day before. Who were they? Who had planted the
bomb? In a country in thrall to mass murderers, or 'regional
commanders', as the Americans prefer to call the *mujahedin*
warlords, the question itself is surreal.

A hundred yards away, men in blue moved stiffly in single file:

mine-clearers. Mines are like litter here, killing and maiming, it is calculated, every hour of every day. Through a line of red flags fluttering in the haze, the silhouette of a man marched, waving his arms and shouting. A refugee recently returned from Pakistan, he was determined to reclaim his home even though it was surrounded by mines. 'It is my right!' he shouted. Two days earlier, another man and his family had done the same, and the men in blue collected their remains in a sheet.

Nearby are the remains of Kabul's famous art deco cinema, where the masonry crackles and falls on children playing in its rubble. There are posters warning that unexploded cluster bombs, 'yellow and from the USA', are in the vicinity. The children chased each other into the shadows, watched by a teenage boy with a stump and part of his face missing. People still confuse the cluster canisters with the yellow relief packages that were dropped by American planes in October 2001, after the invading 'coalition' had stopped relief convoys crossing from Pakistan.

'Does anyone read the posters?' I asked a policeman.

'They can't read,' he replied.

While the number of civilians killed directly by the post-September 11 US bombing and invasion of Afghanistan is conservatively estimated at between thirteen hundred and eight thousand, as many as twenty thousand Afghanis 'may have lost their lives as an indirect consequence', wrote Jonathan Steele in an investigation for the *Guardian*. 'The bombing . . . caused massive dislocation by prompting hundreds of Afghans to flee from their homes. It stopped aid supplies to drought victims who depended on emergency relief. It provoked an upsurge in fighting . . . leading yet more people to flee . . . They, too, belong in the tally of the dead.'[1]

As the first bombs fell, President Bush spoke to his victims from the Oval Office: 'The oppressed people of Afghanistan will know the generosity of America. As we strike military targets, we will also drop food, medicine and supplies to the starving and suffering men and women and children of Afghanistan. The United States is a friend of the Afghan people.' He pledged a repeat of the Marshall Plan that followed the 'moral victory' of the Second World War.[2]

The previous week, at the Labour Party conference, Tony Blair had said memorably: 'To the Afghan people, we make this commitment. We will not walk away . . . If the Taliban regime changes, we will work with you to make sure its successor is one that is broad-based, that unites all ethnic groups and offers some way out of the poverty that is your miserable existence.'[3]

Almost every word Bush and Blair spoke was false. Their declarations of concern were cruel illusions that prepared the way for the conquest of both Afghanistan and Iraq. As the Anglo-American occupation of Iraq unravels, the forgotten disaster in Afghanistan, the first 'victory' in the 'war on terror', may prove an even more shocking testament to the true consequences of modern imperial power.

Through all the great humanitarian crises in living memory, no country has been abused and suffered more, and none has been helped less, than Afghanistan. In the international league of worthy and unworthy victims, Afghanis are the unworthiest. Bosnia, with a quarter of the population but embraced as a liberal cause of the West, receives $356 per person; Afghanistan gets $42 per person. Only 3 per cent of all international aid spent in Afghanistan has been for reconstruction. Eighty-four per cent goes to the US-led military 'coalition'. This has paid for the invasion, the establishment of military bases and the training and equipping of a compliant army.[4]

Other foreign 'aid' has furnished the modern offices of the 1,025 United Nations agencies and international 'NGOs' in Kabul's only exclusive suburb, noted for its outrageous rents, air-conditioned jeeps, foreigners-only imported food shops and alcohol warehouse. A foreigners-only Irish Club is guarded by men with AK-47s, and the Afghan staff have been given Irish names: Sean, Kevin, Jimmy and George.

Some NGOs do valuable work, and many do not. British aid workers Chris Johnson and Jolyon Leslie describe how an American NGO called Creative Associates International Inc., with no previous experience in Afghanistan, won a major education contract as part of a consortium that had little to show in the field of education compared with the second, rejected bidder. Creative Associates is now 'developing education' in occupied Iraq with a contract that could be worth $157 million. As the manager of another company bidding for a slice of this pie put it: 'We cannot lose – the guys in Washington have not only insured our assets in this place, but also our profits.'[5]

In January 2002, with the Taliban on the run, the leaders of the rich world met in Tokyo and pledged $4.5 billion for Afghanistan over five years. This was less than half the $10 billion spent on bombing and invading the country. Three years later, little of it had reached the Afghan government, whose placeman-president, Harmid Karzai, flies regularly to Washington to beg for more. What is then announced as 'new reconstruction aid' is the same honeypot from which American multinationals sup contracts in Afghanistan and Iraq worth more than $8 billion. In 2003, Karzai was promised an extra $50 million by the Overseas Private Investment Corporation, a US government agency, on condition that $35 million went on the construction of a five-star Hyatt hotel in Kabul.[6]

The profits from the hotel, which will be mostly for foreigners, will be repatriated from Afghanistan. A few blocks away, the American Embassy in Kabul is being rebuilt at a cost of $300 million, a figure which, coincidentally, Washington and other rich 'donor countries' have allotted for the reconstruction of all Afghanistan's main roads, which barely exist; $300 million will build just 50 miles of road. Illuminating how America exported 'democracy to the world', the head of USAID, Andrew Natsios, described 'aid' as 'a key foreign policy instrument'. Wishing to leave no doubt about what he meant, he said, 'Foreign assistance helps developing and transition nations move towards democratic systems and market economies; it helps nations prepare for participation in the global trading system and become better markets for US exports.'[7]

The Karzai government is a façade. Hand-picked by the United States and duly 'democratically elected' in farcical elections in 2004, it has no control of the economy and is denied a proper budget. Omar Zakhiwal, an adviser to the Minister of Rural Affairs, told me that the government received less than 20 per cent of the aid promised to Afghanistan by its 'donors'. 'We can't even pay wages,' he said.

'How much do you have for reconstruction?' I asked.

'Nothing.'

'Nothing?'

'The government of Afghanistan has no money. Period.'[8]

However, the opium trade, which was banned by the Taliban, is in full swing. Millions of dollars pass through Kabul as drugs money, much of it acquired as CIA bribes to the mafiosi warlords who hold real power in the 'new democracy', as Bush called it. These are the former *mujahedin* whose guerrilla army was effectively created by the Americans in the 1980s as an instrument of the Cold War. As the Bush administration prepared to attack Afghanistan in the wake of September 11, 2001 – despite all the evidence linking the attack on the Twin Towers to Saudi Arabians – CIA agents secretly met their old clients on the border with Pakistan and handed them millions of dollars in cash. 'We were reaching out to every commander that we could,' a CIA official told the *Wall Street Journal*.[9]

By 'reaching out', he meant bribing them to stop fighting each other and instead fight the Taliban. In his semi-official history, the *Washington Post* reporter Bob Woodward reports that the CIA spent $70 million in bribes.[10] He describes a meeting between a CIA agent known as 'Gary' and a warlord called Amniat-Melli:

> Gary placed a bundle of cash on the table: $500,000 in ten one-foot stacks of $100 bills. He believed it would be more impressive than the usual $200,000, the best way to say we're here, we're serious, here's money, we know you need it . . . Gary would soon ask CIA headquarters for and receive $10 million in cash.[11]

Calling themselves the Northern Alliance, the warlords, and the American bombing, drove their former *mujahedin* comrades, the Taliban, into the mountains. Today, regardless of the claims of the Karzai government, whose writ runs no further than the gates of Kabul, the Taliban is returning by stealth. Meanwhile, the CIA's warlords rule Afghanistan by fear and extortion.

America's favourite client-warlord is General Rashid Dostum, an Uzbek factional leader who rules his fiefdom from the northern city of Mazar-I-Sharif. His reputation for brutality includes chaining his enemies to the tracks of tanks; and he is infamous for the siege of Konduz in November, 2001. This ended in a dirt fort, Qala-I-Jhangi, where thousands of Taliban prisoners-of-war were herded by Dostum's men, then cluster-bombed by American aircraft. Those who survived had oil poured on them, and were set alight, or were shot with their hands tied behind their backs. According to a documentary film by the former BBC director Jamie Doran, three thousand prisoners, out of eight thousand who had surrendered, were suffocated or died of their wounds in closed containers, and their bodies were buried in mass graves. One of Dostum's soldiers says in Doran's film: 'I was a witness when an American soldier broke one prisoner's neck and poured acid on others. The Americans did whatever they wanted. We had no power to stop them.'[12]

Isobel Hilton, a *Guardian* columnist, wrote:

Surely the point about civilisation is that it does not descend lightly into terror and barbarism? . . . The Afghans, we hear, have a bent for savagery and it would be absurd to expect a war in Afghanistan to be fought by Queensberry rules. But whose war is this? . . . Were [the Americans] fighting by Dostum's rules or by their own? Or do we no longer bother with the distinction?[13]

Nothing has changed: not the cluster bombs, which were tested in Vietnam; not the barbaric clients, whose lineage goes back to the British in Afghanistan; and not the enduring shock to the liberal conscience when forced to acknowledge that 'terror and barbarism' are altogether standard practice on 'our' side.

General Dostum has since declared himself a pillar of the 'new democracy', even standing for the presidency in the 2004 elections. His power is money, mostly dollars, and his militia, which is deployed at the border checkpoint with Uzbekistan, plundering a fortune in customs revenue. He has added a Roman-style indoor swimming pool, complete with chandeliers, to one of his mansions; he inaugurated this by swimming with his buddies from US Special Operations Forces, known as 'Team Tiger O2'.

Afghanistan today is what the CIA in its Vietnam days called 'the grand illusion' of the American 'cause'. According to

George W. Bush, the country has entered 'a new era of hope'. For a few Afghanis, there is some truth in this; in Kabul, certain freedoms denied by the Taliban have tentatively returned: the playing of music and sport, and the reopening of girls' schools, together with a new constitution that gives women basic rights such as the vote. In the 2004 elections, the first vote was cast for the television cameras by a nineteen-year-old woman; pictures of women queuing to register their votes appeared on the front pages of American newspapers. The Karzai government claimed that 40 per cent of voters were women. In truth, as observers reported, the figure was as low as 10 per cent, and many women who had registered were prevented from voting.[14]

In the 2005 elections – for parliament and provincial councils – farce took over. Having banned political parties from taking part, Karzai reduced the voting to a popularity contest among 5,800 individuals. More than half the seats in the Wolesi Jorga (Lower House) went to warlords, jihadis and former Taliban chieftains, many at war with one another. They include the likes of Al-Haj Mulavi Qalamuddin, head of the Taliban's Department for the Prevention of Vice and the Promotion of Virtue and source of the Taliban's harshest decrees, such as the closing of girls' schools and the stoning to death of adulterous couples. During the campaign, female candidates were intimidated and attacked; in Helmand province, a $4,000 reward for killing them was posted. The chaos is said to ensure the Americans keep ultimate control. Rather, it ensures they are blamed and make new enemies.

For the 90 per cent of the population who live beyond the cities, there is no liberation. For many, it is as if the Taliban had never departed; for some, the ultra-puritanical Taliban mullahs in black, who punished banditry, rape and murder, are missed. In their wake, the warlords have 'essentially hijacked the country', say human rights groups. Soldiers and police kidnap villagers with impunity and hold them for ransom in unofficial prisons. The rape of women, girls and boys, robbery and arbitrary killing are widespread. As soon as they open, many girls' schools are burned down. 'Because the soldiers are targeting women and girls,' reports Human Rights Watch, 'many are staying indoors, making it impossible for them to attend school [or] go to work.'

In the western city of Herat, women are arrested if they drive. Prohibited from travelling with an unrelated man, even a taxi driver, they are subjected to a 'chastity test' if they are caught, squandering precious medical services to which, says Human Rights Watch, 'women and girls have almost no access, particularly in Herat, where fewer than one per cent give birth with a trained attendant'. According to UNICEF, the mortality of Afghani mothers giving birth is the highest in the world. Men are banned from teaching women and girls. Girls and boys are not allowed to be in school buildings at the same time.[15] Until 2004, Herat was ruled by the warlord Ismail Khan, whom Defense Secretary Donald Rumsfeld described as 'an appealing man . . . thoughtful, measured and self-confident'.[16]

'The last time we met in this chamber,' said George W. Bush in his State of the Union address in 2002, 'the mothers and daughters of Afghanistan were captives in their own homes, forbidden from working or going to school. Today, women are free, and are part of Afghanistan's new government. And we welcome the new minister of women's affairs, Dr Sima Samar.'[17]

A slight, middle-aged woman in a headscarf stood and received the choreographed ovation. A physician who studied medicine after she married at eighteen, she was active in the resistance during the Soviet invasion. When her husband was arrested in 1984, never to be seen again, she and her small son fled to Pakistan, where she established the first hospital for refugee women forbidden to visit male doctors. She became a passionate critic of purdah and the wearing of the burqa and revealed that many women suffered from osteomalacia, a softening of the bones caused by inadequate diet and reduced exposure to sunlight, a consequence of their domestic imprisonment. Returning audaciously to Afghanistan, she set up four hospitals and ten clinics in rural areas and ran literacy programmes and medical training courses for twenty thousand female students, often in secret. Even when the Taliban closed two of her hospitals, they baulked at silencing her.

Her appropriation by Bush was short-lived. No sooner had the applause in Congress died away than she was smeared with a false charge of blasphemy and forced out of Karzai's interim Cabinet. The warlords were not tolerating even a gesture of female emancipation. Today, she lives in Kabul, in constant fear for her life. She has two fearsome bodyguards armed with automatic rifles, one at her gate, the other at her office door. She travels at speed in a blacked-out van. 'For the past twenty-three years, I was not safe,' she told me, 'but I was never in hiding or travelling with gunmen, which I must do now . . . There is no more official law to stop women from going to school and work, and there is a [new] law about dress code; but the reality is that even under the Taliban there was not the pressure on women in the rural areas that there is now.'[18]

Gender apartheid may have legally ended, but for as many as 90 per cent of Afghani women, the paper 'reforms' are as meaningless as Bush's gesture to their champion. The burqa remains ubiquitous. As Sima Samar says, the plight of rural women is often more desperate now because, unlike the Taliban, who punished crimes against women, the warlords now commit these crimes 'with impunity on an enormous scale', according to Amnesty International.[19]

One evening, at a bombed-out shoe factory in west Kabul, I found the population of two villages huddled on exposed floors without light and with one trickling tap. They were like a community in hiding, guarded at each access point by steadfast elderly men, the young men having been kidnapped by the 'commanders' to fight in the militias. Small children squatted around open fires on crumbling parapets: the day before, a child had fallen to his death; on the day I was there, another child fell and was badly injured. A meal for them is bread dipped in tea. Their owl eyes are those of terrified refugees in their own land. They had fled their homes, they explained, because warlords robbed them and kidnapped their wives and daughters and sons, whom they would rape and ransom back to them. They pointed to a woman squatting like a wounded bird.

'Raped,' said an elderly man.

'Who by?'

'A commander . . . he took ten women from our village.'

'What will happen to her?'

'We watch her, but she may kill herself.'

'Did this happen under the Taliban?'

'No. We had nothing, no rights, but our homes were secure, the roads were safe.'[20]

Marina corroborated this. 'Marina' is the code-name for a leading member of Rawa, the Revolutionary Association of Afghani Women, which since 1977 has alerted the world to the suffering of Afghani women. Rawa women still travel secretly throughout the country, with cameras concealed beneath their burqas. During the Taliban time, they filmed an official execution and other atrocities, and smuggled the videotape to the West. 'We took it to all the main media groups,' said Marina. 'Reuters, ABC Australia, for example, and they said, "Yes, it's very nice, but we can't show it because it's too shocking for people in the West." '

That was before September 11, 2001, when George W. Bush and the American media discovered the women of Afghanistan. 'The Taliban suddenly became the official enemy of America,' she said. 'They persecuted women, yes, but they were not unique, and we have resented the silence in the West over the atrocious nature of the Western-backed warlords, who are no different. In some ways, we were more secure under the Taliban. You could cross Afghanistan by road and feel secure. Now, you take your life into your hands.'

We met clandestinely and she wore a veil to disguise her identity. 'This is what happens in the countryside under these so-called commanders,' she said, opening a thick file. 'In March, two girls who went to school without their burqas were killed and their bodies were put in front of their houses. Last month, thirty-five women jumped into a river along with their children and died, just to save themselves from commanders on a rampage of rape. That is not uncommon; it is Afghanistan today; the Taliban and the warlords of the Northern Alliance are two faces of the same coin. If America had not built up these warlords, Osama bin Laden and all the fundamentalist forces in Afghanistan during the Russian invasion, they would not have attacked the master on September 11, 2001.'[21]

At the height of the British Empire, in 1898, Lord Curzon, Viceroy of India, wrote: 'I confess that [countries] are pieces on a chessboard, upon which is being played out a great game for the domination of the world.'[22] He was referring in particular to Afghanistan, whose strategic trade routes the British regarded as vital to their holding sway over Central Asia and the Caspian basin. The ruthlessness and 'grand illusions' of the 'great game' are etched on the pages of Afghanistan's modern history, telling us much about the origins of the 'war on terror'. A secret chapter is America's and Britain's support for and collusion with tribal groups known as the *mujahedin*, and the critical part they played in launching and stimulating the *jihad* that led to the attack on 'the master' on September 11, 2001.

The Afghani *mujahedin* – and the Taliban and al-Qaida – were effectively created by the CIA, its Pakistani equivalent the ISI, and Britain's MI6. In admitting this, Zbigniew Brzezinski, who was President Jimmy Carter's National Security Adviser in the late 1970s, has disclosed Carter's secret directive to bankroll the *mujahedin* and America's collaboration 'with the Saudis, the Egyptians, the British, the Chinese [to start] providing weapons to the *mujahedin*'.[23] Regarded in Washington as something of a guru of Pax Americana, Brzezinski believed that the post-colonial liberation movements and their gains throughout the 'third world' presented a challenge to the United States, as demonstrated by the recent American humiliation in Vietnam. Moreover, the Anglo-American client regimes in the Middle East and the Gulf, notably Iran under the Shah, were vulnerable to gathering forces of insurrection.

The immediate problem, however, was the coming to power of Afghanistan's first secular, modernist government, which promised unheard-of social reforms. This was formed by the People's Democratic Party of Afghanistan (PDPA), which had opposed the autocratic rule of King Zahir Shah and, with progressive military officers, had overthrown the regime of the king's cousin, Mohammad Daud, in 1978. Most foreign journalists in Kabul, reported the *New York Times*, found that 'nearly every Afghan they interviewed said [they were] delighted with the coup'.[24]

This may have been true in the cities, but in the countryside the coup provoked bitter resistance from Muslim traditionalists, especially when the new government outlined a reform programme that included the abolition of feudalism, freedom of religion and equal rights for women. So radical were the changes that they remain vivid in the memories of those who were their beneficiaries. Saira Noorani, a female surgeon who escaped the Taliban in September 2001, recalled:

> Every girl could go to high school and university. We could go where we wanted and wear what we liked . . . We used to go to cafés and the cinema to see the latest Indian films on a Friday . . . It all started to go wrong when the *mujahedin* started winning . . . They used to kill teachers and burn schools . . . It was funny and sad to think these were people the West had supported.[25]

For Washington, the problem with the PDPA government was that it was supported by the Soviet Union. At Brzezinski's urging, and unknown to the American public and Congress, President Carter authorised $500 million to fund and arm the *mujahedin*: in effect, to set up what the Americans would now describe as a terrorist organisation. The aim was to overthrow the Afghan government and to draw the Soviets into Afghanistan.

In an interview in 1998, Brzezinski said:

> According to the official view of history, CIA aid to the *mujahedin* began during 1980, that is, after the Soviet Union invaded Afghanistan on 24 December 1979. But the reality, secretly guarded until now, is completely otherwise. Indeed, it was on 3 July 1979 that President Carter signed the first directive for secret aid to the opponents of the pro-Soviet regime in Kabul. And that very day, I wrote a note to the president in which I explained to him that in my opinion this aid was going to provoke a Soviet military intervention . . . We didn't push the Russians to intervene, but we knowingly increased the probability that they would.

Brzezinski was asked if, having seen the consequences, he had any regrets. 'Regret what?' he replied.

The secret operation was an excellent idea. It had the effect
of drawing the Russians into the Afghan trap . . . The day
that the Soviets officially crossed the border, I wrote to
President Carter: 'We now have the opportunity of giving
the USSR its Vietnam War.' Indeed, for almost ten years,
Moscow had to carry on a conflict that brought about the
demoralisation and finally the break-up of the Soviet
empire.[26]

For seventeen years, the United States deliberately cultivated an
extremism against which it would later proclaim a 'war on terror'.
'Central to the US-sponsored operation', wrote Nafeez Mosaddeq
Ahmed in *The War on Truth: 9/11, Disinformation and the
Anatomy of Terrorism*,

was the attempt to manufacture an extremist religious
ideology by amalgamating local Afghan feudal traditions
with Islamic rhetoric . . . The extremist religious 'jihadi'
ideology cultivated in CIA-sponsored training programs
was interspersed with tribal norms, giving rise to a
distinctly distorted system of war-values garbed with
'Islamic' jargon . . . Among the myriad of policies designed
to generate the desired level of extremism, the US funded –
to the tune of millions of dollars – the production and
distribution in Afghanistan of school textbooks promoting
murder and fanaticism.[27]

These primers, disclosed the *Washington Post* in 2002, 'were filled
with talk of jihad and featured drawings of guns, bullets, soldiers
and mines. [They] have served since then as the Afghan school
system's core curriculum. Even the Taliban used the American-
produced books.' According to candid American officials, the
textbooks 'steeped a generation in violence'.[28]

American administrations poured $4 billion into the pockets of
some of the world's most brutal fanatics. Men like Gulbuddin
Hekmatyar received tens of millions of CIA dollars. Hekmatyar's
speciality was trafficking in opium and harassing women who
refused to wear the veil. Invited to London in 1986, he was lauded

by Prime Minister Thatcher as a 'freedom fighter'. Following the fall of the PDPA government in 1992, *mujahedin* warlords attacked Kabul with such ferocity that an estimated fifty thousand people were killed. 'In 1994 alone,' reported Human Rights Watch, 'an estimated 25,000 people were killed in Kabul, most of them civilians, in rocket and artillery attacks. One-third of the city was reduced to rubble.'[29] Hekmatyar, the West's favourite warlord at the time, rained American-supplied missiles on Kabul, killing two thousand people in two days, until the other factions agreed to make him Prime Minister.

Brzezinski's 'great game' coincided with the ambition of the Pakistani dictator, General Zia ul-Haq, to dominate the region. In 1986, CIA Director William Casey approved a plan put forward by Pakistan's intelligence agency, the ISI, to recruit people from around the world to join the Afghan *jihad*. Some hundred thousand Islamic militants were trained in Pakistan between 1982 and 1992; these were *taliban*, which means students. *Mujahedin* camps were run by the CIA and Britain's MI6, with British special forces, the SAS, training future al-Qaida and Taliban fighters in bomb-making and other black arts. In the United States, CIA operatives who would eventually join the Taliban and Osama bin Laden were recruited at an Islamic college in Brooklyn, New York – within sight of the Twin Towers – and given paramilitary training at a CIA camp in Virginia. This was code-named Operation Cyclone.

Osama bin Laden's notoriety was the product of this. In Afghanistan, wrote John Cooley in *Unholy Wars: Afghanistan, America and International Terrorism*, he operated

> with the full approval of the Saudi regime and the CIA . . . He brought in engineers from his father's company and heavy construction equipment to build roads and warehouses for the mujaheddin. In 1986, he helped build a CIA-financed tunnel complex, to serve as a major arms storage depot, training facility and medical center for the mujaheddin, deep under the mountains close to the Pakistan border . . . The CIA gave Usama [bin Laden] full rein in Afghanistan, as did Pakistan's intelligence generals.[30]

According to Michael Springmann, former head of the US Visa Bureau in Jeddah, it was policy 'to bring recruits, rounded up by Osama bin Laden, to the US for terrorist training by the CIA'.[31]

Operation Cyclone, wrote Nafeez Ahmed,

> provided the CIA with the ability to recruit, finance and train terrorist groups throughout the Muslim world. The goal of these policies was to destabilise nationalist and communist movements that threatened US interests . . . Extremists in Pakistan were thus mobilised by the CIA in tandem with the Saudis to proliferate extremist sects in Afghanistan, Pakistan, Algeria, Yemen, Indonesia, the Philippines and elsewhere. Simultaneously, organised criminal financial centers intertwined with the latter were established in Malaysia, Madagascar, South Africa, Nigeria, Latin America, Switzerland, the United Kingdom, Turkestan and elsewhere.[32]

During NATO's assault on Serbia in 1999, al-Qaida militants joined up with and fought alongside the Kosovo Liberation Army (KLA), which was also funded and armed by the United States – and al-Qaida. The Clinton administration's quarry then was Slobodan Milosevic and its goal the final break-up of multi-ethnic, 'socialist' Yugoslavia. This was achieved by enduring bedfellows: American foreign policy (bombing) and 'Islamic terrorism'. Such an important irony, which helped to explain the rise of the *jihadis*, eluded the media reporting of Kosovo's 'liberation'.

In his 1997 book, *The Grand Chessboard: American Primacy and its Geostrategic Imperatives*, Brzezinski writes, 'Ever since the continents started interacting politically, some 500 years ago, Eurasia has been the center of world power.'[33] He defines Eurasia as all the territory east of Germany and Poland, stretching through Russia and China to the Pacific Ocean and including the Middle East and most of the Indian subcontinent. The key to controlling this vast area of the world is Central Asia. Dominance of Turkmenistan, Uzbekistan, Tajikistan and Kyrgyzstan ensures not only new sources of energy and mineral wealth, but a 'guardpost' over American control of the oil of the Persian Gulf.[34]

The first priority has been achieved, says Brzezinski. This is the economic subjugation of the former superpower. Once the Soviet Union had collapsed, the United States looted some $300 billion in Russian assets, destabilising the currency and ensuring that a weakened Russia would have no choice but to look westward to Europe for economic and political revival, rather than south to Central Asia. What Brzezinski calls 'local wars as responses to terrorism', such as the invasion of Afghanistan, are the beginning of a final conflict leading inexorably to the dissolution of national governments and world domination by the United States. Nation states will be incorporated in the 'new order', controlled solely by economic interests as dictated by international banks, corporations and ruling elites concerned with the maintenance (by manipulation and war) of their power. 'To put it in a terminology that harkens back to the more brutal age of ancient empires,' he writes, 'the grand imperatives of imperial geostrategy are to prevent collusion and maintain security dependence among the vassals, to keep tributaries pliant and protected and to keep the barbarians from coming together.'[35]

Surveying the ashes of the Soviet Union he helped to destroy, the Islamic *jihad* he helped generate and the terrorism he supported, Brzezinski mused: did it matter that all this had created 'a few stirred up Muslims'?[36] On September 11, 2001, 'a few stirred up Muslims' provided the answer. When I met Brzezinski in Washington in 2003, I asked him if he regretted the consequences. He became very angry and did not reply.

The potential of the oil and gas reserves of the Caspian basin has excited imperialists since the discovery of oil there at the end of the nineteenth century. It is not only America and the European powers that have wanted the Caspian oilfields. Hitler, in his invasion of Russia, and before running short of fuel and being defeated at Stalingrad, planned 'to take the saving prize of Caspian resources, then drive south for the even greater prize of Persia and Iraq'.[37] For the West, the Soviet Union barred the way to the Caspian, the vast inland sea that was said, perhaps optimistically, to contain a third of the world's oil and gas.

With the Soviet Union gone, dominion in the 'great game' and its 'chessboard' passed to the administration of Bill Clinton. The former

Soviet republics of Central Asia, declared Energy Secretary Bill Richardson, 'are all about America's energy security. We would like to see them reliant on Western commercial and political investment in the Caspian, and it's very important to us that the pipeline map and the politics come out right.'[38]

What he meant was that the region's oil and gas were worthless without the means to carry them to deep-water ports. There were three routes a pipeline to the West could take: through Russia, Iran or Afghanistan. For Washington, dependence on Russia was anathema, and Iran was the country America had spent more than two decades isolating. It was not surprising that when the Taliban, the latest mutation of America's *mujahedin* clients, took power in Kabul in 1996, they found themselves courted by the American oil lobby and its friends in the administration and the media.

Following September 11, 2001, none was more fervent in calling for the overthrow of the Taliban than the *Wall Street Journal*. However, five years earlier, the authentic voice of American capital struck an entirely different note. The Taliban, the paper declared, 'are the players most capable of achieving peace in Afghanistan at this moment in history'. Moreover, the success of these ultra-fundamentalists was crucial to secure Afghanistan as 'a prime trans-shipment route for the export of Central Asia's vast oil, gas and other natural resources'.[39]

In February 1998, John J. Maresca, Vice-President for International Relations at the Union Oil Company (Unocal), re-assured a congressional inquiry that 'the Taliban does not practise the anti-US style of fundamentalism practised by Iran'. He made no mention of the Taliban's extremism, notably its persecution of women. Unocal had secretly signed a contract to export $8 billion worth of natural gas through a $3 billion pipeline which the company would build from Turkmenistan, through Afghanistan to Pakistan.[40] The Taliban would get fifteen cents for every thousand cubic feet the company pumped through Afghanistan.[41] The problem of the Taliban's reputation was foreseen; shortly after the mullahs seized power in 1996, the State Department dropped Afghanistan from its list of governments that 'protect and promote terrorists'. That the Taliban were then harbouring Osama bin Laden was not a factor. When asked about their appalling human rights record, a senior American diplomat said that it was likely that 'the Taliban will develop like the Saudis', running an oil colony with no democracy and 'lots of Sharia law', such as the legalised persecution of women. 'We can live with that,' he said.[42]

In his Yale University study *Taliban*, Ahmed Rashid wrote that 'the State Department and Pakistan's Inter-services Intelligence Agency agreed to funnel arms and funding to the Taliban in their war against the ethnically Tajik Northern Alliance. As recently as 1999, US taxpayers paid the entire annual salary of every single Taliban official.'[43]

The initial plans for the pipeline were drawn up by Enron, the world's largest energy company, which was to collapse in 2002 under the weight of its corruption. According to an FBI official, 'when Clinton was bombing bin Laden camps in Afghanistan in 1998, Enron was making payoffs to Taliban and bin Laden operatives to keep the pipeline project alive. And there's no way that anyone could not have known of the Taliban and bin Laden connection at that time, especially Enron.'[44]

In 1997, with a pipeline 'memorandum of understanding' agreed, Taliban leaders were flown in high secrecy to the United States, where they were courted and entertained lavishly. Their visit was so secret that a search of TV news archives failed to reveal a single item on it. Yet the Taliban themselves were not so shy, and hired a public relations consultant, Laila Helms, the part-Afghan niece of the former CIA Director Richard Helms. Dressed in the traditional flowing *salwar khameez* and loose, black turbans, men accustomed to a life without electricity and running water dined in the luxurious homes of Texan oil barons. At a party in their honour hosted by Unocal Vice-President Marty F. Miller, they expressed awe at his vast swimming pool, six bathrooms and views over a golf course. 'The first day, they were stiff and cautious,' said Miller. 'But before long, they were totally relaxed and happy. They asked what the Christmas tree was for. They were interested to know what the star was.' It was this 'good old Texas hospitality' that clinched the pipeline deal.[45]

At a ceremony at Unocal headquarters, the visitors were presented with their first-ever fax machine, along with a generator to power it. The first document to come cranking out predicted that the pipeline could net them at least $100,000 a year. To complete their American experience, the Taliban were flown to the NASA space centre and Mount Rushmore, where the profiles of presidents of the United States are carved in the hillside, and finally to a vast shopping mall, where they went on a spree in a cut-price Target store, buying toothpaste, soap, combs and, interestingly, women's stockings.[46]

For the American 'oil and gas junta', as the oil lobby is known these days in Washington, everything was going swimmingly. When Unocal cut its deal with the Taliban, it did so on behalf of a consortium of Enron, Amoco, British Petroleum, Chevron, Exxon and Mobil. The principal deal-makers were Dick Cheney, former Defense Secretary and future Vice-President, then chairman of Halliburton, the giant oil facilities company, and James Baker, former Secretary of State under George Bush Senior. Condoleezza Rice, future National Security Adviser to George W. Bush and now Secretary of State, was then a vice-president of Chevron Oil with responsibility for Central Asia.

Enter Osama bin Laden, already a sworn enemy of the United States living in Afghanistan. Worried that if the pipeline deal progressed the Taliban might end up in the American camp, bin Laden is reckoned to have planned the bombing of two American embassies in East Africa in 1998 as a warning to the Americans to get out of 'Islamic countries', specifically Afghanistan. The American response was not to attack Afghanistan, where bin Laden was ensconced, but to send missiles into his former sanctuary, Sudan. The target of this 'smokescreen' attack was the al-Shifa pharmaceutical plant, which Washington described as a 'chemical weapons facility'.

This was absurd; al-Shifa was famous throughout the continent as the manufacturer of chloroquine, the most effective treatment for malaria, and anti-tuberculosis drugs that were lifelines to a hundred thousand patients in sub-Saharan Africa. It was also the only regional source for veterinary drugs that killed the parasites passed from cattle to people, one of the main causes of infant mortality. As a direct result of the American attack, according to the Near East Foundation, 'tens of thousands of people – many of them children – have suffered and died from malaria, tuberculosis and other treatable diseases'.[47]

At the same time, the Clinton administration curiously declared that al-Qaida was 'not supported by any state'. This meant it was attempting to rescue its relationship with the Taliban, and the pipeline deal.[48] Once again, invitations were flashed to Kabul, and in March 2001 – shortly after the Taliban had outraged international opinion by blowing up the ancient Buddhas of Bamiyan – an adviser to the Taliban leader Mullah Omar, Sayed Rahmatullah Hashimi, was flown to Washington. Like a close ally, he was welcomed to the CIA's headquarters in Langley, Virginia, where he met members of the high-ranking Directorate of Central Intelligence. At the State Department, he conferred with the head of the Bureau of Intelligence and Research.[49] Asked about Osama bin Laden, he replied that he 'is our guest' and 'there are no terrorists'.[50]

When September 11, 2001 had finally ended America's affair with the Taliban, a US Justice Department prosecutor, John Loftus, revealed that a captured member of al-Qaida described in detail 'a cover up [that] US energy companies were secretly negotiating with the Taliban to build a pipeline' and that 'multiple sources confirm that American law enforcement agencies were deliberately kept in the dark and systematically prevented from connecting the dots before 9/11 in order to aid Enron's secret and immoral Taliban negotiations'.[51] Enron was a major bankroller of George W. Bush's presidential campaign.

The reason given by the United States for its invasion of Afghanistan in October 2001 was 'to destroy the infrastructure of al-Qaida, the perpetrators of 9/11'. However, there is evidence that the invasion was planned two months earlier, and that the most pressing problem was not the Taliban's links with Osama bin Laden, but the prospect of the mullahs losing control of Afghanistan to other *mujahedin* factions in the Northern Alliance. With each hectare of territory they conceded, the Taliban were deemed in Washington to lack the 'stability' required of an important client. It was the consistency of this client relationship, not the Taliban's aversion to human rights, that exercised the Bush administration.

Believing it was the presence of Osama bin Laden that was souring their relationship with Washington, the Taliban tried to get rid of him. Under a deal negotiated by the leaders of Pakistan's two Islamic parties, bin Laden was to be held under house arrest in

Peshawar. The plan was said to have been approved by bin Laden himself and Mullah Omar. An international tribunal would then hear evidence and decide whether to try him or hand him over to the Americans. Under pressure from Washington, Pakistan's President Musharraf vetoed the plan.[52] According to Pakistani foreign minister Niaz Naik, a senior American diplomat told him on July 21, 2001 that it had been decided to dispense with the Taliban 'under a carpet of bombs'.[53]

The dust blew in gusts as I drove into the village of Bibi Mahru. Under the Taliban, it was possible to travel outside the cities in relative safety. Now, the countryside is a dangerous maze of checkpoints and banditry. As our convoy of two vehicles arrived, villagers stood framed in the shadows of their mud doorways; they looked away and several hurried inside. They are the poorest of the poor. Their graves are marked only by pieces of shale, and ragged green flags. Here knelt Orifa at the graves of her husband, Gul Ahmed, a carpet weaver, seven other members of her family, including six children, and two children who were killed next door.

It was midday on October 7, 2001 when an American F-16 aircraft came out of a clear blue sky and dropped a 'precision' Mk82 500-pound bomb on the small mud, stone and straw house. The crater that replaced it is 50 feet wide. Orifa was away visiting relatives; when she returned, she was told to go to the mosque and collect the pieces of their bodies.

'I couldn't remember what happened next,' she said. 'I became unconscious with shock. When my eyes opened, I was at the mosque, where I had been taken by taxi. My husband lay on a *charpaie* [a special bed for carrying corpses]. There was no space there for washing the bodies, and my sons and daughter were in a terrible state. One was burnt all over and the other was so crushed I didn't recognise her. One of the other girls was almost headless. On another, all the back flesh had gone. I found myself collecting pieces of flesh, and bagging and naming it for burial. I worked until midnight when at last we buried them. Only then I realised I was homeless; I had nothing, just the hand of my surviving son, and God.'

The son who lived, whose name is Jawad, was fourteen at the time. Pieces of shrapnel had to be hand-picked from his face, which is now permanently pocked. He is silent, sitting with his chin on his hand behind Orifa as she works at her ancient sewing machine in their hut behind the crater. She rents the sewing machine, which gives her an income of less than a dollar a day. Her only possessions, she said, were the photographs of her dead husband and children arranged on a window ledge around an almost-empty bottle of blue-coloured hair shampoo.

'Did you get any compensation?' I asked.

'I got [about $400] which has all gone on medical care for Jawad.'

'The Americans gave you that?' I asked.

'No, the Taliban. They came and offered prayers and gave me the money in a cloth bag . . . Later, eleven Americans came and surveyed the crater where my home had stood. They wrote down the numbers on pieces of shrapnel and each one spoke to me and took notes. As they were leaving, their translator gave me an envelope with fifteen notes: fifteen dollars. That's less than two dollars for each of my family killed.'

'Had you heard what happened in America on September 11, 2001?'

'Yes. I don't know all the details because I am an illiterate person. I heard many were killed: children included. But why should my family die, too? What is this freedom the Americans say they have brought us? Please explain this to me.'[54]

At 7.45 a.m. on October 21, 2001, Gulam Rasul, the headmaster of New Project School in the town of Khair Khana, had just finished eating breakfast with his family. He walked outside to chat to a neighbour. Inside the house were his wife, Shiekria, aged thirty-five, his four sons aged three to ten, his brother and his wife, his sister and her husband. There was an explosion and the headmaster turned to see rising smoke 100 metres away, and an aircraft weaving in the sky, coming towards him. The house exploded in a fireball behind him. Nine people, including a boy killed nearby, died in this attack by an F-16 dropping another 'precision' 500-pound bomb. The only survivor was Gulam's nine-year-old son, Ahmad Bilal.

I sat with the headmaster and his son on the balcony of a house nearby. He spoke quickly, fluently, looking directly at me as he called out the names and ages of his dead sons . . . 'Ahmad Khalid, aged ten, Ahmad Haris, aged six, Ahmad Tamir, aged five, Ahmad Sahil, aged three . . .

'Most of the people killed in this war they call a liberation were not Taliban; they were innocents. If we think deeply about the revolution of the Taliban we realise it was America that developed and nurtured them; and it was America that destroyed their authority, which was a terrorist act, because it is us, the people, who pay the price. Was the killing of my family a mistake? No, it was not. They fly their planes and look down on us, the mere Afghan people, who have no planes, and they bomb us for our birthright, with all contempt.'

'What compensation did you receive?'

'Nothing. No-one came. No-one sent anything. My friend, the police chief, even went to the American Embassy. They didn't understand him, and shut the door.'[55]

On December 29, 2001, the village of Niazi Qala was holding a wedding party for the son of a respected farmer, Bahram Jan. Members of the bride's family had travelled across the great arid south-eastern plain. By all accounts, it was a boisterous affair, with music and singing and old rifles being discharged at the night sky. In the morning, there was devastation: on a fence, torn clothing and pieces of human flesh flapped in the wind; houses were demolished with, amid the bricks, more flesh and tufts of children's hair.

The roar of the planes had started at three in the morning, long after everybody had retired for the night. Then the bombs began to fall – 500-pounders leading the way, scooping out the earth and felling a row of houses. According to neighbours watching from a distance, the planes flew three sorties over the village and a helicopter hovered close to the ground, firing flares, then rockets. Women and children were seen running from the houses towards a dried pond, perhaps in search of protection from the gunfire, but were shot as they ran.

The American commander at Bagram military base, near Kabul, said that two Taliban leaders were among the wedding guests and were a 'legitimate military target'. An investigation by the United Nations found no evidence of this, and concluded that the allegation that planes had pursued women and children was 'well-founded'. During two hours of attack, said the UN report, fifty-two people were killed: seventeen men, ten women and twenty-five children. An elderly man, Sher Khan, who lost seven relatives, told the investigators that forty-eight people were still missing.

What was unusual about that atrocity was that it was reported in the West.[56] Like the slaughter of the families of Orifa and Gulam Rasul, countless other attacks on isolated villages have not been reported and no compensation has been paid. A bus carrying fleeing refugees was blown up by American planes and thirty-five people died. The village of Karam was repeatedly bombed, killing at least 160. Low-flying AC-130 aircraft, designed to destroy tanks, strafed two villages, Bori Chokar and Chowkar-Karez, killing ninety-three.

The few journalists able and willing to collect the evidence and present it were repeatedly told in Washington, 'It did not happen.' In the case of Chowkar-Karez, a Pentagon spokesman expressed frustration with his script. 'The people there are dead,' he said, 'because we wanted them dead.'[57] While murderous tactics have been recognised in the assault on Iraq, a similar pattern of atrocities in Afghanistan has not. At the time of writing, independent investigators are denied entry to areas classified 'operational' and the Western media have lost interest.

At Kabul University, I met Professor Kazem Ahang, a sociologist. I asked him about the lack of compensation for civilians killed. 'You must understand,' he replied, with dry-as-dust irony, 'that many foreigners have come to help us. There are eleven thousand international non-government agencies here. Many of their staff get ten thousand dollars a month. To keep just one official here for a year, the United Nations spends two hundred and fifty thousand dollars.'

I stopped outside the Ghazi High School in ruined west Kabul to talk to students. One said: 'Tell me please, where have you ever seen a school like ours?' The school was mostly rubble, with strips of hessian and sheets of plastic covering classes in progress. As I chatted to the students, a man strode out of the gate.

'Who are you?' he demanded.

'I am a journalist from Britain.'

'What salary do you earn?'

'Why?'

'Well, I get thirty-eight dollars a month, and I am the principal of this establishment. I ask you: why should you get more than I get, why should you eat every evening when I miss a meal so that my family can eat? We are both human beings, are we not?'

'Yes.'

'I am sorry if I insult you.'

'You don't insult me: you are right. May I see your school?'

'Yes, please, you are my guest, come inside . . .'

Children sat on mats and shared a single exercise book; here and there was a textbook, old and yellowing and torn and with pages missing. When the principal rang a big brass bell, the children exchanged one derelict site of learning for another. I watched as he and his small staff read to them, persisting heroically. 'These wars have had a truly momentous effect on the morale of all of us,' he told me. 'Take myself: a few years ago, I was able to speak fluent English, but now I have forgotten everything. Wars make one forget one's language, one's education, one's teachings. A student today needs a subject repeated and repeated to him, or he will not understand, because the young have been emotionally invaded and left with only anguish. They constantly worry about shell or bomb attacks, or stepping on a mine; they are terrified of aircraft. These wars have taken away our minds, and the spirit of our lives, and left us with only the shells of our bodies.'

I have seldom heard anyone as fearful, eloquent and brave as this principled man. With his square shoulders and fine moustache, he had what was once known as bearing. Yet his shoes had burst open at the seams. I offered him money 'for the school', which he refused while extending his hand to shake mine. I regret that I have mislaid his name, which he had written for me in a copperplate hand, ending with 'Peace to you'.[58]

On the drive to Bagram base, snow-capped mountains rose from a moonscape through which ran an empty ribbon of road, laid by the Soviet military when they built the base in the 1980s. It is now an American bubble, with air-conditioning, movies, email, all imported food and water. Military vehicles sweep in and out, flying vast American flags. There is a sense of *Catch-22*: of sullen, faintly mutinous, hog-sized soldiers and career officers who either affect a certain comic madness or are indeed troubled.

'How did you get here?' said a soldier on the gate.

'We drove from Kabul.'

'Where's that?'

'It's the capital of the country, one hour away.'

'Gotcha.'

In the base's briefing room there was a blackboard on which was scribbled: 'There is nothing I detest more than the stench of lies – Kurtz, aka Marlon Brando'. Beside this was draped a bright yellow banner that read, 'James Buchanan High School loves the 109th. We're proud to be American. Thanks for protecting our rights.' Beneath this was: 'No pornography in laptops!' An officer with a shiny head and an unusually wide and unfaltering grin skipped into the briefing room and up to the lectern.

'Good morning! I am Colonel Rod Davis, director of public affairs for CJTF 180. This morning I am going to take you on a tour of Bagram airbase, starting at what we refer to as Bagram High School, where the local Afghan youth attend. It's the only school in the area and is supported by the US government. The school is part of our civic action commitment, our humanitarian work. We call it our CAC work. That's C-A-C, which stands for Civic Action Company.'

'Is it like a WHAM unit?' I asked.

'Sir?'

'Winning hearts and minds, like the army had in Vietnam.'

'Hey, I like WHAM: like the sound of it, the ring to it.'[59]

'Come on out, we're your friends!' Sergeant Melvin Murrell had shouted through a bullhorn; not a shadow moved. 'Come on out everybody, we got rice and candy and tooth-brushes to give you.'

Sergeant Murrell had brought his WHAM unit to the village of Tuylon in central Vietnam. Now he cooed into the hot silence, 'Listen, either you gooks come on out from wherever you are or we're going to come in there and get you and maybe kill you!'

*So the people of Tuylon came out from wherever they
were and queued to receive packets of Uncle Ben's Miracle
Rice, chocolate bars, party balloons and 7,000 tooth-
brushes; and in a separate ceremony befitting his station,
the district chief was presented with four portable, battery-
operated, yellow flush lavatories.*[60]

'The people of Afghanistan are grateful to us,' said Colonel
Davis as he led me, at a cracking pace, through 'Bagram High
School'. Opaque faces watched us intently; no-one spoke. The
colonel's aide carried an M-16 automatic rifle. 'Hey, we get shot at
every time we leave the base,' said Colonel Davis. To illustrate this,
he took a pistol from a holster strapped to his thigh and cocked it.
'I like to have my finger on the trigger at all times.'

'But, Colonel, you said these people are grateful . . .'

'Sir, we liberated them. We gave their women freedom . . . Sure,
we've got a lot more CAC work to do. Or WHAM. Hey, I like that:
less bang more WHAM!'

As we accelerated away from the school, the colonel seemed to
relax. I asked him, 'Can I see the interrogation centre?'

'Woo-ah! . . . you must be referring to the detention facility.'

'Who do you have in there?'

'We refer to them as personnel under custody, definitely not
prisoners-of-war.'

'Aren't many of them innocent people, caught up in the war on
terror, who are not terrorists, who disappear into this place, then
end up in Guantanamo Bay?'

'These people are illegal.'

'Under what law are they illegal?'

'It's rather complicated and I guess there is some kind of
continuum or spectrum, if you will, with prisoners-of-war off to
the far left or right depending on your political perspective, and
something less than that off to the far other end . . . America is
somewhere on that spectrum.'

'Colonel, I didn't understand a word of that.'

There was an extended silence.

'I am a Christian, sir.'

'Yes?'

'I will kill but I am a Christian.'

We were now standing outside the 'detention facility', a windowless converted hangar. 'Al-Qaida suspects' are interrogated here before they are flown to Guantanamo Bay or, to use the CIA jargon, 'rendered' to a country, such as Egypt, where they can be tortured beyond the reach of American law. Two former prisoners, Abdul Jabar and Hakkim Shah, have described how as many as a hundred inmates were made to stand hooded, their arms raised and chained to the ceiling, their feet shackled, unable to move, day and night. Abdul Jabar suffered this torture for sixteen days, standing for ten consecutive days until his legs became so swollen that the shackles around his ankles stopped the blood flow. He was naked the whole time, and the air-conditioning, turned full on, kept him awake, along with the American guards who kicked and shouted at him to stop him falling asleep. He was released suddenly, without explanation. The fate of the others is not known.[61]

During a year incarcerated here, Moazzam Begg, the Briton released from Guantanamo Bay in January 2005, reported witnessing the deaths of two fellow prisoners 'at the hands of US military personnel'.[62] Internal military reports obtained by Human Rights Watch revealed that a 22-year-old farmer called Dilawar was so severely beaten during two days in Bagram's interrogation 'facility' that 'even if he had survived, both legs would have had to be amputated'. A death certificate dated December 13, 2002, signed by Major Elizabeth Rouse, a US military pathologist, says he died as a result of 'blunt force injuries to lower extremities complicating coronary artery disease'. She described his death as 'homicide'.[63]

'We treat the people in here humanely and fairly,' said Colonel Davis. 'There is no abuse or torture . . .'

'Colonel, there is the evidence of one of your own pathologists, who described how an Afghan man called Dilawar was murdered. Two former prisoners saw him naked, hooded and shackled, and deprived of sleep for days on end. You know that case?'

'I am aware of the allegations and what I'll say to you is that we aren't known for committing atrocities. That's not the way we do business.'

'But the CIA has described its methods here as "gloves off".'

'All allegations are investigated.'

'Why don't you allow Amnesty International to inspect the facility?'

'Let me explain our position this way. One of the tough things about modern-day warfare, this era of terrorism, is that the lines are grey. Terrorists are not officially sanctioned operators; they aren't provided all the rights in the Geneva Convention . . .'

'Who says they're terrorists?'

'We do.'

'Colonel, I interviewed the brother of a man whose name is Wasir Mohammed. He was a taxi driver who enquired at a checkpoint about a friend, another taxi driver, who had disappeared into Bagram. For that alone, he was arrested, detained here and he is now in Guantanamo Bay. A former minister in the present Afghan government knows this man well. He has told me that not only is he an innocent man, he's well known as an opponent of the Taliban and was imprisoned by them. But now he's in an American cage in Guantanamo . . .'

'Sir, what's your point in telling me this?'

'The point is that his family have been told nothing; they are beside themselves with worry. All of them have been denied the most basic human rights. What do you say to them and to all those like them?'

'Sir, I'm not questioning your credibility or the credibility of that individual; I just can't comment . . .'

'How would you like it if a foreign army invaded the United States and you and your family were treated this way, and denied even information?'

'I don't understand your questions . . .'

'How would you like to be locked up and no-one on the outside knew or was told anything about you?'

'I don't get the motive behind these questions.'

'It's simple: how would you like it?'

'I'm an American, and I'm a Christian.'

The repartee of numerous 'public relations' colonels has served to distract journalists' attention from the most important stage of America's 'war on terror' since its invasion of Afghanistan. This is the establishment of a gulag of detention and torture 'facilities' across the world with Afghanistan as its hub. Bagram is the model of a system in which as many as ten thousand prisoners have been and are being 'processed' and 'rendered' unprotected by international or any country's law.

As in Latin America in the 1970s and 1980s, many are 'disappeared'. According to the director of the Afghan independent Human Rights Commission, 'many thousands of people have been rounded up and detained. Those who have been freed say they have been held alongside foreign detainees who've been brought to this country to be processed. No-one is charged. No-one is identified. No international monitors are allowed into [these] US jails.' These people are known as 'ghost detainees'.[64] An Afghan BBC correspondent who was arrested without explanation said, 'Every time I was moved, I was hooded again. Every prisoner has to maintain absolute silence. I could hear helicopters whirring above me. Prisoners were arriving and leaving all the time. There were also cells beneath me, under the ground.'[65]

On secret CIA flights, the prisoners are shuttled between Afghanistan and Egypt, Jordan, Syria, Malaysia, Thailand, Indonesia, Pakistan, Uzbekistan and, it is believed, the American base on the Indian Ocean island of Diego Garcia, a British colony. Here they are handed over to American 'contractors' or to local interrogators with fearsome reputations. 'What has been glimpsed in Afghanistan is a radical plan to replace Guantanamo Bay,' wrote Adrian Levy and Cathy Scott-Clark in their investigation for the *Guardian*. 'Evidence we have collected, however, shows that many more of those swept up in the network have few provable connections to any outlawed organisation: experts in the field describe their value in the war against terror as "negligible".'[66]

I flew to New York and took a taxi down First Avenue in Manhattan to what used to be a working-class neighbourhood, the Lower East Side; it is now the fashionable East Village. Rita and Ted Lasar moved into a small fifteenth-floor apartment here soon after they were married. Rita came from an orthodox Jewish family and Ted's background was secular. 'My family never really forgave me,' said Rita. 'Ted and I were a political couple in the sense that we cared about this life, about our country and the world.'

On the shelves, among family photographs, was a fine collection of books: Hiroshima, the Vietnam War, Nixon, titles by Gore Vidal, Kingsley Amis's *Lucky Jim*, Germaine Greer's *The Female Eunuch*, Gibbon's *The Decline and Fall of the Roman Empire*.

One of the photographs was of a big, beaming man, his head resting on Rita's shoulder. This was her brother Abe, who worked for the Blue Cross medical insurance company on the twenty-seventh floor of the World Trade Center, the Twin Towers.

'On September 11, 2001,' she said, 'I was sitting at my kitchen table, like every other morning, having my first cigarette and my first cup of coffee and listening to the radio, and a little before nine a newscaster broke in and said a plane had just hit one of the towers of the World Trade Center. I ran across the hall to my friend's apartment and her windows looked out on the World Trade Center. I got there in time to see the second plane hit the second building. And strangely enough, it was only then that I said, "Oh my God, my brother's in that building."

'I ran back and called my elder brother, with whom Abe lived, and he said he had been talking to Abe on his cellphone and shouting for him to get out, and Abe had said, "I'm gonna stay because Ed, my friend, is a quadriplegic in a wheelchair and he can't get out." Abe kept insisting he wouldn't leave his friend, and everybody kept shouting back at the phone, "Get out of there!" And he hung up on them. And the day went on; it's impossible to describe what it was like here in New York on that day, especially for people who had somebody in the buildings. Then the smell started coming through my terrace door, then the buildings collapsed. That moment is the only thing I'm not coherent about . . .'

'Did you have a sense of time?'

'I don't think so. I seemed to be on the phone constantly, calling all the hospitals, here, New Jersey, all over, looking for my brother. Danny, my son's best friend, called and said, "Did you watch the President's speech?" And I said no. And he said, "He mentioned your brother." And I said, "What are you talking about?" And then, I thought, gee, there must have been a lot of people who stayed behind with their friends in wheelchairs. You don't think that it's your own brother; but it was my brother. And immediately, *immediately*, I knew that my country was going to use my brother's death to justify killing innocent people in Afghanistan and wherever else they would look.'

'What did President Bush say?'

'He said our national character was tested. He used flowery words and said, "One man who could have saved himself chose instead to stay behind to help save his friend who was a quadriplegic in a wheelchair," or something like that. I hadn't paid much attention. But I paid attention to the deviousness, the gall to use my brother to justify killing others when I knew that our country had been trying to have a pipeline through Afghanistan for gas and oil and that anything we were going to do would not be to avenge my brother's death, but to acquire some of the resources that this country seems to think God says it should have. You know, there's something so similar between our administration and al-Qaida in its certainty that God is on its side, that it's laughable.'

Rita was one of the founders of a group of the bereaved called 'September 11 Families for Peaceful Tomorrows'. They took the name from a speech by Martin Luther King in 1967 in which he said that 'wars are poor chisels for carving out peaceful tomorrows'.

'When Bush began to bomb Afghanistan, I knew I had to go there. I was seventy at the time. I had never seen war. My elder brother said he would disown me if I went. He said, "If you're going to drop an atom bomb on them, that's fine." I went, and it changed my life completely. First of all, when I got off the UN plane at the makeshift airstrip, it looked as if I was landing on the moon. It was all dust and rubble. Then I began to meet people who had lost family members in our bombing.

'I met so many who had lost loved ones. I met one woman who had lost her entire family. She was standing in a field, crying; she said she had taken a letter seeking compensation to the American Embassy in Kabul and had been told, "Go away, you're a beggar." Every American should go where our bombs fall. In Afghanistan, the generosity of the poorest people in the world overwhelmed me; I was given a beautiful carved box inscribed "To Rita" by the wife of a man who, a few weeks earlier, had been bombed to death as they lay in bed. How do you explain this generosity when it has nothing to do with money and status and power, just the best of people?'

I walked with Rita down First Avenue to a place next to Burger King where we had a cup of sour coffee. The day was hot and sticky; delivery men and taxi drivers sounded their horns, boys skateboarded past us.

'Do you think people in the street will come to share your view?'

'Yes, eventually, because there is no alternative. If there is, I'd like to know what it is. All we have is the promise, as Vice-President Cheney said, of endless war.'[67]

I caught a shuttle flight to Washington, where I had requested appointments with leading members of the Bush administration. I wanted to ask them about the unreported thousands who had been killed in the invasion of Afghanistan, and now Iraq. I had asked to see Donald Rumsfeld, the Defense Secretary, but was told he gave journalists no more than five minutes. This was to ensure, said his candid spokeswoman, that he would not say something he might regret.

All those I had asked to see were 'neo-conservatives', or 'neo-cons', the jargon description of far-right Republicans who had served Ronald Reagan. As founders of an alliance between the fundamentalist Christian Moral Majority, the 'Greater Israel' Zionist lobby and the 'oil and gas junta', they subscribe to the ideological goals of the 'Project for a New American Century', set out in a policy document written by their acolytes shortly before George W. Bush came to power in 2000. Deploying irony, the dissident Israeli writer Uri Avnery described these goals accurately as 'a US world empire as well as a Greater Israel [emerging from] a struggle between the Children of Light, the United States and Israel, and the Children of Darkness, the Arabs and Muslims'.[68]

Douglas Feith, Under-Secretary of State for Defense and Rumsfeld's senior policy adviser in the Pentagon, had agreed to see me. A young, outspoken militarist in the Reagan administration, he opposed the ABM (anti-ballistic missile) Treaty, the Comprehensive Test Ban Treaty, the Chemical Weapons Convention and the establishment of the International Criminal Court.[69] As an advocate of the war policies of Israel's Likud party, he opposed the Camp

David Agreement, indeed any plan for a national home for the Palestinians, even the term 'Palestine'.

The son of Dalck Feith, a leading member of the extreme Zionist militant organisation Batar, whose members wore dark brown uniforms and chanted fascistic slogans, he and his father were honoured by the far right Zionist Organisation of America in 1997.[70] In 1982, he resigned from the National Security Council under the shadow of accusations that he was too closely associated with Israel.[71]

Reinstated at the Pentagon by Donald Rumsfeld in 2000, he set up the secretive Office of Special Plans, which 'competed' with the CIA by gathering 'second track intelligence' on Iraq, much of it the manipulative fiction provided by the expatriate Iraqi National Congress, now discredited, and disinformation supplied by the Israelis. This furthered the myths that Iraq was planning to use nuclear, chemical and biological weapons and had links with al-Qaida: misinformation – lies – that were regurgitated by 10 Downing Street and supplied to the British press.[72]

The Pentagon is the biggest single office block in the world, employing twenty-six thousand people, one of whom is Colonel Mike Humm. Portly, pressed, fussy and resembling the 1950s television character Sergeant Bilko, though without the humour, Colonel Humm has the job of approving, supervising and, if necessary, terminating interviews with senior officials.

'You have twenty minutes, no more,' said Colonel Humm, as we marched, literally, along the polished corridors of American military power. Our steps echoed until we reached the offices of the Joint Chiefs of Staff, which luxuriate in deep-pile blue carpet. Along the walls, beribboned, bemedalled American warlords looked down, stern, genial, blank, like a parade of Norman Rockwell covers for the *Saturday Evening Post*.

'Twenty minutes, do you understand?' said Colonel Humm. 'I've turned down seventy requests for interviews with Mr Feith. We've agreed, however, he should see the British, our comrades in arms.'

We marched into a windowless, cell-like room, which was bare except for three theatrical 'props': a map of the world, an outsized wooden seal of the Department of Defense and a furled Stars and Stripes.

'You will wait here, understand?' said Colonel Humm. 'Do not move to another location. Do not traverse that door.'

After a long wait, I heard whispering outside the non-traversable door. It was Colonel Humm and another. 'We are restricting this, sir,' said Colonel Humm. 'We have this under compatible control.' He then marched in, followed by Douglas Feith, a somewhat distracted-looking middle-aged man in a pin-striped suit. Sitting directly in front of the Great Seal of the Defense Department and flanked by the map of the world and the Stars and Stripes, he faced me and Colonel Humm, who loomed at my shoulder.

'Vice-President Cheney', I said, 'has spoken about the war on terror lasting fifty years or more. What did he mean by that?'

'The idea that the war on terror could go on for decades refers to the fact that there are two major parts to it. One is destroy-and-disrupt: that is, attacking terrorists and their infrastructure . . . the other is the battle of ideas . . . addressing the kinds of thoughts that make people believe they should be terrorists, that the purposeful targeting of civilians is good, is moral . . . and so it is crucial that we [work on] changing the way people think, and that is a project for decades.'

'Why is it wrong for dictators and terrorists to kill innocent civilians and right or excusable for the United States to do exactly the same?'

'The United States does not target civilians like that. The essence of terrorism is that the terrorists obliterate this enormously important distinction between combatants and non-combatants . . . the law of war. That distinction is fundamental, a pillar of civilisation.'

'That's why I brought it up, Mr Feith. I was in Afghanistan recently and I interviewed a number of people who had lost up to eight members of their family because they had been bombed by American planes which targeted their homes. Three thousand people died on September 11, but many more have since been killed by America. Isn't there a double standard there?'

'The numbers you are talking about are questionable.'

'Why are they questionable?'

'I don't accept that we've killed thousands of innocent people . . .'

'There are now plenty of studies that suggest [in Afghanistan and Iraq] about ten thousand; certainly thousands seems a fair assessment.'*

'Let me say this. What our military does is most impressive. They always make careful calculations that weigh the military values, the risk to innocent people. This is a very meticulous process and the result, as in the case of Iraq, is an enormous military achievement with very little damage to civilian infrastructure and to innocent people.'

'Mr Feith, that sounds fine sitting here in Washington, but in Iraq and in Afghanistan, which is my most recent experience, that's not how it looks at all.'

'*Stop the tape!*' ordered Colonel Humm. 'Let me know when you have stopped the tape. Have we now stopped the tape? I was not under the impression that this was going to be confrontational.'

The interviewee looked aghast. 'Mr Feith,' I said, 'you seem fully equipped to answer my questions. I'm surprised somebody at your level should feel intimidated by straightforward questions.'

'I am not intimidated. I am not a wallflower!'

'I made the decision!' said Colonel Humm, already feeling his isolation.

'I am not interviewing you, Colonel.'

'You were being confrontational,' said Colonel Humm.

'Maybe badgering . . .' said Feith, who added, with mock nobility, 'I am prepared to continue.'

So I continued.

'Mr Feith, in Afghanistan, the United States has produced a group of warlords that are considered as bad as the Taliban. Would you describe these warlords as terrorists?'

'I would not.'

'United Nations investigators have found these people guilty of massacre, rape and all sorts of crimes against humanity.'

'There are good people in leadership positions. But it's a mixed

---

* A 2004 study by the British medical journal *The Lancet* and Johns Hopkins University in the US estimated at least 100,000 civilians had been killed in Iraq, the great majority by Anglo-American military action.

bag we're working with . . . I can assure you we are working towards democracy in Afghanistan.'

'*Time* magazine conducted a poll across Europe, asking two hundred and fifty thousand people which country they considered the greatest threat to peace. Eight per cent said Iraq, nine per cent said North Korea and eighty-three per cent said the United States. Do you understand that fear?'

'Well, our history is an open book, a history of which Americans can be very proud, which people around the world admire. Our role in the world has not been to grab things that don't belong to us. Our role has not been to enslave and colonise. We have become a major force for promoting respect for all human beings and the principle that all men are created equal. We are a benign player that has helped liberate countries . . .'

'How does that square with constant American threats and attacks on other countries, from Afghanistan to Iraq, Syria, Iran and North Korea?'

'Those countries that are nervous should not pursue weapons of mass destruction.'

'Hasn't the whole issue of weapons of mass destruction descended into farce?'

'We see the Iranians [building] a nuclear programme. We see the North Koreans repudiating the non-proliferation treaty . . .'

'The governments of the United States and Britain lied to us about weapons of mass destruction in Iraq. Why should we believe you?'

'I don't think that was a lie. We went to war in the large part because of our concern that weapons of mass destruction in the hands of the Saddam Hussein regime, a regime that used nerve gas . . .'

'. . . Which was supplied by the United States and Britain.'

'No, that's not accurate.'

'Yes, it is. Most of Saddam Hussein's weapons of mass destruction weren't built by him. The machine tools and the ingredients for his biological weapons all came from other countries, many of them from America and Britain.'

'I don't think that's right.'

'It's on the record. Just look in the Library of Congress.'

'You've got to understand the threat to the United States, the threat . . .'

'But surely the greatest threat, and the greatest source of weapons of mass destruction, is right here in the United States?'

'I'm not sure I understand your question.'

'Thank you, Mr Feith.'[73]

On the other side of Washington is the Department of State, the bureaucracy of the American imperium. I had an appointment with John Bolton, whose title, Under-Secretary of State for Arms Control and International Security, was an Orwellian creation of the Bush administration; its function clearly was the antithesis of this. Probably the most driven and dangerous 'neo-con', Bolton almost single-handedly led the United States on a path to nuclear war with North Korea.

Bolton is a product of the very far right of the Republican Party. As a lawyer in the Justice Department under Ronald Reagan, Bolton promoted the ideological goals of the shadowy Federalist Society. These were to 'roll back' the purported 'hold' of the 'liberal establishment' on the judiciary. Graduating to the National Enterprise Institute, another extreme right-wing lobby group, he opposed the very principle of international agreement. 'There is no such thing as the United Nations,' he said. 'There is an international community that can be led by the only real power left in the world, and that is the US, when it suits our interests and when we can get others to go along . . . If the UN building in New York lost ten storeys, it wouldn't make a bit of difference.'[74] However, his hostility to the UN did not prevent him from calling for an invasion of Iraq because of its alleged failure to respect UN resolutions.

Known as the 'treaty killer', Bolton was largely responsible for the Bush administration's withdrawal from the ABM Treaty and its embrace of the 'Star Wars' missile 'shield', whose purpose is to give the United States 'full spectrum dominance'. He opposed agreements to ban chemical and biological weapons and to limit the spread of small arms. In a speech entitled 'Beyond the Axis of Evil', he claimed, without evidence, that Cuba was developing biological weapons and sharing its research with America's enemies, a claim investigated and dismissed by former President Jimmy Carter. He renounced any American role in the International Criminal Court and 'celebrated', as he put it, the demise of the Comprehensive Test Ban Treaty on underground nuclear testing. 'John Bolton', said Senator Jesse Helms, doyen of the lunar right, 'is the kind of man with whom I would want to stand at Armageddon, if it should be my lot to be on hand for what is forecast to be the final battle between good and evil in this world.'[75]

Bolton is a man of striking appearance; he has a 1970s-style drooping Zapata moustache and he wears a curiously old-fashioned toupée, which moved perceptibly down his forehead during our interview. I began by reading him Jesse Helms's tribute to him as 'Armageddon Man'.

'I am very flattered,' he said.

'You have extended President Bush's definition of an "axis of evil" to a number of countries. How do you and your colleagues divide up the world between good and evil?'

'First, we identify where we think the gravest threat to our liberty is coming from. We know that threat comes from weapons of mass destruction: from chemical, biological and nuclear weapons, and the means to deliver them.'

'But you have opposed a treaty to limit these weapons.'

'That treaty was aimed at the United States, not at rogue states.'

'The United States is exceptional?'

'Yes.'

'Many now regard the United States as a rogue state.'

'Well, they are just flatly wrong. We have done more throughout our history to create conditions in which individuals can be free around the world than any other country in history.'

'Let's get back to good and evil. Take Afghanistan. The Taliban were described as evil, understandably, but the warlords, who are considered just as bad, are not regarded as evil here in Washington. Why?'

'Afghanistan is a difficult country. We didn't expect Jeffersonian democracy to spring up overnight. But I can assure you: we are not funding warlords.'

'Yes, you are, and you have been doing it for almost twenty-five years.'

'We assisted the *mujahedin* when they were fighting the Soviet Union.'

'They are the same warlords, and the assistance never stopped. In 2001, they were bribed by the CIA to stop fighting each other and to overthrow the Taliban. If both sides commit terrible crimes, why is only one side classified as evil?'

'The concentration of American assistance today is intended to create an effective central government in Afghanistan. We are not in a position to debate who is evil. It's not an issue.'

'I had in mind Osama bin Laden, who is surely America's apotheosis of evil. He came from the *mujahedin*, which was backed by the United States.'

'Let's be clear about what we were backing. We were providing assistance to the *mujahedin* until the Soviet Union withdrew. Osama bin Laden represented a different strain; he was part of the resistance to the Soviets, yes, but he had quite a different agenda. The idea that somehow or another we are responsible for Osama bin Laden is an extraordinary historical inaccuracy.'

'He came out of the massive support the United States gave to the Islamic fundamentalists who were fighting another American-ordained evil, the Soviet Union.'

'Yes, we gave backing to a variety of political factions, and some were fundamentalist. But we never intended to strengthen them. The tragedy of Afghanistan is chaos, the chaos that resulted after the Soviet withdrawal.'

'The other day, you promised to reveal convincing evidence of Iraq's production of weapons of mass destruction. Where is the evidence?'

'I don't think I ever *promised* to reveal evidence. What we are showing now is that the Saddam Hussein regime was inextricably linked to the *capacity* to use weapons of mass destruction, including nuclear weapons.'

'According to President Bush, the United States invaded Iraq because the world was threatened by its weapons of mass destruction.'

'It was absolutely not the reason. The threat came from Saddam's dictatorial regime.'

'So all those very clear statements by Bush and Blair about, for example, a forty-five-minute threat from Iraq . . . they were not the reason?'

'They weren't the premise on which we went to war, that's right; yes, that's right . . . that's right.'

'You have made a number of threats against North Korea. Is it the next target?'

'What threats! List them!'

'Well, you have threatened what you call the interdiction of North Korean ships. You've said often, using veiled language of course, that if North Korea doesn't do what it's told, it's going to be attacked.'

'What we've said is that, along with like-minded countries, we are prepared to take measures to interdict shipments of weapons of mass destruction or ballistic missiles at sea, in the air and on land, where we have the authority to do so.'

'Who will give that authority?'

'That is a matter for discussion.'

'Couldn't that trigger nuclear war?'

'I don't think there's the slightest chance that will happen . . .'

'But if you stop ships, isn't there more than a faint echo of what almost happened, in 1962, in the Cuban missile crisis? Isn't there the risk that the North Koreans will be moved to defend themselves against a superpower with their only means, which are nuclear weapons?'

'We stopped one of their ships, the *Son San*, and they did nothing in response.'

'What if they take action next time?'

'We can't afford not to interdict. Think of the innocent civilians that will die if we wait for *their* mushroom cloud.'

'I would like to ask you about the civilians that have died in Afghanistan and Iraq . . .'

'One of the stunning things about the quick coalition victory [in Iraq] was how little damage was done to Iraqi infrastructure, how low casualties were.'

'Well, it's quite high if it's ten thousand civilians.'

'Well, I think that's quite low if you look at the size of the military operation we undertook.'

'Ten thousand deaths is low . . . ?'

'Sure is.'

He got up, unclipped his microphone and secured his toupée.

'Say,' he said, 'are you a member of the British Labour Party?'
'No, they are now the conservatives in Britain.'
'So you're a communist?'
'No.'
'Well, *what* are you?'
'Thank you, Mr Bolton.'[76]

William Kristal is the editor of the *New Standard*, a Washington-based magazine owned by Rupert Murdoch and regarded as the house journal of the neo-cons. He is an author of the principal document of the Project for a New American Century, whose offices he shares behind vault-like doors. Short of stature and flushed of face, he sits at a desk overlooked by a bust of Saddam Hussein and a framed article from a French magazine with the headline, 'America: après Irak, le monde!' On the walls are photographs of himself with his heroes, Ronald Reagan and Margaret Thatcher; and there he is, sitting with Vice-President Dan Quayle, for whom he worked. During my interview any notion that the neo-cons have an intellectual, rather than an emotional and deeply ideological, base slipped away. I asked him what he meant by the 'New American Century'.

'What is it? What is it? It's American strength and American aggressiveness on behalf of American principles that advance liberty and democracy . . .'

'Isn't it more than that? The policy document, which you helped write, refers to America as the "cavalry on a new frontier that will fight and decisively win multiple, simultaneous major wars". What does that mean?'

'It's saying we need a military big enough to fight in Iraq and Afghanistan and deal with threats in North Korea and all over the world.'

'On your desk you have a framed article from a French magazine with the headline, "America: après Irak, le monde!" '

'That's a little joke.'

'Is it true?'

'Afghanistan and Iraq are just the beginning of the threats we have to deal with. It would be foolish to think that, having liberated those countries, we can go back to assuming we are protected by the Atlantic and Pacific Oceans.'

'Isn't that paranoia?'

'That's ridiculous.'

'Or a paranoid excuse for interfering in other countries?'

'That's also ridiculous.'

'You call yourself an American imperialist, is that right?'

'No, but if what we do *looks* imperial, so be it . . . The problem with America is not that we go marauding around the world, imposing ourselves. The problem with America since the end of the Cold War is that we have been too slow to get involved in conflicts. Lots of people have died, hundreds of thousands have been killed, because Americans stayed home. The problem Europeans should worry about is that America will come home.'

'People all over the world are worried that the United States is conducting unprovoked attacks on sovereign countries.'

'Are they? Are they?'

'Yes, they are.'

'Really, we're going to attack Britain, France, Germany? Any democracy? Any decent regime?'

'Well, the United States doesn't usually attack strong countries.'

'Do we attack decent countries?'

'I said strong countries.'

'Are people really worried that the United States is going to go to a decent, law-abiding country and is going to come in and say, "We don't like the look of you, we're going to depose you." Is that what the US has done quite often? How many countries has the US attacked in the last fifteen years?'

'Well, since World War Two there have been seventy-two interventions by the United States.'

'Oh, is that right?'

'Yes.'

'That's ludicrous.'

'It's not ludicrous, it's true.'

'It's not true. It's a fatuous and ridiculous statement.'

'It's a fact. There have been seventy-two interventions, including the overthrow of governments that have been democratically elected social democracies, the kind you might describe as decent, such as elected governments in Guatemala, Brazil, Iran, Chile, to name just a few . . . Others have simply got in the way of American designs.'

'So what are you saying, that there is no manageable distinction between decency and indecency?'

'No. Many people now regard the present regime in Washington as indecent, but no-one is going to attack it, are they?'

'Ludicrous . . .'

'What gives the United States the right to decide matters of life and death around the world: which country is decent, which country will be attacked or not?'

'What countries are you talking about?'

'Afghanistan and Iraq.'

'So that's the grand total of aggressive American wars, is it?'

'Two countries attacked in two years: not a bad record.'

'It's two *good* wars.'

'That's more than most countries have done . . .'

'It is and I'm very proud that America was able to do it.'[77]

In the years I have been coming to Washington, I have learned to respect a group of uniquely American whistle-blowers. These are former CIA officers who 'turned' and have spoken out against America's secret machinations in the world. They are not all renegades; some leave the CIA with institutional plaudits, but something already has changed them. Having joined the agency with a sense of idealism, of 'service to my country', they leave it with 'the burden and demands of conscience', as one described it.

In 1981, Ralph McGehee, recipient of the CIA's highest commendation medal, exposed the Vietnam War as a series of 'deadly deceits' used to justify the American invasion.[78] Philip Liechty, a former CIA operations officer based in Jakarta, revealed how President Gerald Ford and his Secretary of State, Henry Kissinger, had given the green light to the Indonesian dictator Suharto to invade East Timor in 1975, then secretly armed his invading forces.[79]

Ray McGovern also left the CIA with the high praise of his superiors, notably George Bush senior, who was then President. A fluent Russian-speaker, he was chief of the Soviet foreign policy branch, Directorate of Intelligence, in the 1970s before becoming the author of the President's daily intelligence brief. When George W. Bush came to power, McGovern warned of the danger of 'the crazies'.

'What did you mean by crazies?' I asked him.

'I meant the people who are running the administration of George W. Bush. You have to understand how different they are. They have a set of beliefs a lot like those expressed in *Mein Kampf*; it's all laid out there. The Project for a New American Century makes it abundantly clear that when Paul Wolfowitz produced his first defence posture document in 1991, it was so extreme that General [Brent] Scowcroft, the National Security Adviser, and Jim Baker, the Secretary of State, swallowed hard, and went to the President [Bush senior] and said, "We've got to disallow this; we've got to put this in the circular file," and the President did precisely that. Now we have the son of that President captivated by these ideologues, and these are the same people who were referred to in the circles in which I moved, at the top, as "the crazies". You talked then about "the crazies" and everyone knew who they were: Richard Perle, Paul Wolfowitz, Doug Feith . . .'

'Who referred to them as "the crazies"?'

'All of us.'

'In the CIA?'

'Yes. Policy circles as well as intelligence circles.'

'The cliché is that September 11 changed everything? Is that your view?'

'No, but it was an incredible boost to what the crazies wanted to do. Our response should have been a police action. Instead, the crazies played on the fears of the population, introducing distasteful elements of vengeance, so that at least as many people perished in the attack on Afghanistan as on 9/11. Everything that followed was PR, public relations, black propaganda. This administration has shown itself to be incredibly adept at this. Look at the way they connected Saddam Hussein with al-Qaida, a monumental task under normal circumstances, because there was no connection; September 11 allowed them to achieve that.'

'Is there evidence that a great deal of this was planned before September 11?'

'Yes, there is, in documents I have seen. Some of them actually say that what they are doing is a long-term process, a strategic plan, and there could be intervening events which would be great blessings and would accelerate the implementation of their plans; 9/11 was exactly that kind of event. Now I'm not a conspiracy type of person so I shy away from a lot of the conspiracy theories that are going around.'

'Having spent a lot of your life in the CIA, you must have a respect for conspiracy?'

'I do indeed. If you look back to the assassination of President Kennedy and Martin Luther King, you need to respect the conspiracy element. I have read persuasive evidence that this Bush administration knew chapter and verse as to what was happening on September 11 and allowed it to happen. I take the charitable interpretation that it was gross incompetence.'

'Is the war on terror a fraud?'

'I think fraudulent is not too strong a word. Being at war enables us not only to throw our weight around abroad but to clamp down very tightly on those who would dissent and to paint them as unpatriotic. That's what has happened.'

'Was the episode of Iraq's weapons of mass destruction merely a charade?'

'It was ninety-five per cent charade.'

'How did they get away with it?'

'The press allowed them to get away with it. Here's just one example. I was asked to be on Fox News to discuss weapons of mass destruction. The interviewer said, "Now, Mr McGovern, we just completed a poll here and this shows that sixty-seven per cent of the American people don't care whether weapons of mass destruction are found, or not. So why do you care?" I said. "Sir, you really have to ask yourself why sixty-seven per cent don't care. And why it is that Fox News and your comrades in the rest of the mainstream media don't tell the American people what's going on? How can they care if they don't know?" '

'Are Americans aware of the significant role the United States played in backing Osama bin Laden and the role the CIA played, going back to President Carter?'

'Again, how can they be if their government doesn't educate them? And the media has equally zero incentive because they are embedded, captives, completely domesticated by their wish to serve not only the government but the corporations that own them.'

'Are you worried about the policy of pre-emptive attack? Where will it lead?'

'I am worried about it very much. We thought we left the nuclear threat behind with the end of the Cold War, but now President Bush and indeed Prime Minister Blair have said they are willing to consider pre-emptive strikes with nuclear weapons. It's quite something . . . that the nuclear threat today should be seen first and foremost as coming from the United States of America and Great Britain . . . If I were a North Korean, I would be very, very worried.'

'Norman Mailer wrote the other day that he believed America had entered a pre-fascist state. What's your view of that?'

'Well, and I'm not saying this to be cynical, but I hope he's right, because there are others saying that we are already in a fascist mode. When you see who is controlling the means of production here, when you see who is controlling the newspapers and periodicals, and the TV stations, from which most Americans take their news, and when you see how the so-called war on terror is being conducted, you begin to understand where we are headed. Josef Goebbels had this dictum that if you say something often enough, the people will begin to believe it; and that strategy has been applied with great success by this administration . . . weapons of mass destruction, al-Qaida, Iraq ties, other evidence being deduced to justify an unprovoked war . . . so yes, we all ought to be worried about fascism.'[80]

In January 2003, Ray McGovern and other former intelligence officers established Veteran Intelligence Professionals for Sanity. VIPS now includes more than forty-five former senior officers of the CIA, the Defense Intelligence Agency, the State Department's Bureau of Intelligence and Research, Army intelligence, the FBI, the National Security Agency and other intelligence agencies. It was an unprecedented act of rebellion from within.

On February 5, 2003, the dissident officers sent a paper, 'Memorandum for the President', to the White House. It was a demolition of Secretary of State Colin Powell's address to the United Nations Security Council that day, in which he lied that intelligence had 'proved' that Saddam Hussein had weapons of mass destruction. The paper complained about the 'politicisation' of intelligence that accompanied 'a drumbeat for war'.[81]

'Our concern,' said Ray McGovern, 'is that this is only the beginning: that we have already lost control.'

I left 'liberated' Afghanistan on a not untypical day. As my car drove to Kabul airport, a bus carrying German soldiers of the International Security and Assistance Force (ISAF), a mile ahead, was blown up, killing six. Who did this? Was it Taliban 'remnants'? Or a 'regional commander', one of the West's new allies, expressing his arcane displeasure? At the scene, Western military technology, its buzzing helicopters, armoured vehicles and automatic weapons, displayed both the power and the impotence of the powerful, salvaging the blackened bus and leaving pools of blood in the dust of the road.

The Germans ran Kabul airport, and so incensed were they that they closed it and set up a machine-gun on the main runway. The mayhem in the decrepit terminal building seemed a microcosm of life outside. As the midday heat made itself felt, people struggled for space to stand and sit. Ariana, the Afghan airline, distributed foil-wrapped meals whose eat-by date had slipped away long ago; several of these had fallen on the concrete floor, leaving a gravy-brown slick. Outside, two old Airbus aircraft stood side by side while one had its nose-cone cannibalised so that the other 'might fly', said a disconsolate pilot.

Following an announcement I mistook for the call to prayers, a stampede to the aircraft ensued. And there we stayed as night fell. The Germans refused to budge from behind their machine-gun. Our aircraft, which had once plied domestic routes in India, was visibly falling to bits: festoons of superstructure hung down in the cabin; seats were broken-backed, and the lavatory doors had long surrendered, leaving an airborne hole-in-the-ground. Then the sound of a siren interrupted the fetid air of fatalism, and President Karzai swept into the airport to plead with the Germans to let us go. They relented, and with the Prophet's assistance, we subsequently reached Dubai.

Meanwhile, it was announced that the pipeline deal, originally agreed between the Taliban, the Clinton administration and the Unocal company, was going ahead.[82] A brief ceremony was held at the American Embassy in Kabul, attended by Karzai, who himself had negotiated pipeline deals as a consultant to the Unocal oil company. He was accompanied, as usual, by his twenty-four American Special Forces bodyguards.[83]

The American and British invasion of Afghanistan in 2001 brought to an end an almost total ban on opium production which the Taliban had achieved. An aid worker in Kabul described the ban to me as 'a modern miracle'. The miracle was quickly rescinded. As a reward for supporting the Karzai 'democracy', the Americans allowed their warlords to replant the country's entire opium crop in 2002. Twenty-eight of thirty-two provinces were instantly under cultivation, and refining factories were re-established. The result is that 87 per cent of world trade in opium now originates in Afghanistan.[84] Today, the victims are mostly young people in the West. In 2005, a British government report estimated that thirty-five thousand children in England were using heroin.[85] At the time of writing this, the radio news reports that an eleven-year-old girl in Glasgow has collapsed at her school desk from the effects of heroin. It does not say she is, in all probability, a victim of the 'war on terror' and its 'great game' in Afghanistan.

For the ordinary people of Afghanistan, everything and nothing have changed. Sharia law and its strict rulings are being reinstated. The Chief Justice, Fazl Hadi Shinwari, a cleric in his eighties with no training in secular law, has ruled that television performances by modestly clad women singing about rural life are illegal, along with popular Bollywood movies.[86] The burqa has returned even to the fleetingly libertarian enclaves in Kabul.

In Washington, the Afghans, having 'walked freedom's road' (George W. Bush) and embraced 'a model' of democracy (Donald Rumsfeld), are of little interest now. Since the invasion of Afghanistan, the United States has established thirteen bases in nine countries in the region, with more than sixty thousand troops guarding pipeline routes and the gateways to fossil-fuel sources. Mission accomplished, as Bush might have said. A report by the CIA says Afghanistan has been replaced by Iraq as the training ground for the next generation of 'professionalised terrorists'. The report's 119 pages contain not a single reference to the leading role played by the United States throughout a quarter of a century, in creating and sustaining these 'professionalised terrorists'.[87]

Among the rulers of the world, stars have fallen and risen. Douglas Feith has resigned from the Pentagon, having been described by General Tommy Franks, the American commander in Afghanistan and Iraq, as 'the fucking stupidest guy on the face of the earth'.[88] Paul Wolfowitz has been appointed President of the World Bank. Using an eighteenth-century constitutional loophole, George W. Bush has ignored the opposition of Congress and appointed John Bolton to represent America at the United Nations, which he loathes.

Afghanistan, where the 'great game' began, is no longer a 'story'. The following was a minor BBC news item as these words were written:

> The US military in Afghanistan has revealed that six children died in a raid on suspected militants . . . News of the deaths came shortly after the US apologised for killing nine children in a separate raid in the neighbouring province . . . However, the US warned it would not be deterred by civilian casualties. A US spokesman said [the dead children] were partly to blame for being at a site used by militants . . .[89]

Notes

Introduction

1   As told to the author in an interview, London, July, 2001.

2   Michael McKinley, 'Approaching America Again: Seeing and Understanding the USA as Just Another Country in War and Peace', paper presented at Annual International Studies Association Convention, Montreal, March 18, 2004.

3   Mark Curtis, *The Ambiguities of Power: British Foreign Policy since 1945*, Zed Books, 1995, pp. 166–7, 172.

4   Cited in *In Our Name: US Intervention in Nicaragua*, www.stanford.edu/group/arts/nicaragua/discovery_eng/timeline and *Counterpunch*, September 13, 2002.

5   UN press release GA/7603, December 7, 1987.

6   Letter from Helen Boaden to David Edwards, co-editor of *Media Lens*, forwarded to the author January 20, 2006.

7   As told to the writer Simon Louvish and relayed to the author.

8   See Dahr Jamail's dispatches on www.dahrjamailiraq.com; also *Al Jazeera*, January 3, 2006 and October 31, 2005.

9   John Pilger, *Distant Voices*, Vintage, 1994, pp. 178–9.

10 *Guardian*, December 8, 2005.

11 William Blum, *Rogue State*, Common Courage Press, 2005.

12 Letter from Harold Macmillan to Robert Menzies, February 9, 1952, cited by Frank Furedi, *The New Ideology of Imperialism*, Pluto Press, 1994, p. 79.

13 Furedi, *The New Ideology of Imperialism*, p. 99.

14 *Evening Standard*, August 20, 1990.

15 Furedi, *The New Ideology of Imperialism*, p. 79.

16 M. Perham, 'African Facts and American Criticisms', *Foreign Affairs*,

vol. 22, April 1944, p. 449; cited by Furedi, *The New Ideology of Imperialism*, p. 88.

17   Furedi, *The New Ideology of Imperialism*, p. 88.

18   www.newamericancentury.org.

19   United States Space Command, *Vision for 2020*, Director of Plans, Petersen AFB, Colorado: www.spacecom.af.mil/usspace.

20   Cited by Richard Drayton, *Guardian*, December 28, 2005.

21   Chalmers Johnson, *Sorrows of Empire*, Henry Holt, 2005.

22   *Daily Mail*, January 15, 2005.

23   *Daily Express*, July 13, 2004.

24   *Daily Telegraph*, July 14, 2004.

25   *Guardian*, October 31, 2001.

26   Cited by Noam Chomsky, *9–11*, Seven Stories Press, 2001, p. 15.

27   *Observer*, January 10, 1993.

28   *Guardian*, May 7, 1997.

29   *Guardian*, October 24, 2001.

30   Richard Falk, 'The Terrorist Foundations of Recent US Policy', in Alexander George, ed., *Western State Terrorism*, Polity Press, 1991, pp. 107–8.

31   See chapter 2, note 1.

32   Glasgow University Media Group, *TV News and Public Understanding of the Israeli/Palestinian Conflict*, Causeway Press, October 2002.

33   Richard Sale, 'Hamas Tied to Israel', UPI, June 18, 2002.

34   Mike Davis, *Late Victorian Holocausts: El Nino, Famines and the Making of the Third World*, Verso, 2001.

35   *Guardian*, May 10, 2005.

36   See chapter 4, note 97.

37   See chapter 4, note 39.

38   See chapter 5, note 2.

39   See chapter 5, note 3.

40   Cited by Simon Jenkins, *Guardian*, February 1, 2006.

41   See chapter 5, note 80.

42   'America Has Fallen to a Jacobin Coup',
     www.informationclearinghouse.info/article10303.

43   'Bush Has Crossed the Rubicon',
     www.informationclearinghouse.info/article11578.

44   United Nations Children's Fund (UNICEF) and the Government of Iraq,
     Child and Maternal Mortality Survey 1999: Preliminary Report, 1999.

45   Katherine Hughes, 'Crime of Compassion',
     www.informationclearinghouse.info/article11646.

46   Richard Ackland, 'If the Law Doesn't Suit, Just Ignore It', *Sydney
     Morning Herald*, January 13, 2006.

47   Mike Whitney, 'Bush's Fascist Valhalla',
     www.informationclearinghouse.info/article11175; WXIA TV, Atlanta,
     'ACLU Releases Government Photos', January 27, 2006,
     www.truthout.org/docs_2006/012706A.shtml.

48   Dr Les Roberts, Johns Hopkins School of Public Health, *The Lancet*,
     www.globalresearch.ca/articles/LAN410A.

49   Correspondence from Dr Les Roberts to *Media Lens*, August 22,
     2005. See also Les Roberts, 'Do Iraqi Civilian Casualties Matter?'
     AlterNet, February 8, 2006, www.alternet.org/story/31508/.

50   Abel Bult-Ito, 'Nothing Depleted about "Depleted Uranium" ',
     University of Alaska, Fairbanks,
     www.globalresearch.ca/PrintArticle.php?articleId=1777. See also John
     Pilger, *The New Rulers of the World*, Verso, 2001, pp. 45–97.

51   *Independent*, December 10, 2005.

52   Ibid.

53   Clive Stafford Smith, *New Statesman*, November 21, 2005.

54   Cited by Noam Chomsky, Amnesty International Lecture, Trinity
     College, Dublin, January 18, 2006.

55   Herbert Aptheker, *History and Reality*, Cameron Associates, New
     York, 1955, pp. 49–72.

56   Inter Press Service, cited *ZNet*, www.zmag.org, November 18, 2004;
     Also *New Internationalist*, no. 376, March 2005.

Chapter 1: Stealing a Nation

1   Mark Curtis, booklet to accompany *Stealing a Nation, A Special Report by John Pilger*, Granada Television UK (broadcast ITV network October 2004, July 2005), p. 4. See also Curtis, *Web of Deceit: Britain's Real Role in the World*, Vintage, 2003.

2   *Stealing a Nation.*

3   *Washington Post*, September 11, 1975, cited by John Madeley, *Diego Garcia: A Contrast to the Falklands*, Minority Rights Group, report no. 54, 1982.

4   Curtis, *Web of Deceit*, pp. 414–31.

5   Foreign Office minutes 1966, cited by Curtis, *Web of Deceit*, p. 421.

6   US Department of State, confidential memorandums, 'US–UK Agreement on Diego Garcia', from Jonathan D. Stoddart: December, 16, 1970; May 9, 1972; September 14, 1972; author's interview with Jonathan Stoddart, former State Department official responsible for Diego Garcia, July 2005. See also Simon Winchester, 'Diego Garcia', *Granta* no. 73, www.granta.com/extracts/1225.

7   *Guardian*, September 10, 1975.

8   US Congressional Records, Senate, 94th Congress, vol. 121, no. 133, September 11, 1975, pp. S15865–8.

9   Lord Justice Sedley, an Appeals Court judge, was cited by Tam Dalyell MP in *Hansard*, House of Commons, July 7, 2004, col. 281.

10 Marcel Moulinie, statement to the High Court, November 22, 1999, CO/3775/98, para. 14.

11 Anthony Aust, Foreign Office Legal Adviser, Foreign Office internal minute, October 23, 1968; second minute, 'Maintaining the Fiction' (advise, 'Secret'), reads: 'Purpose of Immigration Ordinance. (a) To provide legal power to deport people who will not leave voluntarily; (b) to prevent people entering; (c) to maintain the fiction that the inhabitants of Chagos are not a permanent or semi-permanent population . . .' Objective (c) is addressed in paragraph 6, headed 'Maintaining the fiction', cited in *R. (Bancoult) v. Foreign Secretary (DC)*, litigation chronology, pp. 1233–4.

12 Document prepared by the Comité Ilois Organisation Fraternelle, Port Louis, 1980, cited by John Madeley.

13   *Stealing a Nation.*

14   *Guardian*, January 26, 1976.

15   High Commission, Mauritius, to Administrator, BIOT, May 11, 1973, in Chagos Refugee Group High Court litigation chronology, p. 46.

16   Cited by Madeley.

17   A petition to the High Commission in 1974 drew this response: High Commission to petitioners, November 11, 1974, in Chagos Refugee Group High Court litigation chronology, p. 47.

18   Foreign Office minutes, 1966, cited by Curtis, *Web of Deceit*, p. 422.

19   Communication to author from Richard Gifford, the islanders' lawyer, December 15, 2005.

20   John Madeley.

21   *Financial Times*, April 5, 1982.

22   *Daily Telegraph*, April 19, 1982.

23   *Guardian*, September 10, 1975.

24   Rome Statute of the International Criminal Court, Part 2: 'Jurisdiction, Admissibility and Applicable Law', Article 7, 'Crimes against humanity', (d). Available at www.un.org/law/icc/statute/99_corr/2.

25   Curtis, booklet for *Stealing a Nation*, p. 6.

26   Letter from T. C. D. Jerrom to F. D. W. Brown, 140/52/01 'Secret', July 28, 1965; United Nations General Assembly, Official Records, vol. 20: 4th Committee, November 16, 1965, p. 240.

27   K. W. S. MacKenzie, Colonial Office, minute, January 6, 1966.

28   Foreign Office memorandum, September 23, 1964, cited in Chagos Refugee Group High Court litigation chronology, p. 2; letter from I. McCluney to D. A. Scott, FO, February 10, 1971, 'Secret'.

29   Letter from C. E. King, UK Mission to the United Nations, to C. M. Rose, Foreign Office, 10510/G15/64, May 30, 1964; cable from J. H. Lambert, Foreign Office, to UK Mission to the United Nations, February 21, 1969.

30   *Guardian*, July 18, 2000; Foreign Office memorandum, September 23, 1964, cited in Chagos Refugee Group High Court litigation

chronology, p. 2; Foreign Office minutes, March 18, 1966, and February 8, 1971, cited in litigation chronology, pp. 7, 33.

31   Aust, 'Immigration legislation for BIOT', Foreign Office memorandum, January 16, 1970.

32   Ibid.

33   Charter of the United Nations, Chapter 11, Article 73, available at www.un.org/aboutun/charter/chapterXI.

34   H. G. Darwin, Foreign Office internal minute, 4/2020 ND, May 24, 1973.

35   E. J. Emery, Letter to Sir Bruce Greatbatch, 'Secret', HPN 10/1, November 13, 1970.

36   Sir Paul Gore-Booth's comments were passed to D. A. Greenhill in a letter from his secretary, P. R. H. Wright, 'Confidential', August 24, 1966.

37   Anthony Greenwood, letter to Harold Wilson, 'Defence facilities in the Indian Ocean', 'Confidential', November 5, 1965 (embargoed November 10, 1965).

38   Foreign Office minute, February 20, 1969, in Chagos Refugee Group High Court litigation chronology, p. 20.

39   Michael Stewart, letter to Harold Wilson, 'Diego Garcia', PM/68/68, 'Secret', July 25, 1968; Foreign Office minute, May 24, 1965, cited in Chagos Refugee Group High Court litigation chronology, p. 7.

40   Cited by Tam Dalyell MP, *Hansard*, House of Commons, January 9, 2001, cols 182–3.

41   Stewart, letter to Wilson, 'Diego Garcia', PM/68/68.

42   Ibid.

43   Approval came in two letters from the Prime Minister's Office: letter from Prime Minister's Office to Michael Stewart, 'Secret', April 17, 1969; letter from Prime Minister's Office to Foreign and Commonwealth Office, April 26, 1969.

44   See note 11 above.

45   Letter from J. F. Mayne, Defence Secretary's Office, 'Secret', to J. A. N. Graham, Prime Minister's Office, May 6, 1969.

46   Madeley.

47   As told to John Madeley, 1977.

48   Foreign Office minute to the Foreign Secretary, December 14, 1966, in Chagos Refugee Group High Court litigation chronology, p. 8.

49   Cited by Ewen MacAskill and Rob Evans, *Guardian*, November 4, 2000.

50   Ibid.

51   Record of conversation between the Foreign and Commonwealth Secretary and the Prime Minister of Mauritius, 'Secret', DP 15/1, London, July 4, 1969.

52   *Guardian*, November 4, 2000.

53   US Department of State airgram from US Embassy, Port Louis, to Washington, 'Confidential', A-77, May 2, 1972; airgram from Department of State, Washington, to US Embassy, London, 'Secret', CA-6087, December 7, 1970; Simon Winchester, 'Diego Garcia', *Granta* no. 73, www.granta.com/extracts/1225.

54   Letter from William D. Brewer, Embassy of the United States, Port Louis, Mauritius, to James K. Bishop, Jr, Department of State (AF/C), Washington, 'Official-informal-secret', February 1, 1972.

55   High Commission, Mauritius, to Foreign Office, January 13, 1971, in Chagos Refugee Group High Court litigation chronology, p. 32.

56   Foreign Office to High Commission, Mauritius, March 12, 1971, ibid., p. 34, cited by Curtis, *Web of Deceit*, pp. 424–5.

57   *Guardian*, November 4, 2000.

58   *Hansard*, House of Commons, July 24, 2000, col. 423.

59   See note 24 above.

60   *Hansard*, House of Commons, July 7, 2004, col. 282.

61   Letter from Professor D. R. Stoddart, University of Berkeley, to Senator Edward M. Kennedy, June 20, 2004.

62   Lindsey Collen and Ragini Kistnasamy cite the full text of the judgment in 'Diego Garcia in Times of Globalisation', available at www.lalitmauritius.com.

63   *The Times*, November 4, 2000.

64   *Eastern Daily Press*, November 4, 2000.

65   Royal Haskoning for the British Indian Ocean Territory, 'Feasibility study for the re-settlement of the Chagos Archipelago, Phase 2B', executive summary, final report, June 2002.

66   Jonathan Jenness, 'Chagos islands resettlement: a review', Harvard University, PO Box 100, 04108 USA, September 11, 2002.

67   See also letter from Professor D. R. Stoddart, University of Berkeley, to Senator Edward M. Kennedy, June 20, 2004.

68   Baroness Amos, 'The Jim Rose Lecture: Nailing the Lie and Promoting Equality', October 15, 2003.

69   *Observer*, July 27, 2003.

70   *Guardian*, October 10, 2003. Relevant court transcript cited to author by Richard Gifford, October 11, 2004.

71   Foreign and Commonwealth Office press release, 'British Indian Ocean Territory: Statement by Bill Rammell on High Court judgment', October 19, 2003.

72   Foreign and Commonwealth Office press release, 'Bill Rammell addresses UN Commission on Human Rights', March 18, 2004.

73   *Official Report*, *Hansard*, cols 32–4WS, June 15, 2004.

74   *Hansard*, House of Commons, col. 58W, July 19, 2004.

75   Cited by Richard Gifford in *Stealing a Nation*.

76   World in Action, *Britain's Other Islanders*, Granada TV, June 21, 1982.

77   Richard Norton-Taylor, 'Bulletins sent to Diego Garcia "could have saved lives"', *Guardian*, January 7, 2005.

78   *Washington Post*, December 26, 2002.

79   Ibid., December 17, 2004. See also *Toronto Star*, July 2, 2005.

Chapter 2: The Last Taboo

1   Edward Said, 'The Last Taboo', www.zmag.org/meastwatch/saidtaboo, December 22, 2001.

2   *Ha'aretz*, March 22, 2005. (See also www.zmag.org.)

3   Amira Hass, *Drinking the Sea at Gaza: Days and Nights in a Land under Siege*, Metropolitan Books/Henry Holt, 1999, pp. 235–6.

4   Amnesty International press release, AI Index MDE: 'Torture Still Used Systematically as Israel Presents its Report to the Committee Against Torture', May 15, 1998.

5   Amnesty International press release, AI Index MDE 15/027/2002, News Service no. 56, April 2, 2002.

6   British notes to the UNCHR via author's communications with UN delegates; see also *Morning Star*, April 16, 2002.

7   *Jane's Foreign Report*, May and July 2001; see also Akivar Eldar, 'Big Pines II – Rumors are Rife of an Invasion Plan', *Ha'aretz*, July 10, 2001.

8   Cited by Alexander Cockburn, 'The War They Wanted', Creators Syndicate, *Znet*, www.zmag.org.

9   Raviv Drucker and Ofer Shelah, *Boomerang*, Keter, 2005, pp. 41–58.

10 Agence France-Presse, April 3, 2002.

11 *Guardian*, November 4, 2002.

12 Mohammad Tarbush, 'Give Palestinians International Protection', *International Herald Tribune*, May 3, 2002; Geoff Simon, 'Israel: All You Wanted to Know?' *New Statesman*, November 7, 2005.

13 Dr Salman H. Abu Sitta, *From Refugees to Citizens at Home*, Palestine Land Society publication, 2002.

14 Noam Chomsky, *The Fateful Triangle: The US, Israel and the Palestinians*, South End Press, 1983, p. 236.

15 Tom Segev, *One Palestine Complete: Jews and Arabs under the British Mandate*, Abacus, 2000, pp. 456–7.

16 Chomsky, *The Fateful Triangle*, p. 95. See also Seymour Hersh, *The Samson Option: Israel's Nuclear Arsenal and US Foreign Policy*, Vintage, p. 298; Tom Segev, *The Seventh Million* (in Hebrew), p. 29; Yossef Heler, *The Lehi*, Keter, 1979, p. 125; Nathan Yelin Mor, *The Lehi*, Shikmona, 1975, pp. 71–81.

17 *New York Times*, December 4, 1948, cited in Patrick Seale, *Asad of Syria: The Struggle for the Middle East*, University of California Press, 1988, p. 299.

18   Begin justified the invasion of Lebanon as a response to the attempted assassination on June 3, 1982 of the Israeli Ambassador in London by the Abu Nidal group, knowing that they were sworn enemies of Yasser Arafat's Palestine Liberation Organisation.

19   Seale, *Asad of Syria*, pp. 377–8, citing Israel Home Service, August 12, 1982, and BBC Summary of World Broadcasts, August 14, 1982.

20   Amnon Kapeliouk, *Sabra and Shatila: Inquiry into a Massacre*, AAUG, 1984, p. 34.

21   Ibid., p. 61.

22   Benny Morris, *Israel's Border Wars 1949–56: Arab Infiltration, Israeli Retaliation and the Countdown to the Suez War*, Clarendon, 1993, pp. 242, 245–6. A photograph of Sharon's original orders was published on the front page of *Ha'aretz* on September 9, 1994.

23   *Department of State Bulletin*, October 26, 1953, p. 552, cited on www.electronicintifada.net/forreference/keyfigures/Sharon.

24   *Independent*, January 21, 2001.

25   Kapeliouk, *Sabra and Shatila*, pp. 45, 53.

26   *Commission of Inquiry into the Events at the Refugee Camps in Beirut: Final Report by Yitzhak Kahan, President of the Israeli Supreme Court, Aharon Barak, Justice of the Supreme Court and Yona Efrat, Reserve Major-General, IDF* [hereafter Kahan Commission], Government of Israel, 1983, pp. 12–13. See also Kapeliouk, *Sabra and Shatila*, p. 27.

27   Kapeliouk, *Sabra and Shatila*, pp. 35, 39. See also Robert Fisk, *Pity the Nation: Lebanon at War*, Oxford University Press, 1991, p. 371.

28   Fisk, *Pity the Nation*, pp. 363–5.

29   United Nations General Assembly Resolution 37/123D.

30   Fisk, *Pity the Nation*, p. 383.

31   Kahan Commission, p. 104.

32   Fisk, *Pity the Nation*, p. 157.

33   Ibid., pp. 388–9.

34   Chomsky, *The Fateful Triangle*, p. 257.

35   *Ha'aretz*, May 6, 2002.

36 Middle East Research and Information Project, www. merip.org/.

37 Reports of B'Tselem, the Israeli human rights organisation; author's interviews with doctors; also *Guardian*, April 27, 2002.

38 *Guardian*, April 27, 2002.

39 Correspondence with Donna Rovera, researcher on Israel and the Occupied Territories, Amnesty International, February 16, 2006.

40 *Guardian*, April 27, 2002.

41 Mustafa Barghouti, 'Palestinians Won't Be Forced Out Again', May 31, 2001, www.pqasb.pqarchiver.com/latimes/index.

42 Chris McGreal, *Guardian*, July 28, 2003.

43 Ibid.

44 Ibid.

45 With thanks to Christine Toomey, *Sunday Times* magazine, March 3, 2002; also B'Tselem and Physicians for Human Rights, Israel.

46 *Palestine Monitor*, December 17, 2002: www.palestinemonitor.org.

47 Toomey, *Sunday Times* magazine, March 3, 2002.

48 B'Tselem, *Impeding Medical Treatment and Firing at Ambulances by IDF Soldiers in the Occupied Territories: A Special Report,* March 2002.

49 International Committee of the Red Cross, 'Memorandum: Lack of Protection and Respect for Ambulances in the Occupied Territories', Geneva, March 7, 2002.

50 Since 1967, when Israel occupied the West Bank, Gaza and east Jerusalem, more than eleven thousand Palestinian homes have been demolished and seventy thousand people made homeless. Source: the Israeli Committee against House Demolitions, www.icahduk.org/hd/hdstats, February 25, 2006.

51 Hass, *Drinking the Sea at Gaza*, p. 247.

52 *Al-Ahram Weekly*, www.ahram.org.eg/weekly/2002/598/op2.

53 *Yediot Aharonot*, March 8, 1994.

54 Ibid.

55 By email from R. S. Skellington, Open University, March 28, 2002.

56   Peter Beaumont, *Observer*, February 3, 2002.

57   Cited in 'Profile', *The Review*, *Guardian*, June 8, 2002.

58   Toomey, *Sunday Times* magazine, March 3, 2002.

59   Ibid.

60   Extracted from a speech by Yitzhak Frankenthal, Jerusalem, July 27, 2002. Cited in *Guardian*, August 7, 2002.

61   Interviewed Tel Aviv, May 2002. For an update on refuseniks, visit 'Courage to Refuse', www.seruv.org.il/defaulting.asp.

62   Yossi Klein, 'Enemy of the People', *Ha'aretz* magazine, May 3, 2002.

63   From an extended interview by the author with Israel Shahak in April 1974. For an abridged version, see John Pilger, *Heroes*, Vintage Books, 2001, p. 374.

64   Ilan Pappe, *The Making of the Arab–Israeli Conflict, 1947–1951*, I. B. Tauris, 1992, pp. 45–6, 82–3.

65   Ilan Pappe, *A History of Modern Palestine: One Land, Two Peoples*, Cambridge University Press, 2004, pp. 129–31.

66   Ilan Pappe, 'Break the Mirror Now', *Al-Ahram Weekly*, April 17, 2002.

67   Pappe, *The Making of the Arab–Israeli Conflict*, pp. 82–3, 93. (The adviser to Ben-Gurion he cites was Gad Machnes, quoted in Ben-Gurion's *War Diary* 1, January 1948.)

68   Pappe, 'What Happened in Tantura?', article sent to the author May 20, 2002.

69   B'Tselem study, *Ha'aretz*.

70   Cited by Noam Chomsky, *Red Pepper*, May 11, 2002.

71   Interview with Noam Chomsky, *Znet*, April 2, 2000, www.zmag.org.

72   *Ha'aretz*, cited in Chomsky, *The Fateful Triangle*.

73   *Le Monde Diplomatique*, December 2004.

74   Dr Derek Summerfield, *British Medical Journal*, October 16, 2004, www.bmjjournals.com/cgi/content/full/329/7471/924?eaf.

75   Chomsky, *The Fateful Triangle*, pp. 550–1.

76   Moshe Dayan, lecture given to the Israel Technological Institute, Haifa; see *Ha'aretz*, April 4, 1969.

77   Toufic Haddad, 'A Portrait of Sociocide: The Challenge of Khan Yunis, the Gaza Strip', *Behind the Lines*, March 2001.

78   Ibid.

79   Ibid.

80   Ibid.

81   Statistics drawn from a study group of 121 mothers and 121 children, aged 3 to 16, by Gaza Community Mental Health Programme Research Centre, over a four-month period in 2002. See also research by clinical psychologist Dr Shafiq Masalha, psychiatrist Dr Eyad Sarraj and Dr Rita Giacaman, of Bir Zeit University; *Sydney Morning Herald*, February 20, 2002; *West Australian*, April 15, 2002; *Guardian*, September 17, 2004.

82   'Israel Backs Off from Top Israeli Official Accusation about PRCS Ambulance in Nablus', Agence France-Presse, August 23, 2001.

83   *Observer*, June 20, 2004.

84   *Guardian*, February 22, 2001.

85   These emails and other records are included in Carlton Television's submission to the Independent Television Commission, October 28, 2002.

86   *Jewish Chronicle*, September 20, 2002.

87   *Independent*, September 21, 2002.

88   Statement to the author by Carlton press officer Laurelle Keough.

89   Letter from Jacqueline Korn to Michael Green, October 17, 2002.

90   Personal communication to the author from Harold Pinter. Miriam Karlin's letter was published in the *Guardian*, September 23, 2002.

91   *Independent*, September 23, 2002; email communication from Nur Masalha, September 30, 2002.

92   *Guardian*, September 23 and 24, 2002.

93   Letter to Stuart Patterson, Independent Television Commission, October 28, 2002.

94 Letter to Carlton Television from Stuart Patterson, Independent Television Commission, October 3, 2002.

95 Avi Shlaim, *The Iron Wall: Israel and the Arab World*, Penguin, 2000, p. 31.

96 Benny Morris, 1948 *and After: Israel and the Palestinians*, Clarendon, 1990, pp. xiv–xviii.

97 Ibid., p. 22.

98 Benny Morris, *The Birth of the Palestinian Refugee Problem 1947–8*, University of California Press, 1987, pp. 204–5.

99 Ibid.

100 Seale, *Asad of Syria*, p. 129.

101 Shlaim, *Iron Wall*.

102 William L. Cleveland, *A History of the Modern Middle East*, Westview Press, 2000, p. 261.

103 *UK Press Gazette*, January 17, 2003; *Broadcast*, January 31, 2003.

104 Glasgow University Media Group, *TV News and Public Understanding of the Israeli/Palestinian Conflict*, Causeway Press, October 2002; Greg Philo, 'Missing in Action', *Guardian*, April 16, 2002. See also Greg Philo and Mike Berry/Glasgow University Media Group, *Bad News from Israel*, Pluto, 2004.

105 *Observer*, June 20, 2004.

106 *Correspondent*, BBC Television, June 9, 2002; *New Statesman*, July 1, 2002.

107 Richard Sale, 'Hamas Tied to Israel', United Press International, June 18, 2002. (Documents obtained from Institute for Counter Terrorism, Israel, analysed by Center for Strategic Studies.)

108 *Observer*, June 17, 2001.

109 *Ha'aretz*, August 25, 1981.

110 Benjamin Beit-Hallahmi, *The Israeli Arms Connection: Who Israel Arms and Why*, Pantheon, 1987.

111 Israel Shahak, *Open Secrets: Israeli Nuclear and Foreign Policies*, Pluto, 1997, p. 125.

112 *Jerusalem Post*, August 26, 1995.

113 John Steinbach, 'Palestine in the Crosshairs: US Policy and the Struggle for Nationhood', *CovertAction Quarterly*, no. 72, Spring 2002; Jeff Halper, www.informationclearinghouse.info/article 10566.

114 'Israel Military Orders in the Occupied Palestinian West Bank: 1967–1992', Jerusalem Media and Communications Centre report, 2nd edn., 1995, p. 241, www.jmcc.org.

115 Robert Malley and Hussein Aga, 'A Reply to Ehud Barak', *New York Review of Books*, June 13, 2002.

116 *Guardian*, October 27, 2004.

117 Kim Bullimore, 'Sharon Adviser Admits Gaza Plan a Fraud', *Green Left Weekly*, October 20, 2004.

118 *Guardian*, August 19, 2005.

119 Ibid.

120 Toufic Haddad, 'The Great Spectacle', *International Socialist Review*, September–October 2005.

121 *Guardian*, October 12, 2005.

122 *Guardian*, October 18, 2005.

123 Halper, www.informationclearinghouse.info/article 10566.

124 *Guardian*, November 2, 2005.

125 Israel Shamir, 'Much Ado About Gaza', www.rense.com, May 5, 2005.

126 Cited by Chris McGreal, *Guardian*, February 7, 2006.

127 *Guardian*, November 3, 2005.

128 Ibid.

129 *Guardian*, November 16, 2005.

130 *Sydney Morning Herald*, January 6, 2006.

131 *New Statesman*, January 16, 2006; *Guardian*, January 6 and 11, 2006.

132 *Guardian*, January 6, 2006.

133 *Guardian*, January 31, 2006.

134 *Sydney Morning Herald*, February 27, 2006.

135 *Guardian*, September 15, 2005.

136 *Guardian*, May 29, 2002; Campaign against the Arms Trade, newsletter, September 2002.

137 *New Statesman*, March 18, 2004; *United Kingdom Strategic Export Controls Annual Report*, Foreign and Commonwealth Office, 2002, p. 470; Letter from Baroness Symons to Stephen Pound MP, April 13, 2004.

138 *Ha'aretz*, April 27, 2005.

139 Chomsky, *The Fateful Triangle*, p. xiii.

140 John Steinbach, 'Israeli Weapons of Mass Destruction: A Threat to Peace', *Mid-East Realities*, Washington DC, March 1, 2002, www.MiddleEast.org; *Ha'aretz*, April 16, 2002.

141 Mark Gaffney, *Dimona, The Third Temple: The Story Behind the Vanunu Revelation*, Amana Books, 1989, p. 165.

142 John K. Cooley, *An Alliance Against Babylon: The US, Israel and Iraq*, Pluto, 2005, p. 219.

143 CRS Report for Congress, *An Introductory Overview of US Programs and Policy*, Congressional Research Service, April 15, 2005; cited by Mark Thomas, *New Statesman*, June 20, 2005.

144 Michel Chossudovsky, 'The Anglo-American War of Terror: An Overview', www.globalresearch.ca, December 21, 2005.

145 *Guardian*, June 3, 2001.

146 US State Department, Human Rights Report, 2001; Report to the UN Committee on the Elimination of Racial Discrimination, March 1998.

Chapter 3: Shining India

1 Nissim Ezekiel, *Collected Poems*, 1989; *Bombay, meri jaan, writings on Mumbai*, ed. Jerry Pinto and Naresh Fernandes, Penguin Books India, 2003.

2 Cited by Nick Robins in 'The World's First Multinational', *New Statesman*, December 13, 2004, with thanks to Nick Robins for his excellent essay as a resource. His book *Imperial Corporation: Reckoning with the East India Company* was published by University of Michigan Press in 2004.

3   Robins, 'The World's First Multinational'.

4   Ibid.

5   Radha Kamal Mukherjee, *The Economic History of India 1600–1800*, Kitab Mahal, 1967, p. 1.

6   Robins, 'The World's First Multinational'.

7   A. Sen and Himanshu, 'Poverty and Inequality in India: Getting Closer to the Truth', *Ideas*, December 5, 2003. Cited by Chris Harman in 'India after the Elections: A Rough Guide', *International Socialism*, Summer 2004, p. 52.

8   Edward Luce, *New Statesman*, January 30, 2006.

9   *The Walkley Magazine* (Sydney), no. 28, August/September 2004.

10 Suketu Mehta, *Maximum City: Bombay Lost and Found*, Penguin Books India, 2004, pp. 26–7.

11 Randeep Ramesh, *Guardian*, January 11, 2006.

12 'India Hits Rock Bottom on Public Health Spending', *The Times of India*, July 28, 2004.

13 *Indian Express*, July 25, 2004.

14 *The Times of India*, July 29, 2004.

15 Vandana Shiva, *India Divided: Diversity and Democracy under Attack*, Seven Stories Press, 2005, p. 165.

16 *Newsweek*, November 22, 2004.

17 Scott Carney, *Wired News*, December 20, 2005, www.truthout.org/issues_05/123005ha.

18 *Guardian*, March 1, 2005; *The Times*, February 17, 2005.

19 *Indian Express*, July 30, 2004.

20 Interview with the author, May 2001.

21 Shiva, *India Divided*, pp. 95–7.

22 See Abheek Barman, 'Barga Works, OK', *Sunday Times of India*, August 1, 2004.

23 Pankaj Mishra, *New Statesman*, January 30, 2006.

Chapter 4: Apartheid Did Not Die

1   Ahmed Kathrada, *Letters from Robben Island 1964–1989*, Mayibuye Books and Michigan State University Press, 2000.

2   Mosibudi Mangena, *On Your Own*, Johannesburg, 1989, pp. 101–5, cited in Harriet Deacon, ed., *The Island, A History of Robben Island 1488–1990*, Mayibuye Books and David Philip, 1996, pp. 105–6.

3   This story was first published in the *Daily Mirror*, February 6, 1967, and expanded in my book *Heroes*, first published by Jonathan Cape, 1986, pp. 291–300.

4   Brian Barrow (photographs by Cloete Breytenbach), *The Spirit of District Six*, Human & Rousseau, 1997, pp. 6–7.

5   *Not Cricket: The Basil D'Oliveira Conspiracy*, directed by Paul Yule, BBC Four, June 22, 2005.

6   Ibid.

7   Pam Golding was interviewed for *Apartheid Did Not Die: A Special Report by John Pilger*, Carlton Television, UK, broadcast April 21, 1998.

8   *Mail and Guardian*, Johannesburg, August 28–September 3, 1998.

9   *Saturday Star*, March 28, 1998.

10 Noor Ebrahim, *Noor's Story, My Life in District Six*, District Six Museum, 1999, cited by Bryan Rostron, *New Statesman*, February 16, 2004.

11 Interviewed by the author, October 14, 1997.

12 Patrick Bond, *Talk Left, Walk Right*, University of Kwazulu-Natal Press, 2004; en.wikipedia.org/wiki/Bantustan.

13 *Daily Dispatch* (South Africa), January 16, 1969, cited by Cosmas Desmond, *The Discarded People*, Penguin, 1971, p. 82.

14 *The Discarded People*.

15 Ibid., p. 1.

16 Ibid., p. 14.

17 Ibid., p. 1.

18 United Nations Development Programme, *South Africa Human*

Development Report 2003: The Challenge of Sustainable Development: Unlocking People's Creativity, pp. 19–20, 42, 48, 186; South African Institute of Race Relations, *Fast Facts*, no. 9/September 2005. www.sairr.org.za/publications/pub/ff/200509/poorer; COSATU, 'End of Year Statement', Johannesburg, December 22, 2003, p. 2; Patrick Bond, *Talk Left, Walk Right*, University of KwaZulu-Natal Press, 2004, p. 14.

19   *South African Medical Journal*, April 2001; Alliance for Children's Entitlement to Social Security (Acess), cited in *Mail and Guardian*, July 6–12, 2001.

20   Charles Meth and Rosa Dias, 'Increases in Poverty in South Africa, 1999–2002', paper presented at DPRU/TIPS Forum, September 8–10, 2003, Johannesburg. For a 2005 conclusion, see Joege Aguero and others, 'Poverty and Inequality in the First Decade of Democracy: Evidence from Kwa-Zulu-Natal', paper presented at Mostertdrift, Stellenbosch, October 28–29, 2005. The authors describe 'the sharp upward drift in market-generated inequality . . . which is in line with global patterns of inequality'.

21   Ruth Hall, Edward Lahiff and Ben Cousins, University of the Western Cape's Programme for Land and Agrarian Studies, 'Charting a new course', *Mail and Guardian*, July 22–28, 2005.

22   Ibid.

23   Nkuzi Development Association and Social Surveys Africa, www.nkuzi.org.za, cited in *Mail and Guardian*, September 2–8, 2005.

24   *Observer*, February 27, 2005.

25   Ibid., November 13, 2005.

26   Cited *New Statesman*, August 23, 2004; see also *Business Day*, January 26, 2006.

27   *Business Day*, November 9, 2005.

28   David Goodman, *Fault Lines: Journeys into the New South Africa*, University of California Press, 1999, extracted in *Femina*, July 1999.

29   *Mail and Guardian*, August 19–25, 2005.

30   *Sunday Independent*, September 26, 1999.

31   Patrick Bond, *Elite Transition: From Apartheid to Neoliberalism in South Africa*, Pluto Press, 2000, pp. 158, 162, 183, 186.

32   *Sunday Independent*, September 26, 1999.

33   Sipho S. Maseko, 'The Real Rise of the Black Middle Class', *Mail and Guardian*, May 21–27, 1999.

34   Statistics South Africa, *South Africa in Transition*, 2001, and *Labour Force Survey, September 2002*. Cited by Bond, *Talk Left, Walk Right*, p. 14. He wrote, 'The official measure of unemployment rose from 16% in 1995 to 31.5% in 2002. Add to that figure frustrated job-seekers and the percentage of unemployed people rises to 43%.'

35   *Sunday Independent*, December 1, 1996. Mark Gevisser's articles are collected in *Portraits of Power: Profiles in a New South Africa*, David Philip, 1996.

36   *Mail and Guardian*, October 7–13, 2005.

37   Marianne Merton, *Mail and Guardian*, October 7, 2005.

38   Quoted by Dale McKinley, *Mail and Guardian*, October 31–November 6, 1997.

39   Patrick Bond, *International Socialist Review*, August–September 2001.

40   *Mail and Guardian*, June 22–28, 2001.

41   Statistics South Africa, *Earning and Spending in South Africa*, 2002, and 'Database on Expenditure and Income, 2000'; *Business Day*, November 22, 2002, cited by Bond, *Talk Left, Walk Right*, p. 14.

42   Landless People's Movement press statement, Johannesburg, January 8, 2004.

43   Cited by Patrick Bond, *Green Left Weekly*, April 7, 2004.

44   Bond, *International Socialist Review*.

45   Bond, *Talk Left, Walk Right*, p. 192.

46   Peter Robbins, briefing paper for Roger Diski, *Apartheid Did Not Die*, Carlton Television UK, broadcast April 21, 1998.

47   Hein Marais, *South Africa: Limits to Change. The Political Economy of Transformation*, University of Cape Town Press, 1998, pp. 150–1.

48   Bond, *Elite Transition*, p. 55.

49   United Nations Development Programme, 'Poverty Elimination, Employment Creation and Sustainable Livelihoods in South Africa',

paper prepared by the National Institute for Economic Policy, Johannesburg, cited in *Sunday Independent*, May 24, 1998.

50   Cited by Jimi Adesina, 'NEPAD and the Challenge of Africa's Development', unpublished paper, Rhodes University Department of Sociology, South Africa, 2002, cited in Bond, *Talk Left, Walk Right*, p. 211.

51   Frantz Fanon, *The Wretched of the Earth*, Grove Press, New York, 1963, pp. 152–3.

52   Patti Waldmeir, *Anatomy of a Miracle*, Penguin, 1997, pp. 78–9.

53   Ibid., p. 105.

54   Ibid., p. 111.

55   Memorandum, Assistant Secretary of State Chester Crocker to Secretary of State George Shultz, October 24, 1985, cited in *South Africa and the United States: The Declassified History*, National Security Archives, New Press, 1993, p. 103.

56   Waldmeir, *Anatomy of a Miracle*, pp. 157–8.

57   Bond, *Elite Transition*, p. 15.

58   *Mail and Guardian*, July 15–25, 1995.

59   Lecture by Ali Mazrui at Stamford University, California, January 2000, cited by Chris Landsberg, 'South Africa Entrapped: Global Interests and Actors in South Africa's Democratic Transition, 1984–94', doctoral thesis, Oxford University.

60   *Star*, Johannesburg, October 6, 1997.

61   *Mail and Guardian*, March 20–27, 2003.

62   Correspondence with Terry Bell, author, *Unfinished Business: South Africa, Apartheid and Truth*, RedWorks, 2001.

63   *Cape Times*, October 8 and 10, 1997.

64   *Cape Times*, October 10, 1997.

65   Bell, *Unfinished Business*, p. 1.

66   Ibid., pp. 21–2.

67   *The Star*, December 16, 1998.

68   Bell, p. 29.

69 Testimony to the Truth and Reconciliation Commission by Dr Schalk van Rensburg, June 9 and 10, 1998, www.doj.gov.za/trc/amntrans/index.

70 *Guardian*, October 28, 1997.

71 Ibid.

72 *Sunday Independent*, November 16, 1997.

73 David Pallister, Sarah Stewart and Ian Lepper, *South Africa Inc. The Oppenheimer Empire*, Simon & Schuster, 1987, pp. 2, 7, 15.

74 Ibid., p. 18.

75 *Business Day*, November 14, 1997; *Sunday Independent*, November 16, 1997.

76 Cited by Kader Asmal, Louise Asmal and Ronald Suresh Roberts, *Reconciliation Through Truth: A Reckoning of Apartheid's Criminal Governance*, David Philip, 1996, pp. 156–7.

77 *Business Day*, October 29, 1997.

78 Asmal, Asmal and Roberts, *Reconciliation Through Truth*, p. 156.

79 *Guardian*, October 27, 2005.

80 Neil White, 'Prevalence of Occupational Lung Disease among Botswana Men Formerly Employed in the South African Mining Industry', *South African Medical Journal*, January 1997, pp. 19–26, and 1998, pp. 577–8.

81 *Mail and Guardian*, February 7–13, 2003.

82 *Sunday Independent*, August 28, 2005.

83 Ibid.

84 Richard Spoor, 'New Order Mining Rights and Informal Land Rights', paper presented to the South African Mineral Development Association conference, Cape Town, September 20, 2005.

85 *Mail and Guardian*, February 7–13, 2003. See also Business and Human Rights Lawsuits and Regulatory Actions against Companies: Selected Major Cases 209.238.219.111/Lawsuits-Cases; Laura Kazan-Allen, International Ban Asbestos Secretariat, www.btinternet.com/IBAS/IKA_comp-forgn-pla-030.htm, March 15, 2003. The Gencor settlement is 'Settlement between Herman Kubari [and 1,600 others] versus Gencor and others, March 12, 2003'.

86 *Business Day*, November 12, 1997; *Star*, November 14, 1997; author's correspondence with Richard Spoor, November 11, 2005.

87 *Mail and Guardian*, November 23, 2000.

88 *Sunday Independent*, July 25, 2003.

89 *Sunday Independent*, August 9, 2003.

90 *Sunday Independent*, June 15, 2003.

91 *Sowetan*, August 26, 2003. (Thanks to Patrick Bond, *Talk Left, Walk Right*.)

92 *Sowetan*, February 19, 1998.

93 John Pilger, ed., *Tell Me No Lies: Investigative Journalism and its Triumphs*, Vintage, 2005, p. 191.

94 Geoff Berridge, *Economic Power in Anglo-South Africa: Simonstown, Sharpeville and After*, Macmillan, 1981, pp. 34–5.

95 William Minter, *King Solomon's Mines Revisited: Western Interests and the Burdened History of Southern Africa*, Basic Books, 1986, p. 216.

96 Memorandum submitted by the United Kingdom–South Africa Trade Association to the House of Commons Foreign Affairs Committee, in *UK Policy towards South Africa and the Other States of the Region*, June 20, 1990, HMSO, p. 38.

97 See note 17.

98 *Guardian*, July 17, 2002.

99 *Guardian*, January 8, 1999.

100 *Mail and Guardian*, August 8–15, 2002.

101 Ibid., and *Guardian*, July 17, 2002.

102 *Guardian*, June 30, 2003.

103 *Hansard*, House of Commons, parliamentary reply by the minister, Hilary Benn, January 26, 2004. Cited by George Monbiot, *Guardian*, October 20, 2004.

104 Monbiot.

105 David Hall, Kate Bayliss and Emanuele Lobina, 'Water Privatisation in Africa', paper presented at Municipal Services Project Conference, Witwatersrand University, Johannesburg, May 2002.

106 Peter Hain, speech in Cape Town, February 3, 2000, www.fco.gov.uk. See also *Fairlady*, April 26, 2000.

107 Bryan Rostron, *New Statesman*, May 15, 2000; *Green Left Weekly*, February 2, 2000.

108 Cited by Donald Woods, *Observer*, September 7, 1997.

109 Donald Woods, *Biko*, Penguin, 1987, p. 124.

110 Timothy Keegan, *Colonial South Africa and the Origins of the Racial Order*, David Philip, 1997, cited by Ronald Suresh Roberts, *Sunday Independent*. See also Antony Thomas, *Rhodes: The Race for Africa*, Jonathan Ball, 1997.

111 *Mail and Guardian*, August 14–20, 1998.

112 The Fifth Alan Paton Lecture, delivered by Helen Suzman at the School of Law, University of Natal, Pietermaritzburg, September 3, 1998.

113 Aelred Stubbs, *Steve Biko – I Write What I Like*, Heinemann, 1987, p. 22, cited by Alister Sparks, *The Mind of South Africa*, Mandarin, 1997, p. 259.

114 Cited by Dennis Cruywagen, 'A Story of Courage in South African Journalism', *Nieman Reports*, The Nieman Foundation for Journalism at Harvard University, vol. 54, no. 3, Fall 2000.

115 Woods, *Biko*, p. 116.

116 Hugh Lewin, *Bandiet*, David Philip, 1981. This was updated as *Bandiet Out of Jail*, Random House, 2002.

117 *Pale Native: Memories of a Renegade Reporter*, Zebra Press, 2003.

118 *Observer*, July 6, 2003.

119 Ibid.

120 *Sowetan*, June 16, 1995.

121 Sifiso Mxolisi Ndlovu is the author of *The Soweto Uprisings: Counter-Memories of June 1976*, Ravan Press, 1998.

Chapter 5: Liberating Afghanistan

1   *Guardian*, May 20, 2002.

2   George W. Bush, televised speech, October 7, 2001.

3   Blair's speech to Labour Party conference, October 2, 2001.

4   *New York Times*, December 8, 2002; CARE, www.care.org; UNICEF Humanitarian Action, 'Afghanistan Donor Alert', March 17, 2003, p. 6; email correspondence between the author and Department for International Development, London, November 9, 2004.

5   Chris Johnson and Jolyon Leslie, *Afghanistan: The Mirage of Peace*, Zed Books, 2004, pp. 99–101. See also Brooke Williams, the Center for Public Integrity, Washington, 'Creative Associates, Inc.', 2005.

6   OPIC press release 3-16, March 4, 2003; US Department of State press release, March 7, 2003.

7   Johnson and Leslie, *Afghanistan*, p. 101.

8   Interviewed by the author, May 2003.

9   *Wall Street Journal*, April 15, 2002.

10 Bob Woodward, *Bush at War*, Simon & Schuster, 2002, pp. 316–17.

11 Woodward, *Bush at War*, p. 143.

12 *Massacre in Mazar*, a documentary film by Jamie Doran, Atlantic Celtic Films, UK, 2002.

13 *Guardian*, November 29, 2001.

14 *Guardian*, October 12, 2004.

15 Human Rights Watch, 'Killing You is a Very Easy Thing For Us', www.hrw.org, July 29, 2003; *International Herald Tribune*, January 21, 2003.

16 Department of Defense, Washington, April 27, 2002.

17 Bush's 2002 State of the Union address, January 29, 2002.

18 In an interview with the author, Kabul, May 2003.

19 Amnesty report, cited in the *Guardian*, October 6, 2003.

20 Interviewed by the author, May 2003.

21 Interviewed by the author, May 2003.

22 Cited *Observer*, August 22, 2004 from historical sources.

23 CNN, cited by Kurt Nimmo, 'From Afghanistan to Iraq: Transplanting CIA Engineered Terrorism', Centre for Global Research, January 15–21, 2005, www.globalresearch.ca/articles/NIM501A.

24 *New York Times*, May 6, 1978.

25 *Observer*, September 30, 2001.

26 *Le Nouvel Observateur*, January 15, 1998.

27 Nafeez Mosaddeq Ahmed, *The War on Truth: 9/11, Disinformation and the Anatomy of Terrorism*, Olive Branch Press, 2005, pp. 8–9.

28 *Washington Post*, March 23, 2002.

29 Human Rights Watch, New York, October 6, 2001.

30 John K. Cooley, *Unholy Wars: Afghanistan, America and International Terrorism*, Pluto Press, 1999, pp. 119–20.

31 *Newsnight*, BBC2, November 6, 2001.

32 Nafeez Mosaddeq Ahmed, *The War on Truth*, pp. 11–12.

33 Zbigniew Brzezinski, *The Grand Chessboard: American Primacy and its Geostrategic Imperatives*, HarperCollins, 1997, p. xii.

34 Ibid., p. 53.

35 Ibid., p. 40.

36 Ibid., p. 73.

37 John Rees, 'Imperialism: Globalisation, the State and War', *International Socialism*, no. 93, p. 13.

38 *International Herald Tribune*, November 9, 1998.

39 *Wall Street Journal*, May 23, 1997.

40 John J. Maresca, Capitol Hill Testimony, Federal Document Clearing House, February 12, 1998.

41 Cited by George Monbiot, *Guardian*, October 23, 2001.

42 BBC News, December 4, 1997.

43 Ahmed Rashid, *Taliban*, Yale University Press, 2001.

44   Cited by Nafeez Mosaddeq Ahmed, *The War on Truth*, pp. 20–1.

45   *Washington Post*, November 5, 2001.

46   *New York Daily News*, October 28, 2001; *Daily Telegraph*, December 14, 2001.

47   *Guardian*, October 2, 2001; Noam Chomsky, *9–11*, Seven Stories Press, 2001; *Boston Globe*, August 22, 1999; Werner Daum, 'Universalism and the West', *Harvard International Review*, Summer 2001.

48   William O. Beenan, *Sun-Sentinel*, August 25, 1998.

49   Lara Marlowe, *Irish Times*, November 19, 2001.

50   *Washington Times*, October 31, 2001.

51   Attorney John J. Loftus, press release, 'What Congress Does Not Know About Enron', May 31, 2002, www.john-loftus.com/enron3.htm#congress.

52   *Financial Times*, September 20, 2001; *Daily Telegraph*, October 3 and 4, 2001.

53   Jean-Charles Brisard and Guillaume Dasquie, *Forbidden Truth: US–Taliban Secret Diplomacy and the Failed Hunt for Osama bin Laden*, Thunder's Mouth Press/Nation Books, 2002, cited by Damien Cave, 'The Conspiracy Theory that Wouldn't Die', Salon.com, August 16, 2002; BBC World Service, September 22, 2001. See also BBC News, 'US Planned Attack on Taleban', September 18, 2001.

54   Interviewed by the author, May 2003.

55   Interviewed by the author, May 2003.

56   *Los Angeles Times*, January 8, 2002; also interviews by the author with UN personnel in Kabul.

57   The details and references for all these and other attacks have been collected by Professor Marc W. Herold of the University of New Hampshire, and can be viewed on www.cursor.org/stories/civilian_deaths.

58   Interviewed by the author, May 2003.

59   Interviewed by the author, May 2003.

60 John Pilger, *Heroes*, Vintage Books, 2001 (first published by Jonathan Cape, 1986), p. 194.

61 *New York Times*, March 4, 2003.

62 *Guardian*, January 25, 2005.

63 *New York Times*, March 4, 2003 and March 12, 2005.

64 Adrian Levy and Cathy Scott-Clark, 'One Huge US Jail', *Guardian*, March 19, 2005.

65 Ibid.

66 Ibid.

67 Interviewed by the author, July 2003.

68 *Green Left Weekly*, April 23, 2003, abridged from www.avnery-news.co.il.

69 *The Nation*, August 15, 2002.

70 'News Release', Zionist Organisation of America, October 13, 1997. See also profile of Douglas Feith, www.rightweb.irc-online.org/ind/feith/feith.php.

71 *CounterPunch*, Special Report, February 28–29, 2004.

72 *The Nation*, July 7, 2003.

73 Interviewed by the author, July 2003.

74 Council for a Liveable World press release, cited www.rightweb.irc-online.org/ind/bolton/bolton.php; *Guardian*, September 12, 2002.

75 Foreign Policy in Focus, www.fpif.org/republicanrule/officials_body.html.

76 Interviewed by the author, July 2003.

77 Interviewed by the author, July 2003.

78 Pilger, *Heroes*, pp. 188–9.

79 John Pilger, *Distant Voices*, Vintage, London, 1994, pp. 297–9.

80 Interviewed by the author, July 2003.

81 'Memorandum for the President', included in correspondence between Ray McGovern and the author, February 2005.

82 Reuters, February 25, 2003.

83 Unocal has denied the connection with Karzai. This is rebutted by the published investigations of former US National Security Agency official Wayne Madsen, cited by Nafeez Mosaddeq Ahmed, *The War on Truth*, p. 321.

84 Simon Jenkins, *Guardian*, February 1, 2006.

85 Department of Health, 'Smoking, Drinking and Drug Use among Young People in England in 2004', August 28, 2005.

86 *Guardian*, November 11, 2004; *Independent*, November 11, 2004.

87 *Washington Post*, January 14, 2005. With thanks to Kurt Nimmo, www.globalresearch.ca/articles/NIM501A.

88 Woodward, *Plan of Attack*; *Los Angeles Times*, January 27, 2005; 'Dumb, but Smart Feith', United Press International, October 24, 2005.

89 BBC News, South Asia, 'More Afghan Children Die in Raids', December 10, 2003.

Picture
Acknowledgements

Endpapers: the army moves in after vigilantes attack residents in Soweto, South Africa, February 1986: © Paul Weinberg/Panos Pictures.

Lizette Talate: © John Pilger.

Palestinian refugee camp, 1948: United Nations Relief and Works Agency; little girl, Gaza, 2002: © John Garrett; Israeli security barrier in Ram on the West Bank, 20 February 2005: © Reuters/Goran Tomasevic.

Ronnie van der Walt, 6 February 1967: Mirrorpix; author and Nelson Mandela: © Guy Tillim; cartoon, 23 February 2000: © Zapiro; Durban races, July 2005: © Martin Parr/Magnum Photos.

Scrapped buses, Kabul, November 2005: © Ahmad Masood/Reuters/Corbis; Dr Sima Samar, 22 December 2001: © Luke Powell, 2002 (LP18k07-05); US soldiers on the road near Bagram, 11 July 2005: ©Ahmad Masood/ Reuters/Corbis; men trying on prostheses, Kabul, December 2001: Abbas/Magnum Photos.

Disabled woman passing a mobile phone advertisement, New Delhi, September 2004: Prakash Singh/AFP/Getty Images.

Index